On the Ground

THE WORKING CLASS IN AMERICAN HISTORY

A list of books in the series appears at the end of this book.

On the Ground

Labor Struggle in the American Airline Industry

LIESL MILLER ORENIC

UNIVERSITY OF ILLINOIS PRESS
Urbana and Chicago

Manufactured in the United States of America
1 2 3 4 5 C P 5 4 3 2 1
∞ This book is printed on acid-free paper.

Library of Congress Cataloging-in-Publication Data
Orenic, Liesl Miller, 1969–
On the ground : labor struggle in the American airline industry /
Liesl Miller Orenic.
p. cm. — (The working class in American history)
Includes bibliographical references and index.
ISBN 978-0-252-03433-6 (cloth : alk. paper)
ISBN 978-0-252-07627-5 (pbk. : alk. paper)
1. Airlines—Employees—Labor unions—United States—
History—20th century.
2. Airlines—United States—History—20th century.
I. Title.
HD6515.A427074 2009
331.88'1138770973—dc22 2008045960

For Floyd and Elizabeth Miller

For Frances and Lucinda Orenic

And especially for Kenneth J. Orenic

Contents

Illustrations

Acknowledgments

There are many people to thank when a first book finally comes together. I will start by thanking my parents for a lifetime of love and support. My mother, Elizabeth H. Miller, an excellent and creative history teacher, always encouraged my interest in the subject. My father, Floyd G. Miller, a professor of mechanical engineering, introduced me to the airline industry through his work. His commitment to worker safety is part of what brought me to labor history.

During my senior year at the University of Illinois, I took three courses that indirectly helped put this project on track. A labor history course with Dorothee Schneider, a women's history course with Sonya Michel, and a history of science and technology course with Richard Burkhardt together created one of those "lightbulb" moments that make the learning process so wonderful. My interest in the intersection of work, technology, and gender just needed a place to grow.

After college I headed off to the airline industry without knowing where it would lead me. As a temporary passenger-service agent, I guided international passengers through the maze of O'Hare Airport in Chicago. The natural progression of this job led to work as a ticket agent. I turned instead to the higher-paying, unionized, and passenger-free work of fleet services. I found a job on the ramp. As a baggage handler first at American Airlines and then at American Eagle, I began to understand many of the ideas that inform this study. I have many former coworkers to thank for these ideas, which grew from helping a new hire stay hired and to hours of working, talking, arguing, and joking around together on and off the ramp. I would like to thank the fleet-service clerks at the (old) International Arrivals Building in the summer of 1991 (especially Joe Carter), the K-8 crew in the winter of 1991–92, and my coworkers at American Eagle in 1992 (especially Denny Ginko), a much smaller and more informal workplace. Since then, others at American Airlines, including Tom Byrne and Bill Sanker and especially my good friends Walter Sierzega, Michael Brennan, Timothy M. Murphy, and John Trzaska, have added insight to this project.

I thank Wendy Goldman at Carnegie Mellon for the edict that straightforward writing is the best way to tell a story. Thanks also to Judith Schachter (Modell) and the late Barbara Lazarus for their guidance on ethnographic methods. Barbara's enthusiasm for this project always made me glad to share it with her. I know she is missed by many. Thanks also to Peter Stearns and John Modell for their support along the way. Most of all I must thank my advisor, Joe W. Trotter. His guidance, encouragement, patience, and clear commitment to my work were unfailing. As a mentor and a scholar he is a tremendous model.

My research took me across the country several times, and so there are many I must thank for their hospitality. Lisa Z. Sigel opened her home to me on my visits to Pittsburgh during the completion of my dissertation. Thanks also to Mary Broderick Vardaman, Kristen Schultz Murtos, George Orlowski, Robin and Serena Nanda, and my cousins, Sam Smith and Kathryn Schneider Smith, for food, lodging, and friendship. I must thank Lisa Z. Sigel for cheering me on as I scrambled to finish the dissertation and expand my family at the same time and Diane O'Callaghan for all the laughs, cookies, and babysitting.

More recently, this project has been shaped by my experiences in somewhat tangential ways. Thanks to Lynn Weiner at Roosevelt University, I made my way into the adjunct labor market. At Roosevelt I worked with other part-time faculty to organize. I became president of the Roosevelt Adjunct Faculty Organization, IEA-NEA, and then a higher-education organizer for the Illinois Education Association. I thank Tom Suhrbur, Joe Berry, Beverly Stewart, Frank Brooks, Peter Miller, Diane Davis, Jamie Owen Daniel, and Kat McLellan. With them I learned a lot about organizing as well as competition and collaboration in the labor movement. My years working with them were exhausting and exhilarating, and I'd like to think that I am a stronger and better person because of our journey together.

Over the last seven years, readers and commentators on pieces of this study have sharpened my thinking about the place of the airline industry and baggage handlers in labor history. I gladly thank Patricia Cooper, Eric

Arnesen, Joseph McCartin, Daniel Katz, Simon Cordery, Andrew Kersten, and Toby Higbie. Their collective questions about workplace culture and leisure, suburban workers, race on the ramp, and cross-skill cooperation have all found their way into this study.

For many labor historians, scholarship and activism go hand in hand. Since 2001, it has been my pleasure to work with a remarkable group of scholar activists at the Chicago Center for Working-Class Studies. Our work together inspires me, and even our meetings are fun. Three of them generously shared their ideas about improving my work here. Nancy MacLean read through several chapters and offered very helpful suggestions for fine-tuning my arguments. Leon Fink read an early version of this project. His heartening critique and insightful questions were the first that guided me to dig deeper and rework this study. His questions especially about the organizing chronology helped me see the bigger picture. Most recently, Jack Metzgar read all the chapters twice. His intense interest in postwar labor history, his keen eye for restructuring the narrative, and his willingness to tell me which parts were boring are indelibly reflected on these pages. I thank each of them for their friendship and encouragement.

I must thank the librarians and support staff at the Otto G. Richter Library at the University of Miami, the Paul Kent Collection at the C. R. Smith Museum, the Tamiment Institute at New York University, the Catherwood Library at Cornell University, the Minnesota Historical Society, the State Historical Society of Wisconsin, the Daley Library at the University of Illinois at Chicago, and the Transportation Library at Northwestern University. Their expertise and direction made my stints in their collections all the more fruitful. At Dominican University, librarians and support staff have deftly lobbied for extra borrowing time and offered crash courses in RefWorks. I offer my thanks especially to Molly Beestrum, Corinne Stitch, and Kitty Rhoades. Also at Dominican, my thanks to the faculty development committee for research funding and several students who spent time at the copier, mined microfilm, and crafted bibliographies, including Susan Battersby, Jenny Begich, Kristina Snyder, Ryan Sylverne, and Erin Walker.

My sources for this work literally spoke to me. I am grateful to Transport Workers Union, Local 512, especially Claire Hickey, Sally Jahnke, and Michael Brennan, for helping me contact retired baggage handlers at American Airlines. For their time and recollections I am indebted to the late Robert Slouber, the late Eddie Hall, James P. "Sully" Sullivan, John Gales, Martin Trizinski, Roy Okamoto, George Poulos (pseudonym), Richard Sobczak (pseudonym), and Rob Kranski (pseudonym). The late George Rutledge and the late Otto Becker, managers at American Airlines in the 1950s, also generously shared their stories with me.

Thanks to my friend and colleague at the Chicago Center for Working-Class Studies, Bob Bruno, who opened the door for me at the International Association of Machinists and Aerospace Workers, District Lodge 141. There are many to thank at the Machinists union. The IAM 141 executive board member Karen Asuncion helped me contact the former United Airlines employees Kenneth Thiede and Randy Canale. Randy took time out from his incredibly busy schedule as president and general chairperson of District Lodge 141 to share his recollections of the 1966 IAM strike and his hope for a better future for airline workers. Ken Thiede not only shared his memories of the 1966 strike but put me in touch with Kenneth Ahern, Curtis Johnson, and Richard Del Boccio, retired baggage handlers and aircraft mechanics at United, each of whom generously offered his recollections of the strike and work culture on the ramp.

At the University of Illinois Press, I thank Laurie Matheson for patiently waiting for me to get this all together. Our early discussions about this book occurred most often at the airport on the way to and from conferences. At each encounter she shared her good humor and snacks. My thanks also to Alice Kessler-Harris; her enthusiasm and careful reading of the manuscript propelled me forward in the final months of revisions.

I started my thanks with family and will end there. My brothers, John D. Miller and Andrew G. Miller, and my sister-in-law, Tanya Stabler Miller, have affectionately cheered me on and distracted me when I needed it. I thank Aileen Carey Staffaroni, Nancy Carey, Susan Ciucci Brunner, Jen Creed, Kristen Schultz Murtos, and Marynel Ryan Van Zee for being the old and dear family that makes life sweet.

I offer my greatest thanks to my children and husband. Frances and Lucinda have lived with this book their whole lives. Indeed, they measure important moments against this book with questions like, "Is this as exciting as when they said they would publish your book?" Their joy, earnestness, curiosity, and love are a wonder to witness. Lastly, I thank my husband Kenneth. In 1991 we met at American Airlines and spent our first date riding around Chicago on his motorcycle looking at WPA murals. He vouched for me at TWU Local 512 and shared with me his insights from his many years in the industry. Now a reference and government documents librarian at Dominican University, he has helped me chase down Civil Aeronautics Board reports, strike photos, and dusty tomes on airline management. I thank him most of all for his unwavering love and support. I cannot thank him enough.

On the Ground

Introduction

For a labor historian in the post-9/11 world, it is hard to be optimistic about the airline industry. News reports offer shocking stories of tired and furious passengers spending hours baking in the sun as delayed flights sit on the taxiway. Airline executives offer gloomy pictures of bankruptcy due to lost passenger revenue, high wages, and even higher fuel prices. Airline workers—pilots, flight attendants, and ground workers—all face layoffs, deep wage cuts, outsourced work, and speedups. Their unions face decertification, raiding, and a growing number of non-union airlines.

Today's bleak picture should not obscure the important labor history of the airline industry. Workers in the industry began organizing as soon as planes with mail and paying passengers left the ground. They organized in the air and on the ground for two decades, reaching a union-density rate of over 60 percent even as union membership receded in the private sector of the U.S. economy. The intense interest of unions in the airline industry, federal regulation, the concerned "flying public," and the high skill of many airline employees paved the way for fractious labor relations for decades. A work culture constructed around odd working hours, mobility, technological change, and sometimes a love of aviation contributed to and hindered organizing and inter-union cooperation.

This book charts labor relations on the ground in the airline industry from its inception to the eve of deregulation, using baggage handlers as the touch point for understanding how unskilled workers built tense but mutually useful alliances with their skilled coworkers (aircraft mechanics) and made tremendous gains in wages and working conditions through rapid unionization and nearly constant bargaining under the complicated and constraining conditions set forth by the Railway Labor Act.[1]

This project contributes to a number of conversations among twentieth-century American labor historians. First, as a study of union organizing in the postwar era, it offers an alternative narrative to the myth of labor complacency after World War II. Baggage handlers and other airline workers exasperated the airlines, federal mediators, and the flying public throughout the 1950s and 1960s by striking and "whipsawing" their way into higher wages and better benefits. Second, baggage handlers offer an important glimpse at the postwar working class. Unskilled airline workers are in many ways emblematic of the experiences of much of the postwar working class. Workers on the ramp were not mass-production factory hands, nor were they skilled craftsmen; they were a breed in between. They worked in close association with new technologies and worked and often lived in suburban environments.[2] Transport workers and their unions thrived in the regulated era. The end of some of their good fortune came with the end of regulation.[3] Third, as a study of unskilled baggage handlers in the airlines, a segment of the service economy, it offers a deep look at the consequences of unionization for unskilled service workers. From the 1940s onward, unskilled baggage handlers, cleaners, and porters created important and powerful alliances with highly skilled aircraft mechanics. When unskilled airline workers organized with skilled mechanics they benefited on the strike line and at the bargaining table. Skilled mechanics benefited from organizing with less-skilled workers when contracts clearly defined not only job categories but also avenues for promotion into skilled ranks. These alliances were often complicated by the application of the Railway Labor Act to the industry. Today, craft-based independent unions further complicate these alliances. Lastly, this study of ground workers in the airlines provides a new look at union organizing in the twentieth-century South. Southern airline workers were active members of unions with southern as well as northern roots. Indeed, some of the earliest organizing in the industry occurred in Texas and Florida.

This work also contributes to a small but growing body of literature on labor in the airline industry. The airlines are the subject of many corporate and industry "hero" histories and titillating tell-alls by stewardesses and pilots.[4] Airplanes, too, are the subject of an extensive body of "enthusiast" histories. More recently, historians and cultural commentators have examined the impact of airplanes on American culture and society and airports as political and cultural spaces.[5] However, until recently historians have paid little attention to U.S. airline workers. In 1971 George Hopkins published a history of pilot unionization, and in 1982 Georgia Panter Nielsen, a flight attendant, published a labor history of the American Flight Attendants Association. More recent works by Dorothy Sue Cobble, Kathleen Barry, Sandra Albrecht, and Drew Whitelegg have offered a gendered examination of flight attendants, their work, and their activism. Recent articles by Isaac Cohen consider politics and pilot unionism. To this point, none has considered airline work on the ground. This book is a contribution to this history.[6]

This study examines baggage handlers and unionization at four U.S. airlines: Pan American Airways, American Airlines, Northwest Airlines, and National Airlines. Workers at other airlines are part of the larger discussion of airline labor relations, particularly in the chapters that address the 1966 airlines strike and workplace culture on the ramp. However, taken together, these four airlines offer the opportunity to study airline workers in the North and the South, in major international airlines as well as smaller corporations. All four airlines are (or were, in the case of Pan Am and National) legacy carriers. They were part of the industry from the pre–Civil Aeronautics Board era, when small airlines competed for airmail contracts and political favor. Studying legacy carriers means it is possible to examine from the beginning of the industry how airline jobs on the ground were constructed, how workers chose among unions, how they crafted their own shopfloor culture, and how federal labor policies as well as industry regulation increased and hindered airline workers' bargaining power. Certainly the size, corporate character, route system, and headquarters locations influenced the labor relations on each of these airlines. Therefore, readers will benefit from a brief description of the airlines discussed in this book.

Pan American Airways was formed to bid on early airmail routes in the Caribbean and later to South America. The early airmail system is the birthplace of the modern airline industry. The Wall Street financier and aviation enthusiast Juan Trippe headed Pan Am from its inception through 1968. During the 1930s and 1940s, the airline created an extensive network of overseas bases and sometimes faced hostile governments overseas. The airline never secured domestic routes during the regulated era but served instead as America's flagship airline overseas.

American Airlines was formed to consolidate control over airmail routes in the Midwest and Northeast. From 1934 through 1968, the airline was headed by C. R. Smith, who also oversaw the commercial air industry's role in World War II and later served as secretary of commerce during Lyndon Johnson's presidency. Recognized as an "airline man," Smith closely identified with his airline and the industry. American Airlines maintained its headquarters in

New York City through the era of regulation and was the largest domestic airline during this period.

Northwest Airlines was formed to operate airmail routes in the upper Midwest. During World War II its routes expanded across the northern Great Plains and operated into Alaska. After the war, Northwest was awarded routes to Japan, the Philippines, and Hawaii. From 1954 to 1976 the airline was headed by Donald Nyrop, a former Civil Aeronautics Board chairman who was notorious for his fiscal conservatism.

National Airlines, the smallest of the four airlines examined here, was formed to take advantage of airmail-route opportunities in Florida in 1934. Founded by George T. Baker, a rather secretive auto financier, National cultivated its niche in the postwar sun-seeker market down the eastern seaboard and regularly squabbled with Eastern Airlines over routes and fares during the regulated era. In 1980, National was bought out by Pan Am.

Why baggage handlers? Baggage handlers are workers "in between"—their work is categorized as unskilled. They are not porters, handling bags in contact with passengers; nor are they the highly skilled aircraft mechanics with whom they share unions and workspace. Working quickly and working together all over the airport using heavy equipment around potentially deadly aircraft, moving, loading, and unloading suitcases, mail, freight, fresh flowers, and even dead bodies and wild animals, makes their work varied, social, and sometimes grueling. Much of their work is performed on the "ramp": the area outside the terminal within view of waiting passengers. Lost or damaged luggage is among the most irritating parts of air travel, thus their work when done well or poorly impacts customer satisfaction and an airline's bottom line.

"Baggage handler" is the term I use in this book, but it is not likely that this is what these workers would always call themselves. At American or Pan Am, they were "fleet-service clerks." At National, they were "ramp servicemen" and later "ramp agents." At Northwest, they were "equipment servicemen." These titles grew from union contracts, and to avoid confusion I use "baggage handler" to identify them throughout. As will become apparent, their work was not always clearly defined.

The airlines entered into contracts with over twenty unions during the regulated era. Which unions workers joined and which they rejected was a complicated matter. In the early postwar years, a young and mobile workforce meant that collecting cards did not necessarily lead to votes for a specific union. The two main unions that organized baggage handlers, the International Association of Machinists and Aerospace Workers and the Transport

Workers Union, competed to court skilled and unskilled workers across the country. Which workers were eligible for membership in which unions was not the decision of workers and organizers alone. Under the Railway Labor Act, the National Mediation Board decided on craft and class definitions for airline workers as well as jurisdictional disputes. In several instances, craft and class determinations made in the 1940s remained problematic into the 1970s.[7]

While this book draws upon company and union records, it also incorporates oral histories from two corporate managers at American Airlines and fifteen retired baggage handlers and aircraft mechanics at American and United Airlines. Through the Transport Workers Union Local 512 in Elk Grove Village, Illinois, I sent letters to over 220 retired baggage handlers asking to speak with them regarding work on the ramp in 1997 and again in 2003 and conducted ten interviews with retired American Airlines baggage handlers. In 2007 I interviewed five retired baggage handlers and aircraft mechanics from United Airlines, whom I contacted through the International Association of Machinists and Aerospace Workers, District Lodge 141, in Elk Grove Village, Illinois. These interviews represent the personal experiences and opinions of the individual men. They cannot be tabulated and represented as statistically significant in any meaningful way. However, they uncover important aspects of conduct and expectations on the ramp. These interviews are valuable evidence of the intricacies and richness of baggage handlers' workplace culture.

This book is organized into six chapters. The first chapter presents an overview of the development of the airline industry to the eve of World War II. This background is crucial for understanding the speed with which the industry developed and the central role of the government in the subsidy and infrastructure of the aviation system, the application of the Railway Labor Act to airline labor relations, and the regulation of the industry with the creation of the Civil Aeronautics Board. This chapter also investigates the early work opportunities, job duties, and organizing efforts within the airline industry and examines the work of employees on the ground.

Chapter 2 details the airline industry's role in the war effort, the tremendous expansion of the airline workforce, and the intensification of labor-organizing activities and other forms of resistance among ground-service workers, including the construction of a workplace culture. The third chapter examines the years immediately following World War II, when organizers and airline workers themselves imagined that workers in the industry were a different or new kind of worker. Faced with thousands of potential members across the continent, AFL and CIO unions raced to take advantage of perhaps the most hospitable economic and political climate for unions in American history and organize under the complicated jurisdictional and craft and class issues set forth by the Railway Labor Act. The fourth chapter explores the real gains in wages, benefits, and working conditions made as skilled and unskilled workers together whipsawed contractual gains from multiple airlines. Rapid technological change increased union members' bargaining power as airlines were eager to increase productivity to meet the perishable and growing public demand for air travel. Regular rounds of bargaining with multiple unions, strike threats, and strikes left unions and management ready to experiment with multicarrier bargaining. By the late 1950s, airlines and airline employees would join other industries in a labor-management showdown that marked a "new look" in American labor relations.

Drawing upon oral histories from retired baggage handlers and aircraft mechanics, the fifth chapter provides a snapshot of the workplace culture of the ramp and how technology, race, government, and airline policies and the presence of a strong union shaped work and leisure among baggage handlers in the jet age.[8] The sixth chapter examines the largest strike in airline history, when thirty-five thousand workers at five airlines shut down 60 percent of the industry for nearly two months. This strike, in the glory years of this major service industry, destroyed Lyndon Johnson's economic policy for controlling inflation and forced Congress to grapple with the political fallout of declaring a national emergency and enacting antistrike legislation. For airline workers this strike proved to be a tremendous victory that opened the door for major gains into the mid-1970s. For workers across America, the strike served as the "threshold of a wage explosion."[9] The epilogue argues that the dramatic gains in wages and benefits won through the 1966 strike contributed to the growing pressure for deregulation. This chapter also offers some commentary on working conditions in the airline industry in the deregulated era.

1

The U.S. Airlines through the 1930s

In the spring of 1925, eighteen-year-old George Rutledge worked weekends for Robertson Aircraft Corporation, a company that bought and sold airplanes at Lambert Field on the outskirts of St. Louis. Each Saturday, Rutledge took the streetcar to the end of the line and trudged across the field to the Robertson hangar, where he washed a Curtiss Oriole aircraft. On Sundays he made the same trip out to sell tickets to curious and excited passengers for rides in the same plane. For the first three months he was paid in trips up in the airplane. Within the year, Rutledge made his way onto the Robertson payroll along with a more famous Robertson Aircraft employee, Charles Lindbergh. Nearly fifty years later, in 1974, George Rutledge retired as a regional manager for American Airlines.[1]

Rutledge, like millions of Americans, was captivated by flight, and like a much smaller number, as the saying goes, "he got in on the ground floor." While America's fascination with the technological possibilities of aviation and the youthful antics of its practitioners seemed to culminate in a nation obsessed with aviation, it was actually the U.S. mail delivery that fueled the young airline industry through government subsidy and regulation.

This chapter presents an overview of the development of the airline industry to the eve of World War II. This background is crucial for understanding the speed with which the industry developed and the central role of the government in the subsidy and infrastructure of the aviation system. The role of the federal government in the birth and early success of the airline industry can hardly be overstated. Government regulation fostered investment and experimentation, protected the young industry from competition, and mediated labor conflict.

These early years have captured the attention of several aviation historians and writers, such as R. E. G. Davies, Henry Ladd Smith, and Carl Solberg, whose works remain important standards in aviation history. Their studies of the early industry focus exclusively on the technological advancements, the business strategies of industry leaders, and the role of the government in the fledgling industry. The experiences of employees, beyond some mention of managers, pilots, and stewardesses, are missing from the discussion. This chapter investigates the early work opportunities, job duties, and organizing efforts within the airline industry and examines the work of employees on the ground.

In the first three decades of the twentieth century, the airline industry grew through government support and regulation, the infusion of capital led by high-profile businessmen, and the skill and popularity of former World War I pilots. For businessmen, an airline company was a risky but exciting investment. For former U.S. army pilots, it was access to a job in which they could utilize their recently attained skills. Initially, for men not employed as pilots, working for an airline company was an opportunity to be near the exciting new technology. Jobs around the airfield were somewhat informal. Men took tickets as well as cleaned, loaded, and directed airplanes. Later, jobs for men in the airlines would become increasingly defined and structured. White women joined the industry only as office employees and nurse-stewardesses in the 1930s.

Airline employment opportunities in the 1920s consisted mainly of jobs for flight crews and aircraft mechanics. By the early 1930s, as the airlines experimented with passenger service, jobs in ground services developed. As the size and speed of aircraft increased, the fledgling airlines hired personnel to sell and process tickets and handle luggage and cargo. At smaller airfields, a handful of employees might perform all of these duties. At larger stations, managers formalized duties. By the late 1930s, work on the ground in the industry evolved into distinct categories. Workers on the ground recognized their distinct position as employees, not aviation enthusiasts, and participated in organizing drives during the Depression. These efforts set the stage for important work-related conflicts that erupted during World War II.

From Barnstormers and Daredevils to Commercial Aviation

Orville and Wilbur Wright made their first successful flight at Kitty Hawk, North Carolina, on December 17, 1903. For twelve seconds and 120 feet, man left the ground via mechanization. Five years later, the Wright brothers awed daily crowds in the thousands with their flying machine in Fort Myer, Virginia. Two years later, over one million people watched as the first plane flew over Chicago. While Americans gathered anywhere and everywhere to watch airplanes fly, millions more read about them as scientific and popular magazines as well as newspapers chronicled this new and amazing reality.[2]

In 1910, airplanes were still only half as fast as motorcycles or racing cars.[3] That same year, the largest motor shown at the Boston air show was rated at one hundred horsepower, with most airplane engines at about thirty-five horsepower; these early planes, made of bicycle parts, piano wire, and bamboo, could not hold engines any heavier. They were certainly good for exhibiting flight, but not much more. In 1911, the French army ordered an American plane and requested only that it be capable of carrying 661 pounds and fly continuously for 186 miles at a minimum speed of 37.6 miles per hour.[4]

In the years preceding World War I, two types of pilots dominated the aviation scene. The first group, the inventors and builders of airplanes—including the Wrights, Glenn Curtiss, and Glenn Martin—became well known in aircraft production. The second group, appearing about five years after Kitty Hawk, was the "Birdmen" (and a few "Birdwomen"): aviation daredevils. Often self-taught in airplane flying, these men brought their planes to county fairs and competitions. The Birdmen introduced America to flying as thrilling entertainment. Perceived as national heroes, these pilots wowed crowds with their in-flight antics. One such pilot, Lincoln Beachey, thrilled onlookers by scooping up a handkerchief off the field with his wingtip. Another, Calbraith Rogers, was the first person to fly across the country. Taking off and landing sixty-eight times along the way, it took Rogers forty-nine days with only fifteen crashes to make the trip.[5] Birdwomen like Blanche Scott and Harriet Quimby also spread what the historian Joseph Corn called "the winged gospel": the miracle of human flight and all its extraordinary and uncharted possibilities.

According to the aviation historian Janet R. Daly Bednarek, this sort of exhibition flying peaked around 1911.[6] Many of the Birdmen died in plane crashes sensationalized by the press, including Beachey, who was killed in 1915 when his plane broke up in midair during an exhibition at the World's Fair in San Francisco, and Quimby, the first woman to fly across the English Channel, when her plane crashed during an air meet in Boston in 1912.[7] Thus, the Birdmen both helped and hindered the development of commercial aviation in the United States by introducing many Americans to airplanes as part of a thrilling show, a death-defying experience rather than a means of transportation.

Fledgling attempts at commercial air service occurred despite the dangerous public image of flying cultivated by the Birdmen. Just before America's entry into World War I, the commercial use of airplanes seemed a possibility. In 1914, Percival Fansler started the world's first airline. Small and ultimately unsuccessful, the St. Petersburg–Tampa Air Boat Line used a Benoist XIV "flying boat" to carry passengers eighteen miles across Tampa Bay. For four months the plane flew 1,200 passengers on scheduled trips twice a day without a single accident. A one-way ticket cost twenty-five dollars.[8]

World War I transformed aviation from the hobby of inventors and daredevils to an important wartime industry. The war affected aviation development in several ways. Arial warfare captured the attention of the American public. Although witnesses to the war abhorred the technological advances—such as submarines, tanks, poison gas, and machine guns—that made combat more brutal, Americans did not equate airplanes with this carnage in the same way. Air combat harkened back to an earlier era when men fought as individuals: aerial combat was like a duel between skilled gentlemen. The American press covered the European air-combat "Aces" like Manfred von Richthofen (the Red Baron), England's Edward Mannock, and France's Rene Fonck closely.[9]

The war created a heavy demand for military-plane development. According to the aviation historian Henry Ladd Smith, the airplane manufacturing business before the war was small but healthy. The wartime emphasis on military designs raised performance standards but stunted the possibilities of commercial progress. All manufacturing focused on the war effort instead of the commercial potential of planes such as the one used in Florida by Glenn Curtiss. In May 1917, Congress appropriated twelve million dollars for purchasing new aircraft for the war; forty-three million more dollars were set aside for aviation two months later. In August, Congress appropriated 640 million dollars for purchasing aircraft for the army, at this point the largest amount ever earmarked for a specific cause.[10] As Henry Ladd Smith succinctly put it,

> An industry that was less important than the toy-balloon business was suddenly ordered to produce 29,000 airplanes, although it had not yet produced 200 since the first flight in 1903. Immediately after the declaration of war by this country, the Signal Corps had on order 334 planes. They were of *32 different designs,* and the orders were placed with sixteen different companies, not more than six of which *had ever made more than ten planes before.* There were only forty flying instructors in the entire country and only a few of

> these were familiar with modern flying planes. There were about ten qualified designers available. There were no instrument companies and, what was worse, no engines.[11]

The end results were mixed. While the government spent only half of the appropriated money, it was commonly believed that the engine that was developed came too close to the end of the war for it to be truly beneficial to the war effort. Fewer than two hundred planes were actually produced. Army pilots referred to these "defective observation craft," De Haviland-4s, as "flaming coffins."[12] Despite the defective design in aircraft such as the De Haviland-4, significant advances occurred over the nineteen months of America's involvement in the war, particularly in terms of trained aviators and mechanics. The number of training fields went from two to forty-eight, and the number of trained aviation officers rose from fifty-five to twenty-two thousand. By war's end there were 175,000 trained mechanics and ground forces; at the start of the war there had been only 1,300. The aviation industry developed a production line with a rate of 224 planes per year and a potential rate of seventeen thousand.[13]

After the war, without the government as a customer, most aircraft plants closed and emptied their warehouses of surplus airplanes onto the market. The JN4D2, the Curtiss aircraft used for training during the war, a biplane commonly known as the "Jenny," sold for three hundred dollars. Worthless for passenger travel, former army pilots and others new to flying, known as "Gypsy Flyers" or "Barnstormers," used Jennies for entertainment and recreation.[14] Much like the Birdmen of the prewar era, these pilots flew around the country taking people for rides or doing stunts. While their antics and feats did little to develop the concept of safe passenger travel, the Gypsy Flyers introduced thousands of Americans to aviation. Nonetheless, investors and aviators attempted passenger service after the war.

During the 1920s, Americans became "air-minded." The decade ushered in an exciting and promising era for commercial aviation. Airplanes were the perfect symbol of modernity, epitomizing scientific progress, efficiency, and business acumen as well as danger, excitement, and even frivolity. Entrepreneurs and those with wartime aviation experience experimented with aviation business ventures and attention-grabbing stunts. Men and women of the 1920s took everyday life to the air. In 1922, Lt. Belvin M. Maynard, the "flying pastor" of the U.S. army, delivered his Easter sermon from his airplane cockpit while a larger audience listened over the radio. A group of Philadelphia socialites invented "arial bridge"; the practice caught on among the wealthy, with Eleanor Roosevelt playing a hand. In 1929, Mrs. T. W. Evans, with her doctor-husband, another doctor, two nurses, her mother, and a pilot, rushed to the air as she went into labor. Soon after, as they circled Miami, Aerogene was born, laying claim to the first birth in an airplane.

Beyond air bridge and air births, publicized use of airplanes for important business also contributed to America's air-mindedness. In 1920, almost certainly as a publicity stunt, but one with important symbolism, the "first flying saleswoman," Helen McLean, flew from New York to Boston to bring back orders for her drug-company employers. The ticket cost three hundred dollars, comparable to a three-thousand-dollar ticket today. By far the most famous flight of the decade was Charles Lindbergh's across the Atlantic Ocean in 1927. This event, perhaps more than any other, encouraged Americans to be air-minded. Other "routine" journeys also captured the public's attention. After his election in 1928, the Connecticut senator, pilot, explorer, and scholar Hiram Bingham embarked at meetings from a blimp in one instance and from an autogiro (early helicopter) on another. In 1932, Franklin Roosevelt expressed his air-mindedness when he flew to Chicago to accept the Democratic party nomination for president.[15]

One of the first commercial airlines found its passenger base in another 1920s phenomenon, Prohibition. In August 1919, Aero Limited launched a private passenger service between New York and Atlantic City. At the end of the summer the operation moved to Florida, where six-seater Curtiss seaplanes flew to the Bahamas and Cuba. Because of Prohibition, the Caribbean islands were a popular vacation spot, and during its first season in Florida, Aero Limited flew over two thousand passengers to the Bahamas.[16] However, the high cost prohibited all but the wealthy from flying to the islands, as tickets for travel from Miami to Nassau were $150, and a round trip to Havana cost $100. This early service had little space for baggage. All but hand luggage was most often shipped ahead by rail or ship.[17]

A second early airline, Aeromarine Sightseeing and Navigation Company, an offshoot of an airplane-manufacturing company from the war, offered passenger flights in Florida. In 1919 it merged with a small West Indies airline to form Aeromarine and West Indies Airways. In 1920 this new company won one of the first airmail contracts, carrying mail between Florida and the Caribbean.[18] By 1922, Aeromarine and West Indies Airways had absorbed Aero Limited's routes and set up several new ones between Cleveland and Detroit, New York and Atlantic City, and Key West and Havana. During that fiscal year, the company reported that it had flown 17,121 passengers more than a million miles.[19]

Competitive prices, the convenience and speed of its service, and a good safety record attracted passengers to Aeromarine. The airline's prices remained close to those charged by railroads for comparable trips. While most passengers on the Caribbean routes traveled for pleasure, the route between Detroit and Cleveland attracted businessmen. Flying on a schedule and using a reservations system, seaplanes left the Detroit and Cleveland waterfronts at 9 AM, heading for their prospective destinations. Well-appointed houseboats functioned as passenger terminals in each city. "Signal towers" along the way tracked the planes and phoned in their progress. The distance of 112 miles took only ninety minutes by plane, as opposed to five hours by train, for a fare of forty dollars each way.[20]

Aeromarine was not run by former Gypsy Flyers or aviation manufacturers but by a former auto-industry executive, Charles Redden. Redden developed the airline as "an efficient organization," with trained pilots and mechanics incorporating the "safety-first idea." Clearly recognizing the public's hesitation to fly, Aeromarine cultivated its niche. According to Redden, people seemed more confident about flying when it was done in a plane with a hull that could land safely on the water and when they flew closer to the earth. People who feared flying at three thousand feet above ground, considered safe for over-land flight, accepted flying at under one hundred feet over water. While these water-versus-land factors might have attracted passengers, they also allowed the company to save the expense of acquiring and leveling landing fields.[21]

Aeromarine's tenure as a pioneering airline was short-lived. By 1923 the company went out of business; aviation historians disagree on the reasons. According to Carl Solberg, the company folded because of public concerns about safety after two highly publicized seaplane accidents.[22] Henry Ladd Smith states that it was due to the end of its contracts for mail service between Florida and Cuba.[23] According to R. E. G. Davies, Aeromarine had overextended itself, covering winter travel in Florida and summer travel in the North.[24] Nonetheless, Aeromarine holds its place as the first commercially successful airline in America. Its success in carrying the mail and passengers opened the doors for the development of other commercial airlines. Still, more than a decade would pass before commercial aviation could depend primarily on passengers for profit.

The U.S. Postal Service stimulated the rise of modern commercial air transportation in the United States. Serious interest in transporting the mail by air first appeared in a bill introduced to the House of Representatives in 1910.[25] The post office granted fewer than forty short and temporary airmail contracts in 1912, in part to draw attention to the possibilities of airmail.[26] Little more than discussion followed these first novelty airmail flights until 1916, when the government advertised eight bids for air-mail routes in Alaska and on the East Coast. Only one interested party came forward because the routes were so difficult.[27]

The attention World War I brought to aviation resulted in a one-hundred-thousand-dollar appropriation to the post office for the development of airmail service in 1918. Advanced by the National Advisory Committee for Aeronautics, an independent government organization founded in 1915, the plan was to provide expert advice on aviation issues.[28] The committee included representatives from the War Department, the navy, the Weather Bureau, the Bureau of Standards, and civilians with extensive experience in aeronautics.[29]

The post office opened its first regular airmail route on May 14, 1918, between Washington, D.C., and New York City. Using army planes and pilots, a relay was set up between Washington and New York with a stop in Philadelphia. The mail service recorded only two notable mishaps. First, as President Woodrow Wilson and others looked on at the inaugural ceremony, a mechanic at the field in Washington discovered that the airplane's fuel tank was empty. The second problem occured when the pilot headed south instead of north and landed in a cow pasture in Maryland before heading back north to Philadelphia.[30]

The post office began its own airmail service independent of any help from army planes and pilots in August 1918. The postmaster general, Albert S. Burleson, initially planned for a trunk-and-feeder routing system for airmail service across the country. Although this system did not materialize for another ten years, Burleson and his second assistant postmaster general, Otto Praeger, advanced airmail service toward this plan.[31]

Early airmail pilots flew without the aid of weather reports, radio beacons, or cockpit instruments. Flying from city to city, they used only compasses and landmarks to guide their way. Flying the mail could be dangerous to those in the air as well as those on the ground. Carl Solberg describes a flight by E. Hamilton Lee, a pioneer mail pilot:

> If a pilot got caught in clouds or fog and lost sight of the horizon, it was not long before he lost control and fell. Ham Lee had barely escaped that fate in the fog off Staten Island. When the clouds were low, you had to fly close to the ground, close enough to see it; the lower the clouds, the lower you flew, dodging steeples and jumping trees and telephone lines. Doing just this, Ham

> Lee almost rammed into the ship coming out of New York harbor. Elsewhere the fliers followed the railroads from town to town; in bad weather they almost collided with oncoming locomotives.[32]

In July 1919, not long after this harrowing trip to New York, Otto Praeger fired Lee and another pilot for not flying when directed to do so. Both pilots refused to fly their route between Washington and New York in zero visibility. Their removal from the airmail service led to the first strike in aviation history. All six pilots assigned to that route walked off the job. After three days, the pilots and Praeger compromised. Before the strike, Otto Praeger made the decisions regarding the flying of the mail from his office in Washington, D.C., no matter the weather elsewhere in the country. After the strike, the local field manager made the decision. However, if the pilot disagreed, the manager had to fly (or be flown, if he was not a pilot himself) once around the field to prove that conditions were safe enough for flying.[33] Within a year of the incident, airmail pilots employed by the post office formed the Air Mail Pilots of America, an association they vehemently denied was a labor union. The organization had no paid employees or formal offices, and dues were rarely collected. Open only to pilots employed by the post office, it was the first organization of employees in the American airline industry.[34]

Airmail drew little attention from the public before pilots flew at night. Before night flying, the post office shipped mail across the country during the day by air and at night by train, thus not dramatically reducing the time a regular surface delivery would take. Pilots first carried mail at night in 1921, and by 1924 the post office regularly flew mail across the continent around the clock. Americans took notice when letters mailed in New York could reach San Francisco in three days.[35]

Night flying was only possible with a system of beacons and lighted fields. In 1921, the army began testing a beacon system in Ohio.[36] Soon after, the post office tested its own system of beacons and powerful landing lights at airfields between Chicago and Cheyenne. It was a success, and by 1922 the government had built a beacon system covering two thousand miles across the continent.[37] By 1925, the government secured the Appalachian Mountain region between Cleveland and New York, considered one of the most treacherous segments of the transcontinental route. Every ten miles in the hills, the government established emergency landing fields approximately thirty-eight acres in size, installed lights, and hired caretakers. In the first fiscal year of overnight service between Chicago and New York, the post office flew over four million letters.[38]

A healthy but fledgling commercial aviation industry emerged less than thirty years after Kitty Hawk because of the post office airmail system. Although the government never made a profit while flying the mail, it built an extensive system of charted routes, lighted fields, and beacons as well as a weather reporting system that provided the structure necessary for private airlines to develop.[39]

The government never intended to fly the mail indefinitely. In 1925 Congress passed the Air Mail Act, which allowed the postmaster general to enter into contracts with any individual, firm, or corporation to transport mail by air. Also known as the Kelly Act for its sponsor, Representative M. Clyde Kelly of Pennsylvania, chairman of the House Post Office Committee, the legislation designated specific rates and routes. First, the cost of airmail to the public would be ten cents an ounce. Rates paid to the contractors were not to exceed four-fifths of the revenues derived from the airmail by the post office. Contractors could also carry first-class mail by air, again at a rate of not more than four-fifths of the first-class revenue. With this system, airlines had the possibility of flying with full loads of mail because they could carry first-class post. The post office would not operate at a loss when shipping by air because of the four-fifths rule, and the airline operators would not receive a subsidy in payments of equal to or in excess of their operating costs.[40]

In the first two months after passage of the Air Mail Act, the post office fielded over five thousand inquiries regarding flying the mail.[41] It awarded five contracts for routes feeding the New York–San Francisco airmail route, which the post office initially continued to operate. Between February 1926 and April 1927, twelve companies began service; almost all of them focused exclusively on flying the mail, with aircraft designed or modified for that purpose. Ten of these twelve airlines started for the commercial carriage of the mail were the "ancestors" of several major airlines.[42]

Predecessors of American Airlines received the first two routes. The Commercial Air Mail Route No. 1 (CAM-1), from New York to Boston, went to Colonial Air Lines, and the second, from St. Louis to Chicago, went to Robertson Aircraft, employer of the legendary pilot Charles Lindbergh. Routes three, five, eight, and eleven went to predecessors of United Air Lines. CAM-3, from Dallas to Chicago, the longest of the new routes, was awarded to National Air Transport. Varney Air Lines operated CAM-5 across the Rocky Mountains between Washington State and Elko, Nevada. Pacific Air Transport operated CAM-8, flown over the water between Los Angeles and Seattle. CAM-11, the shortest route, from Cleveland to Pittsburgh, went to Skyline Transportation Company. Western Air Express, a predecessor to Trans World Airways

Charles Lindbergh standing next to a Robertson Aircraft airmail plane after his famous trans-Atlantic flight, 1928. Chicago History Museum, *Chicago Daily News.* Negative DN-0084849.

(TWA), won routes four and twelve between Salt Lake City and Los Angeles and from Pueblo, Colorado, to Cheyenne, Wyoming, respectively. The route between Minneapolis/St. Paul and Chicago, CAM-9, after an initial failed attempt, was passed on to Northwest Airways. The Atlanta-to-Miami route, CAM-10, went to Florida Airways, a predecessor of Eastern Airlines.[43]

Ford Air Transport became the first company to fly the mail under the new contracts. Henry Ford, of automotive fame, received CAM routes six and seven, the Detroit-Cleveland route and the Detroit-Chicago route, respectively. On February 15, 1926, the inaugural flight to Cleveland took off. Ford was ready ahead of the other contractors because he had operated a private express-delivery service among Ford auto plants along the same routes since 1925.[44] Ford entered the aviation business before the Kelly Act by financing the fledgling developments of the aircraft engineer William B. Stout, who joined Ford at Dearborn, Michigan, and developed the first all-metal aircraft in the United States, the Ford 2-AT, also known as the Ford Tri-Motor.[45]

While the post office still operated the transcontinental route, by the end of 1926, under the Air Mail Act, over sixteen contracts for airmail routes had been awarded. The success of the private contractors hinged on the success of the transcontinental route. Both the post office and the airlines publicized the speed of airmail. Despite the growing popularity of airmail, the airlines' average income in the second half of 1926 was 42.6 cents a mile, while operating costs were fifty to eighty cents a mile.[46] Streamlining the operation served to create profit. Congress passed an amendment to the Air Mail Act in June 1926 making weight and not postal revenue the foundation for payment. Before the amendment, each letter was counted before flight. This change significantly accelerated the process and expanded the possibility for profit in carrying the mail.[47]

The government fully contracted out the domestic mail by mid-1927 when it awarded the San Francisco–New York route to two airlines, Boeing Air Transport and National Air Transport. For almost ten years, the post office flew the mail unregulated by any governmental body but itself, and during that time, pilots flew almost fifteen million miles and carried over three hundred million letters. In those years the government appropriated seventeen million dollars for flying the mail, two hundred planes crashed, forty-three people died, and thirty-seven suffered serious injuries in delivering the mail by air.[48] Planes in the 1920s carried less than two thousand pounds of mail per flight. While loading the post needed to meet the federal security restrictions for handling the mail, mail could be loaded onto a plane by a pilot, copilot, airline agent, or postal employee. The formal work of baggage handling was yet to appear.

With the mail successfully in the air, the next challenge to the fledgling aviation industry was passenger travel. Federal regulation and increased public confidence in flying encouraged contractors to explore the possibilities of passenger travel. Airmail contractors with hopes of attempting passenger travel were concerned about the unregulated state of the young industry for two reasons. First, with the post office out of the airmail business, questions arose as to the maintenance of the navigational systems already in place, leading to the possibility of risking passengers' safety if these systems were not maintained. Second, without basic standards of operation, new and unsafe companies could open, threatening the new industry with potential disasters.[49] Creating the Bureau of Aeronautics as part of the Department of Commerce, Congress passed the Air Commerce Act of 1926 in response to these concerns. World War I General William Mitchell conducted several surveys, supporting the case for regulation to counteract criticism of civilian aviation. Over 250 witnesses testified before two boards created by Congress on the problems and concerns of the young aviation industry.[50]

As early as 1918, the National Advisory Committee for Aeronautics called for the regulation of civil aviation. By 1925, nearly twenty states had some laws governing aviation. Pressure for the bureau came not only from airmail carriers but also from the American Legion, whose members argued that a structured and controlled aviation system during peacetime was crucial to American defense. Residents of congested areas also called for regulation because of the dangers of unregulated "barnstormers" flying over their towns and cities.[51]

Thus, the Bureau of Aeronautics regulated and promoted aviation. As part of the Department of Commerce, it utilized the various divisions within the department to register individual aircraft, license pilots and mechanics, investigate accidents, aid in the development of airports, publish a newsletter, and maintain and develop airway navigation. In 1927, the post office transferred control of the two thousand miles of lighted airways and emergency landing fields to the Commerce Department. By June 1930, lighted airways covered over thirteen thousand miles, with 319 intermediate landing fields, nearly 1,500 beacons, 303 airway weather stations, and thirty-five airway radio communications stations.[52]

While governmental regulation and airway development were central to the growth of passenger air travel, Charles Lindbergh's flight across the Atlantic Ocean in May 1927 ushered in American aviation mania. In his examination of the creation of the airline industry, Henry Ladd Smith contends that this historic flight took place at the perfect time. The industry and its regulatory bureau were ready for the aviation mania that followed the event. In the year after the flight of Lindbergh's *Spirit of St. Louis*, pilots' license applications to the Bureau of Aeronautics grew from 1,800 to 5,500, mechanics' applications rose from 1,600 to 5,000, and applications to license aircraft jumped from 1,100 to 4,700.[53]

Airmail grew increasingly profitable in the boom years following Lindbergh's flight. In August 1928, the postal rate for mail dropped to five cents an ounce, instead of ten cents a half-ounce as established in the 1926 amendment to the Air Mail Act. Airmail volume increased by 95 percent. Because airlines were paid for the volume of mail they carried and not for the cost of postage, a decrease in postal rates, which led to a higher volume of airmail, worked to their advantage, although the post office lost revenue.[54]

Within months of the passage of the Air Commerce Act, three airlines experimented with passenger service. The first, Philadelphia Rapid Transit Service, or the PRT line, was launched by several prominent Philadelphia businessmen in honor of the 150th anniversary of the signing of the Declaration of Independence. The PRT flew passengers between Philadelphia and Washington, D.C., three times a day between July and November 1926. The trip cost fifteen dollars one-way or twenty-five dollars round-trip. The Dutch Fokkers used, the F.VIIa-3ms, also carried mail to fill the plane to capacity weight if there were not enough passengers, much like airlines work in the early twenty-first century.[55]

The second company to start passenger service after the Air Commerce Act was Standard Air Service, which began service in February 1926 flying one demonstrator's model Fokker Universal from California to Arizona. The line began as a scheduled shuttle for Hollywood people with "hideouts" in the desert. The route was dangerous when loads were heavy because of the long distance and the high altitude of the Arizona desert. The long ride between Phoenix and Los Angeles had one unscheduled stop, Desert City, Arizona, where no more than a gas pump and two outhouses served as a rest stop of sorts for passengers. The stop did more than make the trip comfortable. The trip was safer because of the fuel service; airplanes did not have to leave Phoenix with full tanks, thus lightening the load for liftoff in the thin desert air.[56]

Western Air Express (WAE) was the third and most successful airline to experiment with passenger service. It first flew passengers from Los Angeles to Salt Lake City in May 1926. The cost of a one-way ticket was sixty dollars. Western Air Express, like the PRT line, continued to carry mail. Flying passengers augmented an already healthy profit for WAE as airmail flights for the airline brought in $1,500 a trip in mail revenue but cost only $360 to fly.[57]

Philanthropy funded the first attempt at developing first-class passenger service. In January 1926, the mining fortune heir Daniel Guggenheim created a fund for the study and promotion of civil aviation. The nearly three million dollars in the Daniel Guggenheim Fund for the Promotion of Aeronautics financed several graduate and undergraduate university programs in aviation, as well as aviation education in primary and secondary schools. Guggenheim money also funded a nationwide tour by Charles Lindbergh after his flight to Paris.

In October 1927, the Guggenheim fund lent money to WAE for the purchase of "multi-engined planes designed for safety and comfort." The airline ordered three Fokker F-Xs at fifty thousand dollars each.[58] For comfort and size, each plane could carry twelve passengers plus five hundred pounds of cargo. For safety, the plane had three Wasp FX engines but could fly on one and climb to an altitude of seven thousand feet on two engines.[59] WAE chose a route between Los Angeles and San Francisco to inaugurate this luxury service. Chosen for its distance and for the proximity of both airports to their respective downtown business districts, the route demonstrated the feasibility of air travel between the two cities. The trip covered 365 miles in four hours, with the new Fokker trimotor planes with cruising speeds of 120 miles per hour. The trip by train took thirteen and a half hours. Service began in April 1928, with lunch on board as well as "magazines, the latest editions of newspapers, and radio entertainment and market reports," as forecasted by Harris Hanshue, president of WAE, in a press release months earlier.[60] The speed and comfort of the WAE service between San Francisco and Los Angeles attracted enough passengers that the company paid back the Guggenheim loan of $150,000 plus 5 percent interest within two years, all from profit from passenger service.[61]

The success of WAE is only one example of the 1927–28 boom in the airline industry. The maintenance and development of airways by the Department of Commerce, the mania for aviation following Lindbergh's solo flight, and concerted efforts by airlines and the Guggenheim Foundation to promote aviation resulted in a dramatic increase in passenger traffic in the United States in the last three years of the 1920s. According to the aviation historian R. E. G. Davies, passenger travel in the United States rose from 60,000 passengers flown in 1928 to 160,000 in 1929.[62]

U.S. aviation interests also expanded overseas through foreign airmail contracts and concern for German aviation interests in South America. In 1927, Pan American Airways began mail service from Key West, Florida, to Havana, Cuba. Starting in 1928, Pan Am won a series of foreign mail contracts to fly mail from Florida and Texas into Mexico, the Caribbean, and South America. By 1932, Pan Am, through stock ownership or merger, constructed an extensive routing system for mail and passengers from the United States into the Southern Hemisphere.[63]

The number of airlines and airports increased dramatically as well. Prior to this surge in airport building, the military and the post office encouraged local civic groups and municipalities to construct airfields. Further, the Air Commerce Act of 1926 formally gave local municipal bodies the responsibility to establish airports.[64] According to a report from the Aeronautics Branch of the Department of Commerce, at the end of 1927 there were 240 municipal airports and 263 private and commercial airports in the country. Private airports might only be a landing strip for the use of a single aircraft owner, while commercial facilities could mean a flying school or other nonpassenger businesses in aviation.[65] While these figures did not include emergency-landing or auxiliary fields, in almost every case these airports were not comparable to even a small city airport of the late twentieth century.

In 1928, the civil engineer B. Russell Shaw described the majority of American airports as airports in name only. In an article titled "What Is an Airport?" Shaw explained the distinctions among landing fields, airports, and air terminals. Landing fields were tracts of less than one hundred acres of level land, with only small hangars and gasoline service. An airport was a larger field that included hangars, gasoline service, telephones, pilots' quarters, rest rooms, waiting facilities for passengers, night lighting, first aid, and maintenance and fire-fighting equipment. According to Shaw, an air terminal had all these things at the highest quality standard as well as service from established airlines. Shaw explained that the air terminal had to equal the best railroad facilities in the nation's largest cities in terms of comfort and services. He asserted that the United States in 1928 had no air terminals and only a handful of airports. By Shaw's measure, the significant majority of municipal air facilities were airfields.[66]

By November 1930 there were 531 municipal airports and 589 commercial airports in the United States, not including emergency or auxiliary fields in either year.[67] While the increase in both types of airports is significant, the dramatic increase in municipal airports signaled an important acceptance of aviation by the general public and local governments. Increasingly, these facilities included restrooms, restaurants, ticket offices, administrative offices, observation decks, and, importantly, room for expansion.

By 1930, having an airport was a matter of civic pride. Promoters of municipal airports likened a city or large town without an airport to a coastal town without an adequate harbor; airplanes, like ships full of cargo and passengers, would go elsewhere, relegating the municipality to the backwaters. Archibald Black, a civil engineer interested in airport construction, warned cities in his article "Has Your Town a Landing Field?" that if they did not locate and purchase the "one or two really suitable sites for air terminals" available in or near them, the airlines might instead establish the airport and restrict service, which would not suit the interests of the community. Writing in the trade magazine *Airway Age* in 1928, Black encouraged terminal builders to be mindful of the comfort of the "*specially high class of traffic*" that used air travel. He envisioned a comfortable waiting room, a baggage room to keep luggage dry and safe, a lunch counter or restaurant, a news and candy counter, and even a gas pump. Ideally, Black explained, an air terminal conveniently located near a main road could serve as a comfort station for motorists, who would increase sales in food and commissary goods.[68]

Beyond local municipal concern about airport ownership, the development of municipal airports was crucial for the creation of a national air network because airlines carrying transferring passengers, mail, and cargo used the same airfields and terminals, thus avoiding time-consuming crosstown transit between (presumably smaller) privately owned airports. The development of municipal airports, like the airways system built by the post office, was essential to the progress of the industry as a whole. According to Patricia Michaelis, the expense of constructing airports with long-range expansion possibilities was beyond the abilities of individual airlines. One example of such an expensive municipal project was the Chicago Municipal Airport (known today as Midway Airport, on Chicago's southwest side). By 1929, this airport maintained its own post office, stationed a division of the National Guard, and handled thirty-two arrivals and departures of passengers, mail, and cargo daily. At the airport, a Chicago police officer handled auto traffic during rush hours. The air-traffic director, wearing a white coat, handled airplane traffic with red-and-white checkered flags, a system that would not be able to withstand any significant increase in air traffic. The cost of developing Chicago Municipal Airport was approximately ten million dollars.[69]

Crowds like this one at Chicago's Municipal Airport (today Midway) gathered to watch airplanes arrive and depart at the new airports, 1928. Chicago History Museum, *Chicago Daily News*. Negative DN-0086738.

Enthusiasm and funding for airports withered with the onset of the Depression. Municipalities and private financiers could not allocate funds for airport construction in the face of competing fiscal demands and uncertain future business. However, federal funding through New Deal programs rekindled airport building. The Federal Emergency Relief Act (FERA) and the Civil Works Administration (CWA) provided cities with the funding to hire workers for projects at airports owned or leased by cities. The Public Works Administration (PWA) funded airport-improvement projects, and after 1935, the Work Progress Administration (WPA), which required that airports be owned by local government, also employed workers on airport construction.

Access to federal funding fueled intense competition between cities. For much of the 1930s, New York and Newark battled for funds and the prize of eastern terminus for the transcontinental airmail route. Newark, with WPA funding, spent millions on its airport, and New York built two state-of-the art airports. Importantly, federal funding also paid for the construction of National Airport in Washington, D.C. In this case, the U.S. government emulated the airport construction plans prevalent in western Europe, where the national governments of England, France, and Germany all financed the construction of their showcase capital-city airports.[70]

By the early 1930s, the basic structure of the airline industry and its route system were in place. Central to this transformation was the postmaster general, Walter Folger Brown. Appointed by President Herbert Hoover in 1929, Brown's agenda followed that of the president: to create a stable world-class aviation system for passengers and mail through federal regulation that assisted private capital. Airmail by most accounts could be considered increasingly successful throughout the 1920s. The significant increases in volume through the second amendment to the Air Mail Act of 1925, as well as the growing system of lighted airways for the night flying of mail, were impressive. However, only one transcontinental route existed, and few other routes covered even one thousand miles. To make airmail faster, longer routes needed to be established.

Commercial passenger service faced similar inadequacies. Service did not expand beyond relatively short routes within California, the Northeast, and the upper Midwest. Weather and low population density made service in the upper Midwest somewhat unique. However, Northwest Airways successfully operated routes in the early 1930s among Minneapolis, Duluth, Fargo, Billings, Bismarck, Green Bay, Madison, Milwaukee, Chicago, and Detroit.[71] In

1928, the airline coordinated air-rail service connecting the upper Midwest to the coasts via trains in Chicago. As late as 1929, commercial aviation, concerned with the risks of flying passengers at night, only offered combination long-distance trips by air and rail. Several airlines, including Transcontinental Air Transport (TAT), Universal Aviation Corporation, Western Air Express, and Southern Air Fast Express, developed air-rail combination service across the country. The most famous and luxurious of these lines, the "Lindbergh Line" from New York to Los Angeles, developed with the very public participation of Charles Lindbergh, took forty-eight hours, a full day shorter than the shortest trip possible by rail alone. Using Ford Tri-motors now designed with small kitchens for passenger meals, this route offered air service by day and rail service by night. Amid great public fanfare, particularly at the elaborate air-rail exchange points, TAT made its inaugural transcontinental trip in July 1929.[72]

A third amendment to the Air Mail Act provided the impetus for a consolidation of routes and a concerted effort by airlines to attract passengers. This amendment, designed by Walter Folger Brown, encouraged the consolidation of existing airlines into extensive networks, the purchase of larger aircraft, and passenger service. It also discouraged the opening of new airlines through strict guidelines for airmail contracts. The aviation historians W. David Lewis and F. Robert van der Linden have argued that perhaps more than any other individual, Brown shaped the structure of American commercial aviation.[73]

Known as the Watres Act, this amendment, approved in April 1930, gave the post office the power to grant long-term contracts to airlines with two years' operating experience on established routes. Furthermore, these routes could be extended by the post office if the postmaster general believed that extensions would improve the nationwide system. To be considered for these routes, or new ones, the lowest bid had to come from an airline that had operated a scheduled service for the previous six months over a route of at least 250 miles. The Watres Act also changed the payment plan for flying the mail. Instead of paying by weight, airlines were paid for space offered. Rates under the Watres Act were up to $1.25 per mile for cargo space set aside, whether it was used or not. This system encouraged airlines to purchase larger airplanes because the rate for mail was reasonably profitable, but limited. Increased profit could come only from flying passengers. If the mail did not take up all the space in the larger aircraft, airlines would install seats and fly passengers. Passenger comfort and confidence would in turn pressure aircraft manufacturers to develop faster and safer airplanes. The post office further encouraged speed and safety by granting extra payment to airlines using two-way radios, multi-engine planes with cabins, and navigational aids.[74]

The Watres Act was not the only motivation for the merger frenzy of 1930 in the aviation industry. The mania following Lindbergh's flight three years earlier had not yet ended. According to Henry Ladd Smith, "unreasonable optimism" also played a significant part in the boom of investment in aviation at the turn of the decade. In 1929, investors put almost four hundred million dollars into aircraft manufacturing plants alone, and this figure did not include investments in airports, hangars, or accessories. For returns on this enormous investment, manufacturers needed to sell twenty-five thousand commercial and private airplanes. In 1929, however, at the peak of production, airplane manufacturers sold only 3,500 aircraft.

The crash for aviation came approximately four months before the general market crash that marked the full onset of the Depression. The collapse came after months of overpromotion of an industry not yet necessary to the public. Capital poured in to develop routes that could not sustain themselves through mail or passengers or to compete on routes already oversaturated with service. Many aircraft builders and airline operators entered the new decade seriously overextended.[75] However, the airmail service continued to keep some of the airlines aloft.

Soon after the Watres Act, Walter Folger Brown took another step in aiding the larger airlines carrying the mail. The "Spoils Conferences," as they were known by those critical of these meetings, proved to be the first stage of a scandal that brought the cancellation of the Air Mail Act of 1925. In May and June 1930, Brown held unpublicized—but not secret—meetings with representatives of the larger airline corporations to discuss the distribution of new airmail routes, particularly regarding new transcontinental routes designed to compete with the New York–San Francisco route already serviced by United Airlines and National Air Transport. According to F. Robert van der Linden, Brown, a Progressive Republican, intended through these conferences to avoid cutthroat competition from "unprincipled bidders" who would enter the airmail arena with poorly financed and organized airlines. Rather, Brown hoped that through this process the young but established airmail carriers could stake their claims for routes in their areas of operation, and through this regulated bidding an orderly and secure air-transportation network for mail and passenger service would emerge.[76]

R. E. G. Davies and Henry Ladd Smith portray Brown's intentions in a less generous light. New legislation set down by the Watres Act regarding length of operation in time and miles locked out smaller independent airlines in the bidding for new transcontinental routes. Furthermore, it was Brown's intent to grant each new route to one company, not to split them up so that transferring of mail between lines was necessary. A flurry of mergers ensued. Larger airlines with the prerequisites set forth by the Watres Act bought up smaller lines to increase their route share. Twenty of the twenty-two contracts available after the Watres Act were awarded to United Aircraft, the Aviation Corporation (AVCO), WAE, TAT, and Eastern Air Transport—all corporations with representatives present at the Spoils Conferences. The southern transcontinental route was awarded to AVCO's subsidiary, American Airways. The central route was given to Transcontinental and Western Air (TWA; later Trans World Airlines), a merger of TAT and WAE that was technically not completed by the time the routes were awarded.[77]

American Airways, as it was known in 1930, the predecessor to American Airlines, is an excellent example of the merger mania. American Airways was a subsidiary of AVCO, a holding company created in 1929. Put together by the Lehman brothers and W. A. Harriman, AVCO purchased nine airlines within six months of its inception. Within a year, AVCO had a transcontinental route pieced together through its takeovers. In 1930, it created American Airways to consolidate this sprawling airways system.[78] The newly consolidated American Airways acquired nearly one hundred aircraft in 1931 and flew sixty thousand passengers, fifteen thousand pounds of express cargo, and over one million pounds of mail over seven million miles.[79]

Scandal over the Spoils Conferences bubbled to the surface after the election of Franklin D. Roosevelt. In September 1933, a Senate committee investigated ocean mail contracts, but the focus quickly shifted to airmail due in part to a journalist's investigations into the refusal of the post office to accept the lowest bids on airmail routes from qualified airlines. Dissatisfied over routing in Wisconsin and Montana, corporate heads of United Air Lines and National Parks Airways also asked the committee to investigate the airmail situation. On September 28, 1933, the Interstate Commerce Commission (ICC) seized airline records across the country, and the hearings became national news. Although the committee did not find former Postmaster General Brown or the airlines present at the Spoils Conferences guilty of any illegal act, they were accused of conspiring and interfering with the "freedom of competition contemplated by the statutes."[80] Roosevelt canceled the airmail contracts on February 9, 1934, and ten days later the army took over flying the mail. The army's pilots were not familiar with the routes or rough February flying conditions, nor were their aircraft large enough to carry the volume of mail.

Four pilots died over the five months the army flew the mail, and while the public was outraged by the scandal surrounding the airmail, the inconvenience caused by the unprepared state of the army was also unacceptable.

The end to airmail contracts was catastrophic to the commercial airlines. R. E. G. Davies estimates that the public paid the airlines ten million dollars in subsidies to carry the mail.[81] Monthly losses after the army took over flying the mail were estimated at $375,000 for American Airways, $300,000 for United Air Lines, and $250,000 for TWA—crushing blows to the airlines during the Depression. A public dissatisfied with army airmail service and a new industry on the edge of destruction led the post office to demand new airmail bids. In March 1934, Roosevelt called for private bids for airmail contracts with a top rate of forty-five cents per mile. By June, the airmail was back in the hands of private corporations.

After a series of sensational hearings, Congress passed the Air Mail Act of 1934, known as the Black-McKellar Act, which brought civil aviation under the jurisdiction of three governmental agencies. The post office continued to award airmail contracts, but the ICC controlled rates within the scale prescribed by the act, and the Secretary of Commerce oversaw the speed, safety features, and load capacity of equipment used by the airlines carrying the mail. Section 13 of the legislation required carriers holding airmail contracts to conform to the decisions of the National Labor Board regarding the rate of compensation and the working conditions for all "pilots, mechanics, and laborers" employed by the airlines. Thus, the act granted collective-bargaining rights to airline workers. However, the National Labor Board was dismantled within the month by the creation of the National Labor Relations Board. The airlines would come under the jurisdiction of a different labor law, the Railway Labor Act, in 1936.

The ICC and the post office monitored the accounting practices of the airmail carriers. This legislation forbade any airmail contractor from holding an interest in any other aviation enterprise except landing fields. Other aviation enterprises, including aircraft manufacturers, were not permitted to enter the airline business. Furthermore, the act forbade anyone who had participated in any unlawful combinations to prevent competitive bidding on airmail contracts (meaning those at the Spoils Conferences) to be in a managerial position at an airline. The act also capped salaries for airline officials at $17,500 annually (approximately $275,000 in 2007). Lastly, the act assembled the Air Commerce Commission to study all aspects of aviation in the United States. Arguably, the punitive aspects of this act reflected the anticorporate sentiment of many Americans, including Senator Hugo Black, during the Depression.[82] The Air Commerce Commission recommended that air transport be granted the same status as other transportation industries and be regulated by an appropriate agency.

According to the aviation historian W. David Lewis, frantic technological competition among the airlines pushed executives toward comprehensive regulation of the industry. The Guggenheim grants and the Air Mail Acts had encouraged airlines to work with manufacturers to build faster and safer aircraft with more seats for passengers. Subsequently the airlines competed for cross-country passengers using new designs by Curtiss, Douglas, and Lockheed aircraft corporations as each new aircraft outperformed the last.

In 1936, the Douglas DC-3, which could carry twenty-one passengers and fly 180 miles an hour, changed the playing field. Constructed originally for American Airlines and funded through a line of credit from the federal government's Reconstruction Finance Corporation, at the request of the president of American Airlines, C. R. Smith, this aircraft made it possible to turn a profit flying passengers alone. Now any upstart airline could fly profitably on a route of their own making. Mail contracts could no longer be the defined starting point for aviation legislation.[83] Republicans, Democrats, airline executives, and the public were all ready for comprehensive regulation after a tumultuous decade of transformation. In June 1938, Roosevelt signed the Civil Aeronautics Act regulating air traffic, safety guidelines, and commercial competition—many of the goals set forth by Walter Folger Brown in 1930.[84] Importantly, the act also required routed air carriers to comply with the Railway Labor Act.

The Civil Aeronautics Act transferred the Department of Commerce's role in aviation to the newly created Civil Aeronautics Authority (CAA). Although the CAA was part of the Department of Commerce, its functions were significantly more circumscribed than before. This legislation gave the CAA the power to regulate airline fares and grant air-carrier-route certificates, essentially creating a formalized highway system in the air. In 1940, an offshoot department of the CAA was created: the Civil Aeronautics Board (CAB), held the power to make safety rules, conduct accident investigations, and oversee the economic regulation of the airlines. The CAA, renamed the Civil Aeronautics Administration, maintained control of the Air Traffic Control system, introduced by the Department of Commerce in 1936; the certification of aircraft, pilots, and mechanics; safety enforcement; and general airway development. Regulation and the reorganization of airlines in 1934 led to increased cooperation among the airlines. In 1936, the industry created the Air Transport Association (ATA) to protect its interests in the face of future government action.[85] In the same year, the organization proposed a strategic defense arrangement between the airlines and the government.

On the eve of World War II, through subsidy, regulation, and personal and political ties between the industry leaders and the federal officials, the airline industry was prepared to participate in international affairs. Technologically, the industry was ready for overseas flight. Politically, the industry served American business and political interests around the globe.

With its South American and Caribbean routes in service, in 1934 Pan Am started to build bases on small islands in the Pacific, such as Midway and Wake Islands, as refueling and rest stops on the way to the Philippines and Guam. In 1936, Pan Am service extended all the way to Hong Kong and invested in Chinese aviation interests. In 1939 the airline inaugurated the first scheduled passenger service from the United States to Europe after securing landing rights in Portugal and France.[86] By the end of the 1930s, American Airlines, Northwest Airlines, and Pan American Airways, among others still flying in the late twentieth century, were well-established corporations, carrying mail and passengers profitably.

Airline Employment Opportunities in the 1920s and 1930s

Employment opportunities in the 1920s and early 1930s in the airline industry existed almost exclusively for white males. Former army and post-office pilots and copilots found work with the airlines, as did aircraft mechanics trained by the armed forces. As passenger service developed in the late 1920s, jobs for ticket agents, ramp agents, and porters became available. It was not until the late 1930s that jobs resembling that of baggage handlers developed. As table 1 shows, employment opportunities grew significantly between 1930 and 1940. Employment opportunities for white women expanded as stewardesses and in some office jobs. Employment figures for operations and office personnel, jobs not directly related to flight or maintenance, surpassed those of mechanics, ground crew, pilots, and copilots. Overall, employment in the airlines expanded sixfold over the decade.

In the mid-1920s, nonflying, nonmechanical jobs in the airlines included a variety of duties. George Rutledge, a retired manager for American Airlines, started his aviation career in March 1925 working for Robertson Aircraft in St. Louis. On Saturdays he washed the Curtiss Oriole aircraft, and on Sundays he sold tickets for passengers rides. For the first three months, before his official hiring by the company, he was paid with rides in the Oriole.[87]

In 1927 the company operated only nine aircraft but could boast that

Table 1. Airline Personnel Employed in Domestic, Foreign and Territorial Service

Year	Mechanics and Ground Crew	Pilots and Copilots	Hostesses and Stewards	Other Hangar and Field Personnel	Operations and Office Personnel	Total
1930	1,800	675	—	1,000	—	3,475
1935	2,618	995	—	1,518	—	8,351
1940	5,409	2,278	—	4,249	—	22,056

Source: Claude Puffer, *Air Transportation* (Philadelphia: Blakiston Co., 1941), 646.
Note: Dashes indicate that statistics are not available.

Charles Lindbergh had been its chief pilot before his famous trip across the Atlantic. With those nine aircraft, Robertson flew over thirty-four thousand pounds of mail but only ten passengers in 1927. In 1928, Robertson carried 2,492 passengers. The dramatic increase was due in part to a ticket-interchange agreement with the Illinois Central Railroad.[88]

Municipalities built their airports on the outskirts of town; St. Louis's Lambert Field was no exception. According to Rutledge, the airfield was outside the city and not easily accessible. Nonetheless, Robertson and later Universal Aviation Corporation, which purchased Robertson in 1928, had little difficulty hiring men willing to travel out to the field.[89] According to Rutledge, men interested in working ground jobs for the airline "just showed up for the job. But it was hard because we were fifteen miles from the city, and transportation was very poor. There was a streetcar line that came out to the end of the field, which I used and the mechanics used that I worked with when I first started in '25. We walked across the field to the shop." Ground employees were hired through word of mouth. According to Rutledge, the company hired young men who were interested in being a part of the new industry. He and others were drawn to the airfield by the thrill of aviation; working at the field was for men who "liked being around the planes." According to Rutledge, only men worked for Robertson or Universal in the 1920s. Initially they did not have uniforms and dressed in "outdoor clothes." He earned approximately eighty dollars a month, which "wasn't that much money, about the same amount of money as the office girls downtown."[90]

By 1929, Universal Aviation operated several faster aircraft, including the Boeing B-4, which carried four passengers; the Fokker F10A, which carried twelve passengers; and the Ford 5AT, which carried fourteen passengers. Convincing potential passengers that flying was safe was one of the hardest parts of Rutledge's job as a ticket agent. "We had an intensive selling job getting people to fly, they didn't want to fly, they were afraid to fly. It was something brand new. People didn't accept flying, so we had to sell them on the idea. Then, once they were sold, we had to do a tremendous job of service, and that's why we selected these flight attendants or stewardesses, as they were called at that time, to take care of the customers."[91]

While young women as attendants in the air would become the industry standard, not all airlines employed women in this capacity from the start. According to an article in *Aviation* magazine in 1931, who, if anyone, should attend to passengers in the air was up for debate. Directors' meetings were called "over no weightier problem than whether a given line should have its passengers looked out for by 'aerial couriers,' by 'flight companions,' by 'airplane attendants,' by 'cabin boys,' or by mere 'stewards' who would have to content themselves with the reflected glory of an aeronautical-looking uniform." The author, C. B. Allen, pointed out that Pan American Airways employed "the cabin boy type of aerial attendant, insisting on alert and good-looking youngsters who are carefully trained in the regular duties expected of them and just what they are to do in an emergency." On the New England and Western Airways, African American Pullman porters were used as cabin attendants with "very good results." Allen explained, "The porters, once they overcame their nervousness about flying, were tremendously proud of their jobs and, of course, had the necessary training and background to render the right sort of service. From the novice passenger's point of view the experiment was very reassuring, for it supplied the familiar atmosphere of the Pullman car and made flying seem a lot less strange."[92]

In May 1930, Boeing Air Transport, a predecessor to United Airlines, first employed young nurses as "stewardesses." Eastern Air Transport employed women in the air soon after. According to Allen, the success of this experiment rested on three factors. First, they were attractive. Second, as nurses, they were "trained to discipline and accustomed to looking after the comfort of others." They could judge how much attention an anxious passenger actually needed. Third, "hostesses," as they were called at Eastern Air Transport, increased the volume of female passengers because they "answer the average woman's desire for the company of another woman on a flight."[93] The publicity this experiment generated contributed to increased passenger loads.[94] Nursing certification became the standard for pre–World War II stewardesses; there were also age, marital, weight, and height standards. These young women had to be white, attractive, and polite.[95]

The increasing number of passengers stimulated a new division of labor on the ground. By 1929, two jobs developed: that of the ticket agent, and that of the ramp agent. The latter job encompassed some of the duties that would later be delegated to baggage handlers. According to Rutledge, with the increasing number of passengers, the airline opened a ticket desk at the field where the ticket agent wrote out tickets by hand. The handling of luggage up to the airplane was done by the ramp agent: "The loading was done primarily by agents . . . they were ramp agents, [they] loaded the passengers and loaded mail and that sort of thing." These ramp agents, along with ticket agents, wore uniforms they purchased from the company.

Before boarding and loading the aircraft, the airlines used large scales to weigh passengers and luggage. Passengers were only permitted thirty pounds of luggage each without extra charge. Seating on board was arranged for optimum weight distribution. According to Rutledge, ramp agents loaded items onto the Fokker. They would wheel out a ladder-like structure to the front cargo door just behind the cockpit. For the Ford 5AT the baggage was handed through the cabin and up into the wing, where it was placed in a compartment. While the ramp agents handled the cargo to the plane, it was actually placed in the aircraft by the copilot. Besides handling the baggage and airmail, these ramp agents signaled the planes in and out of the ramp area, and they chocked and unchocked the wheels when the plane was parked. According to Rutledge, formal training for ground employees was almost nonexistent in the late 1920s and early 1930s. Training consisted of "you stick around and watch what I'm doing. It was all pretty 'pell mell' for many years.

Men pulling an airplane in a flooded airfield at Municipal Airport (today Midway), 1929. Chicago History Museum, *Chicago Daily News*. Negative DN-0087936.

Ramp agents didn't use flags, just their hands for flagging" airplanes in and out of the ramp area.[96] Within ten years, such casual training and relatively informal operations procedures would pass.

The mergers and rapid growth of airlines at the end of the 1920s led to a dramatic increase in employment. In 1927, the American airline industry employed only 462 people, including foreign and territorial personnel. On domestic flights, the industry carried nine thousand passengers that year. By 1929, that number, again including foreign and territorial employees, jumped to 2,345. That year domestic airlines flew 160,000 passengers.[97] In 1931, the U.S. Department of Labor's Bureau of Labor Statistics surveyed approximately 95 percent of the domestic airline industry and found 3,509 males and 88 females employed by 26 companies serving 138 cities in 40 states and the District of Columbia. These numbers did not include crop dusters or companies that mapped and surveyed air routes, nor those that operated as sightseeing businesses or flight schools.[98]

This Bureau of Labor Statistics survey of the industry not only chronicled the number of employees but also their average wages and hours worked and categorized them by region. By far the highest-paid employees were pilots, who by law could only fly 110 hours per month, although on average they flew closer to eighty per month.[99] In 1931, on average, the 123 pilots who flew in the East North Central region, which included Illinois, Indiana, Michigan, Wisconsin, and Ohio, earned $762.22 per month, comparable to $10,536 a month in 2007. The 112 pilots who flew in the Western region, which included Arizona, California, Colorado, Idaho, Montana, New Mexico, Wyoming, Utah, Washington, Oregon, and Nevada, made $887.28 in average full-time earnings per month. This higher compensation reflected the difficultly of flying in the Rocky Mountains.[100] In comparison, the highest-paid male workers in the auto industry in 1930 earned $153.84 per month, comparable to $2,115 a month in 2007.[101]

The same survey examined the wages and hours of nonflying employees. Only 10 percent of the employees in this section of the study earned an hourly wage. The other 90 percent were compensated on a weekly, monthly, or yearly scale, regardless of the hours worked. The forty-three male traffic agents in the East North Central region made $31.17 in average full-time earnings per week. In the Western region, the thirty-one traffic agents made $33.20 in average earnings per week. A small number of women also worked on the ground. According to the report, women worked as traffic agents, clerks, stenographers, seamstresses, fabric workers, and in other categories.

During this period, airlines operated their own limousine service to and from the airport and the city center. Twenty chauffeurs employed by the airlines in the East North Central region made $25.45 in average earnings per week. In the Western region, five chauffeurs made $29.77 in average earnings per week. One hundred and thirty-two licensed male airplane and engine mechanics in the East North Central region made $34.54 in average full-time earnings per week. In the Western region, 159 licensed airplane and engine mechanics made $37.33 on average.[102]

Porters, the only job open to African American males in the industry, earned far less. Across all regions, forty-four porters earned only $11.54 per week in full-time earnings. The highest average full-time earnings per week for porters were found in the North Atlantic region at $17.31. Seventy-three janitors across all regions earned on average $19.21 for full-time work per week. The survey also included unskilled male workers. Twenty-three of these workers in the East North Central region made $21.00 per week on average for one week. In the Western region, fifteen workers in this classification earned $24.76 on average for full-time work. All employees in the nonflying categories of this survey worked at least forty-eight hours a week, with janitors and unskilled male employees working on average approximately fifty-three hours per week.

In 1933, the Bureau of Labor Statistics again surveyed the domestic airline industry. This survey included 96 percent of airline workers employed by 15 companies in 156 cities across 43 states and the District of Columbia. Compared to the 1931 figures, the number of companies dropped by 11, the number of male employees grew by 100 to 3,609, and the number of female employees in the industry grew by over 100, from 88 to 207. As in the previous survey, female employees were listed only in a single group covering all female employees on the ground. Although 108 women worked as stewardesses in 1933, the survey did not examine their wages or hours worked. Compared to the rapid growth between 1927 and 1931, the increase in employment figures between 1931 and 1933 is marginal. The number of employees in several categories actually dropped between those two years. The number of pilots in the East North Central region dropped from 123 to 105. The number of male traffic agents in the same region fell from forty-three to twenty-five. The average weekly earnings for this group also slipped from $31.17 to $30.33. Not all regions showed decreases in wages or employment figures.[103]

The rapid growth of the industry as well as regulation by the Commerce Department and the threat of union organization pressed airlines to formalize policy. The newly created American Airlines put together an extensive manual of operations during 1934 and 1935. This manual not only clearly

Works Progress Administration Federal Art Project poster in Ohio publicizing aviation work, 1937. Artist, Blanche L. Anish. Library of Congress, Prints and Photographs Division, Works Progress Administration Poster Collection, LC-USZC2-1095 DLC.

defined a number of jobs but also set forward policy on duties and public behavior of employees. Furthermore, all employees were on call for emergency duty at any time.[104]

According to the 1934–35 American Airlines manual, no specific position of baggage handler or fleet-service clerk existed in this early period. The loading of mail and cargo remained unspecialized. "Station personnel," "cleaners," or "agents" performed such work. Agents' primary duties covered the boarding of passengers and processing of tickets. The manual did not differentiate between ticket agents and ramp agents. The station manager organized his workforce according to the perceived needs of the station.

> It is the responsibility of the Station Manager to see that all routine operations are analyzed, arranged in a logical sequence, and each assigned to a certain individual to be performed at the proper time. This is particularly important for handling arrivals and departures when station activity reaches a peak.

> It will require a careful study of the operations to be performed, the personnel available, and the physical layout of the station to determine the quickest and easiest method of doing the job. If several alternate plans appear feasible, a trial should be given each. The best method, when determined, shall be written in the form of instructions and all personnel carefully drilled in the procedure established. Deviation should be permitted only in an emergency or to meet changed conditions. Improvements should be welcomed but continual change avoided.[105]

Flexibility in operations at a local level was significant. However, porters removed rubbish or airsickness bags from the interior of aircraft, a job performed by baggage handlers at a later period. Porters also delivered supplies to the aircraft, although the stewardess and stock clerk ensured that the supplies had been counted and properly signed for before the porter made his delivery.[106]

The manual also discussed two other jobs later performed by fleet-service clerks. A mechanic pulled the chocks, the blocks that ensure that the aircraft does not roll.[107] Two men performed the second job, signaling the pilot into and out of the ramp area. A "flagman" performed the job during the day when a flag was used, and a "signalman" at night. Presumably this job was part of the overall duties of either agents or mechanics. This job also entailed guiding the pilot for takeoff, a job later controlled through radio contact with the air-traffic control tower.[108]

Baggage handling receives almost no mention in the manual. Mention is made only regarding delivering baggage to passengers at arrival: "At the point fixed for delivering baggage, the checks and tags shall be matched and the luggage delivered to the cab driver, porter, or passenger. Both portions of all baggage checks so collected must be destroyed to prevent fraudulent claims against the Company. At stations where the Company operates its own limousines, tags shall remain on the baggage until the downtown destination is reached, when the checks shall be matched and destroyed as above."[109] The manual does not specify who transports the baggage to this location, but the size of aircraft during this period still did not necessitate the hiring of personnel to load and unload baggage exclusively.

By the early 1930s, American Airlines operated three types of aircraft for passenger service. The first, purchased in 1933, the Curtiss Condor, accommodated twelve passengers for regular service and even fewer for sleeper service. The second, the Vultee V-1A, purchased in 1934, carried only eight passengers but flew 235 miles per hour, almost a hundred miles per hour faster than the Condor. The third aircraft, the Douglas DC-2, purchased in late 1934, accommodated fourteen passengers at a cruising speed of 170 miles per hour. None of these aircraft held enough passengers to make passenger service alone profitable.[110] It was not until the development of the DC-3 by the Douglas Aircraft Company in 1936 that flying passengers became profitable. The DC-3 carried twenty-one passengers, or fourteen in the sleeper berths of the Douglas Sleeper Transport version. Profit came with improved aerodynamics, a more powerful engine, and the increased passenger load with an increase in operating costs of only 10 percent over the DC-2.[111] Until the DC-3, mail continued to be the airline's main source of revenue.

The manual's extensive focus on airmail-handling procedures points to its continued financial necessity to the airline. Careful control of the mail at all times was the responsibility of pilots and ground employees alike. The U.S. Postal Service required mail handlers to take an oath. Employees directly handling the mail were not to let it out of their sight.

> Mail must be in the custody of at least two employees, either of the Post Office Department or of American Airlines, Inc., at all times except when in actual flight or in transit between the Post Office and the airplane in a locked truck. No bystanders may be permitted to approach the mail unless known to be an employee of the Post Office Department or American Airlines, Inc. In cases of interrupted flight or other emergencies, mail may be in the custody of the Pilot or other employee alone. If the mail is carried in an automobile with passengers, it must be in full view of the Pilot or other American Airlines employee.[112]

Concern over theft of the mail required that certain personnel handling the mail carry guns. Early airmail was most used by the banking industry to more quickly process financial transactions.[113] The manual elaborated, "Dispatchers or Station Managers handling mail and Pilots carrying mail must be armed with a pistol or revolver of not less than .32 caliber, to be carried in a holster worn outside the outer clothing. For revolvers, all chambers but one must be kept loaded and the gun carried with the hammer on the empty chamber."[114]

The company issued a gun at each station for dispatchers and station managers. However, station employees were permitted to use their own .32 caliber guns. This permission included all employees handling mail. The company did not specify to which employees it granted cards to carry firearms while handling mail.[115]

During this period, airline employees of all types worked in close proxim-

Airmail being loaded on a Northwest Airlines plane, 1940. Note holstered gun.
Minnesota Historical Society. Location: HC7.3 p35, Negative 52362.

ity to passengers. Passengers walked out onto the tarmac or ramp to board the aircraft, giving them full view of mechanical and loading operations. American's policies on interaction with passengers, intra-employee behavior, alcohol and tobacco use, as well as behavior outside work hours were clearly defined.

> Drinking of any alcoholic beverage by any employee on duty or in uniform, or by any flight personnel, at any time within a twenty-four-hour period prior to going on duty, is forbidden.
>
> Employees reporting for duty showing any evidence of drinking are subject to immediate dismissal. Any employee who knowingly permits another employee to attempt to perform his duty while under the influence of intoxicants shall be considered equally guilty.
>
> In addition to the requirements outlined in the fire regulations, no employee shall smoke when conducting business with passengers or handling mail or express. Personnel in uniform shall not smoke in the presence of passengers

> or guests of American Airlines, or in passenger waiting rooms. Cigarette smoking only will be permitted in the cockpit of airplanes equipped with ash trays while the door of the compartment is closed and the crew is not in the presence of, or visible to the passengers. . . .
>
> While the Company has no wish to interfere in the personal affairs of the employees, and will not do so unless that duty is forced upon it, those whose conduct outside their hours of employment brings unfavorable reflection upon the Company are subject to penalty or dismissal.
>
> Employees shall not discuss Company business with outsiders except regarding matters about which they are authorized to speak. This is not to be interpreted as meaning that the Company is opposed to—on the other hand, it is urged that employees take advantage of the public's natural interest to increase the use of air mail, air express, and air passenger service.
>
> Each employee should use the greatest consideration when dealing with other employees who are working, limiting their remarks to essentials.
>
> An employee is expected to pay his just accounts, and continued complaints from creditors or garnishment proceedings will subject an employee to dismissal.[116]

Company policy strictly regimented uniforms as well as behavior. Flight and ground employees wore specific uniforms, most often purchased through the company. The uniforms for ground and flight personnel excluding porters and stewardesses included a gray-blue jacket with brass buttons, a dark blue English navy–style cap, an optional matching vest, dark blue trousers, an overcoat, a dark blue silk tie, a blue collared shirt, and black shoes. Job titles were embroidered over the left breast pocket of the shirt, and the American Airlines insignia was sewn to the cap. There is no mention of any variation for female ground employees. Porters wore gray wool uniforms in the style of a suit.[117] Due to the oils and fluids used in servicing aircraft, mechanics wore coveralls.[118]

Labor Organizing in the Air and on the Ground

As the 1930s ushered in the era of a federally funded and regulated airline industry in terms of safety, routing, competition, and airport construction, labor relations came under regulation as well. The call for regulation came from concerns about interruptions in mail service and interstate commerce as well as political relationships. As the economic historian Isaac Cohen explained in his examination of the Air Line Pilots Association (ALPA) in the 1930s, New Deal politicians, sympathetic to labor's interests or at least sensitive to their growing voice at the ballot box, also proved to be friends of airline labor during the Depression.[119] As long hours, low wages, and the threat of layoffs and in some cases reduced wages diminished some of the glamour of aviation employment, these issues also opened up the airlines to organizing attempts by several national unions as well as company unions.[120]

Numerous historians have argued that the New Deal was a watershed for many American workers.[121] Federal employment programs, wage protections, Social Security, and unemployment benefits, among other programs, created an unprecedented safety net for the American working class at home and at work. For American workers and unions, the most critical legislation of this era was the National Labor Relations Act of 1935. Known also as the Wagner Act, this law created permanent institutions to facilitate union organizing for a substantial portion of American workers. It became legal for workers to organize into unions and illegal for employers to create "company unions," and the act outlined unfair labor practices and required employers to negotiate with a union chosen through elections held by the National Labor Relations Board. This law encouraged an already energized labor movement, particularly among workers in industries such as steel and auto manufacturing, to organize.[122]

Airline employees secured the right to organize prior to the Wagner Act through lobbying efforts on the part of the pilot's union. In April 1932, a bill supported by the Democrat Fiorello LaGuardia in the House and the Republican Hiram Bingham in the Senate granted pilots at all airlines with airmail contracts the "privilege of collective representation." Weeks later, ALPA introduced a bill to bring the airlines and their employees under the Railway Labor Act, which would effectively give all airline employees access to regulated collective bargaining. Discussion over the nature of the airline industry compared to the railroads ensued. Effective lobbying by the airlines kept it from ever leaving committee. However, the issue of collective bargaining in this growing "public utility" industry remained.[123]

In 1933, during National Recovery Administration code hearings on the airline industry, David Behncke, president of ALPA, wrangled with the airline and aircraft industry trade association, the Aeronautics Chamber of Commerce, over the inclusion or exclusion of pilots in the code (because they were "professional" employees) and the rate of pay, based on the post-office model, which the trade association wanted to change. A national strike was averted through the intervention of the secretary of labor, Frances Perkins, and the National Labor Board. In May 1934 the National Labor Board hearing resulted in Decision 83, creating a complex wage formula for pilots, including base pay, an hourly rate, a mileage rate, and hazard pay.

While Roosevelt's Second New Deal and the Wagner Act in particular transformed the political climate for workers in America, in 1936, airline workers fell under the jurisdiction of a different labor law, the Railway Labor Act. This 1926 act grew in part from the railroad unions' dissatisfaction with the Railroad Labor Board (RLB). Established in 1920, the RLB was a tripartite coalition of labor, capital, and the public that oversaw railroad disputes. The public and capital factions of the RLB often ruled against the interests of labor. Wage cuts and changes in work rules under the RLB culminated in the railroad strike of 1922. Through an injunction against the strike, declaring it illegal, railroad workers and their unions lost significant power. The unions failed to dismantle the RLB through their Democratic allies in Congress and replace it with more hospitable regulation. The railroads, also dissatisfied with the RLB, agreed through the Republicans to discuss change. The unions and the railroads, with Herbert Hoover as the middleman, agreed to support the Railway Labor Act. The act marked a significant change in labor relations, as it was perceived as neutral state intervention that benefited workers and employers. The Railway Labor Act recognized and endorsed employees' right to organize and outlawed national strikes on the rails. It also permitted collective bargaining for railroads on a systemwide but not a nationwide basis, a benefit to railroad management.[124] Under the act, railroads and airlines participated in collective bargaining covering a whole class or craft of employees. Employees elected their representative agents through a majority vote, and the law prohibited employers from influencing or discouraging employees from seeking organized representation.

Lobbied by the Machinists and the pilot's union, President Roosevelt amended the Railway Labor Act in 1936 to include the airline industry. While these craft unions strongly supported inclusion under the act, the airline industry was less engaged in the question at hand. According to the aviation scholar William V. Henzey, the airlines were so concerned with the industry's survival "in its rawest sense" that officials gave little thought to long-term labor relations. During congressional hearings to include the airlines under the Railway Labor Act, the chairman asked for management comment: "Is there somebody here that is interested in the other side of this question?" There was no answer.[125]

Under this amendment to the Railway Labor Act, the National Mediation Board investigated and certified labor organizations for the representation of employees and mediated disputes regarding rates of pay and changes in working conditions or rules for employees of the American airlines. The board also supervised arbitration when mediation failed. Under the Railway Labor Act, the president of the United States could appoint an emergency board when arbitration failed. When disputes between airlines and their employees developed during the life of a collective bargaining agreement, the National Mediation Board was empowered to create a National Air Transport Adjustment Board to make final and binding decisions regarding these disputes.[126] Under the Railway Labor Act, workers organized into bargaining units by "craft or class," but the job of baggage handler was especially difficult to categorize according to craft or class for the purposes of organization. Across the industry, it was unclear whether these employees were part of the mechanical craft or class or the service craft or class.

Even before specific legal statute, skilled employees, including pilots, mechanics, and radio operators, were the first to attempt organizing. In 1931, led by David L. Behncke, a pilot at United Air Lines, pilots made their first successful move to organize when they confronted United over possible changes in hourly wages and their method of computation. The airline agreed to continue its current practice despite a dip in passenger revenue as the Depression worsened. Emboldened by this maneuver, ALPA affiliated with the American Federation of Labor (AFL) to protect the interests of the "craft of airline pilot." According to the historian George Hopkins, although the threat of wage cuts and workload increases impacted relatively few pilots in the first years of the Depression, it was the fear of change and the belief that they protected air safety that motivated them to organize. Further, the substantial number of unemployed but eager pilots threatened the status and wages of those flying for airlines with mail contracts.[127]

Low wages and longer flying times for pilots resulted in the first labor showdown in the industry in February 1932. The California businessman E. L. Cord, famous for his successful auto-manufacturing ventures, started Century Air Lines out of Chicago. Cord hired pilots willing to fly for $350 a month, less than half the going rate. A few months later, Cord opened Century Pacific Airlines on the West Coast and had no trouble hiring pilots at $150 a month. Because Cord's airlines did not have mail contracts, they were not bound by the pay rules originally structured through the post-office contracts. Cord further challenged the "mystique" of the airline pilot by publicly stating, "I feel that 'aviators' have fostered an erroneous conception of flying. . . . It is my conviction that any normal person can safely and easily handle an airplane."[128]

In February 1932, Cord demanded that his Chicago pilots take a pay cut to put them on par with their California counterparts. After an attempt to negotiate with Cord, the Chicago pilots, who had recently joined ALPA, were locked out. ALPA took the issue to Congress, which was considering Cord's airlines for airmail contracts. A public-relations campaign—including aerial picketing and the help of labor allies in Congress, including New York Representative Fiorello LaGuardia, who publicly accused Cord of paying pilots "less than a union truck driver gets in New York"—crushed Cord's plans for a mail contract.[129] In April 1932, Cord exchanged both Century Air Lines for 140,000 shares of American Airways stock and soon after became a director of AVCO (American's holding company). In 1934, Cord named C. R. Smith, a promising young executive from Southern Airways, as president of American Airways. The pilots' union historian George Hopkins argues that through Smith, Cord continued to run American Airways as the "grey eminence behind the corporate structure which controlled it" until 1936, when he severed ties with the airline for four million dollars, afraid that he might jeopardize its ability to secure airmail contracts because of his notoriety.[130]

Despite significant resistance by the airlines, pilots were not the only airline employees to attempt organizing. In 1933, the International Association of Machinists (IAM), affiliated with the AFL, made inroads into the industry by organizing aircraft mechanics at Eastern Air Transport in Atlanta. However, the fledgling local collapsed after an unauthorized strike that same year.[131]

Even with the aid of ALPA members, the IAM faced a difficult struggle against the airlines and other unions attempting to organize the industry. American Airways discouraged its workers from joining the union by intimidating supporters and firing organizers. In a letter to the general vice president of the IAM, H. J. Carr, Paul Ottman, the recording secretary of IAM Lodge 737 at Eastern Air Transport in Atlanta, wrote,

> We are hearing persistent rumors from several pilots flying into this city for American Airways who have connections that enable them to hear of the various practices that are taking place throughout our industry trying to stop our organizing. We have been told on very good authority that Mr. C. R. Smith, Vice President of American Airways, just recently held a meeting at Fort Worth, and at that time he told the employees that they did not need to join any Union and that the Company would grant them an increase in wages of five cents per hour.
>
> You undoubtedly know that American Airways is controlled by Mr. E. L. Cord, who is very antagonistic towards organized labor, and of course we can look for a great deal of opposition from this Company. They have used their intimidating practice to such an extent that one of the pilots, who has been very friendly and helpful in the past, in carrying messages etc., he has been scared to the extent that a few days ago when we asked him to take a message through, relative to the McFarland case, he refused to do so. Of course, you realize that all of these rumors are hearsay, and we are not in a position

> to definitely pin anything on any individual. We have also been told that Mr. Smith let it be known that it was on account of brother McFarland's organizing activities that he was discharged.[132]

During the week of a representation vote in Fort Worth in 1935, American Airlines implied that voting in the IAM would mean layoffs for the mechanics in that city. As IAM organizers explained,

> On what all supposed to be a gentlemen's agreement to let the employees select representation either for our organization to represent the mechanical department employees or for the employees to have no representation, an election was conducted December 14, at the Fort Worth shops of the American Airlines between the hours of 11:30 AM and 9:30 PM. Mr. Hugh Smith representing the American Airlines, Inc., had met with me in the office of Dr. Edwin A. Elliott, Regional Director of the National Labor Relations Board, and agreed that there would be no intimidation nor coercion used by the officials of the American Airlines, to prevent the mechanics from voting for our organization. But after making this agreement with me, and in good faith on my part, Mr. Smith personally took a representative of the Wright Aviation Company through the plant and introduced him to several of the mechanics, something very unusual, and shortly thereafter the rumor got started around the plant that if we carried the election that the company would transfer the work to Glendale, California (near Los Angeles), [and] contract the work out to the Wright company. This happened on December 13, the day before the election. During the election it came to my attention that one of the foremen, a Mr. Paul Moore, had canvassed every man in the Service hanger and had told the men that if we carried the election that there would not be more than 18 men left, as the company would cut off the men to keep from doing business with us. Naturally, with all these rumors and pressure on the part of the officials, which was happening while I was at the voting booth, the men were scared to vote their honest convictions in regard to representation.[133]

Despite the intense pressure against organizing, some mechanics at American Airlines and its predecessor, American Airways, joined the IAM. However, the union never gained a strong enough hold at the company, and by 1939, mechanics at American Airlines voted in another organization, the Air Line Mechanics Association (ALMA).

Despite such anti-union activities, American Airlines, perhaps with the Norris-LaGuardia Act of 1932, which outlawed "yellow dog contracts," officially recognized the employees' right to organize. Its 1934 manual stated, "Employees shall have the right to organize and bargain collectively through representatives of their own choosing, and shall be free from interference, restraint, or coercion in the designation of such representatives or in self-organization or in other concerted activities for the purpose of collective bargaining or other mutual aid or benefit. No employee and no one seeking employment shall be required as a condition of employment to join or refrain from joining, organizing, or assisting a labor organization of his own choosing."[134]

The IAM won its first successful organizing drive on the airlines at Pan American Airways' shop in Brownsville, Texas, part of Pan Am's Western Division, in 1939.[135] Brownsville mechanics, facing an 8 percent wage decrease and impressed with the bargaining power of the pilots, contacted ALPA in August 1933 regarding organization. The AFL directed the mechanics to the IAM, and by the end of the year a struggling local had been established although the company refused it recognition.[136] By 1934, Pan Am attempted to counter the organizing drive by developing its own "education society," or company union. To increase its appeal, employees chosen by foremen were given access to training materials and classes that others, members of the IAM in particular, were not allowed to access.[137]

Initially the IAM intended only to organize aircraft mechanics. The IAM leadership was hesitant to organize beyond mechanically skilled groups, particularly in the case of laborers whose job it was to grade the airport fields and remove weeds and grass.[138] At this early point the IAM held no contracts with any airline, and setting a precedent regarding which workers they would organize was a significant concern. However, the Brownsville local signed up any trusted or interested employee in part because Pan Am started to train unorganized men from other departments to replace union mechanics.[139] This would prove to be an important lesson for future organizing plans. Employees who met these criteria (trusted or interested) included mechanic's helpers, painters, cleaners, storeroom clerks, field laborers, auto mechanics, upholsterers, night watchmen, and welders. Including these groups gave the IAM a majority of votes for representation at Pan Am's Brownsville operations.[140]

A large number of the workers in Brownsville were Mexican or Mexican American, a group that some IAM officials believed were "hopelessly difficult" to organize.[141] Contrary to this impression, Mexican Americans played an active role in the IAM in Brownsville. In 1934, Victorino V. Lopez and a fellow worker filed a complaint with the government charging Pan Am with violating the New Deal's Code of Fair Competition. Lopez stated that the company purposely held down wages because of union activity.[142] Mexican Americans also took active roles as union officials at the local level. Rufino Lopez, a mechanic and an officer and active member of IAM Local 736 in the late 1930s and early 1940s, was of Mexican descent.[143]

By May 1938, the IAM sought representation of three groups of Pan Am employees in Brownsville. The mechanical category included mechanics, helpers, stockroom and stores clerks, field workers, plane cleaners, field laborers, and watchmen. This group contained 140 employees, of which 105 authorized the IAM as their representative. The operating department included thirty-three stewards, clerks, and porters, twenty-four of which authorized the IAM. It is likely that workers from both categories participated in baggage, cargo, and mail handling. The third group, the communications department, employed twenty-six radio operators, Teletype operators, and parts clerks, twenty-one of which authorized the IAM as their representative.[144] Pan Am refused to accept the IAM's claim of representation of the above-mentioned groups of workers. Later that summer, the IAM again contacted Pan Am regarding representation at Brownsville. This time it claimed three different categories of workers, including only mechanics and their helpers, stockroom and shop clerks, radio operators, stewards, and unskilled workers. It is unclear as to how many workers made up this last category.[145] By 1939, the IAM secured the right to represent Pan Am's Brownsville employees. Their 1940 contract included mechanics, stockroom clerks, and unskilled workers. Unskilled workers in their first three months of employment earned sixty-five dollars per month for forty-eight-hour workweeks and seventy dollars per month for the rest of their first year. By their third year they earned eighty dollars, and by their fifth year they earned ninety dollars per month (about $1,350 in 2007).[146]

The IAM had its most critical prewar success at Eastern Air Transport, where it organized aircraft mechanics across the airlines' system in 1939. Following the collapse of an ALMA strike due to lack of organization and resources and the strident anti-unionism of Eddie Rickenbacker, the president of Eastern Air Transport, the IAM organized 347 mechanics, specialists, helpers, and apprentices at the airline and bargained their first contract, which included an eight-hour day, a forty-eight-hour week, overtime, a seniority system, vacation time, and substantial wage increases.[147]

* * *

By the late 1930s, the structure of the airline industry was in place. Its development as a transportation system in less than twenty years rested on the enormous investment of the government in infrastructure, subsidy, and regulation and the capital of wealthy investors. By the 1930s, aviation gained the confidence of the American public. The initial flying of the mail by the post office and its later contracting out not only introduced the public to a safer image of aviation but also made the business of flight possible. No commercial airline or even group of airlines could have supported the development of a lighted airways system, radio and navigational technology, landing fields, and weather stations. Governmental regulation through the Department of Commerce ensured that airlines would operate with the interests of public safety, both in the air and on the ground, during the developmental stage of passenger service. Stipulations in the Watres Act further promoted the development of passenger service through the space-available policy for mail as well as the encouragement to purchase larger and safer aircraft.

Rapid growth during this period and the dramatic increases in passenger traffic in the 1930s required the influx of hundreds of workers into the industry. The combination of industry growth and increased specialization of work duties matured into a distinct categorization of "skilled" and "unskilled" and "inside" and "outside" jobs. Class as well as gender and race would be important components of these differentiations. The new jobs in the late 1930s, skilled and unskilled, were available almost exclusively to young white men. The military supplied the industry with trained radio operators, meteorologists, pilots, and mechanics. For young white males without formal training, especially those fascinated by aviation, like George Rutledge, the industry offered jobs around airplanes as ticket agents, ramp agents, janitors, and chauffeurs. African American and most Hispanic men could only hope for positions in the industry as porters or other lower level jobs. White women found work as stenographers, office girls, sometimes as traffic agents, and as stewardesses as well, although height, weight, poise, and education requirements served to reduce the eligible pool of women interested in the position.

The pro-labor spirit of the New Deal era created critical possibilities for airline workers to organize. Pilots, aircraft mechanics, and other ground workers struggled to organize in the face of layoffs, pay cuts, and strained working conditions. For aircraft mechanics, the "runaway shop" or contracted-out work were real threats during the Depression. These mechanics turned to craft unionism and at least in one case encouraged their unskilled coworkers to join them. The growing gender and racial diversity of the workforce would produce new challenges during the war and postwar years.

2

Airline Work during World War II

The World War II era brought tremendous change to the American airline industry. By the end of the war, the airline industry proved itself central to U.S. defense as well as commerce. The war was also a turning point for airline workers. It ended the era of the small and somewhat informal workplace; opened the industry, at least temporarily, to women and minority workers; and increased the role of labor organizations in the industry. The industry not only demanded thousands of new workers on the ground but introduced new technology and transformed the ramp from a grassy field with a cluster of sheds to acres of concrete, cavernous hangars, and overcrowded terminals. At the same time, the combined efforts of the military and private industry to design more efficient aircraft and related equipment brought important improvements in safety, air pressurization, and cargo loading.

The 1940s formally initiated the position of "fleet-service clerk," "equipment serviceman," "ramp serviceman," or baggage handler within the airline industry. Despite the gradual employment of white women and minorities, white men dominated this category of work. As baggage handlers confronted long hours, low pay, and poor working conditions, they developed their own work culture around their youth, their masculinity, their ability to control the pace of their work, the noise and potential physical danger of the ramp as a workplace, and the informal specialized knowledge they gained on the job. This work culture on the ramp created a sense of camaraderie among baggage handlers across company boundaries and facilitated the development of a variety of resistance strategies, including quitting and labor organizing. This chapter details the role the airline industry played in the war effort, the expansion of the airline workforce, and the intensification of labor-organizing activities and other forms of resistance among ground-service workers.

The Airlines Go to War

A strategic defense arrangement between the government and the airline industry developed in the 1930s. In 1936, a group of executives from fourteen airlines met in Chicago to create the Air Transport Association (ATA), a trade organization for the industry. That year the ATA proposed an emergency mobilization plan for the industry to the War Department. Using personal and political ties to the military was critical to the industry's growth during the war. Recognizing the important role the airline industry could play during U.S. involvement in the war, the ATA president Edgar S. Gorrell carefully maintained information on commercial routes and equipment as well as the aeronautic infrastructure of weather and radio stations across the country and into the Pacific.[1] Gorrell developed a "structure of action" for the industry in case of war. Throughout 1937, Gorrell and his staff worked closely with the Army Air Corps and the Army War College as well as the airline executives C. R. Smith of American, William Patterson of United, and Jack Frye of TWA.[2] The plan, revised monthly through 1941, was designed to maintain the autonomy of the airlines, restrict competition during the war, and aid the war effort through contracts with the U.S. government.[3] Gorrell's plan, which satisfied the airlines' need to continue domestic service during wartime, utilized existing commercial infrastructure (maintenance bases) so that the airlines would conduct domestic and war-related operations in familiar territory.

According to the aviation author Reginald Cleveland, the promise of the full cooperation of the industry during the war by Gorrell and Gen. Henry "Hap" Arnold, chief of the Army Air Forces, prevented the nationalization of the industry by Franklin Roosevelt. Gorrell and Arnold worked to convince the president that nationalization would be a disaster for the young industry. Edgar Gorrell's role as head of the ATA and his close ties to the military played an important role in Roosevelt's decision. In the early 1930s, Gorrell was appointed to the Baker Board, a special committee of the War Department that developed promotion procedures for airmen in the army. Gorrell (later a colonel) was close friends with Gen. George C. Marshall, chief of staff for the armed forces.[4] The wartime government body that oversaw the airline industry's role in the war effort, the Air Transport Command, included a significant number of ex-airline officials in its ranks.[5]

Close cooperation with the government proved to be essential to the war effort and for the continued private operation of the airline industry. Eighteen domestic and three international airlines gained lucrative wartime service contracts. In December 1943, the Office of War Information proclaimed, "[B]oth military and commercial war activities have been profitable to the airlines, several of which had been operating at a loss before Pearl Harbor. . . . [T]he Civil Aeronautics Board states that in the 12-month period ending Aug. 31, 1943, the domestic airlines made a net profit of $31,958,072, more than twice the total of the period, Aug. 31, 1941–Aug. 31, 1942." According to the Office of War Information, the commercial airlines more than doubled their prewar volume of cargo, mostly through carrying military equipment and supplies on a cost-plus-fixed-fee basis. The increase was also due to rescheduling, eliminating nonessential stops, standardization, and better utilization of equipment despite the significant decline in available aircraft. During this period, the airlines also carried nearly twice the amount of U.S. airmail as in 1941.[6] These dramatic increases in cargo and mail loads demanded expanded hours and manning for ground operations.

The airline industry's initial participation in the war effort fell under the jurisdiction of two organizations: the Ferrying Command and the Air Service Command. Before the bombing of Pearl Harbor, the Ferrying Command supplied aid to U.S. allies through the Lend-Lease program. Through this program, Pan American Airways improved landing fields in Africa and ferried aircraft to Britain. By early 1942, the Ferrying Command organized the work of contracted domestic airlines according to their maintenance-base locations. Donald H. Connolly, the military director of civil aviation, divided the country into five zones, taking into consideration maintenance facilities and bases of operation. The airlines were satisfied with this plan because it avoided direct competition for contracts among them. American Airlines covered the East, Eastern Airlines the Southeast, Braniff the Southwest, United the West Coast, and Northwest Airlines the Northwest and Alaska.[7] Pan American Airways routes to South America, established in the 1930s, were crucial to the war effort for transporting raw materials such as rubber and aluminum to defense plants in the United States.[8] Of the 360 aircraft flown by the domestic airlines, two hundred were contracted for the war effort. Contracts were also organized around the types of aircraft available and experience. For example, Northwest Airlines, with experience flying through Alaskan winters, held contracts for flying along the Arctic Circle. TWA owned four-engine Boeing Stratoliners capable of flying the Atlantic; therefore, TWA held contracts to fly to North Africa.[9]

A second government body, the Air Service Command, offered contracts to airlines for transporting cargo to free up military transport planes for tactical work. With two sets of contracts, conflict and duplication of services arose, and by June 1942, the two commands reorganized to become the Air Transport Command (ATC) and the Naval Air Transport Service (NATS). Under the direction of the chairman of American Airlines, C. R. Smith, the ATC controlled aircraft ferrying, the movement of men and materials by air, and the control of operations and maintenance of air routes and fields for the army.[10] The NATS functioned primarily to quickly supply navy vessels with crucial parts, medical equipment, and medicine. Over the course of the war, American Airlines flew the equivalent of twenty-six thousand times around the equator on military business. They flew eight billion passenger-miles and 850 million ton-miles of cargo. At the end of the war, the airlines played an important role in bringing troops back to the United States.[11]

The airlines participated in the war not only by transporting military personnel and materials under contracts with the ATC but also in the training of pilots and mechanics and modifying existing aircraft for wartime use. Over the course of the war, the Douglas Aircraft Company built ten thousand C-47s, the military version of the DC-3.[12] The development of the DC-3 in 1936, by the Douglas Aircraft Company at the behest of C. R. Smith, gave the commercial airlines their first profitable aircraft and the military the C-47, the backbone of much of the war effort in the air. However, the demand for planes by the United States and its allies outpaced production. Most factories were not equipped to build or install the more complicated airframes and systems for military aircraft. United Airlines modified over five thousand Boeing B-17s at its maintenance base in Cheyenne, Wyoming. In the process, the airline trained five thousand technicians in such work.[13]

The modification centers sprang up overnight and often without much shelter and infrastructure. Mechanics and other workers often retooled planes outdoors. As in other wartime operations, thousands of men and women were quickly hired to build and staff the centers. According to the publicity arm of the American war effort, the Office of War Information, "Beauty shop operators, barbers, soda fountain boys, school teachers, milkmen were recruited and given intensive courses of instruction. The manager of one center in the heart of Western cattle country had to post notices urging new employees to remove their spurs before getting to work."[14]

By December 1943, the modification plants functioned indoors and were running full-force. Continental Airlines' modification center for B-17 Flying Fortresses alone cost more than twelve million dollars. The center covered sixteen city blocks, with almost four million square feet of airplane parking space and hangars more than six hundred feet long and four hundred feet wide, "large enough to house all present installations at the airport with room to spare." Continental's modification center also included power and heating plants and a cafeteria with room for eight hundred diners.[15] In St. Paul, Minnesota, Northwest Airlines opened a modification center in March 1943. The company employed 3,500 workers at the facility; approximately half of these workers were women.[16] By September 1945, workers at the St. Paul Modification Center serviced over three thousand airplanes for the war effort.[17] Beyond specific war-related missions and modification overseen by the ATC, domestic airlines served the war effort through efficient use of aircraft still operating in the private sector on domestic routes. Flights between cities with important military-production operations carried blueprints for defense factories and crucial spare parts, as well as specialists when factories needed troubleshooters.[18]

Civilian travel changed dramatically during World War II.[19] Airplanes were no longer filled with salesmen and well-to-do travelers. With over 50 percent of aircraft owned by domestic airlines contracted for the war effort, the remaining commercial seats available came under regulation. The ATC through its Priorities and Traffic Division created four categories of travel for all commercial flights:

1. Persons traveling on direct orders from the White House or the War or Navy Departments.
2. Military pilots en route to aircraft ferry bases or military installations.
3. Military or civilian passengers on essential war-related business.
4. Military cargo.[20]

Seats left open after priority passengers boarded went to civilian passengers. Seats were most often available on underutilized routes, those with many stops, and at off-peak hours. Eastbound flights had more open seats than westbound flights because of the number of Priority 2 passengers heading to California to pick up aircraft to ferry to Europe. Most manufacturers' representatives and salesmen who made up the core of airline business in the 1930s now traveled by train. The scarcity of seats available to civilian passengers led to an illegal market for these seats despite public assurances by the airlines that extra service fees for purchasing seats were unnecessary.[21] Some famous Americans lost their seats to priority passengers. In 1944, newspapers enthusiastically reported how a serviceman with priority papers bumped the president of Eastern Airlines, Eddie Rickenbacker, from one of his own planes. The First Lady, Eleanor Roosevelt, flying Priority 3, lost her seat to an army pilot flying Priority 2.[22]

Although the airlines curtailed commercial service, they actually increased their cargo and passenger loads through more efficient use of available equipment during the war.[23] Continued commercial service was essential to the airline industry despite the lucrative wartime government contracts. While the contracts were profitable, much of the profit during the war years came from increased passenger loads, which rose from 64 to 91 percent between 1941 and 1944.[24] During the war, the airlines attempted to continue some level of comfortable commercial service. Domestic airlines flew with maximum loads on almost every flight. The "load factor," the proportion of seats occupied, reached 89 percent—an all-time high. All sixteen trunk lines turned a profit for the first time during the war. Throughout the war, airlines continued to serve food and beverages on the flights but cut back service in other ways. Cardboard instead of plastic was used for meal trays. The requirement that stewardesses be nurses ended during the war. The glamour and luxury of airline travel also diminished, at least temporarily, during the war because of late flights, lost luggage, crowded terminals, and large numbers of disappointed standby passengers.[25]

Wartime Employment

Under the impact of wartime production, the airline workforce dramatically increased. By 1940, the scheduled airline industry employed 22,051 people. By 1945, that figure more than tripled. As table 2 shows, employment gains in the industry during the war particularly impacted mechanics and communications and office workers, three categories affected by modification and related war-work. The service category, which included baggage handlers, nearly doubled from 4,277 in 1940 to 9,447 in 1945.

Women and African Americans made some inroads into some areas of the industry, but the baggage- and cargo-handling job remained overwhelmingly white and male throughout the war. Of the 20,878 men employed in the industry, only 729 were African American, and ten were counted as "other races." African American men made up only 3 percent of male air-transportation employees. Over half of these men worked in the South. Of the 2,297 women employed in the airline industry nationwide, only thirty-one were African American; over 98 percent of the female workforce was white.[26] Table 3 shows the breakdown of national airline-industry employment figures by race, gender, and region.

Table 2. Personnel Employed by the Scheduled Airline Industry, 1940–45

Year	Pilots	Flight	Stewards	Comm.	Mech.	Service	Office	Other	Total
1940	2,279	33	1,036	193	5,413	4,277	7,689	1,131	22,051
1941	2,664	49	1,210	220	6,389	4,931	9,710	1,285	26,458
1943	2,332	241	992	2,196	10,411	5,191	12,832	4,995	39,279
1944	3,345	277	1,516	2,501	9,963	5,748	15,234	4,023	42,607
1945	5,897	1,046	2,486	3,477	15,943	9,447	23,904	6,081	68,281

Source: Air Transport Association, *Air Transport Facts and Figures* (Washington, D.C.: Air Transport Association, 1959), 14; Air Transport Association, *Air Transport Facts and Figures* (Washington, D.C.: Air Transport Association, 1965), 32.

Note: The categories include personnel as follows: Pilots: pilots and copilots; Flight: other flight personnel; Stewards: pursers, stewards and stewardesses; Comm.: communications personnel including meteorologists and dispatchers; Mech.: mechanics; Service: aircraft and traffic servicing personnel; Office: office employees including ticket and reservations agents; Other: all others.

While a national breakdown of airline employment is informative, an examination of employment statistics for cities served by American, Northwest, Pan American, and National Airlines presents a clearer regional picture of airline workers at these companies. In 1940, American Airlines was based in New York, Northwest was based in Minneapolis/St. Paul, and Pan Am maintained its largest operation in Miami. National served Miami and New

Table 3. Air-Transportation Employment in the U.S. by Region, 1940

	Northeast (%)	Northcentral (%)	South (%)	West (%)	U.S. Total (%)
			Male		
White	5,654	4,805	5,406	4,274	20,129
	(87)	(83)	(87)	(90)	(86)
Negro	137	140	381	71	729
	(2)	(2)	(6)	(1)	(3)
Other	2	2	1	5	10
	(<1)	(<1)	(<1)	(<1)	(<1)
			Female		
White	676	800	413	376	2,265
	(10)	(14)	(6)	(8)	(10)
Negro	15	4	12	—	31
	(<1)	(<1)	(<1)		(<1)
Other	—	—	1	—	1
			(<1)		(<1)
Total	6,482	5,749	6,214	4,726	23,175

Source: U.S. Bureau of the Census, *Race of Employed Persons (Except on Public Emergency Work) and of Experienced Workers Seeking Work, by Industry and Sex, for Regions: 1940,* Washington D.C., 1943.

York. Chicago is also included in this examination because of its role as an important transportation center.

Employees loading and unloading baggage and cargo from aircraft and related duties were classified as operatives.[27] According to the U.S. Census of Population, 1,486 men were employed in air transportation in Florida in 1940. Of that number, 1,382 (93 percent) were classified as white and 104 (7 percent) were classified as Negro. Table 4 shows the breakdown according to occupational group of men and women employed in the air-transportation industry and nonwhite men and women employed in the industry in Florida in 1940. No detailed statistical breakdown is included for Miami. Almost half of the state's airline workers lived in Miami. In Miami, 719 men and fifty-four women worked in air transportation in 1940. Of those counted, forty-three were identified as nonwhite men and one as a nonwhite woman.[28]

White workers also made up the overwhelming majority of air-transport workers in Illinois. Of the 1,382 men employed, only 40 (2 percent) were classified as Negro. One male worker in air transportation in Illinois was classified as "other race." Of the 379 women employed in Illinois, only two (less than 1 percent) were counted as Negro, and none were counted as other races. Of the total numbers for the state, 822 men and 303 women worked in Chicago. In Chicago, thirty-seven (5 percent) of the men and two of the women were classified as nonwhite. Classification for the city did not

Table 4. Air-Transportation Employment in Florida, 1940

	Pro. (%)	Prop./Mgr. (%)	Clerical (%)	Craftsmen (%)	Operative (%)	Service (%)	Laborer (%)	Total (%)
				Male				
All	340	86	205	483	151	100	95	1,460
	(23)	(6)	(14)	(33)	(10)	(7)	(7)	(100)
Non-white	—	—	—	1	5	52	44	102
				(<1)	(5)	(51)	(43)	(100)
				Female				
All	6	1	67	4	4	2	—	84
	(7)	(1)	(80)	(5)	(5)	(2)		(100)
Non-white	—	—	—	—	—	2	—	2
						(100)		(100)

Source: U.S. Bureau of the Census, *Detailed Industry of Employed (Except Emergency Work), and of Experienced Workers Seeking Work, by Color and Sex, for the State, and Cities of 100,000 or More: 1940*, Washington D.C., 1943.

Note: Pro. represents professional and semiprofessional employees. Prop./Mgr. represents proprietors and managers. These figures exclude the protective-service-workers category and workers whose occupations were not reported.

include the category "Negro."[29] Table 5 shows the breakdown according to occupational group of men and women employed in the air-transportation industry and African American men and women employed in the industry in Chicago in 1940.

Minnesota's air-industry employment levels were significantly lower than those of Florida and Illinois. Across the state, 432 men and sixty-one women worked in air transportation in 1940; 297 of those men and fifty-five of those women worked in St. Paul/Minneapolis. Throughout Minnesota, the census classified as Negro two men and no women employed in the air-transport industry. No men or women were included in the "other races" category.[30] Table 6 shows the breakdown according to occupational group of men and women employed in the air-transportation industry in Minneapolis/St. Paul in 1940. Figures for Minnesota did not include separate categories for race.

The air-transportation industry in New York employed a far larger number of workers than in Florida, Minnesota, or Illinois in 1940. Across the state, 3,507 men and 490 women worked in the industry.[31] Of those totals, eighty-eight men and ten women were classified as Negro, and two men and no women as "other races." Over 80 percent of the state's air-transportation employees lived in New York City: 2,429 men and 416 women. African American men and women made up 3 percent of the city's air-transportation workforce. Table 7 shows the breakdown according to occupational group of men and

Table 5. Air-Transportation Employment in Chicago, 1940

	Pro. (%)	Prop./Mgr. (%)	Clerical (%)	Craftsmen (%)	Operative (%)	Service (%)	Laborer (%)	Total (%)
				Male				
All	206	40	241	188	50	44	33	802
	(23)	(6)	(14)	(33)	(10)	(7)	(7)	(100)
Non-white	2	—	1	2	4	25	3	37
	(5)		(3)	(5)	(11)	(68)	(8)	(100)
				Female				
All	129	—	150	5	1	18	—	303
	(42)	(1)	(49)	(2)	(<1)	(6)		(100)
Non-white	—	—	—	—	—	2	—	2
						(100)		(100)

Source: U.S. Bureau of the Census, *Detailed Industry of Employed (Except Emergency Work), and of Experienced Workers Seeking Work, by Color and Sex, for the State, and Cities of 100,000 or More: 1940,* Washington D.C., 1943.

Note: Pro. represents professional and semiprofessional employees. Prop/Mgr. represents proprietors and managers. These figures exclude the protective-service-workers category and workers whose occupations were not reported.

Table 6. Air-Transportation Employment in Minneapolis/St. Paul, 1940

	Pro. (%)	Prop./Mgr. (%)	Clerical (%)	Craftsmen (%)	Operative (%)	Service (%)	Laborer (%)	Total (%)
				Male				
All	79	25	53	98	16	10	16	297
	(27)	(8)	(18)	(33)	(5)	(3)	(5)	(100)
				Female				
All	19	2	33	—	—	1	—	55
	(34)	(4)	(60)			(2)		(100)

Source: U.S. Bureau of the Census, *Detailed Industry of Employed (Except Emergency Work), and of Experienced Workers Seeking Work, by Color and Sex, for the State, and Cities of 100,000 or More: 1940,* Washington D.C., 1943.

Note: Pro. represents professional and semiprofessional employees. Prop/Mgr. represents proprietors and managers. These figures exclude the protective-service-workers category and workers whose occupations were not reported.

women employed in the air-transportation industry and all African American men and women employed in the industry in New York City in 1940.

The airline workforce was a relatively young one in 1940. According to the census, the nationwide median age for male workers was 30.7 years; for females it was 26.8 years. These median ages are far lower than for workers in other transportation industries. The median ages for men and women in the railroad industry were 45.5 years and 40.5 years, respectively. For street

Table 7. Air-Transportation Employment in New York City, 1940

	Pro. (%)	Prop./Mgr. (%)	Clerical (%)	Craftsmen (%)	Operative (%)	Service (%)	Laborer (%)	Total (%)
				Male				
All	478	121	641	871	162	118	65	2,429
	(20)	(5)	(25)	(36)	(6)	(5)	(3)	(100)
Non-white	1	—	4	6	7	50	7	75
	(2)		(5)	(8)	(9)	(67)	(9)	(100)
				Female				
All	81	1	307	8	7	12	—	416
	(19)	(<1)	(74)	(2)	(2)	(3)		(100)
Non-white	—	—	3	—	—	6	—	9
			(33)			(67)		(100)

Source: U.S. Bureau of the Census, *Detailed Industry of Employed (Except Emergency Work), and of Experienced Workers Seeking Work, by Color and Sex, for the State, and Cities of 100,000 or More: 1940,* Washington D.C., 1943.

Note: Pro. represents professional and semiprofessional employees. Prop/Mgr. represents proprietors and managers. These figures exclude the protective-service-workers category and workers whose occupations were not reported.

railways and bus lines the median ages for men and women were 41.3 and 36.2 years, respectively. The median ages for men and women in the airline industry were more comparable to those of workers in another relatively new industry, radio broadcasting and television. In 1940, the median ages for men and women in that industry were 31.7 and 28.7 years, respectively. The median age for males was lower in only two categories: in the category "national defense," the median age was 25.8 years. For males working in "aircraft and parts" manufacturing, the median age was 29.8 years.[32]

As the U.S. Census shows, 87 percent of the air-transportation workforce consisted of white males. Together, white men and women made up 96 percent of the workforce. White males continued to hold the highest-paid and most skilled positions in the industry before and during the war. While white women in Chicago (42 percent of all women in the workforce), Minneapolis/St. Paul (34 percent), and New York (19 percent) found work in positions classified as professional or semiprofessional, this work was less open to them in Florida (7 percent). Between 50 and 75 percent of white women were relegated to clerical and sales positions in the industry in the four regions examined. Over half of all African American men employed in air transportation worked in the South. Of the thirty-one African American women employed in the industry, approximately half worked in the Northeast, and the majority of the rest found work in the South. Again, the work of baggage handlers fell under the category "operative." Only 3 percent of operatives in all three cities and Florida were classified as nonwhite, and only 2 percent as female.

Although white men dominated the airline workforce, white women and African Americans made some inroads into the industry. White women found more employment options in the airlines than black women. White women found work for the duration in the aircraft-modification centers and in commercial operations in airline offices, in baggage handling, and even as aircraft mechanics at the airfields. Race proved to be a greater obstacle than gender for African American men and women moving into the industry. According to averaged figures supplied by nine airlines during the war, white women made up about 15 percent of the air-transportation workforce in December 1941, and by September 1943 they made up 29.7 percent of the workforce.[33] At Pan Am alone, figures for female employment increased fourfold from December 1941 to the same month in 1942, from 390 to 1,642 female employees. Women found work for the company in commercial and modification operations.

These employment rates for women at Pan Am reflect a dramatic increase in female employment across the industry after 1940, when only fifty-four

Table 8. Female Employees at Pan American Airways, 1941–42

Operations	As of	As of	Executive	Comm.	Traffic	Maint.	Operations
Base	12/41	12/42					
Miami	200	449	21	102	77	156	93
New York	65	391	68	15	37	217	54
Brownsville	35	274	5	40	39	163	27
San Fran.	56	331	78	15	8	191	39
Seattle	31	176	24	17	17	87	31
Mexico City	3	21	3	4	13	0	1
Total	390	1,642	199	193	191	814	245

Source: Pan American Airways, *New Horizons* (December 1942): 10, Pan American Airways Collection, Otto G. Richter Library, University of Miami, Coral Gables, Fla., "1941–1960, Women—Ground Jobs" file, box 257.

women worked in air transportation in Miami and 420 in New York City. Women found employment in some of the most skilled ranks of the industry as "radio to ground operators; dispatch clerks; guards; passenger and traffic agents; counter and outside saleswomen; direct traffic managers—only four reported; aircraft engine instructor (one with an 'E' license); cartographers; aeronautical engineers; junior engineering analysts; draftswomen; Link trainer operators and instructors; junior meteorologists and weather chart plotters; women's counselors; medical assistants."[34]

Women's work in the industry also reflected the larger "Rosie the Riveter" phenomenon of the war era, as women replaced men on the job when they left for military service. Women hired by the airlines filled a wide variety of positions on the ground at modification centers and as commercial-service employees. According to one industry journal, women worked as "overhaul shop and hangar mechanics—welding, riveting sheet metal, tube bending, radio, electrical, upholstery, paint, and instrument testing departments and in supervisory capacities as crewleaders; cargo handlers—most lines believe too heavy but some are performing successfully in critical labor areas; ramp agents—calculating weights and as manifest clerks; timekeepers and stock clerks; plane groomers and cleaners; plane gassers and oilers; trouble shooters."[35] This list covers work that was predominantly new to women in the industry at the start of the war, including cargo handling.

Prior to the war, white women worked in the industry as stewardesses, office clerks, cafeteria workers, and janitors. A small number of white women found jobs as baggage handlers during the war. Of nearly fifty baggage and cargo handlers at American Airlines in Fort Worth, Texas, in August 1945, at least eleven were women.[36] According to George Rutledge, an American

Airlines employee from 1925 to 1974, women were hired as baggage handlers at LaGuardia Airport in New York during the war. As he recalled, some of these women were "society gals" who even invited him to a party on Park Avenue. After the war, most women left their airline jobs. According to Rutledge, "I would say probably most of them went back home, especially the New York society girls. They weren't going to hang around working on the ramp."[37] Some women did remain on the ramp as baggage handlers after the war. Most often they were permanently relegated to cabin-cleaning duties and did not load and unload planes or perform other outdoor duties.[38]

Similar to "Rosies" in other industries, depictions of these women emphasized their patriotism and concern for their fighting men. Pan Am's company magazine for passengers, *New Horizons,* contained several lengthy articles about the dedicated performances of women on the job as mechanic's helpers and passenger-service agents. A 1943 article described their work at Pan Am's hangar in Brownsville, Texas: "Society girls, mothers, beauty operators, salesgirls, school teachers; women of all types, ages, sizes, dispositions, and backgrounds have come to Pan American's big Brownsville hangar to actively help win the war. Most of them have sons, brothers, or husbands in the service [and] are proud to help keep the essential carriers of men and materials in the air." Not all the women working for Pan Am in Brownsville were native-born; Greek-born Mary Koutiroulares worked among them. The article notes that she was fluent in Spanish, implying that this skill was useful on the job.

Much of the publicity surrounding the women workers focused on the maintenance of their "female traits" while doing a man's job. According to the Pan Am article, women working as lower-level mechanics were quick to learn their jobs. Despite working in traditionally male jobs, the company magazine was quick to point out their "female" attributes of concern for others' opinions, silly jealousies, and the ability to "laugh away" challenging suggestions: "Only discoverable difference between masculine and feminine personnel is the near-jealous interest each woman has for her own work. Riveters resent opinions that theirs is a noisy job. Banana oil dopers proudly assert the fumes are not bad. Women on the line working in face-scorching eye-burning wind and sun laugh away suggestions that they might prefer to work indoors." The women held their own in the mechanics department. The fastest crew in the Brownsville shops consisted of all women.[39]

Articles in *New Horizons* focused exclusively on white women entering the workforce for the war effort, although Pan Am employed African American women as plane cleaners and maids. The young white women, average age twenty-three, performed cleaning and sewing tasks in the hangars.[40] The article explained, "Most of the new girls went to work in the Fabric and Equipment shops, working on fabric-covered Clipper control surfaces and on emergency equipment (rubber life rafts, etc.). Others performed such duties as cleaning spark plugs, windows, and the luminous dials on Clipper flight instruments, assembling cowl brackets, removing pillows and blankets, splicing ropes."

These articles also downplayed any conflict the new women employees had with their more experienced male counterparts: "Though it was the first time women had actually been employed in the hangar, the innovation caused hardly a ripple in Pan American's smooth-working Maintenance procedure. Male employees had received instructions that the new comers were to be treated as men, proceeded to address the girls by their last names."[41]

An article in an industry journal included a less enthusiastic view of women in the airlines and attributed the problems to "female" behavior. According to the article, a man at Western Airlines told the reporter that he had "watched womanpower burst into tears over nothing, throw earphones at the control board, slap a foreman in the face with a dripping paint brush, pull hair, go on won't talk strikes, try coy man-plays so they can goldbrick, pout when they're reprimanded, and they've even accused me of stealing 25 cents off their pay."[42] Goldbrickers or model employees, overwhelmingly white women left their jobs in the maintenance shops at the end of the war.[43]

African American men and women also gradually increased their presence in the airline industry during the war, mostly as porters, maids/janitors, or plane cleaners. In Chicago, 75 percent and in New York, 73 percent of nonwhite men (nearly all African American) found employment as service workers or laborers. In Florida, 95 percent of nonwhite men (all African American except one) were employed in these low-skill categories despite the fact that over half of all African Americans employed in the industry worked in the South.[44] African American men and women were not hired as baggage handlers, although some of their job duties as plane cleaners and porters at times blurred with those of higher-paid white male fleet-service clerks.[45]

Pan Am's company papers celebrated and praised its black employees. On one occasion, the company noted employment anniversaries of two African American "handymen" employed by Pan Am since 1929.[46] One particularly well-liked African American lead plane cleaner in San Francisco started with the company in 1936. Pan Am's company newspaper for employees, *The Clipper*, highlighted the good work of several African American women in its Alaska Sector edition in 1944. A large photo appeared of four African American women cleaning an airplane in Seattle with the caption,

> BRUSH-OFF GIRLS: This smiling quartette giving airplane joints a thorough brush-off are left to right DOLORES "DUCKY" BENTON, GWENDOLYN MITCHELL, NORMA TURNER, and VASSIE MOSLEY. Using spray guns and stiff bristle brushes, cleaners are performing the first step in removing corrosion, caused by exhaust smoke filtering up inside the wing. After cleaners scour the surface, Paint Shop applies a chromic acid solution neutralizing corrosion. To prevent further exhaust smoke from entering, flap in back of wing will be sealed with dope fabric and sealing compound.

The work of plane cleaners required a certain amount of skill. Beyond the "elbow grease" needed to make the aircraft exterior shine, these workers needed to understand the strength and danger of the chemicals they used and how to use them around the delicate instruments they cared for. The paper continued,

> Corrosion removal is only one of many jobs performed by hangar plane cleaners. Under supervision of Chief Cleaner HASKELL CAMPBELL, they keep plane exteriors mirror-shiny, bilges and cockpits spotless. Careful not to use agencies that will fray or damage cables, cleaners must know how to handle inflammables, how to clean plexiglass, names of every airplane part, how to handle delicate radio equipment. Other airplane and hangar cleaners are Bill Duncan, Hattie Holliday, M. L. Jones, A. Purnell, Clarence Jackson, Vera Carter, E. M. Jones, LeRoy Raine, G. D. Copeland, A. D. Driver, J. J. Owens, T. Walden, and O. L. Williams.[47]

African Americans were rarely promoted past the job of lead plane cleaner during the war.[48]

Across the industry, the work of cleaning planes was not the exclusive domain of African American women. White men like Robert Slouber, an aircraft cleaner and then baggage handler for American Airlines in Chicago, polished airplane exteriors during his first weeks of employment on the night shift in 1941. For six months, his duties included thoroughly cleaning aircraft interiors, another night-shift job. In Miami, African American and white employees at Pan Am completed the same tasks, such as driving trucks and buffing aircraft exteriors, under separate job classifications and pay scales. African Americans were classified as aircraft cleaners or handymen and white men as "fleet-service clerks."[49] Workers frustrated by this disparity were some of the first in the industry to organize.

Work Culture on the Ramp

Work duties and work culture in the industry and on the ramp changed significantly over the course of the war. Prior to the war, the classification of "fleet-service clerk" (baggage handler) was only just emerging. Except in large cities like New York, Miami, and Chicago, there was little need for a work group to perform such specialized duties.[50] With the development of the DC-3, the dramatic increase in hiring, and the increased utilization of aircraft for civilian and military passengers and cargo, the need for workers who exclusively loaded and unloaded and cleaned aircraft grew.

Airlines and the army influenced the work process by developing new methods and equipment for loading and servicing aircraft during the war. Research and testing improved aircraft tires, wheels, propellers, instruments, the pressurization of cabins, and safety equipment. The army developed a forty-eight-foot-long mobile ramp that served as a bridge between the terminal and plane for workers to carry cargo on hand carts. Maj. J. A. Devereux invented an electrically powered lift platform capable of carrying up to ten thousand pounds. This lift, called "Devereux's Folly" by skeptics, rolled up next to the aircraft for level on- or off-loading. While significant advances were made in aviation equipment by the army and by private manufacturers through the demands of commercial airlines, their needs appeared to be at odds in some cases. For example, two companies designed conveyor trucks for loading during the war. The army did not adopt this new technology because it was not suitable for loading the large and heavy equipment flown on many of its planes. Conversely, these conveyor trucks were perfect for loading commercial cargo and baggage, and a modern version is still used today.[51]

Industry-magazine advertisements encouraged airlines to modernize their operations. One company, depicting a smiling African American carrying a box on his shoulder, declared, "Loading air cargo is no job for a Mississippi River stevedore. But cargo loading is a big job for the aircraft operator. With transoceanic flying time measured in hours, days can't be spent taking on the load. 'Stevedore' methods must not delay the achievements of modern aviation."[52]

Airlines utilized new technology as well as processes to expedite aircraft loading. Cargo was no longer handed piece-by-piece up into the cargo hold; instead, conveyor trucks, "skyloaders," and specially designed airport tractors and trailer units transformed the work of baggage handlers, replacing the "bucket brigade" style of loading.[53] Advertisements in *Air Transport* magazine touted the newest developments for loading planes: "This newly acquired

Lyon-Raymond, Ford-tractor-driven, belt loader enables AA to handle air express and its new air freight at LG Field at high speed. Adjustable to the door height of a DC-3 now or to a DC-4 or CW-20E later, this conveyor can discharge cargo directly to waiting panel trucks or load it so fast that the men doing the stowing have to work fast and think fast."[54]

Taylorism, or time-and-motion studies, also transformed the work process for baggage handlers during the war. George Rutledge, the superintendent of planning station operations during the war for American Airlines, believed that increased efficiency in cargo handling was the key to postwar financial success for the airlines. In an *Air Transport* article he surmised, "We must take a page from the book of industries, older than ours, where efficiency, plant, and manpower utilization are geared to movement. We should make careful time and motion studies of every operation performed in the handling of cargo. Every operation no matter how infinitely small should be studied, for every moment can cost time and money. The analysis should be in terms of seconds. In air transport, seconds count and fractions of minutes are invaluable."[55] Workers on the ramp resisted the increased pace expected in their work.

The cold in Alaska also demanded specially designed equipment for loading and servicing aircraft in below-zero temperatures. Alaska during the thaw presented equally difficult conditions, with deep mud runways that required a covering of steel plates for planes to land. Swarms of mosquitoes engulfed mechanics, fleet-service workers, and pilots alike as soon as a plane stopped on the runway. Even in flight, pilots wore gloves and netting to protect themselves from the insects.[56]

The weight and durability of packaging became a life-or-death issue during wartime. According to the Office of War Information, "[T]he Army and Navy have insisted first of all that materials be packed stoutly to prevent damage from rough handling. Often the packing case, made of inch-thick, reinforced pine boards, was heavier than its contents." The high volume of military supplies and equipment necessitated the development of lighter packaging materials. The Office of War Information announced,

> The NATS and the ATC, with the cooperation of the airlines, have developed much less bulky packaging. Strong, specially processed cardboard and fibreboard have been substituted for wood and metal wherever possible. Heavy wrapping paper and burlap are also used in place of weightier materials. For example, the NATS states that the pay load of one type of seaplane has on occasion been increased from 4,000 to 6,000 pounds by reducing the tare weight of cargo carried. A shipment of airplane engines which, under the old methods, would have weighed 26,625 pounds and required the entire

> space of five or six transports, was reduced by the NATS to 8,862 pounds and shipped complete in one plane. New types of gadgets to secure cargo aboard planes have not only added to the safety of operation and reduction of damaged cargo, but have helped materially in making possible the use of lighter packaging material.
>
> Research in the field of light, tough packaging has already turned each of our cargo carriers into the equivalent of several craft.
>
> Implications for post-war airborne commerce are enormous.[57]

Advances in packaging and loading equipment, developed during the war, changed cargo service and the work of loading planes after the war. By war's end, the airfield was no longer a small informal place on the outskirts of town but instead a modern air terminal. The entire industry formalized procedures and operations.

Airline employees saw themselves as an important part of the war effort. Indeed, they played a crucial role in transporting military personnel and cargo as well as retooling hundreds of planes for the effort. Importantly, airline employees saw themselves as distinct from workers in other defense-related industries. While ship and aircraft building were also industries essential to the war effort, airline workers did not identify with workers in these industries. Some airline workers saw themselves as superior to production workers. Concerned about the "bitter feeling" among airline employees when referred to as "aircraft workers," IAM organizers created the Airline Division to differentiate between the two types of aviation work.[58] Others focused on the variation in their jobs and the freedom of movement on the ramp. Robert Slouber recalled feeling fortunate that he found work in the airlines just out of high school. He said that "people felt what they were doing in the airlines was important for the war effort. . . . We needed to do a good job. I never felt sorry that I was working for the airlines. . . . It was exciting. I liked the variety of it."[59]

During the war the position of baggage handler also underwent change. The work was nestled between those positions at the bottom of the airline industry that still directly involved airplanes, such as airplane cleaners, and those demanding specific skills, such as ground servicemen who fueled aircraft and maintained ground-service equipment, semiskilled junior aircraft mechanics, and skilled licensed aircraft mechanics. In 1942, a baggage handler's duties could include chasing cows off the runway in Louisville, Kentucky.[60] By war's end, thousands of baggage handlers across the industry worked in modern air terminals, performing specific duties spelled out in union contracts. At the onset of the war, wages for baggage handlers and other unskilled workers in the industry were substantially lower than those in other jobs available to young men. Robert Slouber earned sixty-five dollars a month when he started with American Airlines just out of high school in July 1941.[61] The Wage Stabilization Act of 1942 also covered the industry.[62] This controversial legislation, designed to stabilize wages and control inflation, attempted to hold wages at levels set in the first nine months of 1942.[63] Employees in the airlines worked eight-hour days six days a week. Wages on this scale equaled thirty-three cents an hour, while wages for laborers in shipbuilding in the Great Lakes region during the same period earned seventy cents an hour. Unionized guards on Chicago's elevated railways earned seventy-seven cents an hour.[64] Unionized helpers on trucks hauling building materials in Chicago that summer earned sixty-five cents an hour for a fifty-four-hour week.[65]

Moreover, the modern air terminals increased the hazards, discipline, and rigors of fleet-service work. The number of aircraft arrivals and departures increased as well as passenger and cargo loads, speeding up and increasing the volume of work for baggage handlers. Baggage handlers worked not only around airplanes but on construction sites, as airfields were transformed into air terminals. Maneuvering new tractors, bag carts, "skyloaders," and cargoveyors across a crowded ramp could be dangerous. Working six days a week loading and unloading commercial as well as military baggage and cargo was exhausting work.

Baggage handlers and other unskilled workers responded to long hours, poor wages, and inadequate working conditions in a variety of ways. First, they left their jobs for better-paying ones in the war years, when most industries experienced manpower shortages. Organizers for the IAM lamented the youthful indifference and transience of some of the cargo handlers they encountered during their organizing drives in the mid-1940s.[66] Turnover due to unsatisfactory conditions was high, particularly among unskilled white and African American workers in Miami:

> The average Air Line Mechanic is rather fond of his job and Company. I have been petting them along for over a year now in our Lodge and I know. One of the reasons that our organization was under the influence of the Company for so long was this very reason. There are many new employees, however, who do not know what it is all about and other new employees, who don't like conditions as they find them. These people move on so fast that they do not form a permanent part of the picture.
>
> These were the people that the CIO was working on and many of them were negro laborers. The turnover among those people is terrific.
>
> Nearly 50 percent a month.[67]

These workers were unwilling to trade low wages for the glory of working in the new and exciting industry. Workers on the ground also resisted low wages and long hours through unionization. Baggage handlers played a central role in these organizing efforts.

Despite rapid turnover, baggage handlers also developed a workplace culture that reflected their masculinity, their youth, and the technology they worked around. The airplanes themselves played a central role in their work culture. For some of the old-timers, the love of aviation was why they worked on the ramp. For others, at least initially, the glamour of aviation was attractive. For old-timers and new hires alike, the ramp could be a noisy, crowded, and dangerous place to work. The crowded conditions near the terminals, the activity of quickly servicing a plane, the tractors, bag carts, and loading equipment all created a workplace that required vigilance. The airplane was a machine that demanded cautious behavior on the part of those working around it. Even a propeller blowing in a breeze could cause serious injury. Baggage handlers were aware of the dangers of their workplace and transmitted knowledge necessary for protecting their lives and limbs.[68] Indeed, baggage handlers took satisfaction in the informal skills they developed. Robert Slouber recalled playing a guessing game about the weights of baggage on the ramp: "Porters did not bring baggage out to the plane unless it was a last-minute bag. We had a little game that we would play. We would sit there by the aircraft, and it would be all loaded except for maybe a last-minute bag or something like that, and we'd see the porter carrying it and say, 'Okay, a quarter to the guy who gets the closest weight to it.' And it would have on the tag how much it weighed. I was pretty good at it. You could tell how much it weighed by how the porter was running with it, even though some porters were stronger than others."[69] Proving specialized knowledge learned through their own tasks was one way of making work entertaining and satisfying. This knowledge related to the men's experience regarding their own strength but also hinged on what they knew about the physical strength of others.

Baggage handlers controlled the pace of their work on the ramp. During the daytime they organized tasks around the arrival and departure of aircraft. They might work very quickly to load or unload a plane and transport its contents and then spend a significant period of downtime between planes socializing with their coworkers. If management tried to fill up that time, baggage handlers could extend the time it took to load and unload. This cut into their own downtime, but it also slowed down operations and could frustrate waiting passengers. On the night shift, baggage handlers cleaning the aircraft

DC-4 sliding into a DC-6 on an icy ramp, Midway Airport, Chicago, circa 1950. Photo from Robert Slouber, author's collection.

developed their own norms for the cleanliness of the planes. Robert Slouber recalled his first night on the job, working exceptionally hard to make the section of the aircraft he was polishing look good. His section looked the best, but he was embarrassed and soon eased up, not wanting his coworkers to look bad.[70] After one night, Slouber's job performance was circumscribed by the norms set by his coworkers.

* * *

The World War II era brought tremendous change to the airline industry. The airlines' role in the war was central to this change. The relationship between the ATA and the U.S. government through the ATC and lucrative government contracts allowed the industry to turn a profit, maintain control of its domestic operations, and prove to the nation the practicality and necessity of commercial aviation. This relationship allowed for smooth operations for the war effort and no government interference in the form of nationalization, an idea industry leaders abhorred. Technological advancements in aircraft design and loading operations developed during the war poised the industry for extensive growth in the postwar years.

The expansion of the airlines forever changed the industry from a small niche in transportation utilized by the wealthy to an essential mode of trans-

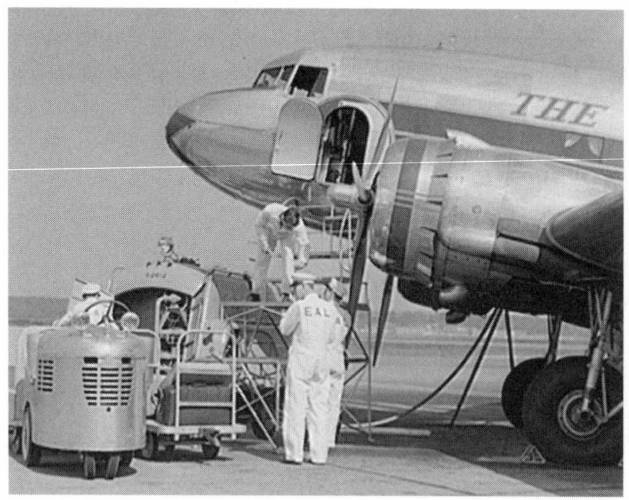

An airliner taking on baggage and fuel at National Airport, Washington, D.C., 1941. Library of Congress, Prints and Photographs Division, FSA-OWI Collection, LC-USF34-045036-D.

portation for the American war effort and economy. The airport changed from a rather informal and sometimes rustic workplace to a modern bustling terminal set amidst dozens of acres of concrete. Employment figures more than tripled over the course of the war. Workers were needed in domestic commercial operations as well as modification centers. Women and minorities made temporary and permanent inroads into the industry. White women found work as junior mechanics and sometimes baggage handlers as well as clerical positions, while African American men and women made inroads into the industry at the lower levels. Particularly in the South, black men found work in the industry as porters, handymen, janitors, and aircraft cleaners. Black women worked as janitors, cafeteria workers, and aircraft cleaners. Despite such inroads for women and minorities, the industry remained predominantly white and male. The war-era expansion was central to the development of the position of baggage handlers. Larger planes, increased cargo loads, and new loading technology demanded more workers to perform these tasks. Thousands of young white men came to work for the airlines as baggage handlers. On the ramp, these men developed their own work culture separate from other work groups at the airlines. Baggage handlers and other unskilled workers also reacted to disproportionately low wages and long hours compared to other industries by leaving the airlines or participating in union-organizing drives. Baggage handlers and other ground-service workers stood at the forefront of the battle to organize the industry.

3

Organizing the Airline Industry, 1945–49

In November 1945, from his post in Cincinnati, the journeyman aircraft mechanic and union organizer Claude Houser weighed in on the state of organizing in the airline industry in a three-page typed letter to the Grand Lodge of the International Association of Machinists. With the IAM and its main competitor, the Transport Workers Union (TWU), in heated battle over the airline industry, Houser explained that a new industry needed new strategies. Regretting the poor showing the Machinists made in organizing at American Airlines, Houser noted that the IAM had overlooked hundreds of employees working outside the largest stations in a "business whose employees are scattered across the United States" and was not faring well against the TWU, which worked "in packs, use[d] airline transportation . . . and [had] a twin engine plane for their use . . . they do spend plenty of money to buy these people's good graces in a number of ways." Houser argued for a union plane, explaining,

> It is my opinion, that our organization could do a far better job of contacting these employees with the least resistance by owning their own plane for the advertising of our organization and the approach to these employees, especially in certain instances where it is impossible to approach them in any other manner than to land right on their own airport and taxi right up to their hangar and make a direct contact and with their interest stimulated from the time the plane comes in for a landing, as these fellows have a habit of scrutinizing every plane that lands and will always become very interested in any plane that is used for transportation or advertising purposes . . . the

> plane is of inestimable value in stimulating interest in our organization and to overcome the weak link in the chain.

Indeed, in his year organizing, Houser attributed his successes to the drives he had flown to in his own plane. In his plea, Houser hit on three of the most important factors facing the IAM and its competitors, all which could

> feel the coming size and tremendous possibilities of the air transport industry, . . . [I]f our organization proposes to be the Bargaining Agent for *all the airline employees* we must overhaul our method of contacting these people and modernize our method of organizing these AIRLINE workers, please note I say AIRLINE workers instead of aircraft workers because there is a bitter feeling stimulated immediately when we refer to these people as aircraft workers, as they feel they are superior to aircraft workers whom they automatically associate with production workers.[1]

In the years immediately following World War II, organizers and airline workers themselves imagined that this industry had inaugurated a different or new kind of worker. Faced with thousands of potential members across the continent, AFL and CIO unions raced to take advantage of perhaps the most hospitable economic and political climate for union organizing in American history. For the "young and aggressive" union leadership[2] and airline workers the question was not so much whether they would organize but how thousands of skilled and unskilled airline workers would choose among competing unions and how this would happen under the complicated jurisdictional and craft and class issues set forth by the Railway Labor Act and decided by the National Mediation Board. This great organizing wave in the airline industry took place against the backdrop of the great strike wave of the postwar era. Airline workers participated in the great strike wave most often over union recognition, not the more common strike issue of wages.[3]

Getting Organized

Patterns of union organizing in the airline industry fall outside the traditional surges of organizing by AFL and CIO unions. While historians have highlighted the AFL unions and federations increasing power and political influence in the years prior to 1920, at least a decade before the birth of the commercial airline industry, an examination of AFL affiliates in the airline industry showcases the federation's continued militancy and even flexibility as it carved out the majority position in what would become a highly organized sector of the economy.[4] Historically, transportation was a critical point of membership and power for the AFL, particularly among the railroad brotherhoods and longshoremen. Indeed, the fantastic growth of the airline industry during World War II sparked the interest of several AFL unions with roots in the railroad industry and ultimately provided the federation with an important and militant membership base among aircraft mechanics and ground-service workers through the end of the twentieth century. In the 1930s, the IAM struggled to organize aircraft mechanics in the airline and aircraft industries and ALPA, affiliated with the AFL, paved the way for organizing the airline industry through their successful lobbying efforts and national organizing strategy.

CIO unions too made headway in organizing airline workers, more often building membership where local reputation or racial politics paved the way. Testing the new possibilities created through New Deal legislation, John L. Lewis of the United Mine Workers and the Organizing Committees organized the steel and auto industries between 1935 and 1937 as the airline industry emerged from its infancy. Like the AFL unions, CIO organizers approached the industry through other transportation workers. The TWU, with roots in the New York transit system, and the United Auto Workers (UAW), with a foothold in aircraft manufacturing, approached workers in the airline industry during World War II.

While airline workers developed myriad responses to their position in the wartime workforce, union organizing drives gained increasing importance by war's end. Baggage handlers at American, Pan Am, National, and Northwest Airlines all participated in the organizing campaigns of the 1940s. Which organizations they chose to represent them reflected how they recognized themselves in relation to other airline workers as well as how these organizations viewed them as part of the airline industry. Baggage handlers' participation in organizing activities reflected their attitudes about the perceived glamour of the industry itself and the reputation of the union soliciting their support, as well as important differences in the racial makeup of the workforce and the area of the country in which they lived and worked.

While these organizing campaigns also focused on aircraft mechanics and porters/cleaners, the position of baggage handlers fell precariously between the other two groups and complicated the issues of class, race, gender, and skill that airline unions faced. In the South, some white male aircraft mechanics and semi- and unskilled workers opposed organizing with African American porters and cleaners. In the North, organizers believed that female junior mechanics hired for the duration of the war hampered efforts to organize aircraft mechanics and baggage handlers. In both regions, skilled aircraft mechanics variously demanded the inclusion and exclusion of the unskilled baggage handlers in their organizing efforts. Unskilled airline workers benefited by organizing with skilled mechanics when the mechanics stood with their less-skilled coworkers on the strike line and at the bargaining table. Skilled mechanics benefited from organizing with less-skilled workers when contracts clearly defined not only job categories but also avenues for promotion into skilled ranks.

Throughout the mid-1940s, AFL affiliates, the Brotherhood of Railway, Airline, and Steamship Clerks (BRC), the CIO-affiliated TWU, and the IAM made vigorous attempts at organizing ground workers in the airline industry. In addition to contesting company and federal policies, these organizing attempts included challenges to the independent ALMA, particularly at Northwest, National, and American Airlines. The TWU and the IAM focused primarily on aircraft and plant mechanics and baggage handlers and similar employee titles, and the BRC focused on clerical and office employees. However, Railway Labor Act jurisdictional issues resulted in competition between the BRC and the IAM over stores and baggage-handling employees. While employees across each airline's system eventually organized, the IAM, TWU, and BRC initially focused their energies on workers at large airports and maintenance facilities—at Pan Am in Brownsville, Texas, and Miami; National Airlines in Jacksonville and Miami; American Airlines in New York and Chicago; and at Northwest Airlines in Minneapolis/St. Paul. Before union contracts were secured, the work of baggage handlers was somewhat dispersed and informal. Thereafter, baggage handlers, under various job titles, became a more distinct and coherent component of the workforce, their duties and titles clearly defined.

By the onset of World War II, the industry's elite workers, the airline pilots, had already secured representation through ALPA, affiliated with the AFL. Skilled and unskilled employees—including baggage handlers, aircraft mechanics, and stewards and stewardesses—looked to the pilots as an example and at times for guidance in their own organizing.[5] However, airline workers were selective about which unions interested them. Unions such as the IAM, affiliated with the craft-based AFL, appealed to the most skilled aircraft mechanics. Many of these men, recognizing their skill-based interests with the pilots, also considered affiliation with the Air Carrier Mechanics Association (ACMA), an organization created by the pilots' union. Other unions, including the UAW, affiliated with the industry-based CIO, appealed to unskilled airline workers, including baggage handlers, airplane cleaners, and porters. The TWU attracted workers from all these groups. For many baggage handlers and some aircraft mechanics, organizing across skill lines made sense. Moreover, for African American cleaners and porters, the union's pledge against racism was fundamental.

Two of the most active unions organizing in the airlines came out of the South and the railroad industry: the BRC and the IAM. The BRC, founded in Sedalia, Missouri, in 1899 by "white-collar" clerks on the railways, affiliated with the AFL and claimed jurisdiction over clerical personnel in transportation industries. After significant struggle against powerful anti-union railroads, the BRC grew from 6,000 to 186,000 members when the federal government assumed control of the railroads during World War I. Postwar depression and the explosive railroad shopmen's strike of 1922 halved its membership. During the 1930s, the BRC's position improved under the leadership of George M. Harrison, who successfully lobbied for the Railroad Retirement Act and served on New Deal commissions to study Social Security legislation, the National Recovery Act, and the Transportation Act of 1940.[6]

Railroad machinists chartered the first National Association of Machinists in Atlanta in 1888. Among its first members were "boomers"—machinists who followed the construction of railroads across the country. Lodges throughout the South, West, and Midwest served members through help with employment, information on local lodging, and even lending money. An aura of secrecy and ritual surrounded the formation of new lodges and membership initiation due in part to the founding members' links to the Knights of Labor. After the turn of the century the Machinists extended membership beyond skilled craftsmen on the railroads and chartered locals for craftsmen, journeymen, and apprentices in city job shops and other industries. In 1895 the Machinists joined the AFL after removing an antiblack clause from their constitution; however, they added a "white-only" clause to their secret initiation rites. By 1915 the union had seventy-five thousand members, including a handful of white women. While the Machinists were militant in their organizing efforts, building a substantial, active, and loyal membership, they were generally politically conservative. In 1928, the union ruled that members could not be Communists and in several instances removed Communist lodge leaders from office. Until the 1930s its identity remained firmly rooted in the white male skilled-craftsman world of railroad mechanics, despite the fact that its membership included thousands of auto mechanics, construction machinists, and tool-and-die mechanics in factories across the country. The IAM formally left the AFL over a conflict with the Carpenters Union from 1943 to 1950, although the split was not complete.[7]

The Machinists made their first foray into industrial organizing when the AFL awarded it jurisdiction over the aircraft industry. In September 1935 the IAM chartered its first aeronautical mechanics lodge at the Boeing Company in Seattle. Up and down the West Coast, the IAM and the UAW, a CIO union, battled for members in aircraft production. The IAM captured key plants in Southern California, including Lockheed Corporation, where membership soared from four hundred to thirty-seven thousand over the course of World War II.[8]

The IAM was the first AFL union to attempt organizing ground workers in the airline industry. The IAM organized aircraft mechanics at Eastern Air Transport in Atlanta in 1933, although the lodge collapsed after an unauthorized strike that year. It had better but temporary success at Pan Am in Brownsville in 1939. That same year, the IAM built a stronghold at Eastern Air Transport with a systemwide contract for airline mechanics. Its efforts at American and Northwest Airlines took place primarily during its years in conflict with the AFL.

In 1945 the IAM began a concerted effort to organize across the airline industry, with thirty representatives assigned to the task. Workers at United, Colonial, Northwest, Eastern, Trans World, National, and Capital Airlines all voted in the IAM in 1945 and 1946.[9] Claude Houser got his airplane, *The Flying Billboard,* a twin-engine, five-seater, as part of that campaign; it shuttled organizers around the country for two and a half years.[10] The IAM acted on another suggestion by Houser and created its Airline Division to counter the "bitter feeling" airline workers sometimes felt when misidentified as aircraft workers.

The TWU, the only CIO union under study here, organized airline workers at American Airlines and Pan American Airways. Founded in New York City in 1934 by impoverished Irish transit workers in cooperation with the Communist Party of the United States, the TWU had a strong ethnic identity and deep roots in radical activity. Many of its founding members were associated with Clan na Gael, a secret society that backed Irish independence and admired James Connolly, the famous socialist and founder of the Irish Transport and General Workers Union. In 1937 it became one of the first unions to charter itself with the CIO. In the 1940s the TWU expanded its organizing beyond New York City to transit workers in Philadelphia and Chicago. It also organized in new industries, including public utilities and the airlines. Like the IAM, the TWU recognized the tremendous potential in organizing the airlines. As the TWU leader Douglas MacMahon told the executive board in 1943, "[I]f we can crack into the air transport field, we will have an opportunity to become one of the most powerful forces in the country."[11] Like the IAM, the TWU created a separate division, the Air Transport Division, under the leadership of Maurice Forge, its most "American" executive, to organize exclusively in the industry.[12] The TWU found its strongest centers of support in New York and Chicago but also won critical victories in Miami.

During the war, the airline industry joined the no-strike/no-lockout pledge honored by other American industries. Patriotism and a tight labor market contributed to wartime labor peace in the industry. However, the rising cost of living and concerns about the postwar economy increased interest in labor organizations among airline workers. Skilled and unskilled airline workers joined "system associations" similar to company unions, as well as unions affiliated with the AFL and the CIO. The number of trade agreements between labor organizations and air carriers rose from thirty-four in 1939 to ninety-eight in 1945. Of the 168 agreements negotiated between unions and airlines from 1937 to 1947, more than half were negotiated between 1945 and 1947, with seventy of the 168 negotiated in just two years, 1946 and 1947.[13] In 1949, airline labor cases made up one-third of the National Mediation Board's work. That year there were fewer than eighty thousand airline employees, compared to 1.25 million railroad workers, in the United States. By 1950, union density among the five largest airlines, which employed over 70 percent of all airline workers, reached nearly 60 percent.[14]

Despite federal legislation against unfair labor practices, airlines interfered with organizing efforts by forming company unions, firing or promoting workers, and threatening to move operations. National Airlines' president George T. "Ted" Baker, notorious for his anti-union stance, pushed the majority of his workforce to strike in 1948.[15] Pan Am took extensive steps to keep unions off the ramp. In Miami during a prewar organizing drive, the company fired one hundred workers to get rid of eight union men.[16] In St. Paul, Minnesota, a BRC organizer at Northwest Airways noted, "The management doesn't like any form of a bonafide organization, as soon as anyone starts talking organization they either promote him or discharge him, he moves one way or the other, if he is a good worker he is promoted, if he drags his feet he is out."[17]

Labor organizers not only had to overcome the persistent resistance of airline management but the conflicting outlooks of old and new workers as well. The influx of new employees into the industry during the war worked for and against union organizing efforts. On the one hand, these new employees were less likely to be working in the industry because of their love of aviation, and they had not shared in the building up of airlines and the flexibility in job functions and promotion of the 1930s. These newer employees felt less connected to the companies they worked for than men like George Rutledge of American Airlines, who entered the industry in the 1920s.[18] Rapid growth through the war period depersonalized airline relations, according to one trade journal in which the author warned of losing the former "closeness of management and employees." It was that "touch" that was invaluable in the early days of the industry, when presidents and operations vice presidents had a first-name acquaintance with the majority of employees.[19]

According to George Rutledge, American Airlines, desperate to replenish its ranks, resorted to advertising on the subways for its operations in New York City. "If you could see lightning and hear thunder, you were hired. They [the wartime hirees] weren't as well selected or educated, because we just picked anybody that would show up. . . . Another big difference was women. We finally had women working for the company out on the ramp and every place else."[20] From his perspective, the results were mixed. While the growth of the company during the war was exciting, the new employees, in his opinion, were not as dedicated to the industry as those hired before the war. Moreover, the rapid growth of the workforce undermined the confidence of some older and more skilled workers. As one IAM representative explained, "The Air Line worker is a funny fellow. His mind is very complex. He has a fierce pride in his work but it is changing so fast he doesn't have too much confidence in himself or his superiors."[21]

The youth and transience of the new airline workers frustrated unions attempting to organize baggage handlers and aircraft mechanics. The workforce was very young. Men working in the airline industry were exempt from the draft, thus making the industry attractive to high school students hoping to avoid war service. Furthermore, few airline workers were immigrants, although many were first-generation Americans. In 1940, over 92 percent of the men employed in air transportation were native-born and white, and fewer than 4 percent were foreign-born.[22] The glamour of the industry attracted some middle-class employees into its blue-collar ranks as well. Their youthfulness, lack of union experience, and sense of American individualism made the task of organizing airline workers more difficult.[23]

Robert Slouber, a retired baggage handler, started work on the eve of full U.S. involvement in the war during the summer after finishing high school in

1941. The son of Czechoslovakian immigrants, Slouber found the job through a pilot he knew. After enlisting in the army, he left the industry from 1943 through the war's end. He returned four months before a second vote for union representation was held for mechanics and baggage handlers at American Airlines. Slouber recalled that when he started working at American, "If a guy was thirty years old, he was old. Most of us were in our late teens or twenties." He did not recall anything specific about the ALMA, the independent union representing baggage handlers and aircraft mechanics since 1943, nor did he have any strong opinions at the time concerning which union should represent him upon his return from the military.[24] However, he felt that they needed a union because their wages were so low. In 1943, under the ALMA, contract wages for baggage handlers at American increased, when first-year baggage handlers earned sixty cents an hour, comparable to $7.29 an hour in 2007.[25]

Turnover, due to low wages and an abundance of available jobs during the period, was high enough that when Slouber returned from the war he was more than three-fourths the way up the seniority list for baggage handlers at Chicago. According to Slouber, jobs were plentiful; men tired of the low wages and long hours could find other work.[26]

Correspondence between IAM organizers also points to the high turnover among baggage handlers during the war. During the IAM's organizing drive at American Airlines, a union representative lamented the lack of interest among baggage handlers in Cincinnati. In April 1945, the organizer found that "[t]here are approximately fifty employees of the American Airlines working at the Cincinati airport, this includes the entire personnel of this Company at this point, namely, clerical workers, supervisors, baggage handlers, maintenance and repairmen. Of all this group, I have only been able to contact two employees that were employed by American Airlines and both of these were baggage handlers who knew nothing about an election and didn't seem to know very much about anything else."[27]

Six months later, another IAM organizer faced heavy turnover and disinterest in Memphis. He reported, "All the mechanics and ground service employees have signed authorization cards. There are thirteen other Cargo Handlers, that have not signed cards. We can get a few of this number. Some we will not get, for reasons they are all young kids, and have no interest one way or the other. On the other hand, they come and go most every day. We will continue to get every card possible."[28] While many baggage handlers might have had no interest in the company or long-term intentions for the industry, their indifference might also indicate that they were not interested in the union soliciting them. The IAM as a craft union that organized workers by skill was ambivalent about organizing unskilled workers like baggage handlers.[29]

Organizers witnessed a lack of long-term interest in airline unions on the part of many women, particularly those at the modification centers. Organizers for the BRC at Northwest's operations in St. Paul were frustrated by women's lack of experience or interest in the labor movement, believing that although they were not especially happy with their wages and conditions, they were dazzled by the glamour of the industry and expected their foray into it would be brief, hopefully ending in marriage. In 1944, the organizer Charles Kief reported to the BRC president George M. Harrison,

> 1. The attitude of the employees toward our Brotherhood or any form of organization is very unpleasant. They do not like the Company Union, they would prefer us but they don't have the initiative to do anything about it. It being impossible to get into either of the airports the employees will accept appointments and then refuse to show up or give any reason other than to say they were busy, or forget, or some other minor excuse.
>
> 2. The majority of the employees are females, brought in from the surrounding localities, never heard anything about labor unions only the stuff that appears over the radio or in the daily papers. They tell you they are only in the industry until the war is over so why organize, or they intend to get married as soon as conditions will permit. That the industry will not operate after the emergency and many will be laid off and if they organize the boss will pick on them first. When they are hired they attend school for a limited length of time "pay while learning plan" and then given a slate colored coverall with NORTHWEST AIRLINES written across the back in red and they think they have the best job in the world.[30]

Perhaps frustrated by the campaign generally, Kief referred to the ALMA, which represented mechanics at Northwest Airlines, as a "company union" and blamed women employees for the poor showing in the campaign. As historians of women workers during the 1940s have pointed out, women, even those employed "for the duration," could and did participate in union activism. Indeed, women were among the first workers in bargaining units at Pan Am and Northwest Airlines. Further, stewardesses, among the most temporary of all airline employees, organized their first union in 1946.[31]

The glamour of the decade-old industry and its critical role in the war effort also contributed to the difficulty unions faced in organizing the airlines. Its most prestigious positions, pilot and stewardess, captured the imaginations of many young Americans. Indeed, the unions organizing the industry recognized the appeal of the industry and its ability to exploit its glamour, particularly by maintaining its focus on its high-profile employees. According to a researcher for the IAM, "The Air Transport Industry has wrapped itself in such a cloud of romanticism that there is no available evidence as to the conditions of the Labor Force that keeps the planes flying. In fact, going through material concerning this industry, one would get the impression that a few handsome pilots and charming stewardesses make up the entire working force."[32]

Despite the romanticism, labor was optimistic about its organizing efforts. A 1946 BRC report on the airline industry anticipated success on the part of unions. The report predicted, "[T]he time has come when airline employees are no longer willing to work for the low wages which have been traditional in the industry. Even the relatively well paid pilots are demanding increased compensation for flying newer and larger planes; other groups are organizing. All airline labor will soon demand decent wages because they have learned that it takes more than glamour of the job to meet the cost of living."[33] Low wages and long hours were the key to this optimism.[34] Although the rapid growth of the industry and the perceived possibility of rapid promotion seemed to justify at least low starting wages, airports functioned twenty-four hours a day, and as the BRC recognized, the undesirable night and weekend shifts during six-day workweeks also reduced the industry's appeal.[35]

Organizing the industry was not only complicated by high turnover and lack of interest on the part of young American-born white men and female workers.[36] Issues of jurisdiction also complicated the matter. Jurisdictional boundaries decided under the Railway Labor Act for organizing groups of workers in the industry were unclear to the unions as well as management. The essential question of jurisdiction focused on whether or not these employees, variously called "groomers," "baggage handlers," "fleet-service clerks," "ground-service workers," "equipment servicemen," "commissary employees," "utility employees," and "cargo handlers," were service workers to be grouped with clerical and ticketing staff or mechanical workers to be grouped with aircraft and maintenance mechanics. In inter-union disputes lasting into the early 1970s, the work of baggage handlers hovered over a thin line of definition between "service" and "mechanical" work. On the one hand, baggage handlers performed nonmechanical tasks such as the loading and unloading of baggage and freight and cleaning aircraft interiors. On the other hand, particularly during the war and the immediate years after, in many cases these workers performed some tasks that were related to the work of aircraft and plant-maintenance mechanics. Over a half-dozen job titles were used to describe these employees. Among the unions this dispute centered on not only which unions held the right to organize baggage handlers according to the National Mediation Board, but also the definition of the work they did. Whether or not these workers were grouped with airline mechanics or clerical staff was the crux of the issue.

Organizing in the South

Airline workers in the South were among the first to organize. The IAM made its first inroads into the industry at Eastern Airlines, based in Atlanta in the late 1930s. By the mid-1940s IAM organizers fanned out across Pan Am and National Airlines in Florida. Miami proved to be a hotbed of organizing on the airlines with vigorous competition, particularly at Pan Am, between the IAM and TWU.

Organizing drives at Pan Am by the TWU preceded "Operation Dixie," the largely unsuccessful million-dollar organizing drive by the CIO in the South, which began in May 1946 and focused on southern workers in textiles, tobacco, oil, and steel industries through 1953. TWU organizing at Miami was initially orchestrated by Charles Smolnikoff, an organizer for the Industrial Union of Marine and Shipbuilding Workers and director of the Florida CIO, who discovered discontent among black workers at Pan Am. Smolnikoff contacted the TWU president Mike Quill, who came to Florida and met quietly with a handful of Pan Am employees and representatives of the Communist party in Florida.[37] By March 1945, the union elections at Pan Am "caused quite a stir in the town."[38]

At Pan Am, race, job classification, and the task of loading planes made the organization of baggage handlers particularly complex. During the war in Miami, African American men loaded airplanes under the job title of "porter," which in most cases referred to men who helped passengers with their luggage at the terminal. The job title "fleet-service clerk" did not exist at Pan Am until after the war under TWU contract. However, white workers also performed the tasks that would become those of fleet-service clerks. Therefore, to understand the identity of baggage handlers at Pan Am in Miami, it is essential to include African American workers called "porters."

By the end of World War II, Miami laid claim to one of the nation's largest airports, with nearly ten thousand employees at the field. The city's position as an important center for tourism and trade with Latin America made the airport all the more crucial to the city's economy and the interest of organized labor. At the height of the organizing drives at Pan Am, the company was the largest employer in Miami.[39] Workers who handled baggage stood in the middle of much of this action.

Organizing campaigns at Pan Am started in the South in Brownsville and Miami.[40] Prior to the war, the IAM organized aircraft mechanics and baggage handlers as well as other unskilled workers at Pan Am's southern operations. White and Hispanic workers played active roles in these organizing drives. By 1943, aided by Hispanic members and union leaders, the IAM and Pan Am entered a contract with more specific job classifications pertaining to unskilled workers. That year, field maintenance men, plane cleaners, janitors, and porters earned $85 as a starting wage and up to $125 per month after six years. The same contract gave master mechanics up to $1.40 per hour, more than triple the starting wage of the ground workers' scale.[41] Importantly, workers in this case demanded that the IAM include workers across skill lines, despite the union's traditional skill-based organizing agenda. Starting in 1943, the TWU organized white, African American, and Hispanic skilled and unskilled ground workers. During the TWU's 1944 organizing drive at Pan Am, union representatives counted over 160 African American men and women paying union dues while employed by Pan Am in Miami.[42] Mexican Americans also participated heavily in the organizing drives of the TWU in Brownsville. In September 1945, the TWU collected over seventy initiation cards from Pan Am employees in the Brownsville overhaul shops. Over half of the cards came from Mexican American men and women employed as mechanics, mechanic's helpers, porters, cleaners, and fuelers. Mexican Americans held union offices in Brownsville's fledgling TWU Local.[43] Roberto F. Colunga, Lino Ramirez, and Bertha Ramirez stood in as acting vice president, secretary-treasurer, and recording secretary, respectively, of TWU Local 503 at the time of its application for a charter in 1945. Of the thirteen original members of the local, eight were Mexican American.[44]

In Miami, the African American porters and cleaners, 10 percent of the workforce, were the first to meet with the TWU about organizing.[45] Over two years, a substantial portion of Pan Am's blue-collar workers in Miami looked to CIO unions, specifically the TWU, to represent their interests. White unskilled workers and African American porters and cleaners allied themselves with the CIO. As IAM organizers explained, "Brother King and Brother Davis have been working primarily on the mechanical employees of PAA. I feel this is as it should be. To begin with, other kinds of employees are rather a new thing in the organized Labor picture and we do not understand their problems very well at all. . . . Again, there are many people in the unskilled labor, who are predominantly CIO in their thinking as they have no skills to offer."[46]

White unskilled workers and African American cleaners and porters believed that organizing with a CIO union was their best option. For black and white workers this belief stemmed from skill issues, but black workers were also motivated by the CIO's policies on racial equality and job upgrading. As a competing IAM officer put it, "As for the unskilled workers such as plane cleaners, janitors, and porters, practically all of them are negroes, a large percentage of whom are negro women and this is the group among which the CIO Transport Workers have their greatest strength."[47]

Although the IAM had cautiously permitted the local to organize unskilled Pan Am employees in Brownsville, the union chose to organize only skilled workers in Miami.[48] This decision stemmed from the color of some of those workers as much as their lack of skill. In that city, Pan Am employed whites and African Americans as well as Cubans. White Cubans were employed as Port Stewards, a position dealing with the comfort of passengers at the airport.[49] African American men and women predominated in the unskilled jobs of porter, plane cleaner, maid, and janitor. Skill, race, turnover, and support for other unions were deciding factors for the IAM in Miami. In a letter to the general vice president of the IAM, the organizer B. W. King surmised, "The situation here is somewhat different from that at Brownsville and in my judgement will have to be handled accordingly. We have been centering most of our efforts on the mechanical group for the reason that they are the most responsive. The stockroom group is at present firmly in the grasp of the company union, in fact the company union has only a few days ago completed negotiations for a renewal of their stockroom agreement." Race relations in Miami were also a primary consideration for the IAM. As King warned,

> Frankly, I am opposed to the I. A. of M. battling it out with the CIO to obtain bargaining rights for the negroes for two reasons. First, the CIO as previously mentioned is firmly entrenched among this group, and second, such a campaign on account of the acute racial prejudice existing in this locality, all the progress we have made among the mechanical group would be wiped out if we made any overtures to this group. I imagine that the unskilled group at Brownsville is composed largely of Mexicans which makes an entirely different situation from what we have here in Miami.[50]

The fear of alienating skilled white mechanics overrode the possible gains of higher membership by organizing unskilled workers.

By the summer of 1943, the TWU had made significant inroads at Pan Am's operations in Miami, initially among African American workers.[51] Men like David Spicy and Roosevelt Winfield, both porters in Miami, participated in the organizing drive. Spicy was later elected to the local's executive board, and Winfield became section chairman for the porters. Also appealing to the cleaners, maids, and janitors was the TWU position on equal pay for women, a stand not taken by the IAM. For the African American women employed by the airline in Miami, this position could only increase their earning power.[52] In the 1940s, many IAM locals still banned African Americans from membership.[53]

Territorial issues relating to Pan Am's corporate structure soon complicated this initial success on the part of the TWU at Miami. The IAM as well as various local company unions representing Pan Am workers on the West Coast were also involved. Prior to January 1944, Pan Am's corporate structure consisted of several territorial units, each autonomous in terms of labor agreements. In January 1944, Pan Am consolidated its Western (including Brownsville) and Eastern (including Miami) Divisions into a Latin American Division and its operations in the Pacific, including Seattle, Alaska, and San Francisco, into a Pacific-Alaska Division. Pan Am changed its labor policy at this point as well; the company intended to deal with its employees on a systemwide basis.[54]

African American porters and cleaners were the first Pan Am employees to vote in the TWU. In January 1944, the TWU petitioned the National Mediation Board to hold an election for workers at Pan Am's Miami operations. In February 1944, porters and cleaners elected the union as their representative.[55] The union aided the unskilled workers in establishing a training program for learning semi-skilled trades and fought the company on behalf of drafted porters and cleaners for thirteen months' retroactive pay totaling sixty-nine thousand dollars.[56]

In March 1944, a second election was held to determine representation for three groups of employees in Miami only: (1) mechanics and helpers (including radio mechanics, flight mechanics and engineers, beaching crewmen and boatmen, and seamstresses); (2) stockroom clerks; and (3) porters, cleaners, janitors, maids, and scrubwomen. The TWU won the election to represent the third group. However, no organization received a majority vote to represent the first two groups. Three months later an election for the mechanics group for the Atlantic Division of the company (including Miami) was held without the TWU on the ballot. The National Mediation Board questioned its validity and permitted a third election for the mechanics at Miami.

In March 1945, the IAM filed an application to dispute representation with the National Mediation Board for airline mechanics across the Pan Am system. This application was the first attempt by any union to organize at Pan Am this way. Elections in this case covered all three work groups. The mechanics group voted in the TWU. That union won 1,534 votes, and the IAM received 1,017 out of a total of 3,552 eligible voters. Stockroom personnel elected the IAM, and the unskilled workers elected the TWU. Of 470 eligible voters in the unskilled group, 291 voted for the TWU, 34 for the IAM, 11 for the World Air Transport Employees Association, and 5 for other organizations or individuals. There were 17 void ballots in that group's election; 112 unskilled workers did not vote in this election.[57] In October 1945, a contract covering four thousand Pan Am employees was ratified. TWU members at Pan Am made significant gains. The contract included a forty-hour workweek with forty-eight hours' pay, shift-differentials, six-cent raises every six months within job classifications, time and a half after an eight hour day and for the sixth day worked, double time after a twelve hour day and for all work on a seventh day, two weeks of vacation after one year with the company, seven paid holidays, and a strict seniority system. Importantly, this contract also included a clause for equal treatment regardless of sex, color, race, creed, or national origin.[58] In April 1945, the TWU was certified to represent the mechanical group in Miami. The TWU won 784 votes from 1,532 eligible workers. The IAM received 191 votes, and the local company union received 162.[59]

Although the TWU campaigned to organize African American workers, it did not disregard the racism of white skilled and unskilled workers at Pan Am in Miami. Race relations in the organizing campaign were tense, and white rank-and-file members opposed mixed-race union meetings, despite the fact that the black porters and cleaners were the first to participate in TWU organizing activities. TWU organizers in Miami also had to contend with what one called the "extreme Negro nationalism" among the black membership.[60] Organizers for the TWU in Miami held meetings for the white mechanics and unskilled workers separate from those held for African American workers. They also kept separate lists of employees who had joined the union—one list designated employees by their occupation, and the other listed only African American employees.[61] The TWU organizers Roy and Elizabeth Whitman delicately maneuvered through this racial minefield. In March 1945, a letter to TWU headquarters from Elizabeth indicated that their careful dues records had successfully cemented the place of black porters and cleaners "who merit the privilege of Charter Member" on the local charter. In her report she asked for a charter with an "Airplane or Clipper on it and with space for the Charter Members to sign" to build unity around aviation, not race.[62]

The IAM and TWU battled bitterly for the allegiance of workers in Miami. The IAM accused the TWU of anti-Americanism and collusion with Communists.[63] The TWU denounced the IAM for charging high membership dues and not developing reclassification programs and claimed the old-style railroad union unfit for handling the airline industry.[64] In the crowded conditions of war-weary Miami, some AFL representatives, hoping to aid an IAM victory, fueled white racist sentiments by distributing leaflets of Ku Klux Klan propaganda claiming that the CIO (the TWU) was "pro-Negro" and then equating "pro-Negro" sentiments with sedition.[65]

The various elections at Pan Am served as a starting point for the organization of the airline industry. Pan Am's company unions vanished, pointing to a decreased sense of loyalty to the company. Skilled and unskilled workers and different racial groups could coexist within the same union. The TWU and the IAM used their victories as examples of their strength in future elections at National, American, and Northwest Airlines, but the position of workers performing baggage-handling and related tasks remained unresolved. This work straddled the job groups of unskilled and mechanical employees. This problematic situation would fully come to light during the organizing drives at American and Northwest Airlines and later at National Airlines.

After defeat at Pan Am and sensing frustration among aircraft mechanics at National Airlines over the merger of the ALMA with the UAW-CIO in July 1945, the IAM began an organizing campaign in Jacksonville, Florida. The IAM faced some competition from the TWU organizer Roy Whitman, particularly among unskilled workers, as well as the threatened interest of the pilot's union. Further, the Air Line Mechanics Department–UAW (formerly ALMA) had no intention of losing their membership at National.[66]

IAM organizing at National was swift but frustrated by a problematic election and craft and class confusion. By October 1945, the National Mediation Board docketed a certification election (R-1548) for "employees servicing and maintaining airplanes and equipment . . . including mechanical employees, fleet or commissary employees, and utility or unskilled employees."[67] However, it was unclear whether baggage handlers at National could vote in this election. While internal telegrams and letters among IAM organizers described cargo or baggage handlers as part of the "stores, commissary employees—including cargo handlers," they also exposed National's objection to including this workgroup in the election and the Mediation Board's agreement with their exclusion.[68] The campaign at National was muddled further when the first election in late November was thrown out because the local mediator assigned to the election improperly denied the Airline Mechanics Department–UAW the election observer of their choice.[69] Frustrated employees at Jacksonville, with the support of National's pilots, threatened to strike over the uncounted ballots. Such a strike would ground the airline.[70] Ground workers at National voted in a second election, December 10 through 12. Eligibility in this certification election followed a determination set down in National Mediation Board hearings in September 1945, which concerned several airlines, including American. Baggage handlers did not vote in this election, and the IAM won an overwhelming victory with 83 percent of eligible mechanics, stores, commissary, and unskilled workers.[71]

However, baggage handlers would be included in the first mechanical and stores contract bargained by the IAM. In January 1946, while the union was considering a campaign for operations and clerical employees at National, the IAM representative J. C. McGlon sent a petition signed by all the baggage handlers (twenty-two) employed at Jacksonville (approximately 85 percent employed on the total system) to George "Ted" Baker, president of the airline, with the expectation that the company would recognize the IAM as the representative of baggage handlers without an election. Given Baker's anti-union reputation, it was a surprise when he agreed, and baggage handlers were classified as "ground-service employees" and covered by the first mechanical contract between the IAM and National. The number of "ground-service employees" at National tripled between January and March of 1946 to seventy-five.[72]

Organizing American Airlines

While Pan Am served as a crucial organizing opportunity in the South, particularly for the CIO, organizing mechanics and ground-service workers at American Airlines, one of the largest domestic airlines, would provide a critical foothold for any union. Baggage handlers and mechanical workers at American Airlines in New York City, New England, and the Midwest participated in the heated organizing drives carried out by the ALMA, the TWU, the IAM, and the pilots' affiliate, the ACMA. Issues of skill emerged at the forefront of these campaigns. Baggage handlers recognized that they did not necessarily share the interests of skilled aircraft mechanics. In heavily unionized cities like New York and Boston, workers readily signed union-authorization cards.[73] In New York, the TWU appeared to have the hometown advantage of solid name recognition; it represented thousands of transit workers on the city's subway and bus lines.

Although a contract between American Airlines and the ALMA covered baggage handlers, the TWU, the IAM, and the ACMA nonetheless carried on organizing campaigns directed at aircraft mechanics and baggage handlers at American. IAM strategists believed that carrying on several drives at once at the largest airlines would aid each individual organizing effort simultaneously.[74] Furthermore, after its loss at Pan Am, the IAM recognized the importance of baggage handlers as a substantial group of workers who could not be overlooked if they intended to organize in the industry.[75] The ACMA courted aircraft mechanics based on their position as skilled workers (like pilots) who faced an uncertain future at the end of the war as American Airlines prepared to transfer much of its maintenance work to a new base in Tulsa, Oklahoma.[76] For their part, fleet-service clerks recognized that skill-based unions, particularly the ACMA, did not represent their interests and looked to the TWU.

Effective April 7, 1943, the ALMA contract included employees whose job description specifically included baggage handling, "fleet-service personnel." Under this contract, "fleet-service personnel" work included "maintaining the appearance of airplanes, interiors and exteriors, the servicing and control of cabin service equipment, the handling of mail, express, and other cargo, the air conditioning of airplanes, the cleaning of airport hangars, buildings, hangar and ramp equipment, and the driving of crew cars at stations where the company maintains personnel for such purpose."[77]

Four job titles existed within this work group: cleaners, junior fleet-service clerks, fleet-service clerks, and senior fleet-service clerks. Employees covered by this contract worked six days a week for eight hours a day. Cleaners and junior fleet-service clerks earned fifty cents an hour. Fleet-service clerks earned sixty cents an hour their first year and seventy cents by their third year. Senior fleet-service clerks earned eighty-five cents an hour.

Overtime pay for all employees covered by the ALMA contract equaled time and a half. Overtime pay started after eight hours of work per day or after forty-eight hours in a seven-day period. Meal periods were unpaid and lasted between a half hour and an hour. Not including overtime, junior fleet-service clerks earned twenty-four dollars for a six-day workweek. Senior fleet-service clerks earned $40.80 for the same period. The contract did not detail the differences in the grades of fleet-service clerks. Starting salaries in other job categories covered by the contract, such as apprentice mechanic, parts washer, junior stock clerk, and ground serviceman, were comparable. The highest-paid employees covered by the ALMA contract with American Airlines were lead inspectors; these employees received $290 per month. In the mechanics' group, lead mechanics were highest-paid at $1.20 per hour.[78]

By 1944, despite the ALMA contract, the IAM, the ACMA, and the TWU started organizing campaigns among American Airlines mechanics, ground-service workers, and baggage handlers (fleet-service clerks) at LaGuardia Field in New York. The TWU was a formidable opponent. In January 1945, the organizer Frank Heisler informed H. W. Brown, the international president of the IAM, that "[t]he TWU is giving us very strong opposition here due to the support given them by former ALMA members. Each time they distribute literature they have at least ten representatives to cover three gates and are spending money like a bunch of drunken sailors."[79] By August 1945, ALMA was also losing ground. Members of the organization were unhappy with its most recent settlement with the company. In July 1945, the ALMA merged with the UAW-CIO. As at National Airlines, questions arose immediately as to whether or not workers covered by ALMA contracts would be automatically handed over to the UAW.[80]

For the unions, organizing American Airlines employees at LaGuardia was essential to larger efforts in the industry. American was the largest employer at the field with some 2,700 mechanical and fleet-service workers, but organizers were frustrated by the perceived indecisiveness of workers on the ramp, complaining that they signed authorization cards for the ALMA, the TWU, and the IAM with abandon.[81]

The TWU's strength in organizing workers at American Airlines stemmed from its significant presence in organized labor in New York City and the allegiance of former members of the ALMA.[82] By December 1944, the TWU contacted American Airlines, stating they had the support of the majority of American's employees at LaGuardia and wanted to pursue representation at the company. The company and the IAM disputed this assertion. In February 1945, the TWU officially invoked the services of the National Mediation Board to investigate a representation dispute at the airline. In March the TWU officially applied for representation of American's ground workers. The IAM followed with its own application in September.[83]

ALPA's president, David Behncke, a powerful personality in the industry since the 1930s, and the pilots' union shifted their support several times throughout the period. In the 1930s, ALPA supported the organizing attempts of the IAM, at least informally, by ferrying messages for them.[84] In 1944, the IAM still held at least some support from Behncke and ALPA, if only because of their mutual (and temporarily suspended) association with the AFL.[85] At the same time, ALPA supported the ALMA and the IAM during the American Airlines organizing drive. However, ALMA lost ALPA's backing after it began talks with the UAW concerning affiliation with that CIO union.[86] In October 1945, weeks before a representation vote was held for American's mechanics, baggage handlers, and other ground workers, ALPA sponsored the formation of a new organization, the ACMA.

The ACMA's affiliation with ALPA served as a strong incentive to vote for the organization, particularly among aircraft mechanics.[87] The ACMA focused its attention on the aircraft mechanics, pointing to the confusion surrounding the ALMA merger with the UAW-CIO, competition from the TWU, and questions regarding jurisdiction. The ACMA called for the aircraft mechanics to join "clean cut, effective, and lawful organizations."[88] The strength of the pilots' union as well as the high level of skill required of aircraft mechanics contributed to their interest in a union affiliated with ALPA. Aircraft mechanics, like pilots, could rely on their position as absolutely essential to the operation of any airline.

Baggage handlers and other ground employees whose skill levels were far lower did not enjoy such certainty in their positions. The ACMA was a direct affront to the philosophy of industry-based organizing, the most secure position baggage handlers and other unskilled workers could take. For Lawson Caldwell, a baggage handler in Boston, the decision was clear. Caldwell signed a TWU card because he felt it had the best chance of beating the ACMA.[89]

Baggage handlers and aircraft mechanics were keenly aware of the organizing activities at other airlines. LaGuardia workers at American watched the organizing at Pan Am,[90] and workers on the ramp, skilled and unskilled, debated the best strategy for organizing. Some mechanics, particularly those at the highest level, with Airframe and Engine licenses and years of experience, opposed being organized with lower-skilled employees.[91] Not all mechanics felt this way, and they were not the only employees to question the groupings of employees unions worked to organize. While organizing Eastern Airlines in Atlanta, a concerned IAM organizer wrote to a lodge representative in Washington, D.C., "When I approach mechanics they ask me why we do not organize the Cargo Handlers of Eastern and other Airlines, and the cargo handlers ask why they should support the IAM when we are not interested in cargo handlers on other Airlines."[92] G. B. Summers, the representative, assured the organizer that such concerns were not exclusive to workers at Eastern Airlines: "In some instances our representatives encounter an antagonistic attitude on the part of certain mechanical employees who learn we are including the cargo handlers in their bargaining unit. On the other hand, as you state, some encounter a situation where the mechanical employees practically demand that *all* other employees be included in the same bargaining unit."[93]

Questions of how to categorize workers on the ground for organization and which unions should hold jurisdiction over these groupings plagued unions other than the IAM. In 1945, the National Mediation Board stepped in to oversee jurisdiction decisions. Elections at American Airlines were the catalyst for this action.

The State and Jurisdiction Disputes

The organizing wave of 1944–49 clearly exposes the complicated application of the Railway Labor Act to the airline industry. Not only were organizers, employers, and workers confounded by the "class and craft" framework set down by the act but the National Mediation Board itself struggled with how to apply this labor law to this industry.

The questions of how and with whom baggage handlers should organize were in substantial part a governmental decision. Through the National Mediation Board, the body that rules on labor disputes covered by the Railway Labor Act, baggage handlers were grouped with "mechanical forces." Therefore, they could organize with aircraft and other mechanics. Industrial unionism was not an option for airline workers despite the gains made by the CIO through the TWU. The airline industry's coverage by the Railway Labor Act meant that workers could organize by "craft or class," not across the industry. As the results of the votes at American Airlines in the fall of 1945 and the summer of 1946 will show, aircraft mechanics initially allied themselves with the airline pilots by voting for the ACMA. By the following summer, significant numbers of aircraft mechanics shifted their alliance to the TWU. The representation dispute at American Airlines forced the National Mediation Board to address issues of jurisdiction and employee groups, although this was not the only case of its kind. In the first half of 1945, the board was faced with similar representation disputes at Colonial Airlines, Pennsylvania-Central Airlines, and Transcontinental and Western Air.[94]

As the organizing drives at Pan Am, National, and American show, workers considered a variety of work-group combinations for organizing. However, the structure of the Railway Labor Act and particularly the intentions of its mediation boards paved the way for a specific kind of unionization. As the labor economist Edward Shils reflected in 1964, "Certainly the development of the many fragmented craft unions in the airlines resulted from the experience of the National Mediation Board in dealing with fragmented craft unions in the railroad industry. It can be safely assumed that the National

Mediation Board did nothing to create a context in which an industrial-type union might thrive."[95]

Facing several complicated jurisdictional issues, in August 1945 the National Mediation Board conducted hearings for all parties interested in airline organization. Through these hearings, the board sought to define employee groups throughout the industry. The mediator Lawrence Farmer conducted the hearings, and the resulting decisions ruled out industrial unionism. Satisfying management and craft labor, the airlines would continue to follow the railroad model of labor organization. For baggage handlers and other ground-service workers, their classification status was temporarily resolved as mechanical in nature. The secretary of the National Mediation Board, Robert F. Cole, explained the importance of the issues under discussion:

> The issues in this case are quite important, and their disposition will set a pattern for the handling of subsequent representation disputes among ground employees in the air line industry. Primarily, they involve the application of the principles of Section 2 of the amended Railway Labor Act to air line employees. This section of the Act deals with employee representation, and the determination of representation disputes among the employees on the basis of craft or class. The problem presented here and in the several other air line representation disputes is how to apply the principle of representation by craft or class well established in the railroad industry to the young and growing air transport industry, a duty which devolves on this Board through the provisions of Section 201, Title II of the Railway Labor Act, amended.
>
> Basically the issues in this and other related cases are:
>
> 1. Shall the ground employees of the air lines determine their choice of representation on the basis of crafts or classes, as specified in Section 2, Ninth, of the Railway Labor Act, amended;
> 2. Shall such air line employees be grouped on an industrial basis for representation purposes.
> 3. If representation is to be determined on the basis of craft or class, what are the proper allocations of air line employees to such crafts or classes.[96]

The other cases mentioned above included employees at Pennsylvania-Central Airlines Corporation, Transcontinental and Western Air, and Colonial Airlines.[97]

Hearings conducted for six days addressed the six disputes over jurisdiction. Management and labor presented arguments for and against industrial organization of the airlines. According to Cole, the author of these "Findings," representatives of airline management agreed with craft labor that "some well-defined occupational groupings among ground employees do not lend themselves readily to inclusion in an industrial representation unit."[98]

Furthermore, because the Railway Labor Act, which deals only in craft or class terms, applied to the industry, the issues of industrial organization proved to be a moot point. According to Cole, the National Mediation Board was thus saddled with defining classes or crafts within the industry:

> It therefore seems quite clear that it is the duty of the National Mediation Board to determine the representation desires of the airline employees on the basis of craft or class, rather than on the basis of an over-all industrial type of unit combining many occupations, which might in some instances be preferred for various reasons by certain organizations and managements. It further seems clear that a "craft or class" in the air transport industry means a well-knit and cohesive occupational group which has developed over a period of years in the course of general voluntary association of the employees into collective bargaining units. The fact that a number of well-defined occupational groups may now be covered in one working agreement is not conclusive evidence that such coverage determines the "craft or class" in that particular instance. Accordingly, it becomes necessary to examine the occupational groupings as they have emerged over a period of years in the airline industry, and to determine whether such groupings are uniform to the extent that they might now be termed "crafts or classes" under the provisions of the Railway Labor Act.[99]

Although a system of crafts and classes developed over nearly a century on the railroads, the decade of growth in the airline industry did not lend itself to succinct categorization. Through the hearings that August, the board found that "[t]he most striking fact emerging from the mass of evidence presented at the hearings, and from a study of occupational representation and association for collective bargaining purposes in the air industry, is the almost complete lack of uniformity in these respects among all but a very few rather well-defined occupational groups."[100]

The board also found that the labor organizations representing airline workers exacerbated the confusion over craft and class:

> Another rather surprising development is the complete change in attitude on the part of certain organizations as to what constitutes a "craft or class." Expediency, and a tendency toward an industrial or semi-industrial form of organization, perhaps quite largely due to the type and constitutions of some organizations seeking the right to represent certain groups of air line employ-

> ees, may be responsible for this change. In any event, certain organizations which a year or two ago held quite positive views as to the proper crafts or classes among airline employees have abandoned or completely reversed their previous positions. The Board therefore must examine the history of organization among airline employees in an effort to gain the proper perspective.[101]

According to Cole's report, the board examined union representation of workers on the ground in the airline industry from 1938 through 1944. While agreement coverage for pilots and aircraft mechanics was uniform, and almost complete across the industry in the case of the pilots, union representation for dispatchers, navigators, stewards, stewardesses, clerical groups, janitors, porters, stores, and plant-maintenance groups was scattered throughout agreements and unions.

Part of the perplexity in analyzing these agreements stemmed from the fact that there was "no standard classification of occupational titles and duties among airline employees, such as exists on the rail carriers. Therefore, job titles for the same kind of work are almost as varied as the number of operating airlines. One airline may have a classification known as commissary clerks, while on another the duties of such jobs would be performed by ground service personnel or utility workers."[102]

The National Mediation Board had on file at the time of these Findings agreements that covered twenty-four separate and distinct groups determined as crafts or classes. Among them, relating to the work of nonmechanics on the ground, were "commissary clerks," "cargo handlers," "fleet-service personnel," "utility personnel," "ground-service personnel," "agents," and "aircraft cleaners." Cole stated that the board contended that so many categories were unnecessary; he reported that the groupings fell naturally into two categories: "[F]irst, employees who man the airplane in flight, or what might be called the 'operating' group; and second, all other ground employees, or the 'non-operating' group."[103]

Cole's report divided these groups into two distinct classifications. The board divided the second group, "non-operating" employees, as "[e]mployees engaged in maintaining and servicing aircraft and equipment. Employees maintaining and disbursing stocks of parts, equipment, and supplies used in the maintenance and servicing of aircraft and equipment. Clerical employees. Janitors and unskilled workers." The board considered as separate and smaller, specialized groups "radio operators, agents, station managers, commissary employees, porters and red caps, protective firemen, guards."[104]

In terms of employees whose job it was to maintain and service aircraft and equipment, Cole explained that on the railroads, clear class and craft demarcations had been established within the "shop" category. However, for the airlines, such demarcations among mechanics had not been established. The Civil Aeronautics Board, which required aircraft mechanics to be licensed, set down the only stringent requirement in that category.

The board found that some groups of employees without aircraft licenses were associated with the mechanics' group. These included aircraft cleaners, parts washers, plant-maintenance mechanics, and service employees whose titles varied depending upon the airline employing them. Titles for these employees included "ground-service personnel," "fleet-service personnel," and "utility personnel." The general functions of these workers included

> [w]ashing and cleaning airplane, engine, and accessory parts in the overhaul shops;
> Fueling of aircraft and ground equipment;
> Maintenance of buildings, hangars, and related equipment;
> Cleaning and maintaining the exterior and interior appearance of airplanes;
> Servicing and control of cabin service equipment;
> Air conditioning of airplanes;
> Cleaning of airport hangars, buildings, and hangar and ramp equipment;
> Other miscellaneous duties at stations and shops not requiring mechanical work on aircraft, engines, or related equipment.[105]

Cole reported that the board felt that such duties naturally placed workers within the mechanical classification. According to Cole, the classifications of "fleet-service personnel," "utility personnel," "plant-maintenance personnel," and "ground-service personnel" appear in only a total of eleven agreements held with the eighteen principal airlines holding contracts with labor unions in 1945. The board assumed that in most cases where such work was not specifically covered under a contract, "mechanical forces" carried it out.[106]

Addressing the work of baggage handling or fleet-service personnel at American Airlines, the focus of these Findings, Cole explained that among these employees were workers assigned the "handling [of] mail, express, and other cargo to and from the airplanes at the air terminals." The board's records showed that on only three airlines were "cargo handlers" or "cargo clerks" given special status as a separate group. In one case a Passenger Agents Association represented these employees. In the second case they were represented as a separate craft or class, and in the third case they were covered in an agreement that included stock clerks, cargo clerks, and fleet-service clerks.

The National Mediation Board found that in most cases service employees known as ground-service or fleet-service personnel performed the work of handling cargo. Although the BRC laid claim to these employees during the hearings that August, no case involving the BRC was before the board at that time. Regarding the case at American Airlines, the board found that the cargo handlers should be included in the general group of fleet-service personnel, which in the Findings Cole stated should be categorized with the mechanical group. The board found that maintenance-of-equipment employees, including airline mechanics, (and radio mechanics), ground-service personnel, plant-maintenance personnel, and fleet-service personnel, should vote together on one ballot. The board also found that stock-and-stores personnel should vote on a separate ballot. Both findings applied only to Case No. R-1447, concerning American Airlines.[107]

In November 1945, the National Mediation Board certified the TWU to represent stores personnel at American Airlines but did not rule on the representation of airline mechanics, the group that included fleet-service personnel, although the mechanics group also voted. Over three thousand American Airlines employees participated in the election. The results are listed in table 9.

For this certification, election ballots were also sent to seventy-three foreign-based employees included in these crafts or classes, despite the fact that union and company officials could not agree on the right of union representation for workers overseas. Only eleven ballots were returned, which would not have affected the vote outcome, and the board, therefore, did not decide on this issue. The TWU was authorized to represent stores personnel.

Table 9. American Airlines employees voting for contesting organizations, November 1945

	(1) Airline Mechanics	(2) Stores Personnel
For Air Line Mechanics Department, UAW-CIO	383	16
For Transport Workers Union of America, CIO	825	157
For International Association of Machinists, AFL	344	21
For Air Carrier Mechanics Association	807	62
For other organizations or individuals	9	0
Void ballots	26	1
Number of employees eligible to vote	2,868	2981

Source: National Mediation Board, "Case No R-1447, Certification, November 28, 1945, in the matter of Representation of Employees of the American Airlines, Inc., (1) Airline Mechanics (2) Stores Personnel," 2, BRC Collection, "September 1945–June 1946, Organization–Air Transport Industry" file; Frank Heisler to Mr. H. W. Brown, November 23, 1945, IAM Collection, reel 296, vol. 1.

Although interest in the pilot-affiliated ACMA was high, no organization or individual received a majority of legal votes cast for the mechanics group. The votes cast for the ACMA were invalid because its authorization cards had not met with the minimum requirements set by the Railway Labor Act. The votes it received were write-in votes.[108]

While R-1447 applied only to employees of American Airlines, the Findings for the case became a benchmark for future disputes over the classification of baggage handlers. The Findings concisely illuminate the difficulty the industry and the unions experienced in defining work and workers in this period of rapid expansion. As the next chapter will show, case R-1447 was not the last word on the matter.

By July 1946, airline mechanics at American Airlines and ground-service and fleet-service personnel voted for representation by the TWU by a significant margin. Of the 3,374 employees eligible to vote, 1,811 voted for the TWU. The second runner-up, the ACMA, created by the pilots' union and dismissed in case R-1447 for improper authorization cards, received 639 votes. The IAM did not participate in this election. As in the earlier election, those mechanics most intent on craft-based organization voted for the ACMA.[109] The Airline Mechanics Department, UAW-CIO (formerly ALMA), which prior to the certification of the TWU represented the airline mechanics at American, received only 145 ballots in its favor.[110] The first systemwide contract for maintenance employees at American increased wages by nine cents an hour on average and implemented shift differentials, double-time on the seventh day worked, and a promotion procedure for mechanics. Baggage handlers started at eighty-four cents an hour and topped out after two years at $1.14 an hour. In an attempt to stave off unionization, American had already instituted the forty-hour workweek for forty-eight hours' pay after the TWU won it at Pan Am.[111]

Organizing at Northwest

The organizing drives at Northwest Airlines also raised important questions of jurisdiction and classification of baggage handlers before and after the important decision made by the National Mediation Board at American Airlines. At Northwest, these workers were variously called "groomers," "cargo handlers," and "equipment servicemen." The BRC, a union with a large membership of office and clerical employees, investigated the possibility of organizing these workers at Northwest. Conflict regarding this investigation arose after the IAM was certified to represent them; a fifteen-year dispute ensued.

Early in the war, the BRC investigated the possibilities of organizing airline workers. Their efforts focused on workers on the ground at Northwest Airlines. While the BRC's organizing attempts at Northwest challenged the ALMA, the IAM also conducted an organizing campaign at Northwest. Initially the BRC and the IAM campaigned simultaneously and honored an unwritten understanding over jurisdiction.[112] On the eve of the BRC's campaign, "groomers"—workers who cleaned the inside and outside of planes as well as loaded all the baggage, mail, and express packages—were represented by the ALMA. The BRC organizer investigating Northwest estimated that nearly 1,800 employees at Northwest Airlines could be organized by the BRC.[113]

After further investigation, the BRC considered a number of work groups to be under their jurisdiction for organizing. These groups included caretakers, cargo handlers, loaders, loading supervisors, groomers, schedule clerks, stenographers, mail clerks, time clerks, stores clerks, stores foremen, janitors, reservations clerks, passengers agents, guards, watchmen, and crew drivers.[114]

While the BRC was confident of its jurisdiction over clerical employees, questions arose over the proper classification of workers who loaded and cleaned the planes. In a letter to the BRC organizer Charles Kief, George M. Harrison, president of the BRC, addressed the position of these workers:

> It is noted that representatives of the Air Line Mechanics Association, International, as it is officially known, are apparently actively engaged in soliciting membership of employees of our craft or class in the employ of this carrier. Of course, under the Railway Labor Act, class or craft lines are pretty generally defined and the nature of the work performed will determine [into] which group employees of more or less border line classification will be placed. For instance some airlines have classification described as "cargo handlers." . . . [W]e will have to determine [whether] these positions [are] analogous to "freight handlers or baggage and mail handlers," etc. Then there are employees known as "groomers" who, as you state, clean the inside and outside of planes and "load all mail, baggage and express." These are undoubtedly jobs requiring no particular mechanical skill or ability and may be roughly classified as "laborers–freight handlers." Undoubtedly the handling of mail, baggage, and express to and from passenger planes required but a minority portion of their time. These positions should be explored further.[115]

The question of how groomers spent their time as well as the job progression to passenger agent would become central issues to the jurisdictional dispute.

In a letter to Harrison, Kief described the job definition and pay scale of "groomers" versus other employees. According to Kief, in an agreement between Northwest and the ALMA, mechanics were paid from $1.00 to $1.10 an hour, senior mechanics made $1.10 to $1.20, and master mechanics were paid from $1.20 to $1.30 an hour. These rates were based on whether a mechanic had no license, an Airframe (A) or an Engine (E) license, or both. These rates were comparable to those of aircraft mechanics employed by American Airlines. The title "crew chief" described "a person employed by the Company, whose work assignments include supervising other employees but who may be required to have an airplane engine or an airplane license." These titles brought up to thirty-five dollars more a month for the crew chief position within the ranks of mechanics. It was also used in the stores and stockroom department, but higher wages for the position did not apply. According to Kief, "[T]hey have given the employees the title to make them feel good but do not want to apply the rate because they are not mechanics, but male crew chiefs in the stockroom received some kind of an increase but not the agreement rate but the majority of the stores employees are women and they are not getting the rate that is being paid the males." Regarding the groomers, Kief wrote,

> The word "Groomer" as defined in Section 2 paragraph (A) of the agreement reads as follows: The term "Groomer" as used herein shall mean a person employed by the Company, a majority of whose work assignments consist of the cleaning of aircraft, interior or exterior, cabin equipment, including items of supplies used by passengers, handling of mail, express, baggage and military equipment, and cleaning and minor repair of equipment used in the Company's operations. Section 8, paragraph (1) reads:
>
> The following rate of wages are hereby established for groomers:
>
> | | |
> |---|---|
> | 1st three months of service | $100.00 |
> | 2nd three months of service | $110.00 |
> | 3rd three months of service and thereafter | $125.00 |
>
> A. In addition to the foregoing rates of wages, groomers assigned to the Chicago station shall receive $5.00 per month.
>
> B. In addition to the forgoing rates of wages, groomers assigned to the Seattle station shall receive the same living increment above the base rate as is applied in the case of all employees based at Seattle.
>
> From the information I can gather about groomers they are a combination mail and baggage handler, janitor and coach cleaner. The repairs they make are about on the same principle of the repairs made by a station janitor.[116]

Groomers' wages in 1943 were comparable to those paid to American Airlines fleet-service clerks the same year, and their work duties were also similar. Northwest Airlines only used the term "groomer," which emphasized the cleaning aspect of this job, up to the mid-1940s. This job title was replaced with that of "equipment serviceman" in 1944.[117] The conflict between cleaning and loading and light mechanical work is apparent in Kief's letter.

By July 1943, the BRC started its organizing campaign at Northwest. In a letter addressed to "All Clerical, Office, Station, and Storehouse Employees of the Northwest Airlines, Inc.," Charles Kief told employees that the BRC had been asked by the employees to represent them. According to Kief, under the Railway Labor Act the BRC could represent "clerks and clerical workers, typists and stenographers, telephone switchboard operators, office boys, messengers, stockroom and storehouse employees, groomers, janitors, scrubbers, cleaners, mail baggage and express handlers, and loaders, station and property watchmen and all others performing similar work."[118] This letter, mailed to employees of the listed craft or class, included representation-authorization cards and information about BRC meetings in Minneapolis.

In August, the BRC stepped up its campaign by tying together unionism and patriotism. In a letter addressed to clerical, office, station, and storehouse employees, George M. Harrison pointed to the importance of the transportation industry in the war and the threat of fascism at home: "In order to insure that Government does not turn to Fascists methods in this emergency the organized labor movement is on guard. Organized Labor has accepted the challenge and will be true to its responsibilities as the guardian of democracy in America. It will not permit democracy to be destroyed and fascist controls set up in this country. IF TRUE COLLECTIVE BARGAINING WERE STOPPED, WE WOULD LOSE DEMOCRACY IN AMERICA. In order to PROTECT YOUR interest you should, therefore, become a part of the Organized Labor Movement."[119] Harrison highlighted the BRC's affiliation with the AFL and its record of representation in the railroad industry, where the union represented employees on "more than 99 percent of the mileage of Class I railroads in the United States" and "more than 75,000 other employees of Express, Freight Forwarding, Steamship and other transportation agencies in the United States, Canada and New Foundland." To appeal to the clerical workers at Northwest, Harrison pointed out that the BRC "represent[s] today the largest organized body of 'white collar' workers in the world."

In February 1944, Charles Kief addressed Northwest employees in a letter to clerical, office, station, and storehouse employees regarding their representation. Kief seemed somewhat frustrated by the progress of the BRC's organization attempt over the last several months and reminded readers that "[f]or some time employees of our craft or class employed by the Northwest Airlines have urged us to organize them for the purpose of improving their working conditions and rates of pay." Kief reiterated the right to organize under the Railway Labor Act and called into question the ability of the ALMA, which represented some Northwest employees at the time: "The employees of the Northwest Airlines are in dire need of representation by a bona fide labor organization. The present type of representation is merely a 'smoke screen'; a pretense set up in lieu of bona fide representation to avoid dealing with the kind of representative contemplated in the Law—to prevent you from obtaining just and equitable conditions. You know that such things as the 'Trade Test Standards' examination are methods devised for the purpose of legalizing discrimination."[120] In this letter, as in previous ones by Kief and Harrison, Kief encouraged Northwest employees to sign authorization cards and attend BRC organizing meetings.

By 1945, the BRC was not the only union challenging the ALMA's position at Northwest Airlines. The UAW as well the IAM conducted organizing drives at the airline. In the months before the ALMA became the Air Line Mechanics' Department of the UAW, the competition between the two organizations was fierce.[121] Their merger improved the IAM's position at Northwest.[122]

Initially, relations between the BRC and the IAM over the issue of baggage handlers were guarded but friendly. In the summer of 1945, the IAM considered a joint effort with the BRC to organize the airline industry, in part because of workers' confusion over too many choices for representation. As the organizer Lee Chapman explained,

> (1) It appears that possibly it would be advantageous to us if President Harrison of that Organization could be contacted to the end that a coordination of assignment between his organization and ours be brought about. As it now is, we have a representative visit a given point and later comes along a representative of the Clerks Union.
>
> This system only adds to the present confusion and chaos inasmuch as the employees of this industry know very little if anything about the trade labor movement and cannot differentiate between the various organizations.
>
> (2) The organizational effort in the air transport industry should be thoroughly discussed with the Clerks Union with the intent and purpose of definitely drawing a jurisdictional line of demarcation.

The IAM recognized the precarious position between the unions regarding baggage handlers. Chapman continued: "As you know, we have petitioned for the cargo handlers on some carriers, and at the same time the Clerks are interested in these cargo handlers. This situation is not alarming at the moment since President Harrison has told his organizers not to interfere with our activity, . . . not to claim jurisdiction over any group of people we presently have organized. Not withstanding this fact, sooner or later, unless a definite understanding is reached, difficulty will develop."[123] The unwritten agreement regarding baggage handlers at Northwest Airlines survived until after both unions won certification for separate work groups.

After exhaustive campaigns by the BRC and IAM at Northwest, the IAM collected enough authorization cards among airline mechanics to call for an election for representation. In February 1946, the National Mediation Board certified the IAM to represent Northwest's mechanics. This group included inspectors, all levels and types of mechanics, and baggage handlers. Of 921 employees eligible to vote, 499 cast ballots for the IAM. The UAW's Airline Mechanics Department received 277 votes. At least one hundred employees eligible in this election did not cast ballots.[124] After months of negotiation and a two-day strike, Northwest and the IAM finalized an agreement covering these workers in September 1946. Soon after, the BRC and IAM dispute over baggage handlers erupted.

In July 1946, the BRC won certification of transportation agents (ticket agents and others engaged in the paperwork for passengers and freight), and the IAM won certification of stores and stockroom employees as well as unskilled employees. At the time of the IAM election, the stock and storeroom employees and those in the unskilled category were represented by the Airline Mechanics Department, UAW-CIO. The UAW did not participate in this election at Northwest, and the IAM went unchallenged. Eighty stock and storeroom employees and fifty-seven unskilled employees were eligible for that election.[125]

The BRC gained its foothold at Northwest with its certification to represent transportation agents. The transportation agents voted in the BRC without a challenger. Of 545 employees eligible to vote, the BRC received 361 votes.[126] By September, the BRC and Northwest negotiated an agreement for the transportation agents; this group included the reservations agents. Transportation agents were responsible for "load supervision, passenger service, departure control, counter sales and check-in."[127] Reservations agents and their supervisors did not work at every station served by Northwest Airlines and took reservations for flights by phone in most cases.

Airline Workers and Communism: The Cold War on the Ramp

Immediately after the war, the federal government continued regulation and bureaucratic control of wage adjustments, and American corporations demanded limitations on labor's power. The strike wave of 1945–46, fueled by rising prices, layoffs, and fears about the postwar economy, further irritated business leaders, who connected this rebellion to Communist sympathies among union members. As many historians have argued, the cold war battered labor's political power, curtailed union organizing, and eroded the cultural and social worlds of the American working class.[128] The growing cultural power of corporations and their associations (such as the National Association of Manufacturers and the Air Transport Association) led to the passage of the Taft-Hartley Act of 1947, which permitted the president to delay strike action up to 140 days in disputes considered "national emergencies," banned strikes related to jurisdictional disputes, reconfigured much of the administrative and procedural components of the National Labor Relations Board, and required union officers to sign affidavits stating they were not Communists.[129]

The anti-Communist fervor of the business community, the fear of Communism among Catholic unionists, and the preoccupation with red-baiting on the part of the press all culminated in a crisis for the TWU in Miami. Originally organized with significant participation among Communists, the TWU was a prime target for the anti-Communist fervor of the late 1940s. A 1948 attack on Communism in the TWU stemmed from the overarching political climate as well as an internal power struggle. In Miami, Local 500 at Pan Am challenged not only the racial and anti-Communist mores of the postwar South but leftists among its ranks struggled against national TWU leadership.

In the summer of 1948, when TWU Local 500 staff members met with Communist spokesmen in a local diner, the Miami press launched a vicious crusade against the union. The *Miami Daily News* ran photos of the diner meeting and for weeks printed articles about the TWU International representative Charles Smolikoff's Communist associations.[130] Over the next several months, several factors contributed to the extensive attention paid to the meeting and the suspicion of rampant Communism in Local 500. The local was the most important one for the TWU in Florida, with over two thousand members, and served as a strong base for the Left.[131] Within the previous year the TWU had organized an additional 450 workers and led a mass meeting in Miami to fight the Taft-Hartley Act. This meeting, held in a public park and attended by six thousand people, according to the TWU, was the largest ever in Florida. It was also racially mixed; "[F]or the first time in Miami history, hundreds of Negroes attended the lily-white park and delivered a smashing blow to Jim-Crow."[132]

At the same time, the TWU was attempting to organize at Eastern Airlines, where the son of the owner of the *Miami Daily News* held a seat on the board of directors; alarmist coverage of the TWU at Pan Am could only damage the TWU's campaign at Eastern, while the UAW began raids on the union at Pan Am. From within, the situation was aggravated by a dissident group of TWU members who had recently lost a union election. These members, affiliated with the Association of Catholic Trade Unionists, an anti-Communist group, called themselves the Committee for Democratic Action and demanded an end to the "Communist domination" of their union.[133] Members of the Communist party had indeed been central figures in the development of Local 500. Charles Smolikoff was a member of the party, as were two of the original organizers of the Local, Roy and Elizabeth Whitman. Smolikoff's public affiliation with Communism and his urging that the local endorse the Progressive party's presidential candidate Henry Wallace, further focused the public's attention on the Red Scare at the community level.[134]

The attention focused on Local 500 spurred a House Committee on Un-American Activities investigation of Communism in Miami. City officials and police participated in what one observer called "terror let loose" on the local. They threatened to "run out of town" TWU president Mike Quill during a trip to aid the local, thirty police officers intimidated the chief steward, police arrested Smolikoff for using a different name (charges later dismissed), and the county district attorney questioned the local's president, M. L. Edwards, his wife, and other members of Local 500.[135]

Cold-war witch hunting did not end with Smolikoff and the Left-oriented leadership of Local 500. In April 1948, Mike Quill publicly severed ties with the Communist party over support of Henry Wallace and transit-fare issues in New York City. This break led to rifts within the TWU, between the International Executive Board and Quill, and between the Air Transport Division and Quill. At the TWU's December 1948 convention Quill flushed the union of its last party members and leftists, including the Air Transport Division leader Maurice Forge.[136] Angry at the ousting of Forge and the lack of autonomy of the Air Transport Division within the TWU, dissident airline workers formed the Committee for Air Transport Autonomy (CATA) to push for structural change within the union. Airline workers in Miami and New York stood at the center of the battle. Quill viewed the CATA as an attempt to "create an international within the International" and sought to destroy it. The International Executive Board and Quill called the CATA a Communist front.[137] Again, accusations of Communist activity served to silence dissident voices in airline locals. Amid rumors of connections with a Latin American Communist network and scandal over mismanagement of funds, Miami's Local 500 leaders and Smolikoff were removed from their positions. The CATA also fell to the pressure.[138]

Some members of the dissolved CATA decided to leave the TWU altogether and organized a new union, the Federated Airline Workers of America (FAWA). With substantial support in New York and Miami, the FAWA challenged the TWU and called for industrial unionism in the airlines with the slogan "One Union of Airline Workers." Among Pan Am workers in Miami the fledgling union had enough support to call for elections. The FAWA lost by a narrow margin to the TWU, marking the end of the revolt of airline workers within the TWU.[139]

Airline Workers in the Postwar Strike Wave

The mostly successful shopfloor peace of the war could not withstand the oppositional pressures of management's intention to restore managerial prerogatives and labor's hope to maintain wartime regulation to boost wages to offset the loss of war overtime and counter inflation. Initially, labor leaders and liberal capitalists publicly announced intentions of hammering out a postwar plan, a "Labor-Management Charter"—a set of agreed-upon values defining a "people's capitalism" that centered around labor's right to bargain, high wages and efficient productivity, and management's right to manage its enterprise. The project failed in part because the AFL and CIO did not hold a shared vision for the postwar era. AFL traditions of voluntarism and the majority of their membership in the booming sectors of the economy (construction, transportation, and service) made them suspicious of the pattern wage increases the CIO supported. Frustrated by this stalemate, workers across basic industry and beyond went on strike as this public debate played out.[140]

In most cases workers walked off the job and won significant wage increases even if much of labor's social agenda was not realized. In the latter half of 1945, the nation lost over twenty-eight million man-days to strikes, double the figure for 1943. In many cases these strikes were wildcats, spontaneous action by the rank and file. Workers on the airlines joined hundreds of thousands of others in steel mills, bus companies, drug stores, lumber yards, harbors, oil refineries, electrical plants, meatpacking, and auto production and walked off the job. However, the nature of the airline strikes differed from those carried out by the millions of workers employed in most other industries. Airline workers were among the less than 15 percent of all workers striking for union recognition in the immediate postwar years.[141]

Porters and baggage handlers at Pan Am participated in two cross-skill and cross-race job actions in Miami in the years immediately following the war. One of the first postwar strikes in the industry was a wildcat strike at Pan Am. In October 1945, two thousand Miami Pan Am workers participated in a two-day, sit-down strike to protest violations of a precontract agreement between the TWU and the airline.[142] On October 23, worker representatives presented a list of eight complaints pertaining to violations of the precontract agreement to the airline. The complaints were directed to Pan Am headquarters in New York, where contract negotiations with the TWU were under way. The Pan Am workers did not wait for a response. They sat down on the job within minutes of the complaints presentation. White aircraft mechanics, unskilled workers, and African American porters all took part in the strike. The TWU leader Michael Quill called the strike "illegal" and ordered the workers back on the job. The fifty-hour, sit-down strike ended when the strikers unanimously agreed to a settlement hammered out in New York regarding seniority in layoffs and grievance procedures.[143]

In July 1946, Pan Am fired seven porters for refusing the extra task of unloading ballast sandbags from an aircraft. As a result, one hundred African American porters led a job action at Pan Am, and white aircraft mechanics and unskilled workers threatened to follow. Seventeen white and four black union officers confronted Pan Am's management. The airline reinstated the seven porters and paid them for lost time. Such militancy on the part of the black porters and biracial cooperation among airline workers did not sit well with some whites. Members of the Ku Klux Klan threatened Roosevelt Winfield, the chair of the porters-and-cleaners section of the local, with drowning if he continued to handle grievances from black workers at Pan Am. White union officials publicly denounced the Klan and its intentions, stating, "[T]here's nobody . . . who's going to split us white workers away from our Negro co-workers . . . when it comes to color, race or politics, Local 500, TWU-CIO has no weak links."[144]

In July 1946, ground-service workers at Northwest Airlines walked off the job, completely shutting down the airline for over thirty hours. It was the first time that aircraft mechanics, baggage handlers ("equipment servicemen" at Northwest), and other ground-service workers closed an airline coast to coast. In February 1946, the National Mediation Board had certified the IAM to represent mechanics and baggage handlers at Northwest Airlines. By May of that year, negotiations for a contract between the IAM and the company had reached a standstill. For all practical purposes, the mechanics and baggage handlers had been in negotiations with the company for a contract since 1944, under the representation of the ALMA and later the UAW's airline department.[145]

By mid-May, frustrated mechanics and baggage handlers in New York were ready to confront management at the local level. Frank Heisler, a union officer in New York, let his counterpart in St. Paul know that "[t]he membership as a whole are 100 percent behind the [negotiating] committee, and they state that they will let local management know in no uncertain terms that they do not appreciate the attitude of the officials in not negotiating in good faith."[146] Union demands included a liberalization of vacations and sick leave, a longevity allowance, continued premium pay for licensed mechanics, night-shift differential, an 18.5 percent general wage increase, and the elimination of classification inequities.[147]

At the same time, workers in Minneapolis/St. Paul lost patience with the contract situation and recent layoffs. In a letter to the union president, Frank Heisler wrote, "The situation at St. Paul–Minneapolis is highly explosive in the face of the prolonged delays in negotiations our membership have experienced in the past and the reductions in force that are taking place from time to time and it is my opinion that the slightest irregular move on the part of the company or any extended delay in the assignment of a Mediator will be the spark that will cause an immediate work stoppage."[148] Mediation proved less than satisfactory for both sides. IAM representatives complained that the mediator was a resident of Minneapolis and possibly partial to the company's position. Furthermore, the mediator was elderly, in poor health, and did not seem to grasp the intricacies of labor relations in the air industry.[149]

On July 3 at 6:00 AM, mechanics and baggage handlers at Northwest went on strike. Workers in New York, Minneapolis/St. Paul, Spokane, Portland, and Billings walked off the job.[150] In Billings, the union representative Tom Temple reported,

> All but one of the eligible employees are members, and cooperated fully and enthusiastically in carrying out the arranged program. . . . The pilots completely supported the strike. Passenger agents remained on the job, but refused to handle cargo, luggage, or equipment. Mail was removed by post-office employees. . . . Public reaction has been generally favorable, as Northwest

> hasn't too good a reputation in this area. The local press gave a small, distorted notice space in yesterday's paper. Passenger reaction was mostly unfavorable, of course, although many of the 86 people grounded asked as to the reasons and seemed to accept our story in good faith.[151]

Approximately one thousand aircraft mechanics, plant-maintenance men, baggage handlers, and janitors walked off the job, shutting down Northwest Airlines across the country.

As per the Railway Labor Act, President Truman called for the creation of an emergency board to investigate the matter and begin a thirty-day cooling-off period. Northwest's workers returned to the job. Locked in hearings through July and August, the company and union struggled over "company rights" policies and facts and figures regarding sick and vacation time. In August, the emergency board denied the IAM members the wage increase, citing the government's wage-stabilization policy. The board granted improvements in sick and vacation time and gave four- and six-cent shift differentials. Despite the dissatisfaction over the board's findings, the union and company signed a new contract the next month that included small wage increases.[152]

By 1948, airlines and unions increasingly brought their issues to the flying public.[153] The threat of layoffs and outsourcing and hardline tactics by management resulted in strikes at American and National Airlines. In Au-

Northwest Airlines strike, 1946. Photographer Philip C. Dittes. Minnesota Historical Society. Location: HG3.18 r3, Negative 5;7717.

gust 1948, workers at American Airlines in New York City responded to layoffs and transfers with informational picketing at the city's airports. Flyers handed out to passengers questioned the safety of American's flights due to four major layoffs of maintenance employees within the year. The flyer asked passengers to "[r]emember, air safety starts on the ground—in the hangars and repair shops!"[154] Aircraft mechanics at American admonished the airline for disloyalty to its employees and for eroding their financial and community security. A flyer for the membership—"Here We Go Again!"—read,

> Again, the cry is "economy"! Again the Company asserts its "God-given" and "legal" right to scramble the lives of its twenty-five hundred New York maintenance workers in the push for greater profits.
>
> We all remember the rosy promises of a bright future in the airlines—Pan American, American Overseas, American Airlines, and others. We well remember how some airline employees sweated out the war years at low pay while the airlines prospered on government contracts and how these employees looked forward to the security of peace-time jobs in a young glamorous industry.
>
> The glamour has worn off. What has happened? More and more the Air Transport Industry has become an industry for seasonal, migratory workers—an industry that has repeatedly shown that it cares nothing for the well-being or peace of mind of its employees. . . .
>
> [I]t [American Airlines] has a moral obligation to its employees such as is recognized by every intelligent and forward-looking employer. The management of American Airlines has a moral obligation to assure its employees a normal, decent, American existence—which includes the right to establish family and home relationships. The management of American Airlines has no right to expect its employees to live in a state of constant suspension—to be prepared at a moment's notice to uproot their families, disrupt their homes, cancel their obligations, and hop a freight for a new location.
>
> The employees of AA in New York know that this city furnishes a substantial, if not major portion of all revenue collected by AA.
>
> They themselves, as taxpayers and citizens, contribute to the millions of dollars that the City has spent to create facilities for American Airlines and other airlines. They demand that AA retain its employees in the New York area as a matter of common decency and fairness.
>
> The employees of AA *made* American Airlines. They have poured their hearts and their brains and their energies into making AA the largest airline in the United States. They believe that they are receiving a shabby reward for their years of loyalty and service.

> The employees of American Airlines have had enough of lay-offs, transfers, switches, bumping and shoving around. They are not going to take this lay-off lying down![155]

The August 1948 informational picketing and rallying of TWU members pressured American to respond. In a letter to American Airlines employees, president C. R. Smith urged workers to promote, not discourage, customers to fly American and explained that layoffs were necessary when there was not enough work.[156] Within a month, American postponed the maintenance layoffs indefinitely and agreed to explore keeping maintenance work in New York, in part due to the influence of TWU president Michael Quill as a New York City councilman.[157] Nonetheless, the company opened a maintenance base in Tulsa within two years.

Although by most accounts National Airlines, despite its name, was strictly a regional carrier transporting sun-lovers from the East Coast to Florida, its strikes in 1948 were perhaps the most significant and symbolic of the age. The strikes at National that year were the first in the industry to last more than four weeks and the first to involve the hiring of replacement workers. The strikes played out in the arenas of public opinion, the courtroom, and national politics. The Civil Aeronautics Board, not a body concerned with labor-management disputes, found itself tangled in the fracas. Airline unions and airline management, including the ATA, recognized that the battle over National would set the stage for postwar labor relations in the industry.

Among the airlines, National's president, George "Ted" Baker, was among the most notorious for his shrewd tactics and anti-union stance. Baker's combative relationship with the pilots' union dated back to the early war years, when he grudgingly respected the pilots' contract under the threat of Civil Aeronautics Board investigations over irregular wage practices. His relations with the aircraft mechanics' and baggage handlers' union were scarcely better. In the months leading up to union elections among the aircraft mechanics and stores employees in 1945, National repeatedly interfered with organizing and pushed for a company union among its employees.[158] During the reclassification program for mechanics and ground-service workers in spring 1946, frustrated IAM members like Local 368 president Norris P. Thomas of Jacksonville were convinced that "the company is apparently trying to break us as a Union and the state of unrest is such that you may expect anything to happen here."[159] After months of waiting, the company presented its classifications system, which the union deemed to be approximately 90 percent incorrect with twelve violations of the contract in these classifications.[160] After bargaining a second mechanics and baggage handlers' contract (effective January 1, 1947), IAM officials were frustrated, as "promise after promise has been made by various officials of the Company, including President Baker, results being blank with minor exceptions." Indeed, three months after the contract was in effect, the union had no copy of the seniority list, apprenticeship agreements were ignored, wage grievances were unsettled, and the general chairman of the union's travel-pass privileges, clearly allowed by the Civil Aeronautics Board, were revoked. In March 1947, the IAM grand lodge representative J. C. McGlon speculated that "President Baker would like to see a strike on National Airlines, which would probably permit or give sufficient cause for him to cancel contracts he has to purchase new airplanes."[161]

Conflict between the IAM and National grew during contract negotiations for the clerical and office workers. After the close election in May 1947, the IAM requested copies of wage rates, job descriptions, and titles to be used to craft a contract proposal several times over the summer. Without the data, the IAM presented its opening contract proposal for these workers in August 1947. After several delays by the company, negotiations began at the end of October.

National Airlines and the IAM were not the only parties at the table; the Airlines Negotiating Conference, a service arm of the ATA, joined National. This body of the ATA was formed initially in 1945 to attempt joint bargaining with the pilots' union over four-engine aircraft. The pilots refused to bargain with the body, and the conference was dismantled but reorganized in the summer of 1946.[162] Already a tense situation at National, the presence of the ATA negotiating service was a further affront to unionized airline workers.

Two days into bargaining, IAM representatives warned the International that "the conference desires to place itself as a party to the agreement, in fact they are attempting to assume the same relationship or position as that of our International." The conference challenged "long times standard" contract language proposed by the IAM, and the union recognized the ominous effect such a negotiating body could have on airline bargaining. As the grand lodge representative Lee Chapman explained, "In fact, it is our opinion that we should do everything possible to prevent success on the part of the conference as a negotiating agency. If this conference enjoys reasonable success here in the National negotiations, it will be in a much better position to sell its services to the employer groups in future negotiations. We think that it will be well to 'foul them up' if possible, thus discounting their possibilities of selling future service."[163]

Within two weeks, the IAM and other unions responded to this threat by forming the Federation of Unions Representing Employees of National Airlines to promote cooperation among the unions and provide mutual support. Twenty-five men and women—National employees and union representatives from mechanical and clerical locals of the IAM, ALPA, and the Radio Officers Union—met to discuss the "strategy and methods that may be used in coping with the situations existing on the National Airlines, Inc."[164] This organization would provide a first step toward building a somewhat strained solidarity among IAM and ALPA members during the 1948 strikes.

During negotiations for the clerical and office workers, considerable time was spent at the table listening to Ted Baker "tell union leaders why there should not be a union." This stalling was followed by a pronouncement that the company could afford no wage increases, a demand for a bargaining recess until December, and then a twenty-dollar-per-month increase for all non-union employees earning less than $275 a month. Frustrated by these tactics, the IAM had requested National Mediation Board intervention for the clerical and office negotiations on October 31.[165]

On November 11 and 12, IAM members from both work groups, mechanical and clerical, voted to set a strike date for December 12, against the judgment of IAM officials.[166] Members of the Miami aircraft mechanics and baggage handlers Local 368 were particularly incensed over the pass-privileges issue for their general chairman and the contracting out of instrument work. As IAM representatives reported, "[T]hey are fully determined to strike and those officers advised me that there was no point in my trying to persuade them otherwise. They had suffered all the indignities they intended to suffer, however, they were willing to follow advice and will strike only after having followed through with proper procedures. Conditions among all employees of this Airline are terrible. They are all wanting to strike and when I say all, I mean from the pilots downward. National Airlines either does not know how, or does not wish to treat the employees with any degree of fairness."[167]

A mediator was requested by the IAM to resolve the maintenance issues; however, already embroiled in the clerical and office situation, the National Mediation Board was slow to follow up. With a board mediator present on December 1, negotiations for the clerical contract resumed, and the IAM agreed to postpone the strike. Back at the table, the company insisted on the right to contract out all work and refused to discuss other terms. Negotiations stalled on December 8, and the mediator formally offered arbitration. National stated that it could not agree to arbitration without the vote of its board of directors, which was not meeting until mid-January. Two days before Christmas, National announced changed policies regarding sick leave, vacations, holidays, notice of layoffs, and grievances, issues it refused to discuss before settling the contracting-out issue. On January 20 National's board of directors voted to decline arbitration. On January 22 the IAM clerical group voted to strike, effective noon January 23.[168]

On January 22, the National Mediation Board frantically followed up on the November request for mediation by the mechanics over the contracting out of instrument work. According to aviation economist Mark Kahn, the board notified IAM president H. W. Brown that board members themselves would mediate mechanical and clerical disputes on January 26. Ten minutes before the strike deadline, Brown wired local leaders in Miami, temporarily calling off the strike so that mediation could resume. It was too late; workers across Florida and in New Orleans walked off their jobs.[169]

Union leadership and the federal mediator convinced some strikers to return to work. Many workers, fearful of company discipline, refused to go back. Other stations again walked off the job and rejoined the strike. The IAM and National drafted a "no discrimination" agreement two days later, which was rejected by the membership because it did not include a process for settling disputes. On Monday, January 26, the IAM arrived at National Mediation Board offices to begin mediation. The airline refused to participate as long as workers were on strike. The following day, mechanics and baggage handlers honored the clerical picket lines. National Airlines maintained diminished service for the next eleven days by immediately replacing mechanics and clerical workers.[170]

IAM members were not the only ones in a showdown with Ted Baker and National Airlines. At 11:00 AM on February 3, National's pilots stopped flying over a long-brewing conflict between the company and ALPA. This action completely shut down the airline, at least temporarily, and focused national attention on it. The long-standing conflict between National and its pilots stemmed from an accident in September 1945. That month, a pilot, Maston O'Neal Jr., "overshot" the runway in Tampa. It is possible that what actually occurred was hydroplaning, a phenomenon where a cushion of water prevents aircraft wheels from actually touching the runway. O'Neal was first suspended and then fired. ALPA processed a grievance through a System Board of Adjustment, which deadlocked over the case. ALPA's president David Behncke corresponded and met with National's Baker, but to no avail. In May 1947, ALPA notified National that it would strike the company, and both sides met at the National Mediation Board offices. With the pressure of a pilots' strike, the two sides agreed to return the case to the System Board of Adjustment with a fifth neutral party added. When Behncke protested the appointment of this party, a safety-bureau employee of the Civil Aeronautics Board, National refused to consider a replacement. Again the pilots set a strike date, and again they returned to mediation.

While the ALPA strike was certainly not in sympathy with the IAM strikers, the mechanics off the job influenced the final strike date. There had been some concern among the pilots over the safety of planes since January 23. On February 3, the pilots walked out; Baker fired them two days later and advertised for replacements. According to George Hopkins, an historian of the pilots' union, Baker used this opportunity to try and break ALPA.[171] A complete shutdown during the peak Florida travel season could devastate the airline. However, National had some planes in the air again by February 11, with replacement pilots at the controls. The Civil Aeronautics Administration, concerned about accidents, tightened operating requirements while the new pilots got "the requisite experience."[172]

As National's operations increased, tensions between strikers and replacements grew, strikers' financial stress compounded, and frictions among union strategists appeared. In February, National Airlines filed an injunction against the IAM in Dade County regarding numerous incidents of vandalism and intimidation against working National employees, including pouring paint on cars, slashing convertible rag tops, and ripping out ignition wires. At the end of that month, violence erupted in a Miami bar when a striking National Airlines stock clerk and war veteran, Nelson Francis (twenty-eight), was shot outside a bar at 3:00 AM after four men beat a mechanic working for the airline. According to a *Miami Daily News* article, the beaten mechanic, Hugh McClain (twenty-six), who claimed that he carried a gun for protection during the strike, shot three times in the air as he tried to escape his attackers. He was charged with attempted manslaughter.[173] An IAM staffer, Lee Chapman, warned that picketers needed to be "watchful against some 'scab' running them down with an auto as [he] passes the picket line."[174] Violence erupted in the pilots' strike as well. Striking pilots harassed replacements with phone calls at their homes and profanities at the airports. Fistfights broke out at airports when National flights landed, and according to Brad Williams, a ground-school instructor for the new pilots was murdered, although the assailant was never caught, and so no motive was determined.[175]

As the strike wore on, some IAM members drifted back to work at National or elsewhere, and the union put substantial energy into maintaining the line, particularly among the clerical employees. A central preoccupation of IAM staff was the distribution of strike funds. IAM staff at outlying stations like New Orleans wrote regular letters to headquarters lobbying for more funds as workers faced mounting bills, evictions, and power shutoffs. Conditions were particularly difficult in the overcrowded housing market of Miami. By May, the IAM staff in Miami reported that strike meetings and the disbursement of funds were getting out of hand. At evening meetings held jointly for mechanical and clerical workers, a "certain element" appeared only at payout time and sometimes drunk. The meetings were moved to the daytime to discourage drinking and strikers with other employment from utilizing the strike fund.[176]

The gravity of the situation was clear to IAM leadership. The strike at National was not only a critical battle for the IAM but for airline workers across the industry. As the IAM representative E. H. Chambers wrote,

> If we are successful in driving this man Baker to the wall, the International will have saved many hundreds of thousands of dollars in its organizing efforts.
>
> If we lose it, practically all I. A. of M. efforts on the airlines will come to a halt, simply because, just as soon as the National boys go down to defeat, the remainder of the Air Transport Companies are going to start in to do a similar job on the rest of us. Let us not deceive ourselves. They are just standing by, watching and waiting. . . .
>
> Everyone is watching to see what comes out of this thing, and many of us have been told by the employers with whom we are normally associated, that they expect this to mark a milestone one way or the other in labor relations on the airlines.[177]

Airline workers and other union members from around the country paid close attention to the National strike and offered their support. In March, the Florida Federation of Labor passed a strong resolution of support for National strikers, and strike-fund donations came in from members of other IAM locals, the bricklayers union, firemen and engineers, the International Brotherhood of Electrical Workers, the Brotherhood of Maintenance of Way Employees, the Typographical Union, the Mail Handlers Association, and the International Cigar Workers. The Teamsters and the BRC refused to make deliveries to National.[178]

Workers on other airlines were particularly supportive. Despite years of competition over airline workers, the TWU in Miami offered its support. Money orders arrived from airline employees at Capital and Northwest Airlines in Milwaukee.[179] From Washington, D.C., employees of Capital Airlines sent a check and wrote,

> The strike of National Airlines employees is of a serious nature. It concerns a principle, one which will or will not involve all of us who [work] for the industry.

> In view of this the employees of Capital Airlines here in Washington have watched the situation with interest. The I.A. of M. members taking part in the walkout and those who are respecting the picket lines are to be commended by employees through-out the air transport industry for their courage. They have shown that they are willing to enter a bitter fight with the ATA if necessary in order that we might continue to enjoy decent wages and working conditions comparable to those in other industries. To the National Airlines employees we say: Stick to your guns, fellows, we are behind you 100 percent. You must not lose. . . . We cannot afford to let you lose.
>
> The enclosed check for $308.05 was collected by the Department Committeemen here at the Washington station and we hope there is more to follow. Almost everyone contributed so please acknowledge the amount received with a letter telling how things are going. Would like to read the letter at our next regular meeting which is scheduled for February 17.[180]

Importantly, the workers at Capital recognized this fight as one between the ATA and labor, not only between the IAM and National.

Pilots at the mostly non-union Delta Airlines also showed their support for striking National employees. At the Jacksonville airport, a flight crew on a Delta DC-4 blocked in a National aircraft and then tried to "blast" the foremen from the wing of the National aircraft as they fueled the plane. When the National plane was ready for departure, the Delta crew refused to move its craft out of the way and forced the National foremen and scab mechanics to push the plane into a position for departure. According to a striking National mechanic who witnessed the event, "All of this was done in a pouring rain and the pushing by man-power. This situation gave the crowd at the airport and even the Police a big laugh."[181]

National's striking workers took their issues to the public and politicians. Striking clerical workers attached bumper signs to the fronts and backs of their cars stating they were on strike. IAM representatives and local leaders wrote to friends of labor like Florida Senator Claude Pepper, local Miami radio hosts, the actor Tyrone Power, and the press to ask for support for their cause.[182] Because of National's route to Cuba, IAM staffers extended their publicity to the Caribbean and South America. Four thousand circulars, written to "fit the hot temperament of the Latin Americans," were sent to "Spanish Clubs" (Latin counterparts to the Elks and Masons). The circulars were then read on the radio as well.[183]

Perhaps the most public display of the National strike came with the aerial picketing campaign. Starting soon after the pilots' strike, the IAM and ALPA sponsored planes towing streamers and skywriting, drawing the public's attention to the strikes at National. While picketing in the sky definitely captured the attention of the press and public, the preoccupation with the glamorous work in the industry resulted in more attention to the pilots' strike than that of the clerical and mechanical workers.[184] After two planes flew over Miami, the first with a streamer stating, "N.A.L. CLERKS ON STRIKE. UNION MECHANICS NOT WORKING!" and a second with one that read, "NATIONAL AIRLINES PILOTS ON STRIKE," a frustrated IAM representative reported, "As usual, the pilots received the newspaper publicity, while we were left out in the cold so to speak. In fact, we are more than disappointed at the amount of paper coverage we received. . . . These Miami papers are not at all fair, much less friendly. We will continue the use of these planes for a few days, the chief value being the 'boost' they gave our people."[185] Relations between the two unions over aerial picketing worsened as they bickered over funding the aircraft and what uniforms would be worn in flight. During strike publicity flights, ALPA members expected the IAM representative Claude Houser to wear a pilot uniform to blend in, although the union was using Houser's IAM plane.[186]

Despite the publicity campaign, National continued to increase its service over the next several months, albeit at substantially decreased rates, particularly in domestic passenger service.[187] National countered the publicity campaign with lawsuits against the IAM and ALPA. Charging libel and slander in connection with allegations that the company's aircraft were unsafe, the airline sued the unions for five million dollars each. ALPA countered with a suit against the airline for one million dollars to offset financial losses, charging that National had caused the strike.[188]

By late March, resolution of the strikes seemed unlikely. The IAM and ALPA hoped that the National Mediation Board would recommend a Presidential Emergency Board; however the National Mediation Board did not believe the strike had caused enough of a disruption in air service to warrant one. At the end of the month, David Behncke and the board of directors of ALPA forced the hand of the National Mediation Board by passing a resolution for all ALPA members to respect the pilots' picket line at National. The result would be that no ALPA pilot would fly into an airport serviced by National during the strike. Air traffic down the East Coast would effectively come to a halt. Behncke notified both the National Mediation Board and President Truman of the resolution. On May 15, on the recommendation of the National Mediation Board, Truman created a Presidential Emergency Board to investigate the ALPA-National dispute. On June 3, a second executive order instructed the Emergency Board to examine the IAM-National dispute as well. The Emergency Board returned its findings on July 9.[189]

According to the language of the Railway Labor Act, when a Presidential Emergency Board is created, workers can return to work during a thirty-day "cooling-off period" in which no changes to the predispute situation can be made except by agreement. ALPA and the IAM offered to send their National employees back to work, but the company ignored the offers. As the aviation economist Mark Kahn pointed out in his study of the strike, "The Act, obviously, had not contemplated a situation in which the Emergency Board is appointed long after the commencement of a strike, and in which the strikers had been completely replaced."[190]

During the Emergency Board hearings, National Airlines accused both unions of striking illegally: the ALPA dispute was still in mediation, and the IAM walkout took place before the thirty-day "status quo" period had expired. The Emergency Board ignored the company's claims regarding the ALPA strike and found that the IAM strike was legal because the thirty-day prohibition of changes applied to employers, not employees, following the failure of National Mediation Board mediation.[191]

The Emergency Board's report was a clear tactical victory for the IAM and ALPA. The board found that National Airlines had made no effort to resolve the dispute with the pilots' union until faced with a strike, despite the reasonable request that the discharged pilot receive an impartial hearing of his case. The board scolded National, stating that the case of the O'Neal discharge indicated "an immaturity and lack of responsibility which is not consistent with the duties imposed by Congress upon carriers in interstate commerce." As for the IAM strike, the Emergency Board found that "the Carrier's disregard of its statutory duty was not isolated or accidental; on the contrary, it was repeated and deliberate. And it contributed directly and immediately to the situation out of which the strike arose." The board recommended the reinstatement of ALPA and IAM strikers, arbitration of the O'Neal case, and the resumption of negotiations for a clerical agreement with arbitration if necessary.[192]

In mid-July the IAM and National Airlines began "back to work" negotiations. Again, a representative for the Airlines Negotiating Conference sat at the table. At issue was not only when clerical and mechanical strikers could return to work but who among them could return. The airline objected to the return of forty-seven employees, claiming that they had let their credentials lapse, had resigned to take other work, had slandered the company in Spanish, or had committed "undue violence" during the strike. Further, the company argued against any accrual of seniority for mechanics and baggage handlers who respected the clerical picket lines. The parties struggled over these issues as well as when to convene negotiations for the clerical contract, a timeline for handling mechanics' grievances, and the placement of baggage handlers whose work had been contracted out during the strike. On July 27, with the direction of the National Mediation Board, the IAM and National reached a back-to-work agreement that granted a timetable for returning, seniority accrual for mechanics, a plan for returning workers whose jobs had been reorganized or contracted out, the dismissal of all lawsuits against each other, and interventions filed in Civil Aeronautics Board hearings in which the company was engaged that summer.[193]

The return to work did not go smoothly. During the strike, porter and ground-service work at the Miami airport was contracted out to a firm called Dispatch Service. With the return-to-work agreement, African American porters, who had been on strike as part of the clerical group, were laid off while the company retained the baggage handlers who now worked as cleaners. This was a violation of the back-to-work agreement and the mechanical contract. The company laid off workers in the mechanical and clerical groups and demoted workers in lead positions. In Miami, lead mechanics supervised the baggage handlers doing the cleaning, and the laid-off porters returned as cleaners. Tensions erupted between "cleaner girls" in Miami and the scab cleaners hired during the strike, and the lead mechanic McClain (from the shooting incident) was back to work again, carrying a pistol on duty. In Miami and Jacksonville, management instituted a series of antagonistic "shop rules" challenging worker autonomy and community. These rules dictated where and when soft drinks from company vending machines could be consumed, where workers could go during their break periods, where and when cigarettes could be smoked, and even where and when joking was appropriate. The union threatened to stall dropping its lawsuits and remove its petitions from the Civil Aeronautics Board dockets the company was embroiled in that summer and fall.[194]

Further complicating matters, ALPA-IAM relations after the IAM settlement disintegrated, and the vestiges of the Federation of National Employees collapsed. According to J. C. McGlon of the IAM, ALPA president David Behncke was working to turn National's pilots and the local labor press against IAM members. While the return-to-work agreement meant that IAM members would cross the ALPA picket lines, McGlon argued that IAM members were honoring their alliances with the pilots. In a letter to other IAM staffers, he wrote, "It is needless for me to say or to try and remind you of how close our organization and membership worked with the pilots during the strike, and in some cases, since our back to work agreement was consummated. We have offered and given moral support and in some instances I fear that our membership has gone beyond moral support and have furnished the pilots with some confidential information they have received from the files or personal knowledge they have with reference to load factors, CAA regulations, etc." For the security of IAM members, McGlon advised staffers to tell them to refrain from sharing information with the pilots because such actions could be turned against them. Individual IAM members expressed solidarity with the pilots but no longer shared information.[195]

The National Mediation Board and President Truman through the Presidential Emergency Board were not the only representatives of the federal government to become involved in the National Airlines strikes. The Civil Aeronautics Board was also embroiled in the conflict at several points. Created by the Civil Aeronautics Act, the board set rates for airmail and certified route systems. Importantly, the act required carriers certified by the Civil Aeronautics Board to comply with the Railway Labor Act. As a regulated industry, violations of labor law could result in changes to an airline's route system, fares, or even its existence as a certified air carrier.

In the first month of the IAM and ALPA strikes, the Civil Aeronautics Board awarded National Airlines a retroactive and continuing airmail rate increase after the airline argued the strikes were not a major contributing factor to its financial woes. The rate increase added over one million dollars in revenue to the airline's 1948 bottom line.[196] On March 5, the IAM lodged a formal complaint with the Civil Aeronautics Board, arguing that National had failed to comply with the Railway Labor Act. On May 24, the board's attorneys agreed that the board must recognize National's violation of the act. The board did not take immediate action, and the case was dismissed as part of the IAM-National return-to-work agreement.[197]

An aircraft- and personnel-interchange agreement between National and Capital Airlines was also under consideration by the Civil Aeronautics Board in March 1948. Such an agreement would substantially increase revenues for National and better manage the seasonal fluctuations in manpower and equipment faced by the airline. Again the board lodged its decision that the agreement would be contrary to the public interest if National was in violation of the Railway Labor Act. This case was settled after the pilots' strike ended.[198]

National's greatest challenge by the Civil Aeronautics Board came in September 1948 when the board began an investigation to determine whether or not it was in the best interest of the public to dismantle National Airlines and distribute its routes and equipment to other carriers. The investigation made no reference to the ongoing ALPA dispute, although according to the historian George Hopkins, the case came to the board under great pressure from the pilots' union and their Democratic allies. The argument for dismantling the airline rested on the fact that National was losing money. While the airline had resumed a full operations schedule, low passenger loads indicated that the strike publicity had succeeded in encouraging passengers to choose other airlines when possible. Baker attempted to counter some of this negative publicity with "package deals" with Florida hotels compelling other airlines, like National's major competitor, Eastern Airlines, to decry this unfair "cost shifting."[199]

During the tumultuous presidential campaign of 1948, Ted Baker was an outspoken supporter of the Republican candidate Thomas E. Dewey, while labor, with exceptions, supported Truman. In the uncertain months leading up to the election, the Civil Aeronautics Board was slow to move on such a dramatic decision as the dismantling of an airline. With the surprising Truman victory, the board moved forward with the dismemberment case, and Ted Baker recognized the gravity of Dewey's defeat for National Airlines.

National and the pilots' union had slowly resumed negotiations in late October 1948. However, after the election, in what may be one of the strangest strike resolutions in labor history, ALPA and National quickly resolved their dispute. According to Hopkins, during the fall Ted Baker became a follower of Dr. Frank Buchman, the founder of the "Moral Rearmament" movement, an anti-Communist Christian evangelical campaign popular among business executives. Shortly after Truman's victory Baker disappeared to a Buchman retreat in Michigan. From the retreat he called individual pilots begging their forgiveness and blaming all the troubles of the last year on the "power of Satan." Baker transported fifty carefully chosen employees—pilots, stewardesses, mechanics, and ground personnel among them—to Michigan to share in their employer's "religious conversion through the sweet healing power of Jesus." Baker asked them to spread the word of his conversion upon their return to Miami.[200]

National and ALPA reached an agreement that substantially favored ALPA's position. The agreement included the settlement of the O'Neal case with an impartial referee appointed to the System Board of Adjustment and the quick return of all ALPA pilots to duty with full seniority rights. The settlement of the ALPA dispute and the seemingly new era of labor relations at National lifted some of the pressure on the Civil Aeronautics Board to press forward on the dismemberment case. Docket 3500 was dismissed in 1951.[201]

Had National changed its labor relations policy? Arguably, no. While the pilots may have won a favorable contract, IAM members and National continued their skirmishes. Baggage handlers in particular faced a tenuous future. By November 1948, baggage handlers at National had not returned to their regular duties. At Miami and Idlewild, New York, their work was contracted out to the Dispatch Service Corporation. In Jacksonville, all baggage handlers had been laid off and their work performed by mechanics and operations agents. Tampa and New Orleans were the only cities with baggage handlers working by the mechanics contract.[202]

The situation for baggage handlers and the instrument shop mechanics whose work had been contracted out in the summer of 1947 was indicative of an increased and organized interest in contracting out. Over the weekend of October 30, 1948, the main topic of the ATA conference in Chicago was the practice of contracting out work. In a confidential IAM memo, J. C. McGlon reported that his source in the National Mediation Board had informed him that the airlines "by unanimous action went on record for all out contracting out of work drive meaning that all airlines from here on out will now sub-contract out as much work as they desire, each airline getting the support from the ATA in any fight they may encounter by so doing." McGlon further noted that since the ATA conference, National's position on contracting out had become even more rigid. While his suggestion to contact the BRC, TWU, and UAW to discuss strategy was rebuffed by the IAM president H. W. Brown, his plan to align negotiating deadlines with Civil Aeronautics Board hearings was put into effect.[203]

IAM leaders attempted to reverse the contracting out of ground-service work by amending their standing National Mediation Board case related to the contracting out of mechanics' instrument work. With the Civil Aeronautics Board dockets for dismemberment and the National-Capital equipment interchange agreement still pending, IAM strategists believed that the airline needed their cooperation for these cases. Indeed, testimony of improved relations with labor would be important for the dismissal of Docket 3500. In March 1949 the union testified in support of the company in Docket 3500. In May, the parties began settling the contracting-out disputes for baggage handlers, porters, and instrument mechanics. That same month the Civil Aeronautics Board approved the equipment interchange, and the IAM entered into job-protection agreements with Capital and National Airlines.[204]

Interconnected with the contracting-out issue was the application of National Mediation Board case R-1706, which effectively classified National's baggage handlers as part of the clerical unit. While the IAM was negotiating contracting-out issues as they violated the mechanical agreement, baggage handlers were actually being transferred to the clerical contract. Correspondence among the National Mediation Board, National's industrial relations director Jerome Rosenthal, and IAM officials paints a complicated picture of conflicting timelines and strategies.

In December 1948 the company and the IAM hammered out a wage amendment to the mechanics agreement from January 1947. This amendment included wage rates for baggage handlers and lead baggage handlers. A month later the company and the IAM finished bargaining the clerical, office, and related employees contract. However, the question of inclusion of baggage handlers (called "ground servicemen" at National), to be classified as "ramp agents" in this contract, remained under discussion.[205] In May 1949, the IAM president H. W. Brown stridently opposed shifting baggage handlers to the clerical unit despite the National Mediation Board's decision, even as IAM representatives were bargaining with National over the new category of "ramp agent." By July baggage handlers were amended out of the mechanical contract and amended into the clerical agreement. A memorandum to the changed agreements included a "joint service" contract among National and the Dispatch Service Corporation and the IAM covering ramp agents (baggage handlers) and porters at Miami, Washington, D.C., and New York. This agreement gave supervision of the employees to Dispatch Services but applied the wages and working conditions bargained in the IAM–National Airlines clerical contract.[206]

National kept management prerogative at the center of the issue. Within two months of crafting the "joint service" agreement, National's vice president of industrial relations, Jerome Rosenthal,[207] asked for its cancellation but with the right to reinstate if the costs of running the stations without subcontracted supervision were deemed unacceptable. IAM representatives recognized the game being played as part of the longer-term problem of contracting out at National and demanded that any such cancellation include deadlines for the experiment and protection from layoff. The parties proposed and counterproposed changes to the July "joint service" agreement for several months.[208]

Technically, the ramp agents and porters working for National under the direction of Dispatch Services enjoyed the protections of the IAM contract. However, in reality these workers faced a hostile employer. Dispatch Services, possibly with the silent approval of National, pressured ramp agents working overtime to sign a letter agreeing that "any work performed by me during my regular off duty hours for Flight Dispatch Service, Inc., a New York Corporation, shall be entirely at my own discretion and convenience, and that I shall in no way hold Flight Dispatch Service liable to enter said extra time on my time card which is submitted to National Airlines for pay purposes. If I agree to work for Flight Dispatch Service during my off duty hours, I shall accept the prevailing rate for extra part time work as paid by Flight Dispatch Service."[209]

Such a letter clearly violated the IAM clerical contract. The IAM attempted to circumvent this pressure on the IAM–National Airlines contract at Flight Dispatch Service by organizing the subcontractor's other employees. However, organizers found that most of the Flight Dispatch employees were university students employed only part-time. Collecting authorization cards seemed fruitless, as most of the students would be gone before an election.[210]

The transformation from "ground serviceman" to "ramp agent" not only diminished the security of these workers through the contracts with Flight Dispatch Service but also in the structural changes to their position in the company and their job duties. Perhaps through negotiation missteps on the part of the IAM, supervisory authority and accompanying wage rate were not incorporated into the clerical contract for lead ground servicemen. As National's Jerome Rosenthal explained, "I think there is sufficient logic supporting my position that these Lead Ground Service employees now performing a different job under the Clerical Contract, in that they have been relieved of what supervisory function they were formerly discharging, are appropriately reclassified and reduced in rate of pay. This is not the situation of the employee having his title changed but discharging the same function, but is a case of an employee having both his title and function changed."[211] The security of ramp agents was further diminished under the clerical contract because of bumping rights. Under the clerical contract, during layoffs and recalls the job title "agent," an employee who worked with passengers at the airport, could bump a ramp agent if he had more seniority and equal qualifications.[212]

The strikes at National proved to be an extraordinary testing ground for union and company power and exposed the constant presence of federal regulation. During the strike, airline unions built useful but fragile alliances, developed sophisticated campaigns for public support, and tested their influence on the federal apparatus of the Civil Aeronautics Board. For Ted Baker and National Airlines the strikes exposed airline dependence on federal goodwill and proved that challenging one federal regulatory body could garner a response from another. For the ATA, the strikes on National were a testing ground for how the industry group could support a member airline and build strategy for later battles against airline labor. For baggage handlers, the strikes at National and National Mediation Board case R-1706 further emphasized the "in flux" nature of airline work.

Raiding as Organizing

By 1949, the number of representation cases before the National Mediation Board declined for the first time, marking the end of the organizing era.[213] However, union representation issues for airline workers were far from over. Across the industry, established unions struggled over jurisdictional issues and expanded their presence into new work categories. Among other conflicts, the IAM and the BRC carried on a protracted battle over the representation of baggage handlers at Northwest Airlines, the IAM announced a raid on the TWU, the ALPA affiliate the Air Line Agents Association (ALAA) raided the IAM at National Airlines, and the Flight Engineers International Association battled with ALPA over the manning and representation of cockpit crews at several airlines.

In November 1950, the BRC again applied to the National Mediation Board to represent workers they believed to be part of their class or craft, including equipment servicemen, at Northwest. The National Mediation Board mediator decided upon a list of eligible workers for an election using colored ballots to differentiate their work groups. Nearly a year later, the board ruled that the votes of equipment servicemen and equipment-service chiefs would not be counted. Over the opposition of the IAM, the election included ballots from janitors and storeroom employees.[214] Both groups had voted for IAM representation in 1946. In this election, however, the BRC won certification by an overwhelming majority of 772 to 289 votes over the IAM.[215]

In 1954, the BRC and the IAM again struggled over the classification of baggage handlers (called "equipment servicemen") at Northwest. The crux of the issue remained whether or not these workers were mechanical or service-oriented in their overall duties. Preceding decisions by the board played an important part in the Northwest case. In the American Airlines case in 1945 (R-1447) and the composite decision in 1947 (R-1706 et al.), the board examined the duties of workers called "fleet-service personnel" and "fleet-service employees." According to their findings, these groups were not one and the same; confusion over classification stemmed from how companies used these job titles as well as how the work changed over time. In 1945, the board found that the duties of fleet-services personnel fit in the craft or class of airline mechanics. In 1947, the board found that the duties of fleet-service employees fit in the craft or class of clerical, stores, fleet-service, and passenger-service employees.[216]

During the 1954 investigation the IAM's Frank Heisler testified that out of twenty-eight airlines, equipment servicemen or ramp-service employees were covered by mechanics' contracts at eighteen. Out of the twenty-eight airlines, ramp-service or fleet-service workers were covered by clerical contracts in six cases. Heisler also claimed that equipment servicemen at Northwest wanted to be represented by the IAM and had signed petitions to that effect as well as re-signed authorization cards. Frank Heisler's testimony underscored the complicated fit of the Railway Labor Act for the airline workforce. According to Heisler, the breakdown deprived workers their right to organize. At Northwest, ticket agents were grouped with office and clerical employees who were not interested in unionization. Heisler explained that the changes in classifications pressed workers performing dissimilar duties into awkward associations:

> In addition to that, it has created a tremendous amount of unrest in the industry because of changing the association of the employees, whereas they were more closely related in the performance of their duties under prior operations before this determination, but they now find that they are being pushed over into another group with which they have no common relation whatsoever.
>
> I don't say that in a derogatory manner toward the office and clerical people, but I think it is common knowledge that the office and clerical people, as Mr. O'Neill cited, the equipment service people of Northwest are a breed of cats of their own.[217]

The duties of equipment servicemen were covered in "mechanical" and "service" classifications, according to the decisions of 1945 and 1947. As stated by a Northwest Airlines manual, duties one through six were mechanical in nature, while seven through eleven were service-oriented.

1. Drives fuel trucks and operates bulk storage facilities.
2. Services aircraft and automotive equipment with fuel and oil.
3. Picks up and delivers passengers' meals from the flight kitchen to aircraft with the use of automotive ramp equipment.
4. Operates the air conditioning units.
5. Operates energizers, placing wheel chocks, and safety pins on landing gear of aircraft while on ramp, handles fire extinguishers during engine warm up and installs and removes surface control blocks on equipment which requires the use of such devices.
6. Sterilizing oxygen equipment of emergency equipment.
7. Physically handles mail, freight, cargo, and express from and to terminal building and cargo room to the aircraft and places all such cargo in the proper compartments in the airplane.

8. Places and arranges in the aircraft all passenger service equipment, including but not limited to magazines, blankets, clothes, etc.
9. Cleans, washes, and polishes the interior and exterior of airplane ramp equipment, hangar, and other facilities.
10. Removes snow from aircraft and de-ices airplane with the use of special fluids.
11. Handles other general utility service work of a similar nature as requested and directed by supervisors.[218]

In February 1954, the National Mediation Board urged the airline, the IAM, and the BRC to work together to survey and then classify the duties of equipment servicemen into mechanical and service jobs. The board also recommended separating the equipment servicemen into two groups to be represented separately.[219] Cooperation among the unions and the company proved nearly impossible. According to an organizer for the BRC, the IAM refused to participate in the process and implied that if the National Mediation Board took action to divide the equipment servicemen into two groups, these workers would walk off the job.[220] The IAM was not the only party to refuse cooperation in this matter. Northwest Airlines declined to accept the BRC's investigation into equipment servicemen's duties or participate in any survey.[221] Both the IAM and the company wanted the National Mediation Board to consider the equipment servicemen as a separate craft or class for representation purposes.[222] In 1959, the board rejected a BRC survey showing that most equipment servicemen performed duties falling under BRC jurisdiction during most of their shift.

Accordingly, the National Mediation Board ruled in favor of the IAM. The ruling for the IAM in the Northwest Airlines equipment-servicemen case set another important precedent for these workers. Their affiliation with skilled aircraft mechanics rather than clerical employees affected their position within the airline in terms of class and gender identity as well as wage realities. Aircraft mechanics were working-class skilled white males with bargaining power within the industry second only to that of pilots. By associating with male mechanics rather than office or passenger-service employees, whose ranks included a significant number of women, equipment servicemen hoped to claim a more powerful position in terms of wages and perhaps gendered identity. Conflict over the classification of baggage handlers, particularly challenges to the R-1706 ruling, would continue to appear before the National Mediation Board into the 1980s.[223]

In 1954, as TWU negotiations with Pan American Airways heated up and the IAM began developing a multicarrier bargaining strategy, the IAM publicly announced plans to begin organizing drives at American and Pan Am.

Table 10. Equipment Servicemen Duties Survey, August–October 1959

Functions:
1. Loading, unloading or otherwise handling mail, baggage, freight, express, etc., including pick-up and delivery time.
2. Loading and unloading of food-service equipment, including pickup and delivery.
3. Cabin service, including stocking and destocking.
4. Fueling, equipment cleaning, and/or any other assigned duty.
5. Standby time. Waiting for flights and/or work assignments.

City	ESM 8 hrs work on functions 1, 2 3, 5 (BRC)	ESM 8 hrs work on functions 4, 5 (IAM)	ESM 8 hrs work on functions 1–5	No. of ESM duties checked
Mpls.	47	16	20	83
Seattle	49	—	17	66
Chicago	48	12	5	65
New York	26	6	1	33
Detroit	9	4	20	33
Milwauke	6	—	13	19
Spokane	9	—	6	15
Portland	2	—	7	9
Anchorage	11	2	2	15
Billings	—	1	7	9
Cleveland	—	—	2	2
Rochester	1	—	—	1
Grand Forks	—	—	1	1
Madison	—	—	2	2
Pittsburgh	—	—	3	3
Tampa	2	—	4	6
Wash.D.C.	—	—	11	11
Miami	3	—	3	6
Shemya	—	—	—	7
Fargo	—	—	—	5
Yakima	—	—	—	3
Missoula	—	—	—	2
Helena	—	—	—	1
Total	213	41	124	396

Source: "Chart Showing All Locations of Northwest Airlines and Number of Equipment Service Men Whose Duties Were Checked or Observed by Local Chairmen of the B. R. of C. on August 20, 1959, or Another Date," BRC Collection, box 448.

Note: ESM in Shemya, Fargo, Yakima, Missoula, and Helena were counted in the study, but their duties were not tabulated.

The IAM president Al Hayes proclaimed that the interests of airline employees could be best protected by a single union for all nonflight workers. Although the AFL and CIO had signed no-raiding agreements, neither the IAM nor the TWU had joined in these agreements. Mike Quill and TWU leaders challenged Al Hayes to join them in public debates on wages and working conditions at airfields across the country.[224] Despite the threats, the

IAM and the TWU rarely went head to head over maintenance and ground-service workers in the airlines.

In 1946, ALPA began a long-range campaign to organize airline workers outside its traditional jurisdiction by creating affiliates for stewards and stewardesses, flight engineers, mechanics, dispatchers, and clerical and communications employees. Supporters of the measure included Wayne W. Parrish, the editor and publisher of *American Aviation* magazine. Parrish and the ALPA affiliates argued for a "family" of airline unions, as opposed to unions with a vested interest in other industries.[225] Association with the powerful ALPA proved to be an attractive option to workers in the airline industry.

At National Airlines, the ALPA affiliate, the ALAA, found support among workers who had formerly been strong supporters of the IAM at the airline after a prolonged round of negotiations, which went to arbitration, and the controversial firing of a ticket agent in New Orleans. In 1954, male and female clerical employees (including baggage handlers) at National Airlines voted out the IAM in favor of the ALAA by a three-to-one margin.[226]

ALPA's battle with the Flight Engineers International Association (FEIA) during the 1950s and 1960s proved to be the fiercest fight among airline unions during the regulated era. Flight engineers were first used by Pan Am in 1937. According to E. B. McNatt of the University of Illinois Aviation Institute, they were little more than flying mechanics until the postwar period. The introduction of four-motored Constellations and DC-6 aircraft with more complex instrument panels created the need for a third person in the cockpit. This became a Civil Aeronautics Board requirement in 1948 over the objection of the ATA. Flight engineers looked to join ALPA, but the union's by-laws required that members be males legally classified as pilots or copilots on commercial flights. Initially ALPA created an afflilliate for flight engineers but had limited success in building membership among them, many of whom came from the ranks of aircraft mechanics. According to the aviation historian Nick Komons, the AFL strongly encouraged ALPA to accept flight engineers as members anticipating conflict over jurisdiction. ALPA refused, and the FEIA-AFL was formed in 1948. Two unions in the cockpit proved to be one too many as the right to represent flight engineers shifted between ALPA and the FEIA at three airlines seven times in ten years. Nonetheless, by the mid-1950s the FEIA represented flight engineers at all but four commercial airlines. In 1956 ALPA changed course and allowed any person on a flight crew to become a member. However, with the coming introduction of jet aircraft, ALPA took a hard-line approach to its rivalry with the FEIA and adopted a resolution stating that all turbine-powered or turboprop aircraft must be manned by a qualified pilot in all cockpit positions. ALPA argued that the new technology required a higher level of skilled coordination that only a full pilot complement could provide. Further, a third pilot would be an added safety precaution in case a pilot or copilot was incapacitated.

The FEIA stood its ground, and airlines buckled to ALPA pressure rather than face a strike as new airplanes arrived. Planes flew with four men in the cockpit, and the airlines paid for an extra, basically idle pilot. In 1959, ALPA filed a petition with the National Mediation Board claiming a representation dispute at United Air Lines. In 1961 the board found that the flight crew at United was one craft or class and called for an election to determine representation. ALPA easily won the election with three-to-one representation at the airline. FEIA members responded with a wildcat strike at seven airlines but returned to work when John F. Kennedy formed a presidential commission to investigate the problem and offer recommendations.

The commission recommended that the two unions merge, that the fourth cockpit position be phased out, that flight engineers come from the rank of pilots, and that mechanic-trained engineers receive pilot training at company expense. Over the next six years the FEIA shrunk from over 3,000 members to 1,300, as ALPA members crossed FEIA picket lines, FEIA members left for pilot training, and ALPA membership and further technological changes in avionics made flight engineers obsolete.[227]

* * *

The young airline industry provided tremendous opportunities and substantial headaches for the labor movement by the end of World War II. Often frustrated by youthful indifference, jurisdictional confusion, and awkward classification, craft and industrial unions did find workers eager to organize. Skilled aircraft mechanics shaken by the rapid transformation of their workplace and young unskilled white and black workers facing low pay and long hours played central roles in the struggles for representation. Racial issues and left-leaning politics among unskilled workers in Miami impacted union choices on the ramp for Pan Am workers. In New York and the Northeast, mechanics and baggage handlers balanced their interests in light of local union power structures and organized across skill lines. The substantial success among the airlines during the World War II era set the stage for four decades of union strength, with the IAM and TWU representing the majority of ground workers in the industry.

4

Bargaining in Prosperity, 1949–59

The story often told of midcentury labor relations in the United States has been one of a labor accord, the maturation of the collective-bargaining system in which Big Labor and Big Business, especially in rubber, meatpacking, auto, steel, and mining, bargained industrywide standards and contracts that resulted in cost-of-living increases, pensions, health benefits, and productive and reliable workers. Low unemployment, good wages, and a rational labor-relations system were the keys to a decade of economic growth and spreading affluence. For workers, historians have argued, the formality of these labor relations stifled militancy and rank-and-file participation and opened the door to corruption among union leaders.[1]

At the end of the 1950s, Charles Mason, the vice president of employee relations at United Airlines, described the airlines' collective-bargaining structure as "not yet fully developed," a system of relations that had not yet reached a "mature" or "rational" stage.[2] While airline workers did see real gains in wages, benefits, and working conditions during the 1950s, this was not accomplished through labor-management peace. Airlines and unions struggled under the unwieldy application of the Railway Labor Act to the industry. High levels of union density in the industry, particularly among skilled employees and those sharing craft and class jurisdiction with aircraft mechanics, gave unions the ability to "whipsaw" contractual gains from multiple airlines. Rapid technological change exacerbated intra-union conflict[3] but also increased union members' bargaining power, as airlines were eager to increase productivity to meet the growing public demand for air travel.

Spontaneous action by rank-and-file members exasperated union leadership and aggravated airline supervisors and passengers alike. The perishable nature of airline travel as a commodity made protracted fights with workers expensive to the airlines and unpopular with the traveling public. Airlines joined other corporations in the 1950s with sophisticated plans for cultivating company loyalty. Regular rounds of bargaining with multiple unions, strike threats, and strikes left unions and management ready to experiment with multicarrier bargaining. By the late 1950s airlines and airline employees would join other industries in a labor-management showdown that marked a "new look" in American labor relations.

Industry Growth

A strong economy and a public hungry for vacation and business travel marked the 1950s as an era of impressive growth for the airline industry. Airlines found new profits with the introduction of coach-class service by adding more seats to the planes by changing the "pitch," or the space between the seat backs, from forty-two to thirty-four inches. By 1952, a coach-class ticket from New York to Chicago cost thirty-two dollars, and a coast-to-coast ticket cost ninety-nine dollars. By 1958, coach passenger traffic constituted approximately 39 percent of total domestic trunkline travel and 68 percent of international passenger volume. Coach-fare flights to Europe led to a tremendous upsurge in the number of passengers who flew to Europe. By 1958, two-thirds of North Atlantic business was low-fare.[4]

Transcontinental and trans-Atlantic nonstop service became realities in the 1950s. By 1953, nonstop flight from New York to California was possible on TWA's Lockheed Super Constellation and American Airlines' Douglas DC-7, planes that seated between eighty and one hundred passengers. The trip could be made in less than nine hours. By 1955, Pan Am and TWA introduced trans-Atlantic nonstop service. Using the DC-7C, a plane slower but more comfortable than its DC-7, Pan Am cornered the trans-Atlantic market.[5]

Increases in passenger-load figures for Pan Am, American, Northwest, and National during the 1950s were dramatic. In 1951, according to Civil Aeronatics Board statistics, 1,273,000 passengers "originated" on Pan Am flights systemwide.[6] An "origination" was a passenger counted once at the beginning of a trip. That same year, American Airlines had 4,960,000 domestic and international originating passengers, Northwest had 791,000 originating domestic and international passengers, and National had 623,000. In 1956, Pan Am, American, Northwest, and National carried 2,503,000, 7,829,000, 1,481,000, and 1,353,000 passengers, respectively.[7]

After the economic downturn of the late 1940s, the airline industry stabilized and expanded its workforce. The number of airline workers rose from a postwar low of about 81,000 in 1949 to over 95,700 in 1951 and rose to 166,200 in 1960. Urban headquarters and locales of Pan Am, National, American, and Northwest Airlines experienced tremendous growth in employment between 1950 and 1960. Employment figures in New York, Miami, Chicago, and Minneapolis/St. Paul nearly doubled over the course of the decade. In all four cities white males continued to make up over 60 percent of the entire air-transportation workforce and more than 90 percent of the male workforce. African Americans made slight gains relative to the substantial growth of air transportation. In 1950, African American men and women made up less than 5 percent of the workforce in New York and Miami, major cities for Pan Am. In 1960 they made up 5 percent of the workforce in those two cities. In Chicago, an important city along with New York for American Airlines, African Americans made up 5 percent of the air-transportation workforce in 1950 and 7 percent in 1960. For both years, African Americans made up less than 1 percent of the workforce in Minneapolis/St. Paul, the headquarters of Northwest Airlines. In 1951, Pan Am employed 16,577 people systemwide. For domestic and international operations, American employed 14,734 people, and 5,562 employees worked for Northwest. Six years later, Pan Am employed 21,929 people, 20,721 worked for American, and 5,924 worked for Northwest.[8]

Union contracts, larger aircraft, and an expanded workforce all contributed to the formalization of fleet-service work. Loading and transporting baggage and cargo between terminals and aircraft became the exclusive domain of workers under this title. As table 11 shows, baggage handlers (part of the service category) experienced a steady increase in employment from 1950 through 1960.

Between 1947 and 1955, Gotch and Crawford of Washington, D.C., collected detailed statistical information on employment in the airline industry. This data included the average annual salary, employment levels, and the percentage distribution for numerous job classifications in the industry, including ground operations. Gotch and Crawford collected this data by domestic air carrier rather than for the industry as a whole. Pan Am was not included in their data because it was considered an international carrier. Table 12 shows the average wages, percentage distribution, and numbers of employees at American Airlines and Northwest Airlines and averages for the industry over an eight-year period.

Table 11. Personnel Employed by the Scheduled Airline Industry, 1950–60

Year	Pilots	Flight	Stewards	Comm.	Mech.	Service	Office	Other	Total
1950	7,277	1,521	4,427	3,403	19,606	12,256	31,138	3,158	82,786
1951	8,386	1,708	5,303	3,618	23,477	14,370	35,081	3,810	95,753
1952	8,770	1,852	5,859	3,653	26,162	15,588	37,894	4,294	104,072
1953	9,437	2,146	6,106	3,567	26,105	17,353	40,319	4,359	109,392
1954	9,495	2,525	6,363	3,332	25,173	17,855	40,670	4,128	109,541
1955	10,857	2,762	7,454	3,499	29,196	19,114	45,030	4,291	122,203
1956	11,286	3,384	8,097	3,605	30,962	20,657	49,336	4,076	131,503
1957	13,386	3,797	9,450	4,004	31,162	36,052	31,799	17,640	147,190
1958	12,897	3,667	9,811	3,978	29,580	37,256	32,003	17,958	147,150
1959	14,471	4,075	10,902	4,390	32,823	43,839	32,324	21,346	164,170
1960	13,535	3,811	10,600	4,233	34,181	43,334	35,440	21,101	166,235

Source: Air Transport Association, *Air Transport Facts and Figures* (Washington, D.C.: Air Transport Association, 1959), 14; Air Transport Association, *Air Transport Facts and Figures* (Washington, D.C.: Air Transport Association, 1965), 32.

Note: The categories include personnel as follows: Pilots: pilots and copilots; Flight: other flight personnel; Stewards: pursers, stewards, and stewardesses; Communications: communications personnel including meteorologists and dispatchers; Mechanical: mechanics; Service: aircraft and traffic-servicing personnel; Office: office employees including ticket and reservations agents; Other: all others.

Note: Recategorization of some work groups between the service and office categories after 1956 distorts the figures.

As these figures show, wages steadily improved for ground-operations employees in the airlines between 1947 and 1955. Employment opportunities across the industry also increased over that period, despite periodic layoffs. The average number of ground-service employees at a given airline in 1949 was 420. In 1955, that number rose to 902. Throughout the period, aircraft mechanics earned approximately six hundred to one thousand dollars more annually than baggage handlers. Pilots earned three to four times the amount of ground-service employees during this period.[9]

The Intangibles of Air Travel

As the historian Elizabeth Fones-Wolf has explained, corporations during the 1950s developed complex welfare-capital, recreational, and educational programs designed to capture the loyalty of their workers. For manufacturing industries like auto, electronics, and steel, employers hoped that these programs would diffuse workplace dissatisfaction, which could lead to slowdowns, lower-quality output, or even strikes. After the fact, these disruptions would impact the consuming public.[10] For the airline industry, such disruptions or the threat of such disruptions could cause immediate losses

Table 12. Employment Figures, Percentages, and Wages at American and Northwest Airlines for Operations-Service Employees in the Ground-Operations Department, 1949–55

	American Airlines		Northwest Airlines		National Airlines		Industry	
Year	# of empl. (%*)	Avg. salary	# of empl. (%)	Avg. salary	# of empl. (%)	Avg. salary	# of emp. (%)	Avg. salary
1947	1,855 (16)	$2,672	406 (11)	$2,477	66 (4)	$3,033	373	$2,292
1949	1,687 (16)	$2,943	562 (13)	$3,515	135 (8)	$2,069	420 (12)	$2,755
1951	2,130 (15)	$3,337	646 (13)	$3,361	247 (10)	$2,248	525 (12)	$3,044
1953	3,058 (19)	$3,852	621 (13)	$3,681	417 (14)	$3,321	799 (13)	$3,510
1955	3,404 (18)	$4,415	683 (13)	$4,495	454 (13)	$3,785	902 (13)	$3,843

Source: Gotch and Crawford, *Air Carrier Analyses: A Detailed Analytical Comparison of U.S. Domestic Civil Air Carriers Including Tables of Rank and Relationship,* 6 vols. (Washington, DC: Gotch and Crawford, 1949, 1951, 1953, 1955).

Note: "Industry" represents the domestic airline industry, including statistical information for thirteen airlines: American Airlines, United Airlines, Eastern Airlines, Trans World Airways, Braniff Airways, Chicago and Southern Airlines, Delta Airlines, National Airlines, Northwest Airlines, Pennsylvania-Central Airlines or Capital Airlines, Western Airlines, Central Airlines, Continental Airlines, Inland Airlines, Mid-Continent Airlines, Northeast Airlines.

*percent of total workforce

in revenue and reverberate into future sales. Just the threat of a strike could create a 20 percent reduction in passenger traffic, as travelers rerouted to avoid any potential delays.[11] Lost profits in passenger sales are lost forever, and airline passengers with some choice in air travel could either adhere to or reject brand loyalty. Labor action or even an unpleasant service encounter could result in lost revenues for years to come.

Because the Civil Aeronautics Board regulated fares, how passengers chose among the airlines was determined not so much by fare but by service, convenience, and reputation. In 1957 the *Chicago Tribune* conducted interviews with forty-five regular air travelers to find out the "personalities" of the seven major airlines that served Chicago. Passengers interviewed had clear ideas about the reputations of the airlines. While the interviewees first said that they booked their travel by convenience, further questioning pointed to comfort and reputation as important factors among experienced travelers. The research suggested that airlines indeed had "personalities." United, which was the hometown airline, was the most popular, with a reputation as safe, comfortable, and attractive, with luxurious service and excellent food. American was known for being a large, safe, dependable, prompt, and well-established line that perhaps lacked a "personal touch." Northwest's advertising campaign highlighting its flights to Asia effectively conjured up images of the Orient, cocktails, and "exceptionally good service." Eastern Airlines was known for its flight stewards and routes to Florida; it also proved to be the most controversial, with respondents closely identifying the airline with its president, Captain Eddie Rickenbacker, in the positive and the negative.[12] Building these reputations required the cooperation of airline employees, those with and without direct contact with airline passengers.

To help develop these brand personalities, the airlines sought ways to cultivate loyalty in their new employees. They created welfare-capital programs to motivate employees to recognize themselves as part of a corporate family and as important parts of the service provided. The programs included improved travel benefits and a variety of social activities. Pan Am, American, and Northwest all published monthly newsletters for their employees, highlighting the fun and excitement employees were having across the country or around the globe. Promotions, seniority, exotic vacations, engagements, marriages, and births were announced. Photos of employees "hamming it up" and beautiful stewardesses graced the pages. For example, in addition to athletic teams, a credit union, and picnic outings, Pan Am employees in Miami enjoyed a lakefront clubhouse situated on eleven acres purchased by the Panair Recreational Club.[13]

While pilots and stewardesses were the most recognizable employees of any airline, company publications included articles about baggage handlers, cafeteria workers, porters, mechanics, and reservations agents, focusing on their work as part of keeping the airlines running. In 1950, a *Northwest Airlines News* edition included baggage handlers playing cards on a baggage cart and a second group posed playing baseball in front of an aircraft on the ramp on its front page.[14] A Northwest equipment serviceman (baggage handler), Fritz Marty of Seattle, won a safety-slogan contest in 1953 with his slogan, "For Plane Safety and Plane Economy, Use Plain Sense!"[15] In January 1953, *Northwest Airlines News* put four baggage handlers on the front page of the newspaper. These four, the Jenkins brothers, young white men from suburban Washington, D.C., worked at Washington National Airport. The airline also employed a fifth brother at Holman Field in Minnesota.[16] In April 1953, the *Northwest Airlines News* devoted a cover and a two-page spread to baggage handlers. Titled "Equipment Servicemen Combine Speed and Skill to Keep Planes Flying," the article playfully illuminated the specific duties of these workers and noted that the job was tougher than it seemed. Baggage handlers loaded and unloaded cargo, baggage, and even animals on and off planes, cleaned aircraft interiors, and fueled planes. While the industry continued to hold the image of glamour and excitement, these men did not seem to share in the image. The article announced, "Tip your hat to the equipment serviceman! He sometimes thinks—probably with good reason—that he's the airline's forgotten man. But let him and his fellow workers step out of character for 21 hours, or 60 minutes, and he'll be remembered fast. His isn't a glamorous job. To his way of thinking, it's strictly routine. It's a fact, though, that it's as important as any in the company, save only the basic task of flying the planes." The *Northwest News* article spotlighted, with a touch of humor, the varied duties performed by equipment servicemen: "YOUR EQUIPMENT SERVICEMAN is a combination gas station attendant, stevedore, truck driver, animal trainer and mail clerk, with certain talents of a magician thrown in." Carrying over from the war years, some equipment servicemen's jobs were held by women.

> Lest you think that equipment service is strictly a man's world, we hasten to add that many of NWA's 450 equipment service jobs are filled by women. The girls handle most of the chores inside the planes.
>
> For the most part, however, it's a male domain.
>
> From the time a plane reaches a ramp to the time it leaves, equipment servicemen—as busy as a swarm of ants—rush through the hundred-and-one duties necessary to keep the plane in the air. A partial list of the things they do includes:
>
> * Loading and unloading baggage, mail and freight.
> * Filling the gas tanks.
> * Getting mechanical equipment to places where it's needed.
> * Cleaning the plane, inside and out.
> * Changing headrests and pillow cases.
> * Distributing flight kits and magazines.
> * Redistributing cargo.
> * Loading and unloading food containers.[17]

Three or four baggage handlers had to complete these duties in forty minutes on average. For some aircraft, the turnaround time was only fifteen minutes. While not busy with a recent arrival or imminent departure, baggage handlers spent their "spare time" loading ballast onto check flights, sterilizing oxygen masks, or cleaning up their work areas. The article assured readers that their work was not simple, despite the sound of it:

> Some of the tasks might sound easy to other employees. But few of them are.
>
> Take the matter of gassing planes, for example. During the month of February, at Minneapolis alone, equipment servicemen pumped over three-fourths of a million gallons. In an average summer month they'll pump over a million gallons at this single station.
>
> Loading cargo a snap? Not when some pieces of freight weigh a ton or a few pounds less—which isn't too out of the ordinary. A lift gets the bulky stuff up to the plane, but once inside it has to be moved by hand.
>
> At Minneapolis, Billings and Detroit, all cargo is re-checked and when necessary, redistributed. At times it's necessary to remove all cargo and then reload, arranging everything by stops. That's when the magic talent helps.
>
> ANIMAL TRAINERS have nothing on equipment servicemen. In the space of a year the airline's trouble shooters handled wolverines, dogs, monkeys, lions, poultry, mink and chinchilla, oftimes not without some degree of difficulty.[18]

The article acknowledged the job's position as a starting point within the industry and as one that did not always receive the respect of other airline employees.

> Usually equipment servicemen gravitate into other classifications.
>
> Many have become pilots, mechanics, stock clerks and transportation agents.
>
> But the equipment servicemen need not take a back seat to anyone.
>
> He's a top priority employee. As one ES chief pointed out, "[. . .] The fellows are in a position to get things awfully goofed up if they aren't on the ball all the time."
>
> Fortunately for NWA, they are on the ball![19]

Articles like this one promoted the inclusion of baggage handlers in the "corporate family" of the airlines. Training procedures and their coverage in company publications attempted the same.[20]

During the 1950s, airlines focused their energies on formally training their employees. Through training and incentive programs, airlines encouraged employees to see themselves as part of a "service organization." In her study of flight attendants, the historian Kathleen Barry examines the highly scripted nature of airline work. While stewardesses served as glamorous hostesses and pilots as brave and confident captains, other employees had their roles to play. In the late 1940s and early 1950s, while the airlines encouraged ticket agents and stewardesses to "put the smile back in service," airlines formally trained baggage handlers to improve safety and efficiency and to relay that image to the flying public. A well-trained or experienced crew could reduce handling costs up to 75 percent over a "green," untrained or undisciplined crew. An efficient and clean crew could also send an important message about airline safety to passengers watching from the terminal.[21]

A 1950s Pan Am customer-service manual accented the importance of ramp operations to the passengers' impression of the airline. How baggage handlers loaded planes, handled equipment, and wore their uniforms influenced the passengers' feelings about the safety and efficiency of the airline. In 1958, a Pan Am baggage-handling training program included specific lessons for baggage handlers. In a companywide training program on baggage handling, managers emphasized the importance of carefully handling luggage. The manual suggested remarks for manager presentations that included:

> Almost every person who works for Pan American is responsible in some way for seeing that a bag has a safe trip and is returned to the passenger in the same condition it was received. You have the biggest responsibility of all. It is your job to see that each bag is loaded on the right flight in the right compartment, and that it is off-loaded at its proper destination.
>
> More than that—it is your job to see that all baggage is handled carefully, so that it is not scratched, dented, torn, crushed, soiled, or damaged in any way. . . .
>
> Pan American is proud of its Fleet Service Personnel and you are proud of being Pan American employees. None of you would intentionally mishandle a bag. But a lot of baggage does get mishandled. It gets damaged; it is put on the wrong flight; it is overflown or under flown; and sometimes it gets lost completely. You are not responsible for all of these mishaps, but you are responsible for some of them.[22]

The training program presented the assumption that baggage handlers felt valued by the company and that they in turn felt loyalty to Pan Am. The program included a slide presentation, a lesson on properly filling out and recognizing baggage tags, displays and discussions on properly loading bag carts and aircraft, as well as a picture book entitled "Baggage Happy."[23]

The airlines not only emphasized safe baggage handling but proper dress and demeanor among employees. According to a Pan Am manual, "[S]mooth ramp operations" related to customer service in two ways:

> First, there is the direct service responsibility for safety, efficiency, and careful handling of baggage. Secondly, there is the less tangible but nevertheless important item of the general impression given the passengers. To the general public the men on the ramp are "mechanics."

> If our customer or potential customer observes a smoothly running ramp operation—one in which everyone seems to know his job and goes about it industriously and efficiently—he tends to feel that the aircraft in which he is to make his flight is maintained in the same manner. If, on the other hand he sees a lot of confusion, shouting and slamming around of equipment he may fear that an essential adjustment has been neglected in this mad rush to prepare the aircraft for flight.[24]

Airlines recognized the importance of passengers' visual perceptions of operations even when workers had no personal contact with passengers. "For reasons already listed ramp personnel must be concerned with their personal appearance. Uniforms and overalls must be clean and in good repair. Personnel must develop the proper attitude for good customer service for even though they are not in direct contact with the customer, they are exposed to his view, and he is an interested observer." Future business could depend on how baggage handlers did their jobs: "If ramp personnel have a sincere *interest* in preserving and safe-guarding a passenger's property (baggage or cargo) through careful handling, the watching customer notices it—and forms a favorable impression of the Company. If, on the other hand, they throw his property around and bang it into conveyors and stands, he'll probably make a mental note to use another airline next time." The airport ramp was the idealized stage for the modern efficiency and cleanliness of air transportation: "The terminal ramp is a stage upon which the ramp personnel appear as actors representing the inner workings of the Maintenance and Operations Departments. Conduct of personnel is all-important. There must be no shouting, boisterousness, horse play, profanity, or any other action which will detract from the good impression we're trying to make on the passenger."[25] For the airline, it was important that baggage handlers go beyond just getting their job done. The personal appearance and behavior of even unskilled employees were almost as important to the image as making sure the bags were loaded onto the plane.

Some baggage handlers responded positively to the airlines' welfare-capital and incentive programs. Photos in the newsletters show baggage handlers enjoying congratulations for employment anniversaries and participating in sporting activities. As a crew chief, Robert Slouber proudly received commendations on several occasions for the careful handling of baggage and cargo by his crew. Outside of work duties, baggage handlers also participated in company-sponsored group activities. Slouber played hockey with employees from various departments on the company team. He also regularly attended the annual company picnic with his family.[26] James Sullivan, a retired baggage handler who started at American in 1954, played on the company basketball team in Marquette Park near Midway Airport. Richard Sobczak, a retired baggage handler who started at American in 1952, played Santa Claus at the annual Christmas parties held at a hangar at Midway Airport. As Santa, Sobczak would "arrive" on a freighter with stewardesses dressed as Santa's helpers and pass out gifts to the children of employees. Curtis Johnson, who started with United Airlines in 1964 as a baggage handler, recalled company Christmas parties that lasted two or three days so workers from all shifts could attend with their families. Johnson and a retired United Airlines baggage handler, Kenneth Ahern, hired in 1958, also recalled elaborate celebrations honoring employees at the twenty-fifth anniversaries (and above) with the company. As Johnson explained, "You got flown to San Francisco where they put you up at the St. Francis Hotel and had a big party. All the executives would come to see you."

Baggage handlers also utilized flight benefits, a unique opportunity for airline employees to see the world. Martin Trizinski, a retired baggage handler at American Airlines, hired in 1955, used his flight benefits to travel regularly to the West Coast, Hawaii, and on occasion even flew to Los Angeles and Indianapolis for dinner for the fun of it.[27] Richard Sobczak took first-class trips to Los Angeles, Acapulco, Dallas, New York, and Hawaii. When he took his family to Disneyland in the first-class cabin, his wife "thought she was the queen." Roy Okamoto traveled with his wife and four children to the Caribbean; his favorite destination was St. Thomas. Curtis Johnson recalled how well other employees treated him when he traveled on employee passes: "They knew you were an employee and they treated you real nice. I took my mother to Hawaii and the gals were real good to her." James Sullivan also enjoyed his flight benefits, particularly flying to spring-training baseball games. Among his earliest trips was his honeymoon in California. On the way back from Los Angeles, Sullivan and his wife had plans to fly to San Diego and then San Antonio. His wife, already apprehensive about flying, got off at San Diego and would not get on the plane again. She took a bus to San Antonio and then the train back to Chicago and never flew again. Working at the airport could also mean meeting celebrities. Over the years Sobczak met Humphrey Bogart, Danny Kaye, Liberace, Irene Dunn, Marilyn Monroe, Gene Autry, and John Wayne at the airport, and James Sullivan, a serious baseball fan, recalled meeting the Dodgers baseball team when he cleaned their airplane.[28]

Despite the enthusiastic participation of some baggage handlers in the programs offered by the airlines, not all felt a part of the "airline family." As suggested in the *Northwest Airlines News* article championing the work of equipment servicemen, baggage handlers recognized their low position within the airline and often felt undervalued. They also recognized that their shared interests extended beyond the company they worked for to fleet-service clerks at other airlines. George Poulos, a retired fleet-service clerk at American Airlines, hired in 1956, recalled socializing regularly with clerks from United and Delta Airlines when he worked at Chicago's Midway Airport.[29]

Airline unions created their own social activities and benefits programs to encourage loyalty on the part of their membership. Baggage handlers participated in the organized activities of their unions. TWU locals held dinner dances, picnics, and holiday parties. Union locals sponsored education seminars and held blood drives as well. George Poulos attended union meetings at Local 512 when he first started working at American. According to Poulos, Sullivan, Slouber, and Trizinski, a substantial portion of baggage handlers attended meetings in the 1950s held at a VFW hall in Elk Grove Village, a suburb of Chicago. After the meetings the men regularly remained at the hall, socializing at the VFW bar. According to James Sullivan, sometimes there was a barrel of beer available during the meetings, and "guys would start a riot over what they were arguing about." When they stopped serving the beer, attendance seemed to decline a bit.[30]

Labor versus Management: Whipsawing and Mutual Aid

Collective bargaining in the airline industry during the 1950s was an exhausting process for labor and management. With multiple bargaining units and even multiple unions at most domestic airlines covering over 50 percent of all airline employees, airline human-relations departments and unions faced a constant state of bargaining. According to United Airlines' Charles Mason, because the company-union relationship was not "fully matured," making both sides "reluctant to settle in direct negotiations," bargaining had often moved too rapidly through the process set up by the Railway Labor Act. Unions suspicious of airlines and airlines holding back final offers pushed through direct negotiation, to mediation, to the National Mediation Board offer of arbitration, the refusal by one or other party, to a thirty-day cooling-off period, strike threats, then a return to mediation, and then once more a strike threat.[31]

Technological change also impacted workers on the ground. Immediately after the war, American Airlines bought surplus C-54s from the government for ninety thousand dollars apiece and converted them for commercial use.

These planes helped during the initial postwar transition but were soon replaced with DC-6s, Lockheed Constellations, and Boeing Stratocruisers at a cost of over half a million dollars each. These larger four-engine planes with three landing gears towered over the baggage handlers loading them and required new and expensive equipment such as lift-and-conveyor trucks.[32]

New equipment altered work on the ramp for baggage handlers in several ways. Increased training was required for the operation of new equipment. The larger cargo space available also challenged the airlines to develop more efficient ways of loading baggage and freight. Because of the extremes between peak and low times at airports, workers for individual airlines were idle, waiting to load or unload flights, approximately 50 percent of the time.[33] To speed up loading times, airlines began experimenting with containers and destination-based configurations. However, turnaround times for aircraft did not change dramatically despite the introduction of new equipment and training because the increased volume in freight and baggage took longer to load.[34]

New technology did not weaken workers' bargaining power either. Rather, as Charles Mason explained to an audience at a business-school seminar in 1960, "While the unions have not fought the introduction of advanced equipment, they have seized such opportunities to make major gains in wages and working conditions. . . . Each day of delay is irretrievable. The unions have effectively used the force of this competitive pressure to play one carrier against the other."[35] Twelve- to eighteen-month contracts and multiple bargaining units at each airline meant that airlines were negotiating with one or more unions every month, every year. As Charles Mason explained, "There has been almost a constant whipsaw between carriers, and each time an agreement is signed the next carrier up for negotiations is pressured to better terms. Accordingly, in many cases the first settlement in a new round of negotiations does not set a pattern. It merely establishes a floor."[36]

With one or two unions representing workers in the same craft or class in the industry, bargaining strategies could be applied at more than one airline. By the mid 1950s, the IAM represented nearly 80 percent of all organized aircraft mechanics and baggage handlers in the industry. The TWU represented a much smaller share of mechanics and baggage handlers. Nonetheless, its influence in the industry stemmed from its presence at the largest domestic and U.S international airlines, American and Pan Am. ALPA represented almost 100 percent of all commercial airline pilots.[37]

Information about wages and working conditions across the industry was also available more informally to rank-and-file workers. Airline workers on the ground shared a common workplace, the airport, even when employed by different airlines. Airline employees in the air were highly mobile and also had frequent opportunities to exchange information at airports and layover accommodations.[38] Formally, workers and their unions could bargain a "floor" for various workgroups practically on an annual basis thanks to short contract periods and the predominance of ALPA, the IAM, and the TWU in the industry. Fierce competition between carriers on the same routes,

Right: Robert Slouber, Stanley Socha, and a coworker getting ready to load, Midway Airport, Chicago, circa 1948–50. Photo from Robert Slouber, author's collection.

Below: Ready to unload a DC-6, Midway Airport, Chicago, circa 1948–50. Photo from Robert Slouber, author's collection.

the regular introduction of new technology, and the extremely perishable product of service made strike avoidance a major priority for most airlines. A workforce with a high percentage of skilled employees and a public keenly tuned in to aviation safety further complicated labor relations. Labor in the airline industry not only consumed 40 percent or more of airline operating budgets, but when airlines had six, eight, or even ten labor agreements open every year, a company could spend every month of the year bargaining with one or more employee groups.[39]

During the 1950s, pilots, flight engineers, navigators, stewards and stewardesses, clerical employees, mechanics, baggage handlers, porters, and commissary workers variously went on strike over dragging contract negotiations, wages, benefits, and working conditions. Between 1947 and 1957, the airlines and their employees entered into 141 new labor agreements, and the National Mediation Board handled 680 mediation cases, sixty-two arbitration cases, and ten emergency board cases. Over this ten-year period there were thirty-five strikes in the commercial airline industry.[40] The majority of these strikes were among ground employees.

Baggage handlers recognized that despite their unskilled position, they were capable of disrupting service and forcing their employers to address their issues. A 1950 strike at American pointed to the cross-skill solidarity among airline workers in the New York City area when baggage handlers were the first to walk off the job over contractual issues. American and the TWU negotiated and participated in mediation for four months before the March 1, 1950, walkout. Wages, a job-security clause, subcontracting maintenance work, and the length of the contract were all disputed issues. While the strike began with the 6:30 AM shift of baggage handlers, a total of 4,600 mechanics, baggage handlers, and stores personnel participated in the strike, affecting thirty-four cities with air service by American. Although the airline claimed operation levels of approximately 20 percent capacity during the strike using supervisory employees, the TWU stated that the strike was 93 percent effective. Using either figure, the TWU used this to its advantage by warning Congress and the public of the dangers of improperly maintained aircraft. Mike Quill, the leader of the TWU, called on President Truman to take over the airline during the strike, because the planes were "unsafe for public transportation." He based his request on U.S. airmail subsidies, which he termed the "Government's partnership function" with the airline.[41]

Five days into the action, union members voted overwhelmingly to stay on strike despite a recommendation to return to work by the National Mediation Board. Of the 4,600 strikers, 2,569 voted to stay out, and 284 voted to return to work. In New York City, all but six of the nine hundred members voted to remain on strike. However, a majority of workers in smaller cities such as Nashville, Boston, El Paso, and Washington voted to return to work. With assistance from the National Mediation Board, workers returned to work March 12 after ratifying a new agreement by a vote of 3,100 to 390. This agreement included two firsts for the industry: a severance package for laid-off workers, and a company policy pledging only to subcontract mechanical work that American Airlines employees did not have time to do. The strike was a major contractual victory for ground workers in the airlines. Union members overwhelmingly stayed on the picket lines and off the ramp, and the union's use of the issue of air safety prompted discussion in Congress, public concern, and placed pressure on the company. Despite the important gains made in terms of job security, the union failed to win the twenty-cent-an-hour wage increase it called for before and during the strike. However, strikers did win several firsts in fringe benefits: their first severance package, paid meal time for night-shift workers, and three weeks paid vacation after twelve years of service (instead of fifteen years).

In December 1950, American Airlines and the TWU voluntarily reopened the contract and entered into what the *New York Times* described as a "three-year wage agreement embodying basic features of the General Motors labor-peace formula." Employees covered by the contract won a twenty-eight-cent increase over two years through a new cost-of-living escalator clause, a supplementary wage increase for workers in the lower-paid categories (including stock clerks, cleaners, and entry-level baggage handlers), and dues checkoff for a union shop in anticipation of the passage of an amendment to the Railway Labor Act the following month.[42] The American Airlines vice president of personnel called the contract "an exchange of economic concessions for a long period of stability." Mike Quill called it "a tremendous victory" for the union, one that put membership at American Airlines ahead of all other workers in the industry in terms of wages and working conditions.[43]

Within two weeks of the labor settlements in March and December at American Airlines, TWU members at Pan Am threatened to strike. In March, mechanics and baggage handlers at the airline sought a job-security clause, the elimination of subcontracting of maintenance work, and a systemwide seniority plan and threatened to strike in support of TWU stewards and stewardesses bargaining for improvements in wages, a systemwide seniority package, and severance pay. After a seventeen-hour strike by both groups on May 13, the National Mediation Board worked out a settlement. According to the *TWU Express*, the Air Transport Division director James Horst said

Stanley Socha, Red Berndt, and a coworker doing paperwork on the ramp, Midway Airport, Chicago, circa 1948–50. Photo from Robert Slouber, author's collection.

that the new agreement "paralleled the American Airlines pact, signed at the conclusion of an eleven-day strike." Mechanics and baggage handlers at Pan Am won controls on subcontracting, the employment of foreign nationals, and improvements in severance pay.[44]

In December, TWU mechanics and baggage handlers at Pan Am called for a contract opener and an eight-cent-an-hour wage increase, citing wartime inflation, although their contract did not open until November 1951. Their demands came as added pressure as Pan Am and the TWU negotiated other contracts for two smaller work groups, the commissary and port-steward employees. Within three days, ground crews at New York airports staged sit-down strikes and were joined by workers at Miami and San Francisco. The union and Pan Am agreed to wait until after the New Year's holiday to resume talks. On January 15, 1951, nine hundred rank-and-file mechanics at a Miami maintenance base walked off the job for a few hours instead of returning to work after a ten-minute smoking break, offering the airline a spontaneous show of solidarity. A federal mediator stepped in, and in March 1951, 150 port stewards as well as over four thousand mechanics and baggage handlers won a six-cent-an-hour increase, and stewardesses won a five-dollar-a-month increase. The agreement also included an escalator clause tied to the cost-of-living index of the Bureau of Labor Statistics.[45]

Pan Am faced two more TWU strikes during 1951. In June, five hundred mechanics and baggage handlers at Idlewild Field stopped work in a "spontaneous protest" because eighty-nine workers had been laid off after Pan American purchased American Overseas Airlines (not American Airlines) and moved much of its heavy maintenance to an overhaul base in Miami. The next day, twenty workers at LaGuardia joined them, and according to the union, Pan Am workers in London and Puerto Rico threatened to follow. For the first two days the airline continued to operate a limited schedule; however, when members of the FEIA-AFL refused to cross picket lines, the company agreed to offer work in Miami or Brownsville, Texas, to the laid-off mechanics and pay for relocation. Those mechanics that declined to move received severance pay and compensation for wage losses in taking another job through July 1952.[46]

Six months later, a strike by Pan Am mechanics, baggage handlers, and stewards and stewardesses, all TWU members, left international travelers stranded a full twenty-four hours before a December 17 strike deadline. Pan Am and the TWU began bargaining November 15, and despite mediation, they remained far apart on wage issues when the strike broke out. According to James Horst, the strikers walked off the job a day early when the company declared that supervisory employees were ready to ensure uninterrupted service because the strike was illegal. A strike at Pan Am could potentially disrupt the supply chain for the Korean War, although the TWU promised to continue to service aircraft used for this purpose. On December 17, Truman set up a Presidential Emergency Board to examine the issues, and TWU members voted to return to work while the board conducted its investigation.[47]

Nearly daily coverage of the strike and talks in the press included a chiding in a *New York Times* editorial describing the strike as a "needless" one that disrupted the process of the Railway Labor Act and a report on name-calling across the table as the two sides bargained for paid mealtimes. At the end of February 1952, the Presidential Emergency Board made wage recommendations that fell in the middle of the opening positions of Pan Am and the TWU. The board also condemned the union for "quickie" work stoppages and reprimanded management for dragging its feet in turning over collected union dues. The board concluded that a "thorough and complete change in attitude" was needed on both sides. Soon after, the two sides agreed to a two-year contract based on the board's recommendations.[48]

As the Presidential Emergency Board met to investigate the Pan Am strike, the National Mediation Board reported to Congress that the Railway Labor Act "faced a 'complete breakdown' if strikes in the two industries continued much longer at recent rates." Between July 1950 and July 1951 there had been twenty-four strikes total and five on the airlines, the greatest number of strikes for any year since the Railway Labor Act was passed in 1926. That record was soon broken. The number of airline strikes nearly doubled in 1953.[49]

In June 1952, American Airlines baggage handlers walked off the job on the East Coast. They protested the use of non-union employees and supervisors in place of recently laid-off TWU members. From the union's perspective, the airline badgered its members into the walkout as part of a larger attempt at union busting.[50] On June 4, five hundred TWU members, predominantly baggage handlers, stopped work at LaGuardia without the consent of union officials. At the center of the dispute stood the use of supervisors, clerical workers, and other unorganized employees for duties covered by the TWU contract. According to the union, the company replaced laid-off workers with non-union employees and refused to discuss the situation. According to the airline, these employees stepped in so the airline could fulfill its duty as a certified air carrier. Travel pay appeared as a central issue; while the airport was closed workers commuting from Newark complained that the trip could take four hours a day on top of an eight-hour shift. The airport at Newark was closed for several weeks while authorities investigated three plane crashes in Elizabeth, New Jersey. On June 5, two hundred baggage handlers and mechanics in Chicago and thirteen in Philadelphia sat down for the day in sympathy with their New York counterparts. By July 6, over a thousand workers at LaGuardia and Idlewild participated in the sit-down strike.[51] According to the *New York Times,* some baggage handlers "lounged around and others played cards while white collar workers in the reservation department of the line struggled with cargo loading and unloading jobs. Many of the white collar workers had started with the line as cargo handlers and were familiar with the work."[52]

Three days into the sit-down strike, TWU leaders called on the National Mediation Board to intervene. At the same time, American Airlines instituted a suit for $250,000 in damages against the union for breach of contract due to violation of a "no strike" clause in the December 1950 agreement. The board requested that workers return to the job and the company restore the "status quo"—remove non-union employees from duties covered by TWU contract. Ninety-five percent of the striking workers were back on the job by the second shift June 8.[53] Tensions nonetheless remained high throughout the summer and into the fall. Baggage handlers were singled out for their participation in the job action, and the union complained to the National Mediation Board that the company had not returned operations to the status quo. Furthermore, workers at Philadelphia and LaGuardia were issued disciplinary notices for the strike, which TWU officers considered an affront to their manhood and an attempt to incite the workers into further action.[54]

Baggage handlers resisted work they felt to be unsafe even when it fell under their job description and when they were disciplined for refusing it. Baggage handlers on the East Coast stopped work after several of their ranks were disciplined for not lifting a large piece of cargo at Idlewild. In September 1958, three baggage handlers were given "notices of unsatisfactory performance" for refusing to unload a 290-pound piece of cargo. At 5:10 AM September 19, 150 baggage handlers stopped work at Idlewild to protest the notices given to their fellow employees. Slight delays for departing flights followed. Within three hours, three hundred baggage handlers and maintenance men stopped work at LaGuardia, causing the cancellation of five flights and ninety-minute delays on other flights. At both airports supervisors loaded and unloaded aircraft that night. Over three shifts, a total of 1,500 workers participated in the sit-down strike at Newark, Philadelphia, Albany, and Hartford, Connecticut. The next afternoon, baggage handlers and their supporters returned to work after an agreement had been reached to discuss rules over the maximum weight to be lifted by hand.[55]

Baggage handlers also walked off the job in support of workers in lower-status positions than themselves. Similar to walkouts a decade earlier, Pan Am workers in Miami walked off the job over contracting out work that belonged to commissary employees and porters. On February 12, 1959, more than two thousand workers in Miami, San Juan, and Houston, including baggage handlers, mechanics, stewards, and stewardesses, walked off the job for twelve hours when the company hired non-union porters and food handlers as the company shifted its operations to a new terminal. After two hours of negotiation the company agreed to return to the status quo.[56]

Airline workers' activism produced real gains in terms of wages and benefits. Severance pay, sick leave, vacation time, a union-shop, shift-differentials, "follow the work" transfer rights at company expense, a ban on subcontracting, and the station-to-station transfer rights were several of the gains won through strikes, strike threats, and negotiation during the 1950s.[57] However, generally health insurance, pensions, and death benefits lagged behind those gained in other industries.[58] Wages for baggage handlers at American Airlines rose from $1.12 an hour in 1947 to $2.28 in 1958, an increase of over 57 percent.[59] For baggage handlers, wages increased enough to make homeownership a real possibility. The retired baggage handlers Robert Slouber, Richard Sobczak, and Martin Trizinski started on the ramp after high school in 1941, 1952, and 1955, respectively. Each purchased his first home in the Chicago suburbs when he was twenty-eight years old. John Gales, a Dutch immigrant who came to work on the ramp in 1959, bought his first home in the Chicago suburbs in 1963. He recalled, "Buying the house was no problem when I told the realtor I worked for the airlines."[60]

Airlines attempted to manage the "whipsaw" problem first in 1946 to avert a pilot strike at TWA. Thirteen airlines came together with the ATA to create the first Airlines Negotiating Committee to bargain a multicarrier contract with ALPA. ALPA refused to bargain with the committee even after a thirty-day cooling-off period under a Presidential Emergency Board. TWA and the other airlines put the board's recommendations into effect but never bargained a multicarrier contract.[61]

In 1953, a second attempt at multicarrier bargaining was made, this time at the behest of airline labor. That year the IAM had mechanical contracts open at Capital, National, Eastern, Northwest, and United Airlines. All five cases went to mediation, and upon the request of the union, the National Mediation Board and the airlines agreed to joint mediation. After four months the companies and the IAM reached a wage and contract-duration settlement.[62] The result, via the Emergency Board, was in part de facto multicarrier bargaining.

In January 1954 the IAM began to collect data from its airline lodges to create a set of uniform contract proposals for the airline industry. That May the IAM proposed common contract language regarding over twenty job titles for standardization and pay rates to Eastern, United, Trans World, Northwest, National, and Capital Airlines. The airlines stalled, and Eastern Airlines refused to participate under these conditions. When the IAM threatened a strike, a Presidential Emergency Board convened and recommended multicarrier bargaining. However, none of the parties were required by the Railway Labor Act to implement the recommendations of a Presidential Emergency Board. Under National Mediation Board mediation, the parties hashed out bargaining agreements, which handled the work rules separately for each carrier but the wages and other fiscal matters jointly. The IAM and all the airlines, except Eastern, concluded agreements in March 1955. Three weeks later Eastern also settled. For the first time the IAM contracts included uniform wage rates for aircraft mechanics and uniform longevity pay for all classifications covered in the contracts.[63]

In 1957 again the IAM offered multi-unit bargaining, and the airlines refused. Instead the industry resurrected the Airline Negotiating Conference as the Airline Personnel Relations Conference to evaluate joint negotiations and even consider lobbying for the industry's inclusion in the Taft-Hartley Act. Among the conference's suggestions that most airlines could agree upon was coordinated bargaining by management and a strike-insurance program.[64] Faced with nearly monthly bargaining, growing labor costs, and increasing labor unrest, particularly among flight crews, as ALPA and the FEIA fought bitterly over cockpit-manning issues, the airline industry joined the American management offensive of the late 1950s. As contemporary observers such as the economists Herbert Northrup, Jack Barbash, and Frank Pierson and historians such as Melvyn Dubofsky, Nelson Lichtenstein, Mike Davis, and Jack Metzgar have argued, American corporate management countered dwindling profits in the recession of 1957–58, reduced federal spending, and increased foreign competition with an offensive attack on the collective-bargaining system of the mid-1950s.[65] The airlines joined in on this attack.

For the airlines, the need to counter wage increases and lost time to strikes grew over the course of the decade. Between 1949 and 1955, airline profits rose steadily as passenger traffic increased. However, in mid-1956, profits began to level off as air traffic slowed, operating costs rose, and fares remained fixed. The airlines lobbied the Civil Aeronautics Board for fare increases, but congressional opposition blocked their efforts. Dwindling profits were especially problematic for the airlines as they entered into a period of technological change—the start of the jet age.

For the airline industry, 1958 proved to be a banner year for labor unrest with fifteen work stoppages, eight of them involving ground workers, with a total of over sixty-two thousand airline employees involved.[66] Among these strikes were conflicts between ALPA and the FEIA at Eastern, Pan Am, and American Airlines over crew complement on new jet aircraft and accusations of "featherbirding," or overmanning the cockpit.[67] At Pan Am and Lake Central Airlines, stewardesses represented by the TWU and the Air Line Stewards and Stewardesses Association, respectively, went on strike.[68]

Striking IAM members at eight airlines created the greatest challenge to airline management in 1958. IAM whipsawing at Capital, Eastern, TWA, United, National, Northwest, Northeast, and West Coast Airlines led to new strategies on the part of airline management. With concurrent contract expiration dates among these airlines and a strike fund of more than two million dollars, the IAM attempted to bargain a master contract. Facing short cash flows because of jet aircraft orders, tight competition, and differing labor-relations situations, the airlines refused joint bargaining. Bargaining on several of the lines reached an impasse in October 1958, and the union struck Capital Airlines, the weakest of the group, first. The strike lasted thirty-seven days. With the new contract signed, the IAM next went on strike at TWA and West Coast Airlines. After settling at those airlines, IAM members went on strike at Eastern for the month of December. The other four airlines settled with contracts similar to those at Capital, TWA, and West Coast Airlines. The agreement at Capital was not only more favorable to the union than the recommendations of the Presidential Emergency Board but also included new language that allowed workers at the airline to respect each other's picket lines.[69]

In 1959 the airline industry rolled out its management offensive plan. American, Capital, Eastern, Pan American, TWA, and United banded together and created a Mutual Aid Pact, a strike-insurance policy to offset the fiscal effects of a strike on any one of the member airlines. When workers at an airline disrupted service through a strike, the other airlines reimbursed the struck airline the extra profit gained through the increase in passengers on their own flights. The Civil Aeronautics Board approved the pact over the strong objections of airline unions. In 1960 the pact was amended to include coverage of strikes called even without Presidential Emergency Boards, as long as the airline was in full compliance with the Railway Labor Act. Smaller carriers whose strikes would not create substantial disruptions of air service now had a reason to join the Mutual Aid Pact, and Braniff, Continental, National, and Northwest Airlines joined that year. The ten airlines together accounted for approximately 90 percent of the annual trunkline air traffic in the country, and their union density rate fell between 64 and 88 percent. From 1958 to 1961 airlines used the Mutual Aid Pact eight times and paid out benefits totaling more than fifteen million dollars.[70]

In response to the Mutual Aid Pact, the IAM, the TWU, ALPA, the UAW, the BRC, the FEIA, and the Air Line Dispatchers Association formed the Association of Air Transport Unions (AATU) to counter the airlines' Mutual Aid Pact and research the impact of the recent passage of the Landrum-Griffin Act. The frequent rivals agreed to provide moral and financial support during any strike by one of the member unions and to withhold final settlement with a struck airline until it agreed to reinstate all striking workers and withdraw any retaliatory action. Despite this collective response, the association was inactive by the end of 1960 because of disunity among its members.[71]

* * *

Baggage handlers benefited from their important place in the "staging" of air transportation. The perishable nature of air travel bolstered their strength in informal and formal negotiations with the airlines. The strength of the IAM and the whipsaw tactics of short contracts and pattern bargaining rapidly increased wages across the industry, and growing resistance to constant bargaining resulted in remarkable cooperation among airline competitors through the Mutual Aid Pact.

5

On the Ramp in the 1950s and 1960s

Airports are intriguing and increasingly exasperating places in which to spend time. In the 1920s and 1930s, when airports in cities like Dallas, Milwaukee, Louisville, and Minneapolis shared space with public parks, thousands of people flocked to airports on the weekends to picnic in the grass and watch planes land and take off.[1] Today airports operate twenty-four hours a day, seven days a week. Tens of thousands of employees and nearly two hundred thousand passengers fill up international airports like Chicago's O'Hare, New York's Kennedy, and Los Angeles's LAX each day. As the essayist Pico Iyer and the sociologist Mark Gottdiener have explored, for passengers airports are strange, liminal, "intranational" shopping malls where all the dynamics of the human experience unfold before an audience of global strangers.[2] Among those strangers are the men and women who come to work each day at the airport.

The American fascination with the working world of airplanes and airports has found its way into popular culture. Through film and print, beautiful stewardesses and handsome pilots, especially, represent all that is glamorous about working in the airline industry. Romance, intrigue, and heroism have filled the screen in *Three Guys Named Mike, Murder in the Clouds,* and *China Clipper* in the 1930s and 1940s and today with films like *Catch Me If You Can, The Aviator,* and of course the *Airport* films of the 1970s. More recently the media has offered a glimpse at working on the ground rather than in the air in television shows like the *Airline* series (2004), chronicling the ups and downs of working at Southwest Airlines, and to a lesser extent films like *The Terminal,* starring Tom Hanks as a man trapped in the limbo world of Kennedy International Airport.

For passengers and workers alike, the airport is a combination of "hurry up" and "wait," as weather, technology, crowds, and increasingly the threat of terrorism shape time at the airport. Since the 1990s, the news media has chronicled the diminished glamor of airline work due to cheaper airfares, growing passenger loads, and the seeming decline in the civility of air travel. Since the terrorist attacks of September 11, 2001, troubles for airline workers have compounded with growing concerns over workplace safety, speedups, bankruptcies, layoffs, mergers, and pay cuts.[3]

Despite the bad news airline workers have faced in the last two decades, working on the ramp was a "good job" in the late 1950s and 1960s. The pace of work and the acres of terminal and ramp space offered baggage handlers the time and the place to construct a culture of leisure alongside a culture of work. Drawing from oral histories of retired baggage handlers and aircraft mechanics at American and United Airlines, this chapter offers a snapshot of the workplace culture of the ramp and how technology, race, government, and airline policies and the presence of a strong union shaped work and leisure among baggage handlers in the jet age.[4]

The introduction of jet aircraft to the U.S. airline industry in the late 1950s transformed the industry for passengers, workers, and even the neighborhoods surrounding airports across the country. The size and speed of jet airplanes captured the imagination of the American flying public. Lower ticket prices through "youth" and "family" fares again introduced more Americans to aviation for pleasure travel. The growing popularity of travel to vacation spots such as Las Vegas and Florida as well as Europe helped ensure that investment in jet-engine aircraft was worthwhile for the airlines.

Over the course of the decade, the use of jet aircraft also dramatically increased employment opportunities in the airline industry. From 1960 to 1970, employment in the industry nearly doubled. While baggage handlers were excited by the new job opportunities and the wonders of technological change, they responded to this new technology with concern and fear for their jobs and safety. Despite the larger aircraft, new containerized loading could lead to layoffs for baggage handlers. Indeed, the initial introduction of the new technology, during the recession of the late 1950s, brought layoffs and uncertainty to airline workers. The introduction of jet aircraft also brought new safety concerns for baggage handlers, the workers who spent the most time around operating aircraft. Jet-engine noise and power could cause permanent hearing damage or grisly death. Despite concern over job security and safety, baggage handlers perceived this technological change in their workplace as one of historical importance. They were participants in the dawning of a new era.[5]

The airline industry was not immune to larger changes in the American social and political landscape. The overwhelmingly white male workforce of the industry encountered the civil rights movement of the 1960s with mixed results. As before, baggage handlers were suspicious of their new African American coworkers and questioned their ability to succeed at the job. Along with white-worker resistance, geographic, bureaucratic, and institutional factors hampered racial integration of the industry. Nonetheless, new federal laws such as the Civil Rights Act of 1964, executive orders applied to companies holding government contracts, and other incentive programs helped to overcome inertia. In increasing numbers, African American men found work on the ramp as baggage handlers, a key entry point for new workers into the industry during this decade. Despite their position at the bottom of the corporate structure, baggage handlers understood their important position within the airline. The airlines also recognized baggage handlers' power to affect the passengers' experience and consequently the image of the corporation for which they worked. The industry recognized plane seats as a perishable item. Every missed flight due to labor action was irretrievable revenue.

Technology, Work, and the Changing Composition of the Labor Force

Although jet-engine technology developed for civilian aircraft after World War II in Britain, it was not applied to commercial aviation in the United States until 1957. Pan Am initiated the process with a Boeing 707–120, equipped with four Pratt and Whitney jet engines. Using the 707, with a cruising speed of six hundred miles per hour and seating for 181 passengers, Pan Am inaugurated transatlantic jet service in October 1958.[6] A year later, American Airlines became the first domestic airline to use its own jets in domestic service, with flights from New York to Los Angeles.[7] Jets not only replaced piston-engine aircraft and cut flight times in half but also increased the size and carrying capacity of aircraft. While the Boeing 707s could carry up to 181 passengers, Boeing 727s, the workhorse of domestic air travel through the 1990s, carried up to 189 passengers. The Douglas DC-8 carried up to 250 passengers, while the largest series of DC-10s could carry up to 345 passengers. The largest airplane of its time, introduced in 1970, was the Boeing 747, with a passenger capacity of 490. On average, jet aircraft flew at 600 miles per hour, compared to the 190 to 250 miles per hour of piston aircraft.[8] Jet fuel was relatively inexpensive, and jet engines were more reliable than their piston counterparts. The lack of vibration also lowered airframe maintenance costs, and the size of jet aircraft lowered per-seat costs. Fares in the 1960s averaged five cents per mile, a third of the cost in the late 1930s.[9]

Between 1955 and 1972, the number of passengers in the United States jumped from 49 million to 119 million per year.[10] According to Gallup polls, 50 percent of Americans said they had flown at least once, but businessmen made up the greatest number of air passengers. In 1964, *Time* magazine reported that 86 percent of air passengers were businessmen. In 1969, the Port Authority of New York and New Jersey estimated that 5 percent of all passengers took 40 percent of all the trips out of their airports that year.

Along with business travel, flying remained transportation for the relatively privileged, those with discretionary incomes for holiday travel that included airfare. Miami and Las Vegas topped the list of domestic destinations for personal travel. Europe became the destination of choice for American college students. With jets, the number of students studying abroad rose 150 percent. In the summer of 1960, American students registered over 120,000 times in European youth hostels.[11]

Under the impact of jet-age technology, the air-transportation labor force nearly doubled, from 198,139 in 1960 to 388,455 in 1970. The air-transportation labor force did not merely increase but diversified in racial and gender terms. The percentage of women employed increased from 22 percent of the labor force to 27 percent. Likewise, African Americans increased from 5 to 6 percent between these years. The number of African American men in air transportation more than doubled over the decade, and more than five times the number of black women worked in air transportation in 1970 than in 1960. The number of other minority men more than doubled, and minority women more than quadrupled, in air transportation between 1960 and 1970. Although their gross employment figures rose dramatically, African American and other minority men and women did not make substantial gains as a percentage of the entire air-transportation workforce.

The introduction of jet aircraft caused concern for job security and safety as well as excitement for airline workers in all segments of the industry. George Poulos, a baggage handler who started working for American in 1956 in Chicago and several coworkers, made a special trip to Los Angeles to see the new DC-707s. Poulos recalled thinking the new airplane was a "monster." He

Table 13. Race and Sex of Air-Transportation Workers in the United States, 1960 and 1970

	Male				Female			
	White (%)	Negro (%)	Other (%)	Total (%)	White (%)	Negro (%)	Other (%)	Total (%)
1960	143,958 (93)	8,201 (5)	2,704 (2)	154,863 (100)	41,745 (97)	895 (2)	636 (1)	43,276 (100)
1970	259,134 (92)	17,613 (6)	5,926 (2)	282,673 (100)	97,749 (92)	5,208 (5)	2,825 (3)	105,782 (100)

Source: U.S. Bureau of the Census, Industry of the Experienced Civilian Labor Force and of the Employed, and Unemployment Rate, by Color and Sex, for the United States: 1960 (Washington, D.C.: 1967); U.S. Bureau of the Census, Race and Spanish Origin of Employed Persons by Detailed Industry, and Sex: 1970 (Washington, D.C.: 1973).

wondered how it would ever get off the ground because of its size. However, the excitement surrounding the introduction of jet aircraft soon subsided. As Poulos recalled, "At first we were very careful about everything. But after a while it was just another airplane." Within a few years, jet aircraft were "old news" to baggage handlers like Poulos, who remembered receiving only an hour or two of training on the new 490 passenger DC-747s in 1970. He did not believe that baggage handlers required more training on new equipment. Over the years the technology became commonplace: "If you can work one [jet aircraft], you can work them all."[12]

Nonetheless, jet aircraft transformed baggage handling in ways that threatened to reduce their numbers. George Poulos described their work as more complicated with the jet aircraft. Loading and unloading was now containerized, and baggage handlers needed to operate mechanized loaders, interior track systems that locked the containers in place inside the aircraft, specialized dollies to move the containers, new auxiliary power units, potable water feeds, and lavatory trucks.[13] As the airlines introduced jet aircraft, the TWU estimated a possible 20 to 25 percent reduction in manpower for jet overhaul work compared to piston-engine levels.[14] In the early 1960s, Northwest Airlines contracted out aircraft fueling, a mechanical task, in Minneapolis, where 25 percent of all baggage handlers on the airline worked. The new aircraft, new facilities, and contracting out led to a decrease in the number of baggage handlers employed by Northwest from 650 to 447 over the three-year period from 1959 to 1962.[15]

Along with the introduction of jets, automation of freight and baggage systems threatened the job security of baggage handlers, particularly at larger airports. These new "bag rooms," outfitted with myriad motorized conveyor belts and staging areas, streamlined transferring and sorting procedures. Northwest installed a conveyor-belt system with built-in scales for more efficient processing and loading of freight at Idlewild Airport in New York. The new operation cut "truck-to-plane" loading time in half.[16] Pan Am and American each developed automated baggage-handling systems for LaGuardia and Kennedy Airports at a cost of over seven million dollars. Pan Am's system at Kennedy was designed to handle over 150,000 pieces of luggage a day upon its completion in 1972. Both systems were built with elaborate conveyor networks and computerized mini-carts to transport the bags.[17]

Large-scale containerization of freight, mail, and baggage coincided with jet service. The first cargo-handling system using interlocking parts was developed at the end of the piston era. In 1961, Pan Am developed its AirPak system for use with piston-engined DC-7s. This freight-loading and shipping system used a series of preloaded pallets of freight towed on dollies. The pallets, dollies, and the floor of the aircraft cargo belly were each equipped with a ball-roller and track system so that the pallets could be easily shifted from dolly to plane and secured in place without ropes and netting. As Pan Am announced in its publication for cargo customers, the "New AIRPAK system allows seven 6,700-pound pallets to be preloaded at factory, warehouse or terminal. Speed and efficiency cut loading and unloading time to approximately 45 minutes."[18]

In 1963, Pan Am and American introduced jet freighters, aircraft that carried only cargo. Using 707s, the new freighter could carry more than forty tons at a speed of 575 miles per hour for over three thousand miles. The new freighters were equipped for compatibility with military freighters as well as Pan Am's AirPak system and could be loaded or unloaded in under an hour.[19] As a result of the advances in freight-handling systems and jet service, freight revenues on commercial (including passenger-service) airlines rose significantly during the 1960s.

Passenger aircraft as well as freighters were outfitted with container systems. With the increased number of passengers onboard the jets, preloaded containers of baggage could be offloaded or transferred between planes at specified destinations. Boeing 707s and 727s were equipped with a floor-track system for containers but also had a cargo belly for freeloaded baggage. Douglas DC-10s were also equipped with floor-track systems for containers and had a small freeloading belly in the tail of the aircraft.

Jet aircraft brought on a host of new safety concerns for airline workers, especially baggage handlers. The decibel levels of a jet engine could be permanently deafening. Within a hundred feet of a jet engine at full power, the

Above: Trying out a new DC-6A freighter, Midway Airport, Chicago, 1958. Photo from Robert Slouber, author's collection.

Right: Securing freight at Pan American Airways, 1960s. Pan American World Airways, Inc. Records, series 1, box 230, folder 15, Special Collections, University of Miami Libraries, Coral Gables, Fla.

decibel level was twice as loud as the rate considered safe for the human ear, making earplugs or earmuffs essential to work safety and comfort. While the extraordinary noise of a jet engine could be a persistent irritation on the job, the danger of standing too close to an operating jet engine could prove fatal. With piston-driven propellers, workers on the ramp could see the immediate area of danger and work away from the deadly blades. Jet engines could suck in or throw back a man standing near them. The danger was very real, and, according to the air force, more common than perhaps expected: "Air Force experience during the past five years has been that a man has been sucked into a jet intake on the average of once every 60 days. The victims have been all types—from apprentice mechanics to experienced maintenance personnel. Six out of ten survive their experience, but almost none do so without crippling injuries and long hospitalization. There is no record of a case where the person in a bout with a jet intake escaped without major injuries." The range of the danger area in front of an operating Boeing 707 jet engine was substantial. When the engine was idling, the area went forward from the engine one hundred feet to where the velocity was thirty miles per hour and the temperature one hundred degrees Fahrenheit. The danger area at this distance was about twelve feet wide. When the engine was at dry takeoff power, the danger area was thirty feet wide at a distance of two hundred feet. At that point the velocity was forty miles per hour and one hundred degrees Fahrenheit. Furthermore, the electrical voltage of auxiliary air-conditioning power units for jet aircraft was eight times more powerful than those used on piston aircraft.[20]

As the industry transitioned to jet aircraft, the TWU called for a thirty-hour week for all transit workers to counter job loss through automation, noting in particular the dramatic changes to the workplace in the airline industry.[21] The TWU emphasized safety as a central issue for mechanics, baggage handlers, and others working on and around jet aircraft. Baggage handlers at American attended classes on the thrust and pull of airplanes, as Robert Slouber, a member of the union's safety committee, recalled. As a member of the committee, he helped indoctrinate the loading crews on jet-aircraft safety to keep them from working directly behind or in front of the engines. These were important lessons to be learned because, as Slouber stated, "You could be sucked in, in a second."[22] In March 1960, the union issued a thirty-two-page booklet entitled *ATD-TWU and Jet Safety* to its Air Transport Division members. The booklet explained the dangers of noise, electric current, exposure to radar, jet suction, and exhaust and air-tire pressure. According to the booklet, deafness was one of the greatest hazards of working around jet airplanes.

> If you disregard any of these, this is what you can expect: Exposure to intense noise may cause temporary hearing loss that persists from a few hours to a few days. Continued exposure over an extended period may result in a partial but permanent hearing loss. . . .
>
> Even with all this talk about decibels, it is not too hard to draw a few ground rules about noise. To be safe, wear ear plugs anytime within 400 feet of the engines. Wear ear plugs and ear muffs when you are within 100 feet. And wear a helmet and ear plugs when you are closer than 25 feet. Insist on wearing plugs that are fitted to your ears and keep them absolutely clean.
>
> Before going to work or being reassigned on jet planes, TWU urges the em-

> ployee to undergo a hearing test. He should be tested again in three months and then once a year thereafter.[23]

Workers could be sucked into a running jet engine to their death, and the booklet ominously warned of this danger: "The first rule here is that you must remember that you are working in the vicinity of four giant vacuum cleaners which do not differentiate between the objects they suck into their intakes. Propellers had the advantage of advertising their danger, but jet intakes—while equally as deadly—wait for the unsuspecting to venture near."

Standing behind a running jet engine was also dangerous. While a person could not be sucked into the engine from this position, he or she could be burned. A person or even a service vehicle could be knocked over by "jet blast," with serious injuries resulting. As the booklet explained, "For example, the exhaust of a Boeing 707 jet engine at 25 feet has a velocity of 590 miles per hour and a temperature of 370 degrees F. Even at a distance of 100 feet, the speed is 94 mph and the temperature is 140 degrees. If you must walk or work in the danger areas behind operating jet engines, keep a healthy distance of 200 feet at a minimum. This might not seem necessary when the engines are idle, but it takes only a second to go from idle to a power setting and in that time the damage can be done."[24] A few years later, the union challenged an American Airlines policy that directed baggage handlers to work within twenty-five feet of operating jet engines. According to this procedure, baggage handlers loaded last-minute bags while the engines were running. The TWU advised its members to refuse this unsafe assignment.[25]

Baggage Handling, Civil Rights, and the "Hardcore" Unemployed

Employment opportunities for African Americans and other minority groups in the air-transport industry were affected by institutional, bureaucratic, and geographic factors. As in other industries, several of the largest labor organizations in aviation discriminated against African Americans. ALPA, the ALMA, and the IAM each had racially restrictive "white only" membership policies. While these policies were removed gradually during World War II and its aftermath,[26] in 1961, members of Local 514 employed at Berry Field in Nashville wrote to the TWU president Michael Quill at least twice asking him to keep the union out of civil rights activities. The thirty-three Nashville members who signed the letter strongly objected to TWU donations to civil rights Freedom Riders, among other groups. They felt that the northern leadership of the union could not understand the situation in the South:

> In regard to your editorial in *TWU Express* of June 2, 1961, we the undersigned members of the TWU think it would be best for our union and our country if we, as a Labor Union and elected officials of Labor Unions, serve the union and refrain from getting involved in those things that are not any of our business. Let us refrain from giving aid and comfort to Khruschev and the Communist party by giving aid and comfort to the outside agitators stirring up trouble in the South. . . .
>
> Let us tend to the things of the union, for which we are being paid, and not contribute to the breakdown of all rights and authority guaranteed to the States by the Constitution. Let us refrain from sending a lawless group of atheist hoodlums to the South, a group that does not even want to obey the draft laws of our country, the rules of their schools, the orders of the Federal and State and officials, and the laws of God.[27]

Other southern locals voiced similar concerns regarding the "legality" of some civil rights activities. Members of Local 513 in Dallas refused to donate money to aid the Freedom Riders and objected to union donations to the National Association for the Advancement of Colored People or other organizations they felt conflicted with the U.S. or union constitutions.[28]

To be sure, not all baggage handlers or their unions were hostile or indifferent to racial integration. TWU officials and many rank-and-file members actively participated in the civil rights movement.[29] Michael Quill rebuked the Berry Field Local in the *TWU Express* in August 1961. In a scathing open letter to the chairman, Quill railed,

> The trials and tribulations of all Americans are "things of the union!"
>
> Wherever there are fascist-minded members of the White Citizens Councils trying to destroy our country, it is the business of the TWU.
>
> Wherever Americans do not have the right to vote, it comes under the heading of "things of the union." When there are 6,000,000 unemployed men and women in the U.S., it is our problem. When people are overcharged for poorly constructed homes, it is our business. Where there are long hours and low wages, it is our business. When America is sick and endangered by the cancer of segregation, it is cause for concern by all organized labor—and by each and every member of the TWU.

Quill went on to directly challenge the Nashville membership:

> We gave you the right to speak to your bosses—something you did not have until TWU organized airline workers. We shortened your hours, raised your wages, gave you security and dignity you had never dreamed possible.
>
> But dignity also means equality—for every worker—regardless of race, color

> or creed. *And that is the way it is going to remain as long as there is a section of the TWU organized in Nashville or any other city!* . . .
>
> There are 150,000 members of TWU who respect the Constitution of the United States and of our union. *We intend to continue fighting bigotry and ignorance on every front with our money, manpower and moral pressure. IF YOU DON'T ELECT TO STAY IN THE TRANSPORT WORKERS UNION YOU ARE FREE TO LEAVE. WE DON'T WANT GANGSTERS, DRUG ADDICTS OR TRAITORS IN TWU. WE WANT NEITHER BIRCHERS OR BESMIRCHERS OF HUMAN FREEDOM. WE DON'T NEED YOU.*[30]

Quill made clear in no uncertain terms the position of TWU leadership on segregation. In 1963, Vernon Bassom, a member of Local 514 in Tulsa, informed TWU leaders that he was proud to be a member of a union that practiced what it preached. He wrote that "the iniquities of segregation and inequality should have been corrected long ago, and I think the colored people would feel much better if the other races of people could realize that this problem is also their responsibility." Bassom assured TWU leaders that while not all members of Local 514 in Tulsa felt this way, he was sure those against the union's civil rights policy were in the minority.[31]

Such TWU leadership announcements were insufficient to overcome rank-and-file opposition to black employment. Such racial barriers were reinforced by federal policies as well as geography. The structure of the Railway Labor Act proved problematic for African Americans, in part due to the fact that the airlines and the railroads were governed by the act. Airline-industry bargaining-unit determinations made by the National Mediation Board under the act were influenced by the structure set for the railroad unions. Through "craft or class" bargaining units determined by the act, employees at an airline could not choose an industrial union to represent all workers. Through the craft or class units, airline workers often organized into several unions at the same company. For example, freight handlers and freight clerks, working in the same room, would not necessarily share the same union. The jurisdictional lines between jobs and the unions covering them were often vague, particularly regarding issues of promotion. The craft or class jurisdictions used under the Railway Act limited intracompany movement by employees because different jobs could have different seniority lists. Movement into a new job could mean moving into a new union that placed a person at the bottom of the seniority and wage list, a twofold loss of security. For African Americans at the bottom of the job ladder, moving up could mean taking such risks.[32]

Geography also played a crucial role in limiting the number of African Americans in the airline industry. Airports and aircraft-maintenance facilities almost without exception were located on the outskirts of cities. Airports in Chicago, Detroit, St. Louis, and Washington, D.C., were located in newer sections of the metropolitan area, far from minority neighborhoods. Public transportation to the airport was rarely available to inner-city residents.[33] Eddie Hall, an African American baggage handler hired in 1969, got to work at O'Hare Airport "by hook or by crook." When first hired in Chicago, he took the bus as far as it went and scrambled for a ride from there with other employees. Sometimes he traveled from his home on the West Side to the Palmer House Hotel downtown to catch the airport shuttle for two dollars one way, nearly an hour's wages as a new hire. After a few months on the job, he bought a used car for two hundred dollars and carpooled. According to Hall, a supervisor told him he had to buy a car to keep the job. He felt that this supervisor did not want African Americans working there and thought this "requirement" would force him to quit.[34]

Only the advent of new federal civil rights legislation and executive decisions broke the logjam against black airline employment. In 1961, under the growing pressure of civil rights leaders, President John F. Kennedy signed Executive Order 10925, which established the strongest federal support of equal employment opportunity since the Federal Employment Practices Commission of the World War II period. Industries with government contracts were among the first to be marked for supervision of racial policies. Such industries were formally monitored through the Office of Federal Contract Compliance.[35] The airlines, because of their U.S. mail and military cargo contracts, fell into that category.[36] In 1963, the U.S. Supreme Court ordered an end to discrimination in hiring on the airlines in a case involving an African American pilot and Continental Airlines.[37] A "Plans for Progress" program, implemented by Vice President Lyndon Johnson, encouraged the airline industry to voluntarily increase their recruitment of minorities. American, Northwest, Pan American, United, Trans World, and Eastern Airlines were among those companies to participate in the program.[38] Title VII of the landmark Civil Rights Act of 1964 made discrimination based on race, color, religion, sex, or national origin illegal in the American labor market. The legislation also created the Equal Employment Opportunity Commission (EEOC) to oversee the implementation and adherence to this law.

Between 1966 and 1969, African Americans nearly doubled their numbers in the airline industry, including some white-collar jobs.[39] In 1966, 235,984 people worked in the American air-transportation industry. Of that number, only 9,887 were African American, approximately 4.2 percent.[40] That year only 1.1 percent of all African Americans employed in the industry held white-collar jobs, and most of these were clerical. Of blue-collar jobs, only 2.2 percent of mechanics were African American, while 30.1 percent of the laborers and 14.3 percent of the service workers were African American.[41] By 1969, 326,517 people were employed in the air-transport industry. Of those, 17,731 were African American, approximately 5 percent. Workers with Spanish surnames numbered 8,801. That year African Americans made up 2.4 percent of the white-collar jobs and 8.6 percent of the blue-collar jobs. In the blue-collar category, 2.6 percent of those were recognized as "craftsmen," which included mechanics. African Americans made up 11.2 percent of the service jobs and 12.1 percent of the "operative" category that included baggage handling and other semi-skilled positions.[42]

In 1969, several airlines, including Pan Am, American, Trans World, Delta, Braniff, Northwest, Continental, United, and Eastern, participated in a program to recruit and train what they termed the "hardcore" urban unemployed. The Job Opportunities in the Business Sector (JOBS) program developed by the National Alliance of Businessmen (NAB) and the Department of Labor worked to find five hundred thousand jobs for the unemployed across the nation. NAB-JOBS also developed a summer youth-employment program. The airlines hired inner-city workers as general office clerks, typists, keypunch operators, stockroom helpers, mailroom personnel, aircraft cleaners, commissary helpers, and baggage handlers.[43] By 1970, Dallas-based Braniff's total minority (predominantly Hispanic and African American) employment had risen 94 percent, while its overall employment increase was only 11 percent. United Airlines, the largest U.S. airline in the 1960s, employed over fifty-two thousand people and trained approximately four hundred new urban workers by early 1970. Twelve percent of United's workforce was categorized as minority in 1969. In 1968 Pan Am employed 250 so-called hardcore workers at Miami, San Francisco, and New York, its major cities, and American Airlines trained approximately 350. Outside of the hardcore program, airlines also actively recruited minorities as stewardesses, reservations agents, and pilots.[44]

While airlines recruited and trained approximately one thousand unemployed people for entry-level blue- and white-collar jobs, the permanence of these positions was questionable. Some hires never made it through the training process, others quit during the first year, and still others lost their jobs in a wave of layoffs across the industry in 1969 and 1970. Once on the job, their new coworkers, white or black, did not always accept them. Baggage handlers whose ranks included such new hires viewed their new coworkers as very different from themselves.[45]

For "regular" white baggage handlers, a high-school diploma had been a requirement for employment.[46] By the late 1960s training in fleet services included tests for basic math and English comprehension and a physical examination, as well as learning the three-letter "city codes" used in the industry, operation of equipment, company policy, and the layout of the ramp. This training lasted approximately two weeks. For JOBS program new hires, training lasted up to thirty-six weeks, and a high-school diploma was not a requirement.[47] At Pan Am, trainees were introduced to "the world of work" and given job-retention counseling in the first week. New hires at the eighth-grade academic level went on to technical courses or direct job training. Those below the eighth grade level were given twelve to twenty weeks of job-related basic education and job-skills training. In the last phase, hires worked with job coaches to gradually bring them to the productivity level of "regular" coworkers.[48]

Experienced baggage handlers like Rob Kranski felt negatively about the new hires. Kranski, hired at American in 1967, recalled that many of them "had a bad attitude," which he found frustrating. He said, "They didn't care. That's what doesn't make sense. If you come out of the ghetto someone is giving you a chance, you would think that you would take it . . . that you would better yourself." At the same time, he recognized the obstacles many of the hardcore hires must have faced, although his perception of African Americans remained an important factor. In his recollection of a discussion with an African American coworker, he said,

> I did talk to one guy . . . he said to me, "I'm going to ask you some questions." He was a black guy. He says, "When you were growing up, and you didn't get good grades in school, what happened?" I says, "Well, you go home and your father tells you to straighten up. 'Start flying right.'"
>
> He says, "Well, when you're in a black home, chances are you didn't know who your father was. You didn't have anybody telling you you had to do this, this, and this. A lot of them didn't know their fathers and sometimes their mothers weren't even around . . . so chances for us to progress was a lot less because we didn't get the initial pushing." You know, the incentive wasn't there. And you know, I could see that part.[49]

For Kranski and some others, there was a big difference between the "regular" African American baggage handlers and the new hires. To him, race relations were not really an issue except with the so-called hardcore hires. The "regular" African American workers "set the standard" for the recent hires to follow. Some of the old-timers were men white and black workers could look up to. Kranski remembered, "There were a lot of old-time blacks that were great. I liked them. There were several of them I made real good friends with . . . one guy was like a father to me. . . . We had a lot of black guys that we looked up to, really nice guys." One of these men was popular enough among his coworkers to be the cause of a wildcat job action in 1967. Kranski offered this story abut "Pops" Courtney, an African American baggage handler: "There was one guy in particular, back in '67, when I started. They called him Pops. He was probably in his sixties already. One of the supervisors tried to fire him for almost delaying an aircraft. We liked him so much that we went in and complained and said, 'Hey, he's doing the best he can.' . . . They called him into the office anyway. We walked off the job in a wildcat strike for him." According to Kranski, the whole ramp, all the baggage handlers, walked off the job, and the ticket agents loaded bags and attempted to do the rest of the work.[50]

For some white baggage handlers like Martin Trizinski, the new black workers disrupted what they perceived to be harmonious race relations on the ramp. According to Trizinski, when he started working on the ramp in the mid-1950s there was "no racism" among the baggage handlers. People got along well on the job. To Trizinski, the hardcore program was like a "swinging door," and the men hired did not really want to work. According to Trizinski, the airline had to hire an extra supervisor to make sure the new people came to work. He would even go to their homes and get them out of bed to ensure they did so.[51]

Other white workers at American and United Airlines recalled the "hardcore" program as one that caused tension among workers on the ramp and failed to do much to change the racial makeup of the airlines. Millard Parker, who started on the ramp at American Airlines in 1953, after finishing high school in West Virginia, felt that the program was an "attack on the union and higher wages." The program was especially problematic for him because he believed it had been "forced by the government" onto the airlines and that it prevented other "honest people" from getting jobs in the airlines. He explained, "There were lots of guys who came from Iowa for jobs. They couldn't get jobs because of the hardcores. They felt like, 'What do I have to do? Shout at someone to get a job?!'" Parker believed that many of the hardcore hires brought trouble with them: "They called in sick, wouldn't work when they got there. Some things were gang-related. They smoked marijuana. But I didn't rat on them. I don't like people like that, like spies." For Parker, these workers did not contribute to what was good about working on the ramp; rather, they were interlopers who brought trouble. At the same time, he felt honor-bound to not "rat" on anyone. Like Kranski, Parker recalled race relations on the individual level in more friendly terms. He explained, "There was one young black guy, called Erikson, he called me 'Uncle Parker.'"[52]

Curtis Johnson, who was hired as a baggage handler at United Airlines in Chicago in 1964, had similar recollections. While he could not recall specifically how many African Americans worked on the ramp for United before the hardcore program, he explained, "You all worked close, you got along pretty well. Not everyone loved each other . . . but it was teamwork." Johnson said, referring to the hardcore hires, that even though "these men didn't want to work," some of them were still on the ramp when he retired in 1996.[53]

Roy Okamoto, a Japanese American man, came to work on the ramp for American Airlines in 1968. Born in Santa Ana, California, Okamoto came to Chicago with his family after spending three years interned at the Poston Camp in Arizona during World War II. Okamoto was generally more optimistic about the hardcore program than Kranski and Parker. Although "you couldn't get those guys to work" was Okamoto's first recollection of the program, he also explained that some of them worked out. He recalled, "They got used to the income. Some were terminated, but all in all, it worked out."[54]

For Okamoto, the growing presence of African Americans on the ramp and the Black Power movement changed his own relationship with white and black coworkers. As the only Asian American on the ramp at American in the late 1960s, he remembered being treated differently. Sometimes white coworkers would say things like, "Hey you, Slant-Eye," or, "Slow down, you ain't back on the rice paddies!" if he was working too fast. Okamoto recalled not minding too much, but he said, "The civil rights movement changed things. I could call them 'Creampuff' and 'Whitey' to the white guys!"[55]

Eddie Hall, an African American baggage handler, began his career in the airline industry as a so-called hardcore hire. In 1969, after three years in the armed forces, Hall returned to Chicago. He heard about jobs in the airline industry at the unemployment office. He was told that there were no "regular" jobs available in the airlines, so he was hired as part of the hardcore program. He received two months of training before starting full-time on the ramp. Hall felt that the program was not necessary in his case; he had plenty of self-discipline and work experience as a sergeant in the army. At the time, he entered the program because he needed the job.[56]

Hall also questioned the necessity of the program for other minority workers. He believed that the government and industry used the program to control black workers in response to the airline industry's claim they could find no qualified minorities to hire: "It was an unnecessary program. . . . It was strictly a program to keep an eye on minorities, that's what I think." Hall felt that the job could easily be learned in two weeks and that the extended training was a waste of time.

> A month after I was out of that class on the job, I knew that it wasn't necessary because when we was in the class it was like we were being treated like we were totally illiterates, we was being demeaned to the point where it wasn't necessary for us to be like that because what it takes to learn during that time period . . . what it took for you to do the job did not require nothing but maybe one week or two weeks of training, not no two months. That's what they would usually give their new employees, two weeks of training . . . the biggest part of the training was in the classroom, they wanted you to know the station codes and also safe use of the materials and the equipment that you need to load the airplane.[57]

For Hall the program was degrading, and the two months, instead of two weeks, meant that he had less seniority than if he had been hired through regular channels.

While white workers like Martin Trizinski, George Poulos, Rob Kranski, Millard Parker, Curtis Johnson, and Robert Slouber all felt that overall race relations on the ramp were fairly friendly, particularly on the individual level, Eddie Hall painted a different picture. The racism he experienced was not always overt—he witnessed no name-calling. It was often more a matter of preferential treatment by supervisors and crew chiefs. According to Hall, whites got the better jobs on the crew. African Americans ended up "in the belly" doing the loading by hand inside the cargo hold. In other cases, Hall said, white baggage handlers would sabotage the job an African American baggage handler was doing by loading the wrong bags into his cart or unhooking his carts from his tractor. He heard rumors of supervisors taking bets among themselves over which African Americans would be fired. At the same time, Hall did have friendly working relationships with many of his white coworkers. White and black baggage handlers would eat together during lunch breaks. However, he did not socialize with white coworkers off the job. In the 1980s, Hall served as a member of TWU Local 512's executive board.[58]

Very few of these new hires stayed on the ramp long enough to retire. Anecdotal evidence from retired baggage handlers and aircraft mechanics suggests that "hardcores" were let go for failing to come to work or perform their work duties on the ramp. However, the downturn in the airline industry after 1968 was an important factor in the failure of the program. Pan Am, in an internal memo regarding potential questions at the company's annual meeting in 1972, noted the failure of their hardcore program: "We did train and hire some community hard-core personnel but we fired or laid off approximately 99 percent of them. Later, we recalled 50 workers who had quit jobs with other companies to return to Pan Am and keep their seniority privileges. About 3 weeks after the recall, with the exception of approximately 20 Commissary workers, we proceeded to lay them off again. We are doing practically nothing in this area."[59]

The airlines faced multiple problems in the late 1960s. High wages, overcapacity, increasing fuel costs, a drop in airline stock prices, inflation, and upcoming capital costs of jumbo jets rattled the industry. Between October 1969 and March 1971, Pan Am laid off nearly 4,500 employees.[60] In 1971, total employment in the industry actually dipped below 1969 levels, according to EEOC figures. In 1969, 326,517 people worked for airlines employing over one hundred people. In 1971 that figure was 292,828. By 1975, however, that figure increased to 318,695. That year, African Americans made up 7 percent of the airline workforce, according to EEOC records.[61]

The introduction of nonwhite, hardcore unemployed men to the ramp was disruptive to white baggage handlers for a number of reasons. For men like Rob Kranski, Martin Trizinski, and Millard Parker, the hardcore program was unnecessary and an inappropriate use of government pressure and funds.[62] More importantly, the lower hiring standards and "bad attitude" of new hires challenged their own sense of worth on the job. The failure of the hardcore program reaffirmed their understanding of what attributes made a good baggage handler. Personality was as important as physical strength on the ramp. Whiteness also mattered. Among the white baggage handlers, a good worker could be black, but his ability to work hard failed to fully overcome the color barrier on the ramp.

Crafting Culture in Work and Leisure

As in the 1950s and early postwar years, the predominantly white fleet-service workers elaborated upon their workplace culture and used their unions to counteract management prerogative on the ramp. The following discussion examines the workplace culture of the ramp through the eyes of twelve baggage handlers at American and United Airlines. Their recollections shed light on how predominantly white male baggage handlers constructed the culture of the ramp through the 1960s. The baggage handlers' construction of their identity as workers was by no means a simple process. For these men, success and job satisfaction stemmed from their ability to get along with each other, control the work process, and uphold certain standards of masculinity.

Yet the ability to lift and load heavy or large objects was not the most important measure of masculinity. Rather, it was the ability to be social, participate in group activities, and adhere to group intentions that defined a man. Class issues within the airline structure also defined masculinity for baggage handlers. The absence of women on the ramp also contributed to the masculine identity of baggage handlers. The job remained the domain of men into the 1970s, with very few exceptions.

Working on the ramp often involved nearly as much "downtime" as work time and provided baggage handlers ample opportunities to forge a collective work culture. Loading and unloading and otherwise servicing a plane was completed in less than an hour, and a half an hour might pass before another airplane arrived at that gate. As George Poulos explained, "You do the job, then we sit and bullshit." The men spent their downtime drinking coffee, napping, talking, playing cards, chess, or backgammon, or "people-watching" in the terminal. As Curtis Johnson, who started as a baggage handler at United in 1964, remembered, up in the terminal, "We would people watch and drink coffee. It was interesting. It wasn't just ogling the girls."[63]

Terminal gate crews worked as a team led by their crew chief, who decided which man would take on which tasks. Some crew chiefs might delegate based on seniority, others on personal preference. Eddie Hall witnessed crew chiefs

Stanley Socha, Red Berndt, Joe Hebel, Jack Ellis, and other baggage handlers having fun at Midway Airport, Chicago, circa 1948–50. Photo from Robert Slouber, author's collection.

Baggage handlers Joe Hebel and Bob Gelms at Midway Airport, Chicago, circa 1948–50. Photo from Robert Slouber, author's collection.

assign African Americans the worst tasks on the gate. Martin Trizinski explained that "loners" or "introverts" often ended up with the worst positions because they did not incorporate themselves into the group.[64] Sometimes a baggage handler might perform the same tasks on each plane each day. Other crews might rotate the tasks so the most unpleasant job, "working the belly," would be shared.

A baggage handler's work time was determined by the seasons. In the winter, airplanes needed to be deiced. At Christmas, more baggage handlers were needed in the post-office and freight operations. In the summer, passenger travel usually increased with school vacations. Most large airline ground operations were scheduled in a series of shift bids. Several times a year, baggage handlers (and others) participated in a stationwide bid for new positions in their job category. The bidding was done in order of seniority. For example, a baggage handler who spent the summer working outside loading and unloading planes at the terminal could spend the winter in the freight building moving freight around for shipment. Through shift bids, baggage handlers could work with new coworkers every three or four months or could choose to work with the same four or five people year after year if their seniority permitted. This flexibility was one of the most attractive parts of the job. For James "Sully" Sullivan, shift bids meant that you could "pick which people you wanted to work with and avoid others." For Rob Kranski, bidding different jobs "kept it interesting." Over the years he worked in the freight house, at the terminal gates, in overnight cabin service, in the packing room preparing pillows, blankets, and movie headseats, and deicing aircraft.[65]

Wherever they worked, baggage handlers recognized that a worker's personality mattered more than his brute strength for getting along at the job.

Robert Slouber, hired in 1941, said that his biggest problems at work in more than forty years on the job stemmed from people's personalities. Although he recalls having to regularly unload several dozen heavy boxes by himself off freighters, a task requiring strength, Slouber said that the most important traits necessary to be good on the ramp were "common sense" and "being able to get along."[66] For George Poulos, a good baggage handler had to "get along with others, not take advantage of other people, understand the job, and not tell others what to do."[67] Eddie Hall felt that physical strength was an important factor for the job but that getting along with others was equally important.[68] Rob Kranski said that a person had to be "congenial" to do well on the ramp. In terms of physical ability, while strength was important, persistence mattered more. For Millard Parker, having personable coworkers made the job fun: "With 90 percent of people it was a fun job. Everyone had a good sense of humor, people didn't come in with a cold shoulder."[69]

"Getting along with others" meant getting along with other baggage handlers. More seasoned baggage handlers "helped" rookies learn to get along with others by example but also through pranks. Baggage handlers with seniority socialized new hires by playing tricks on them or making them perform the most unpleasant work assignments, a position sometimes outgrown only when a man with lower seniority appeared. A classic prank at the airport called for sending a rookie for a nonexistent piece of equipment. In the 1940s, experienced baggage handlers sent a new hire on a wild goose chase for a "bay stretcher." As Robert Slouber recalled, the men told the rookie, "Go down to Braniff there and get a bay stretcher for us. . . . [At Braniff] they said, 'Well, we don't have one. You have to go to TWA.' And they kept sending him to different airlines. They all knew what was going on. They did this to guys that were slow. This guy was gone for six hours! He kind of caught on after a while."[70] New hires were especially targeted if they were slow on the job or "smart alecs." Importantly, baggage handlers at one airline could count on their counterparts at other companies to continue the prank.

Pranks could serve purposes other than socializing new hires. Baggage handlers used pranks to get back at supervisors they felt were too strict. George Poulos recalled cutting a supervisor's tie as a joke and greasing a telephone receiver. Roy Okamoto remembered workers taking the keys out of running "blues" (company station wagons) when supervisors got out to check on workers on the ramp. Sometimes the keys would end up down a sewer grate.[71]

Downtime between flights also offered baggage handlers time to play tricks on each other. Richard Sobczak described playing pranks on fellow workers, including Bob Slouber, whom he described as a friend and sometimes an impatient crew chief. Sobczak recalled, "We liked the comical stuff. One time we nailed his lunch pail to the table. When he tried to pick it up, the handle came right off. Bob Slouber hated pizza, it would make him sick. Guys would bring in pizza and put it in his lunch pail. Slouber was always a Dodge man. When he was gone [from the work area], they jacked up his car just off the ground, when he tried to drive away his car isn't going, he can't understand. What happened? He was swearing, he rocked the car off the jack and away he went!"[72]

Time spent sleeping on the job left baggage handlers vulnerable to pranks. Sobczak described how sleeping created the perfect element of surprise: "We worked with this Jewish guy, Harold Brown, I used to say, 'How come you're Jewish and you're working for a living?' He should have owned a business. Anyway, we covered his glasses with ink while he was napping. When the crew chief told us we had to wake up and go outside and work the freighter, he couldn't see. He thought he was blind!" Another naptime prank was played on an African American baggage handler named Willie: "He always wore suspenders. When he was sleeping we would put them through the chair so when he got up the chair would pull him back. We also put them around the door of the freighter—they pulled him back onto the plane." Some pranks required the help of workers from outside the ranks of baggage handlers. Richard Sobczak described a joke played on a baggage handler well-known for his ability to "sleep standing up behind a forklift" in the air freight building. As Sobczak recalled, baggage handlers took this coworker and locked him in the belly of a plane. Aircraft mechanics ferried the plane to the hangar. When they let him out he was greeted with a birthday cake.[73]

Transporting coffins with bodies in them was perhaps one of the most unusual aspects of the job. Several retired baggage handlers remembered coworkers who were uncomfortable with the task of moving "Jim Wilsons," the American Airlines term for human-remains cargo. Millard Parker explained, "Some guys would open the boxes and look at the dead people. . . . Black guys were really afraid to handle these boxes." As a joke, a white baggage handler climbed into an empty casket, and when his coworkers got close enough he started moaning and opened the casket and sat up, scaring especially one of his African American coworkers. According to Parker, some black baggage handlers would not move a body off a plane: "That was their way. It didn't cause hard feelings, we just took care of each other."[74]

Transporting caskets became a particularly difficult task during the 1960s because of the Vietnam War. Of the fifteen retired baggage handlers interviewed, half had served in the military before or during their years on the ramp. As Ken Ahern explained, "The worst part was the days we had to take coffins off the planes from California." United Airlines shipped the remains of servicemen into the interior of the country. Ken Thiede, a retired aircraft mechanic at United, remembered being sent to Fort Bragg to work on a plane in service for the war. "People in the airlines were generally supportive of the war. A lot of guys were ex-GIs. You didn't find too many draft-card burners at the airlines."[75]

While working at the terminal gates brought baggage handlers into some contact with pilots, stewardesses, ticket agents, and passengers, they had little formal contact with other airline employees. They saw stewardesses while they cleaned the aircraft between flights.[76] They met with ticket agents briefly at the gate working on the same flight. They saw mechanics when they were called out to the ramp to check on an aircraft in the process of being loaded. Baggage handlers shared the ramp with pilots when the latter did a visual check of the aircraft before departure.[77]

Baggage handlers' interaction with other employees of their airline was limited but remained an important part of their self-definition. Some felt strongly that other work groups at the airline looked down on them. Eddie Hall thought that the colloquial job title "baggage handler" was degrading and that "most people felt the job was degrading."[78] Martin Trizinski felt that the aircraft mechanics treated the baggage handlers decently, especially since they belonged to the same union.[79] At United, baggage handler Randy Canale and aircraft mechanic Ken Thiede thought the two groups got along well enough, particularly because they shared a union. Curtis Johnson thought baggage handlers and mechanics got along "fair," although "the two worlds didn't really get together." Rob Kranski perceived baggage handlers to be lowest in status at the airline and believed that other employees felt that way.[80] Kranski explained, "I didn't like the image we had with the office employees and flight attendants. We were stereotyped. They always referred to us as 'ramp rats.' And they always had the opinion that we were the lowlifes. That we lived like rats and looked like rats and smelled like rats. We had no credibility." While George Poulos remembered some socializing outside of work with some ticket agents and stewardesses, Rob Kranski described a different experience, "They [ticket agents] would have parties, and they wouldn't invite fleet-service clerks [baggage handlers]. There were a couple of guys who infiltrated the barriers. They were going out with a couple of ticket agents. They would have Christmas parties. They would invite lots of company employees. Sometimes the company would sponsor parties, and they would only have fliers on bulletin boards in the ticket-agent areas. Very, very few men got to date some of these girls that worked as ticket agents.

... They got to go to these parties, and the girls told these men, 'You keep your mouth shut.' We were shunned. They thought that we were a bunch of troublemakers."[81] Roy Okamoto recalled baggage handlers going up into the terminal to flirt or "make conversation" with ticket agents, to no avail: "They did not want to associate with us." This disdain was a challenge to baggage handlers' masculinity. In the eyes of these women, the job made them unworthy as potential dates or even spouses.[82]

Even if baggage handlers had difficulty socializing across work groups, some did forge social ties with each other, on and off the ramp. Richard Sobczak recalled some socializing with other baggage handlers outside of work. For him, his socializing was usually among others who lived in the south and southwest suburbs of Chicago. A few times other baggage handlers came over to his house. He said one event even included "one black guy named Clarence Dair, and a few Spanish." Eddie Hall recalled eating with white and black coworkers on lunch breaks at work but socializing only with black coworkers outside of work. James Sullivan, who started on the ramp at American in 1954, had a birthday party at his house with nearly one hundred coworkers in attendance. Curtis Johnson, who started at United in 1964, remembered socializing often with coworkers outside of the ramp.[83]

Aircraft mechanics at Midway Airport, Chicago, circa 1948–50. Photo from Robert Slouber, author's collection.

The odd days off for airline workers, especially those with low seniority, meant that planning activities with non-airline friends and family could be complicated. As Ken Thiede explained, "We had a lot in common." Airline employees often worked holidays and weekends. Ken Ahern, hired as a baggage handler at United in Boston in 1958, remembered attending weddings and christenings for friends on the ramp. When he was single, he spent off-time with airline friends, going to the beach, playing golf, or fishing. George Poulos socialized regularly with coworkers off the ramp, most often without wives or family. He remembered especially going to "airline" bars near the airport after finishing a shift. Millard Parker also remembered socializing with other baggage handlers, particularly when he was single: "There was ten or fifteen guys in 1953, all young. We went to bars, we were close-knit, we went fishing." Airline employees could also make going to bars or out to eat an exotic adventure thanks to their flight benefits. Parker recalled taking a Boeing 707 with a friend to California. The men would sit in first-class, eat lobster and filet mignon, and drink whiskey "like kings." He said, "We wouldn't even leave the airport and come back drunk."[84]

Holding some control of the work process was central to the baggage handlers' workplace culture. Controlling the speed of loading and unloading planes and moving freight and the level of care they took demanded the participation of baggage handlers as a group. Airlines recognized that these were two important ways that baggage handlers impacted service. With the increased volume of passenger baggage and variety of destinations worldwide, damage and loss of luggage and its contents continued to be a concern for passengers and airline management, which heightened the importance attached to fleet-service work. Most often, a misdirected bag was reunited with its owner within twelve to twenty-four hours.[85] Nonetheless, reimbursing passengers for lost or damaged luggage was costly. In 1963, U.S. domestic trunk lines paid approximately $1,200,000 in claims on 87,000 pieces of damaged baggage.[86]

Airlines continued training baggage handlers to see their work as part of the "service" of the airline. At TWA, a dummy named "Mr. PAWOB (Passenger Arriving Without Baggage) rode around the airline's system in aircraft cargo bellies to remind employees of "stray baggage problems."[87] Pan Am implemented a training program that encouraged employees to "think service" when it came to loading bags.[88] Small airlines, such as North Central in the upper Midwest, also developed their own training campaigns to combat damage to passenger baggage. Some damaged luggage implied a kind of worker sabotage in retaliation against mistreatment by company officials or even passengers. In 1962, North Central printed a series of posters comically portraying good and bad characteristics of employees. "A Masher" portrayed a careless baggage handler: "Why waste steps? If I can toss a bag for a distance of five feet from cart to compartment—then that's the way I do it. The nicks and tears mean nothing to me—it's not my bag. I enjoy the way the luggage flattens out when I pile freight and express on top of it. My foot comes in mighty handy when loading that last stubborn piece of cargo. IF I CAN'T FIT 'EM, I JAM 'EM."[89] Airlines recognized that damaged or lost baggage, no matter how excellent the service experience at the ticket counter or in the air, could leave passengers infuriated and end their business with a given carrier. Roy Okamoto remembered that workers would sometimes delay bags on purpose when frustrated with management. Baggage handlers would "forget to load it" and leave a cart or pod (container) behind: "A fleet service clerk gets a C-3 [discipline], but the company has to deliver all those bags."[90]

Damaged and lost baggage was not the only cause of concern for employers. Late departures also frustrated passengers, and airlines developed

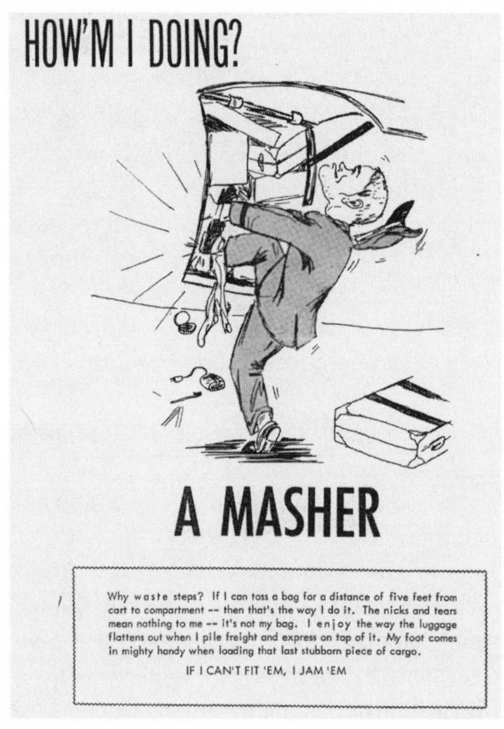

"A Masher," Project '62, North Central Airlines, 1962. Republic Airlines Records, Minnesota Historical Society.

systems to track the causes of late departures. According to Rob Kranski, overwhelmingly, baggage handlers were blamed for such incidents despite the actual fault. Whenever an aircraft was over four minutes late to leave the terminal gate, a written report was submitted explaining why the plane was delayed. According to Kranski, delays were regularly blamed on fleet services even if the actual cause was late passengers or a late crew, and management blindly accepted these reports. Although they were frequently blamed for delays beyond their control, baggage handlers did use work slow-downs as a way to show dissatisfaction on the job. They slowed down operations over rules they felt were unfair, supervisors who played favorites, management clampdowns on tardiness, or when a contract was open for negotiation.[91] "Work-to-rule" was a particularly effective way to make a statement on the ramp. This action, doing all tasks while following all the rules regarding the job, showed how much the company relied on the baggage handlers' innate knowledge of the job for smooth operations. Roy Okamoto explained that there was no way to get a plane out on time if a crew followed all the safety procedures at American Airlines. Although work-to-rule was an important tactic for expressing discontent, Okamoto remembered feeling bad for the passengers stuck on delayed flights. By strictly following the rules, baggage handlers could snarl operations for hours. As George Poulos explained, "A fleet-service clerk can ruin a supervisor . . . if the supervisor gives a hard time, he needs a lesson, go by the book."[92]

In the mid-1970s, a controversy with a single manager over the length of the lunch period erupted at the freight-operations building in Chicago. The baggage handlers at the freight house followed all the safety rules and tagged dozens of pieces of loading equipment for repair. Over 350 containers of freight could not be moved, resulting in delays throughout the airline's freight system. When the manager was removed from the post, operations returned to schedule within a day.[93] Baggage handlers, working within the rules of the ramp, could severely curtail operations to show their dissatisfaction and the importance of tacit skills required to get the job done in a timely manner.

The tremendous increase in airline cargo handling in the 1960s due to increased capacity and deterioration in railroad systems made damage to and theft of cargo as well as snarled operations central concerns to airline management. Between 1948 and 1968, the volume of domestic freight handled by the industry increased by two billion ton-miles.[94] Until the 1960s, theft of baggage or cargo was a negligible problem for the airlines. Prior to the jet age, airlines paid claims for damage and loss that equaled less than 1.5 percent of total freight revenues.[95] However, by the late 1960s, theft and pilferage of airfreight skyrocketed, and claims by shippers and the airlines for cargo losses tripled between 1968 and 1969.[96] According to one study of international air cargo operations in the mid-1960s, approximately 90 percent of all stolen items were relatively small and easily converted into cash, and nearly 60 percent of all thefts were perpetrated by air-cargo-handling employees.[97] Cargo-handling employees included workers for freight-forwarding and shipping companies as well as airline workers. Baggage handlers had ready access to baggage and freight during the loading process as well as in staging areas.

New York airports were the sites of several famous cargo heists in the late 1960s, some of which may have involved baggage handlers as well as organized crime.[98] In July 1969, Kennedy Airport was robbed twice, resulting in losses of nearly one million dollars. On July 13, armed thieves stole $340,000 from an Air France consignment, and a week later armed thieves dressed in Pan Am fleet-service uniforms stole $600,000 in cash from the Pan Am cargo building. These robbers used the colloquial term "crib" to describe the valuables lockup at the facility.[99] Airfreight theft at Kennedy Airport

Loading cars at Pan American Airways, 1960s. Pan American World Airways, Inc., Records, series 1, box 230, folder 15, Special Collections, University of Miami Libraries, Coral Gables, Fla.

Loading freight at Pan American Airways, John F. Kennedy Airport, 1960s. Pan American World Airways, Inc., Records, series 1, box 230, folder 15, Special Collections, University of Miami Libraries, Coral Gables, Fla.

involved organized crime and individual thieves at airline freight buildings and particularly freight-only operations run by freight forwarders. Baggage handlers were only a small factor in freight theft.[100]

High-profile banditry was not the only, nor the main, cause of cargo loss at the airports. According to New York Port Authority reports, in 1966, $877,350 worth of goods was stolen from New York airports. In 1967 that figure jumped to nearly $2.3 million. In 1968, the figure dropped to $1.8 million. The Airport Security Council, a group formed in reaction to a legislative threat to turn over airport security to the Waterfront Commission of the Port of New York, reported that a significant proportion of that loss came from pilferage, meaning the theft of individual items from larger shipments rather than entire shipments.[101] In 1969, the value of stolen air cargo at New York–area airports surged to $3.7 million. That year the airports handled nearly $10 billion worth of cargo. Nearly $3.4 million of that figure was attributed to loss at Kennedy Airport. This high figure related to the volume of cargo handled through that airport and the inadequacy of the facilities. Cargo warehouses at the airport were spilling over with goods. Often, cargo had to be stored out in the open for hundreds of yards along the airport ramp and runways. Pan Am's operations were particularly chaotic, as the airline was in the midst of moving into a new cargo facility.[102]

The Airport Security Council and the airlines themselves worked to combat the chaos and theft at New York's airports, and at Kennedy in particular. Airline employees wore photo-identification badges while on the job. The Security Council and the airlines instituted a series of crime-prevention procedures, including inspections by the Security Council that could lead to recommendations or notices of violation for poorly secured areas. Individual airlines installed dual-lens cameras that photographed cargo drivers and their papers at the same time and employed full-time security detectives and guards. Some airlines installed closed-circuit TV systems and additional secured areas and vaults and made basic changes in their cargo-facility layouts for improved security. These changes brought a dramatic reduction in cargo-theft rates at New York airports. In 1970, the total value of stolen cargo was approximately $1.5 million. Of that figure, $1.4 million was attributed to Kennedy Airport.[103]

For many of his years on the job, Robert Slouber worked in the freight department at Midway Airport and later at O'Hare Airport in Chicago. In the early 1950s, the police and FBI questioned Slouber regarding a robbery at the freight house:

> One day I just got to work, and my wife called me. And she said, "Robert, there were two plainclothes cops looking for you."
>
> I said, "For what?" She said, "They wouldn't say but they're coming out to you [at the airport]." As it turns out, they came over there, and I was waiting for them. . . . There was two FBI guys there too!
>
> Two Chicago detectives and two FBI guys. They said, "Come on with us, we're going upstairs to talk [at Chicago Municipal Airport freight building]." I got there and sat down and said, "Can you tell me what's going on?" So they says, "Never mind, we'll get to that." So they asked me these questions: "Where were you this day? Where were you that day? We understand you've got a new boat." I said, "No, no. I traded in my other boat on that one." And I said, "I can show you that I took the money out of the credit union to pay for it." They said, "Well, you got a new car too." And I said, "No, I didn't get a new car, I got a used car. Who told you that? [They said,] "Never mind that, we know what's going on."
>
> They checked into all this stuff. . . . After two and a half hours of questioning me, I said, "I'm getting tired of this! Look, let's go down to John Reed downtown." Which was the lie detector test at that time. I don't know whether they have it there anymore. . . .
>
> I said, "I didn't steal nothing here. I don't even know what's missing." I found out that there was about fifty thousand dollars in cameras and that, that were in the special room they had, and it ended up where one of the crew chiefs that was on [duty] there on the Sunday night it was missing, and this crew chief was the one that saw to it that the stuff was stolen. He turned his back while friends of his emptied the place out. And the only way to get in there

> is by someone leaving the door open or someone that knew it had a special lock on it. So it turned out this guy got nabbed, and there was about four or five other people involved. . . . I think one was a fleet-service clerk, but the other two were outsiders.[104]

Robbery was not the only reason goods or even shipments of cash could go missing. In the early 1970s, Slouber stumbled across a bag of money in the snow. At the beginning of the spring thaw, he was moving a pile of pallets that had been stacked over the winter. Using a forklift, he came across a registered pouch that was split open. From the forklift Slouber could see that it was full of cash and checks. He notified a company manager and a postal inspector. They returned to the scene where the clean snow showed he had not walked near enough the bag to touch it. The bag, containing nearly thirty thousand dollars, had fallen off a Continental Airlines baggage cart over the winter.[105]

Despite the temptations of millions of dollars of freight, Robert Slouber said, in his experience, freight or baggage theft was rare. As a freight-crew chief, he told his men he would not tolerate stealing and would report anyone he saw pilfering to management. On his shift, he never caught anyone on his crew stealing.[106] Other retired baggage handlers recalled hearing about more theft than they actually witnessed. George Poulos, hired in 1956, said that he never witnessed any stealing from passenger baggage, but if he had, he might have looked the other way. Roy Okamoto, a crew chief, warned baggage handlers on his crew not to steal but said it was even worse to be a snitch. Theft in the "bag room," the underground sorting facility, was also a problem. According to Roy Okamoto, baggage handlers would cover the lenses of security cameras. The company did attempt sting operations by sending tempting items such as "open boxes of booze" through the sortation system. The boxes were empty at the end of the belt system. Eddie Hall, hired in 1969, attributed theft to human nature: "No matter where they work, their hands will stick to something."[107]

Martin Trizinski, a baggage handler from 1955 through the mid-1990s, never witnessed theft from passenger baggage but did hear of one baggage handler who stole a variety of goods from freight shipments and was caught for his carelessness. According to Trizinski, this man's thievery was known among his coworkers. He stole a coin collection and jade statues from shipments. He was caught after fifteen years on the job when he showed a supervisor the new radio in his car. The supervisor suspected it to be stolen and copied down the serial numbers off the item. After he was caught, it was rumored that his house was piled high with company blankets, first-class silverware, and similar items.[108]

Pilferage of company property was more common than theft from passenger baggage. Rob Kranski, a baggage handler from 1967 to the mid-1990s, said that baggage handlers ate food and stole liquor from the planes, particularly during his early years on the job. One man was fired in the mid-1970s for "making a business" of stealing the tiny liquor bottles. According to Kranski, he actually sold the bottles to liquor stores.[109]

Drinking liquor from the planes was common during the overnight cleaning shift. Kranski worked that shift in the late 1960s. As he recalled,

> It was very common for these guys to have a drink during work. There was very little supervision at the time, other than they would check your work when you were done. I didn't drink, so when I came on there, they thought I was a plant. . . . They said, "Come on in back over here, we're having a little party." I said, "I'll be back there later." They said, "No, no. We want you back here now." I said, "Why?" They said, "We want to talk to you." There were six or seven guys back there [in the back of the plane]. I said, "Okay. What's up?" They said, "Well, we want you to have a drink with us." I said, "Sorry, I don't drink." The one guy said, "You don't understand," and got in my face. "Either you have a drink, or you don't work here [on overnight cabin cleaning], or we meet you after work." He said, "Don't ask any questions, what would you like?" I said, "Well, if I have to have something, I'll have a small glass of wine." Then they said I could go back and do my work. The reason is, they felt that you can't go in front of a supervisor and say this, this, and this with alcohol on your breath . . . you have to be in the clique.[110]

Midnight cabin cleaning was done at the hangar, away from possible passenger scrutiny. According to Kranski, some supervisors knew this was going on, and it was common knowledge that the midnight cabin cleaning crew was a job often chosen by alcoholics. James Sullivan concurred: "Everyone wanted to collect those [little bottles]. People had them at home, they'd show them off." The bottles were a problem on the ramp as well. Sullivan explained, "People started drinking them. . . . We'd make a cooler and have beers in the truck. People almost became alcoholics. When traffic backed up and catering couldn't keep up [with deliveries], you'd see thirty guys running to the hangar."[111]

Having such control over work time was one of the "best things" about the job. Almost all retired baggage handlers interviewed between 1997 and 2007 described the autonomy, camaraderie, pay, and benefits as the best parts of the job. Several also remarked on the pride they took in working in the airline industry. James Sullivan, who started on the ramp in 1954, liked his work as a manning coordinator best. In this job Sullivan placed baggage handlers in overtime shifts and covered absences. "I started at 3:00 AM and had ten cups of coffee by 10:00 AM." When baggage handlers would come by the manning office for their assignments, Sullivan said, "I got to see everyone, and I knew everybody there." George Poulos too liked the people he worked with. He explained that even though he was the only Greek on the ramp, "Everyone got along so well, you couldn't wait to get to work." Martin Trizinski, who started on the ramp in 1955, said, "A lot of times it was fun, we had fun. The pay was decent, and the benefits good." For John Gales, an immigrant from Holland who started working on the ramp in 1959, the best job was in air freight. He liked the people who bid there, he liked the work, and he especially enjoyed unloading the flower shipments from Europe. For Rob Kranski and for Millard Parker, the variety of work was important, as Parker pointed out: "Every day was a different job." For Roy Okamoto, the opportunity to work overtime was an important part of the job. Some years he could nearly double his base salary with overtime. Richard Sobczak, who joined American in 1952, "really loved the job," especially because he could meet lots of people—coworkers, the public, and movie stars included—and work outdoors. For others, working outdoors was not among the best parts of the job. In fact, most baggage handlers interviewed said working outside in inclement weather was the worst part of working on the ramp.[112]

Up through the 1960s, airline work maintained its glamorous aura even among baggage handlers. Working in the industry set workers apart from their neighbors, and the unique opportunities possible with flight benefits were highly valued. For Ken Ahern, who started on the ramp at United in 1958, the work was "different from what everyone else did." Millard Parker recalled returning to his hometown in West Virginia and regaling his old friends and neighbors with airline stories: "Airplane talk is kind of fascinating to people who don't know about it." Eddie Hall, hired through the NAB-JOBS program, said that in the early days he felt proud working for a major airline. He was taking care of himself and his family and "serving the public, helping people travelling." For John Gales, the Dutch immigrant, the flight benefits made it a fantastic job. He could take his wife and six children to visit family in Europe.[113]

Retired baggage handlers at American and United recognized the power of union membership, particularly through the contracts, which covered aircraft mechanics and baggage handlers. Contractual power came from cross-skill

Above: The weather could be the worst part of the job. Cartoon from Southern Airways employee magazine, *The Southernaire* 2.12 (December 1951). The Republic Airlines Records, Minnesota Historical Society.

Left: Passengers come first. Cartoon from Southern Airways employee magazine, *The Southernaire* 3.4 (April 1952). The Republic Airlines Records, Minnesota Historical Society.

unionization. As Randy Canale explained, when the IAM began organizing at United Airlines in the 1940s, they challenged the United Mine Workers, CIO, which was trying to organize baggage handlers. According to Canale, the IAM recognized early on that they needed to bring baggage handlers as well as aircraft mechanics into the union. Millard Parker also attributed the TWU's power to organizing the two work groups together. Martin Trizinski felt that relations between aircraft mechanics and baggage handlers were good in the 1950s and 1960s, until some mechanics became "prima donnas" and wanted to bargain separately. Richard Sobczak said, "Some mechanics because they had their license thought they were big wheels. They didn't want to associate with us [socially]. [Even though] the Teamsters were trying to get the mechanics, the mechanics wanted to stick together." Roy Okamoto believed that bargaining with the mechanics benefited baggage handlers: "They had better pay, but we got something too. If they didn't get anything good, we didn't get anything." The retired baggage handler James Sullivan believed that the union's strength came from bargaining together with the aircraft mechanics. Reflecting on the separation of baggage handlers and aircraft mechanics in the TWU local in Chicago in 2002, he explained, "We were holding them back." He attributed his good fortune to the union: "People were overpaid. . . . I never finished high school, and look at the money I was making! I give credit to the union."[114]

* * *

The 1960s was a period of tremendous change for the American airline industry. The introduction of jet aircraft catapulted the industry into a new era. For passengers this meant unprecedented speed and luxury on board. For airline workers on the ground this meant new dangers, new insecurities, but ultimately significantly expanded operations and increased employment. Expanded operations meant a more impersonal workplace but also gave baggage handlers the venue in which to develop their own workplace culture exclusive from, but in part formed by, other airline workers. This culture valued personality and sociability over brute strength. Veteran baggage handlers indoctrinated new workers into the culture of the ramp through lesson and example. Fairness in dealings with each other as well as fair and equitable treatment on the part of supervisory personnel was important to baggage handlers, and they withheld the tacit skills required to make operations run smoothly to get their point across when their working conditions became unacceptable.

This decade also brought the challenge of civil rights and race to the door of the airline industry. Despite government intervention and government-business collaboration on diversifying the workplace, the percentage of African Americans in the industry remained under 10 percent of the air-transportation workforce. Rank-and-file white resistance, federal job classification procedures, and geographical barriers all hampered the employment and ascent of black workers. African Americans who did gain and maintain fleet-service jobs often met hostility. Black workers challenged predominantly white male baggage handlers' perceptions of what kind of person should work on the ramp. Only slowly did some African American baggage handlers gain acceptance among their white coworkers. For white baggage handlers, these men proved their mettle and embodied the values necessary for success on the ramp despite the adjusted standards under which some of them hired on. While African Americans challenged the predominantly white and male workforce, only during the late 1970s would the ranks of baggage handlers give way to a more diverse and somewhat more equitable workplace.

6

Militance and the Mutual Aid Pact, 1960–70

In late June 1966, the United Airlines baggage handler Randy Canale came back to work after months off the job recovering from surgery for a back injury on the ramp. It had been a difficult recovery compounded by anxiety over a sick child. As the twenty-one-year old Canale recuperated, his infant son was hospitalized with spinal meningitis. Friends on the ramp in Philadelphia thought he was crazy to return to work while eligible for workman's compensation. However, Canale wanted to get back to the ramp to go on strike. Canale, now president and general chairman of District Lodge 141 of the IAM and member of the United Airlines Board of Directors, recalls that the airlines strike of 1966 was when "labor grew up" in the industry.

After several years of stilted wage gains as the airline industry invested heavily in jet technology, aircraft mechanics and other ground-service workers represented by the IAM were anxious to share in the substantial profits of 1965. Facing a bargaining impasse between the IAM and the five carriers covered in the industry's first multicarrier labor contract, a Presidential Emergency Board presented a "compromise" package. In the summer of 1966, IAM members rejected this compromise and walked off the job in the largest strike in airline history. For forty-three days during the peak summer travel season, 60 percent of the U.S. commercial airline industry was inoperative as thirty-five thousand workers stayed out on strike.

Labor historians are beginning to uncover the rank-and-file militancy of the 1960s, which was, until recently, understudied, as scholars of the era focused instead on social movements and civil rights. Buttressed by the Landrum-Griffin Act in 1959 and the auto industry's Lordstown Strike in 1972,

Big Labor's reputation for the decade is often one of fierce anti-Communism, corruption, racial entrenchment, violence, and increasing conservatism. Nonetheless, between 1960 and the early 1970s, rank-and-file workers continued to lay claim to postwar prosperity via strikes and aggressive bargaining. During a high employment economy, rank-and-file workers expressed their concerns about inflation, automation, and their share of growing profits by rejecting contracts and leaders that did not address their concerns.

The 1966 strike was a turning point not only for airline workers but workers across U.S. industries. For airline workers the strike proved to be a tremendous victory that opened the door for enormous contractual gains over the next decade. For workers across America, the strike served as the "threshold of a wage explosion."[1] This strike, in the glory years of this major service industry, destroyed President Lyndon Johnson's economic policy for controlling inflation as rank-and-file members soundly rejected a contract offer negotiated at the White House. The strike tested the airline industry's Mutual Aid Pact and forced Congress to grapple with the political fallout of declaring a national emergency and enacting antistrike legislation. The strike also highlighted tensions around skill and wages among baggage handlers and aircraft mechanics, opening the door to raiding by the new craft-based union, the Aircraft Mechanics Fraternal Association.

Bargaining and the Mutual Aid Pact

The Mutual Aid Pact, constructed by the airline industry in 1958 to counteract the wage increases airline unions made through whipsawing, changed the length of strikes during the 1960s and served as the backdrop for the industry's first ever multicarrier bargaining in 1965. Between 1951 and 1958 there were twenty-six strikes in the U.S. airline industry and twenty-three strikes between 1959 and 1966. Although the number of strikes was relatively unchanged, the length of strikes did change. Between 1951 and 1958 airline strikes lasted an average of 13.3 days. From 1959 to 1966, airline strikes lasted an average of 25.3 days. While some airlines now had greater resources via the Mutual Aid Pact to withstand the financial pressure of a drawn-out strike, the longer strikes also indicated continued or even growing resolve among strikers to stay on strike. The pact also seemed to impact the length of contracts bargained in the industry. In 1960 and 1961 the majority of airline labor contracts were set to open after one year. From 1961 through 1969, ALPA, the IAM, and the TWU contracts were bargained for two- and three-year periods.[2]

The Mutual Aid Pact did not change the tenor of contract negotiations. As in 1958, the negotiating process remained long, drawn-out, contentious, and with government intervention. Throughout 1962 the IAM met with seven airlines[3] to hammer out an agreement for industrywide bargaining. No agreement was reached; however, the union and the airlines did agree to simultaneously exchange proposals for seven items, including pay, benefits, and job progression, even if contracts were not set to reopen. After a year of talks, seven strike threats, and two Presidential Emergency Boards, five of the seven airlines made uniform agreements with the IAM, including a wage rate of $3.52 per hour for mechanics, increased shift differentials, 100 percent employer payment for accident and sickness insurance, and improved vacation time. While IAM officers were generally pleased with these gains, there was some dissatisfaction with the attempt at multicarrier bargaining among the rank and file where members felt that contracts should be ratified by local members even in the case of expanded bargaining.[4]

In the spring of 1965, IAM leadership readied its members for bargaining at eight airlines. Buoyed by record airline profits in 1964, the IAM president Al Hayes told members, "We cannot afford limited wage increases. Despite the so-called guidelines, there are not legal wage controls in the USA, just as there are no controls on the profits these companies make." Hayes declared that airline workers would not accept less than recent settlements in auto and other basic industries.[5]

After more than a decade of discussion, five airlines and the IAM agreed to joint negotiations in August 1965. This was the first multicarrier bargaining in the history of the industry.[6] The IAM had pursued multicarrier bargaining since the early 1950s. However, with the advent of the Mutual Aid Pact and the sophistication of jet technology, such a strategy was increasingly important to the IAM. At the 1960 IAM convention, the union passed Resolution 103, approving industrywide bargaining in the airlines as a goal. Set contract dates would make possible simultaneous strikes on all the airlines in the Mutual Aid Pact, diminishing the effectiveness of the agreement. Uniform terms of employment for aircraft mechanics especially could offer greater mobility across airlines and create a disincentive for airlines to move maintenance operations to lower-wage states. This multicarrier bargaining took place against the backdrop of the AFL-CIO campaign to repeal the "Right to Work" section 14(b) of the Taft-Hartley Act. Further, multicarrier bargaining fit the traditional patterns of railroad bargaining, a system most familiar to the IAM.[7]

The IAM entered the negotiations as a growing union under their new president, LeRoy Siemiller. In one year, the IAM had added one hundred thousand members, had a full (ten-million-dollar) strike fund, and claimed to be the third largest union in the nation. At twenty-three, Siemiller first joined the IAM in 1929 and became a grand lodge representative, organizing railroad workers in 1937. His slogan, one that would serve as a rallying call during the strike, was, "A go-go union for workers that want action."[8]

The mid-1960s marked a transitional moment for organized labor. While the number of unionized workers had actually dropped since its peak in 1957, unionization in service, education, and the public sector incorporated new members. Organized American workers enjoyed higher pay, better benefits, and more leisure time than ever before. Increased productivity and a tightening labor market bolstered union demands at the bargaining table. However, concerns about automation, inflation, and waiting for the boom times to bust tempered economic optimism. The concerns and gains of union labor extended to airline workers as well.

The mid-1960s marked the glory years of air travel. Soon after the American airline industry first introduced jet aircraft in 1959, passengers embraced jet travel. The five airlines came to the table with a growing share of commercial passenger and cargo transport. In 1950 only 14 percent of all intercity commercial passenger transportation was by air. In 1965 that number had risen to 59 percent, and flying was cheaper for the American public than in 1950. A comparison between consumer prices in 1950 and 1965 showed a decrease of nearly 10 percent for air travel over those fifteen years. Jet aircraft and containerization contributed to record growth in domestic air freight. Between 1960 and 1965 air-freight cartage rose 90 percent. Industry growth averaged 14 percent annually between 1950 and 1965, as compared to the Gross National Product at 4 percent on average. Although the industry had suffered a fiscal setback during the Eisenhower Recession in the late 1950s, which was compounded by the heavy investment in jet technology and automation, between 1961 and 1965 profits rose with 1965 a record year. While profits were high, at a record 12 percent, nearly 85 percent of that profit was reinvested in expansion and improvements by the airlines.[9]

In August 1965, five airlines—Eastern, National, Northwest, TWA, and United—agreed to a short timeline for negotiations and a structured format for contract proposals. All but National Airlines were members of the Mutual Aid Pact.[10] After years of resisting, the airlines were ready to try multicarrier bargaining. It appeared a reasonable solution for diminishing the costs of union whipsawing. The terms for this multicarrier bargaining agreement included other enticements. The IAM agreed not to delay bargaining by adding new items to the negotiations. Further, the IAM agreed not to sanction any job actions, including slow-downs, sit-down strikes, or refusals to work overtime, for the life of the contract. Lastly, the airlines and the union agreed that no parties could conclude their agreement until all the airlines and the IAM had reached a final settlement. The airlines hoped to avoid the turbulent whipsaw bargaining of 1958.[11]

For nearly two months the parties bargained industrywide items and reached no settlements. Deadlocked on everything, the two sides applied to the National Mediation Board. By March 1966 the two sides remained deadlocked, and the IAM declined an offer of arbitration by the National Mediation Board. A final effort to mediate the dispute over the national issues was unsuccessful, and the IAM set a strike deadline for April 23, 1966. Despite the vehement objection of the IAM, President Johnson created a Presidential Emergency Board to examine the situation and make recommendations for a settlement. The IAM feared the board would recommend a settlement within Johnson's 3.2 percent wage guidelines, a settlement that IAM members would not accept.[12]

This was not the first bump in the road for the Johnson wage-guidepost policy. Auto, aluminum, cement, glass, maritime, and construction workers had all pushed the limits of the wage guideposts at the bargaining table in 1964–65. While Johnson could confidently point to the 1965 steel contract, which held wage increases at 3.2 percent, pressure against the policy was mounting. Labor and management argued that the wage guideposts disrupted "free collective bargaining."[13]

The Presidential Emergency Board held eight days of public hearings in May 1966 and reviewed two thousand pages of exhibits and testimony. While local issues were part of the dispute, the board put most of its energy into resolving eight national issues: wages, vacation allowances, health and welfare, pension, overtime, holidays, hours of service, and license premiums. The only issue the two sides agreed upon was that the contract should cover a three-year period.

On wage issues, the union argued that members should receive their fair share of the profits of 1964 and 1965, a cost-of-living escalator, and the removal of wage progressions. The IAM offered as evidence an increase in the cost of living of approximately 5 percent, airline profits of up to 11.5 percent in 1965, and a productivity increase of 7 percent, compared to a national average of 3.6 percent in the last year. The airlines countered that short-term profits would soon be offset by new investment in supersonic technology, that an escalator clause would increase inflation, that wage progressions reflected the lower productivity rates of newer employees in maintenance and baggage handling, and that wages in the airline industry had already increased 15 percent more than those of production workers over the last decade. The board recommended a wage-increase scale over a forty-two-month contract, which met Johnson's anti-inflation goals and would allow for future fare reduction as set by Civil Aeronautic Board guidelines if profits continued to climb and a wage rate comparable to historic gains in the industry. Table 14 reflects the top rate for aircraft mechanics.[14]

The second point of disagreement between the IAM and the five carriers centered on vacation allowance and the availability of highly skilled specialized mechanics. The IAM wanted to roll back the number of years of service required for three and four weeks of vacation time. The union argued that foreign airlines offered better vacation allowances and that the substantial responsibility of highly skilled mechanics placed extreme pressure on them. More vacation for more senior mechanics would offer relief from this pressure. The airlines argued that extended vacations would exacerbate existing service problems due to the shortage of highly specialized aircraft mechanics. Longer vacations would force the airlines to use more overtime to complete maintenance, a plan the union opposed. While the board did not concur with the IAM's demands on vacation allowances for more junior members, it recommended the four weeks of vacation for employees with fifteen years' service, citing public safety as a factor: "'While relatively few contracts in this country now provide four weeks of vacation after 15 years, the Board thinks that liberalization is justified in an industry which needs stability of service from the skilled men represented by this Union and which requires from the men a special devotion to duty in the interest of the traveling public.'"[15]

On health and welfare issues, the union argued for full coverage for employees and their dependents with costs paid by the carriers. The carriers

Table 14. Wage Rates—Presidential Emergency Board No. 166

IAM Proposal	First Year	Second Year	Third Year
Rate	$3.70	$3.88	$4.04
Carrier Proposal	First Year	Second Year	Third Year
Rate	$3.64	$3.76	$3.88
Board Rec.	First 18 months	Next 12 months	Last 12 months
Rate	$3.70	$3.85	$4.00

National Mediation Board, "Case No R-1447, Certification, November 28, 1945, in the matter of Representation of Employees of the American Airlines, Inc., (1) Airline Mechanics (2) Stores Personnel," 2, BRC Collection, "September 1945–June 1946, Organization–Air Transport Industry" file; Frank Heisler to Mr. H. W. Brown, November 23, 1945, IAM Collection, reel 296, vol. 1.

offered additional payment toward dependent coverage in the second year of employment for IAM members. Both sides argued over what they claimed to be the industry standard. Since the plans themselves were not changing, the board recommended no change, since any increased contribution on the part of the carriers would actually be an increase in compensation.[16]

The Presidential Emergency Board asked the union to withdraw its proposals on the last four national items. The board rejected the union's proposal for a noncontributory pension plan, stating that such a request was inflationary. The board recommended the IAM withdraw its proposal for double-time overtime rather than time-and-a-half overtime because the unpredictability of scheduled air transportation would make such an overtime policy too punitive to the airlines because overtime was unavoidable during bad weather, employee absences, and mechanical malfunctions. Further, while the IAM wanted more workers hired rather than offered overtime, local issues under review indicated that IAM members wanted overtime work. The board expanded the recognized holiday pay for an eighth holiday (Good Friday) but did not recommend expanded overtime rates for holidays. The board asked that the IAM withdraw its proposal for a paid lunch period during an eight-hour day to replace the unpaid half-hour break, which effectively created an eight-and-a-half-hour workday. The airlines argued that the half-hour overlap between shifts was essential for the exchange of tools and information. The board concurred. The last item the board addressed at the national level was license premiums. While the IAM argued that any mechanic required to be licensed by the Federal Aviation Authority or Federal Communications Commissions should receive an extra ten cents per hour because of the added responsibility of signing off on maintenance work completed, the airlines disputed the added responsibility. The board concurred and asked that the item be withdrawn.

The Presidential Emergency Board's recommendations would have cost the airlines approximately sixty-seven million dollars over a three-year period, or seventy-six million dollars over forty-two months. The board's recommendation offered an average annual increase of 3.6 percent, slightly above Johnson's 3.2 percent wage guidepost. Nonetheless, the president supported the board's recommendations, stating that they reflected "the highest order of judgment, imagination, and wisdom," and offered the airlines and the IAM a "framework for a just and prompt settlement" that would avoid supply disruption to the military operations in Vietnam as well as the hundreds of thousands of Americans traveling by air. The airlines accepted the board's recommendations as well. The union did not.[17] The IAM president LeRoy Siemiller told reporters, "The union is more than disappointed with the recommendations made by this board relating to wage rates, duration of contract, protection of wage rate against increased cost of living, and other items of an economic nature. . . . The Wage Policy Committee feels that Emergency Board #166 was mistaken in their understanding of many of the issues and in addition arrived at certain conclusions based on nineteenth-century concepts rather than liberal twentieth-century thinking."[18]

With thirty days to continue bargaining under the Railway Labor Act, the two sides returned to the table, now with Secretary of Labor W. Willard Wirtz attending the bargaining sessions. Despite the federal presence at the table, the airlines and the union did not reach a settlement, and the union set a strike deadline for July 8, 1966.[19]

The 1966 Airlines Strike

On July 7, 1966, as talks between the airlines and the IAM ended, over 150,000 U.S. airline passengers[20] braced themselves for the largest airline strike in American history. Operating airlines, railroads, and bus lines put emergency plans into action to attempt to meet the needs of travelers stranded by the IAM strike. President Johnson addressed the nation, expressing his disappointment that the two sides could not reach agreement and his concern for military operations, space work at Cape Kennedy, and the transport of the U.S. mail.

On July 8, as 6:00 AM dawned across the nation's time zones, over thirty-five thousand IAM members stayed off the job at Northwest, TWA, Eastern, National, and United Airlines, cutting 60 percent of the nation's passenger air traffic and 70 percent of the U.S. mail air transport. The strike eliminated or diminished air service to 231 U.S. cities and twenty-three foreign countries. The remaining six trunkline carriers and twelve local-service airlines could not possibly accommodate the passengers and mail stranded by the strike. In Buffalo, New York, an unnamed American Airlines ticket agent stated, "We're busy as hell," as stranded passengers attempted to rebook onto American. In New York City, twenty thousand passengers faced canceled flights, and in Chicago the number reached forty thousand. Railroads with runs between major metropolitan areas reported traffic increases of over 50 percent, and Greyhound Bus Lines sales were up nearly 20 percent. Hotels in Manhattan were nearly full.[21]

While stranded passengers and harried customer-service agents at the operating airlines felt that the strike had created a national emergency, it had not. In the first days of the strike, the federal government and airline officials classified it as an inconvenience and disruption but not a danger to the nation's economic health. In 1966 only 0.5% of all freight transferred within the United States was carried by air. Quick delivery items, such as emergency replacement parts for industry and perishable items like fresh flowers and some scientific equipment, were grounded by the strike, but the vast majority of freight continued to move. The banking industry faced an expansion of credit because the airlines carried millions of checks between banks, and millions of Americans enjoyed the extra "float" on their checks during the strike. Professional baseball teams were forced to bus between games or charter airplanes, but hardest hit by the strike was the tourism industry. The hotel industry especially faced a chaotic and costly situation. In the first days of the strike, Miami hoteliers expected losses of three million dollars a week during the strike, and New York hoteliers struggled to house stranded conventioneers for the Lions International as they anticipated the start of the American Library Association annual meeting. As one hotel clerk quipped, "If things get bad, we're going to feed the librarians to the Lions."[22]

As the days passed, the IAM and the airlines came no closer to a settlement, although the shape of national air-transportation options shifted to some degree. Military service continued as the IAM agreed to cooperate "to the fullest" in the movement of military personnel and materiel and to continue relevant service at the Cape Kennedy space program. Despite informal objections by the struck carriers, the Civil Aeronautics Board temporarily expanded the route systems for non-struck airlines for cities that had lost 25 percent or more of their service to the strike. Nonscheduled airlines were permitted to lease their aircraft and services to scheduled airlines, and operating airlines were allowed to lend aircraft to struck carriers. However, such adjustments did relatively little to alleviate the shortage in air transport. Nonscheduled airlines added few planes to the air, and other airline unions, such as the TWU at American and Pan Am, refused to service airplanes borrowed from struck airlines.[23]

The IAM welcomed the support of other unions, particularly in the face of growing media and political pressure to settle. As the strike continued, the press reported on shortages in perishable items, including fresh fruits and vegetables, substantial losses in the hotel and tourism industries, and short-tempered travelers. The *New York Times* editorial pages called the strike "unconscionable" and pressured President Johnson and Congress to move toward legally binding arbitration to end strikes that "threaten irreparable damage to the national interest."[24] Members of the TWU, ALPA, the FEIA, and the BRC refused to service aircraft borrowed from struck carriers, and leadership shared important industry information with the IAM. The TWU president Matthew Guinan warned American and Pan Am that the union was monitoring the amount of work during the strike and that members would not allow any speedups or strike-breaking jobs to be snuck into their work. The United Airlines baggage handler and strike captain Randy Canale remembered the support from other organized workers outside the airline industry. "I remember the outstanding support from other workers . . . the building trades, printing trades, across the AFL-CIO, they made contributions to our strike fund. It went a long way to help keep morale up."[25]

At the end of the first strike week, talks heated up as both sides showed their muscle. The IAM negotiator Joseph Ramsey broke off talks with the airlines and accused Northwest Airlines of violating an agreement with the union regarding overseas housing and commissary charges for IAM members in Tokyo. Talks resumed a day later when Northwest withdrew the rent changes in Tokyo, and the IAM indicated some willingness to scale down two or three of its economic demands. Although the IAM signaled that it was ready to reconsider some points, union negotiators returned to bargaining wearing open-necked short-sleeved shirts with the IAM emblem on the front and back rather than the suits and ties of earlier sessions. As Joseph Ramsey explained, "It's going to get hot, so we're ready for action."[26]

The union again broke off bargaining on July 20, this time to take the airlines' "best offer" up to that point to IAM membership for a vote. Reports were not optimistic for a settlement. The *New York Times,* which carried the story on the front page nearly every day throughout the strike, deemed it "unlikely" that the membership would accept the airlines' offer. IAM leaders viewed the July 20 "best offer" as an opportunity to show that IAM members were unwilling to accept a settlement within the framework of the Presidential Emergency Board recommendations. Because of intense pressure from the president, Congress, and the airlines to settle under the recommendations, IAM leaders believed that a no vote at this juncture would show that a "militant membership, rather than a stubborn union leadership was an obstacle to a settlement." This tactic was foiled when the chief negotiator for the airlines refused to make a "best offer."[27]

As the strike headed toward its third week, pressure, particularly on President Johnson and the IAM, continued to mount. Politically at least, Johnson and IAM president Siemiller were firmly locked in conflict over the wage guidepost. Johnson's firm public support for the Presidential Emergency Board recommendations left him with little room to increase pressure on the airlines to improve their offer. Such a move would undermine his wage policy and statements of confidence in the recommendations. As newspaper editorials called for personal intervention, the president reminded reporters during an East Room press conference, "We've done all we can do under the law. We are continuing to persuade the management and labor to continue their discussion."

Siemiller faced pressure to hold firm from a militant IAM rank and file eager for a share of the airline industry's record profits, skirmishes around jurisdiction with the Teamsters and raiding by the Aircraft Mechanics Fraternal Association (AMFA), and his own program for moving the IAM from "the good gray Machinists" into a "go-go" union. A vote after two weeks of strike-time bargaining was a better move than bringing a proposal based on the wage guidelines to the membership for a vote. Such action would have implied some acceptance of the guidelines on the part of IAM leaders. The focus among union members remained on "catching up" with rising costs and the recent wage gains in other sectors of the economy. The publication of airline-industry profit margins in the IAM newspaper *The Machinist* and the release of airline executive salaries in the *New York Times* fanned the flames of discontent. As the *New York Times* reported, under the headline "High Flying Salaries,"

> That closely guarded secret of the working man—how much he makes—is one luxury some highly paid executives cannot afford.
>
> *Air Transport World* has just paraded across its pages the salaries of the 100 top airline executives. The salaries are based on figures filed with the Civil Aeronautics Board with *Air Transport World* adjustments for "known deferred income" not reflected in C.A.B. records. Juan T. Trippe, chairman of Pan American, still flies the highest, while even Mark Kramer, vice president of customer service for Continental, collects $44,000 at the pay window though he barely made the list. Here is a short list to con-the aces.

1. J. T. Trippe	Pan Am	$147,222
3. C. C. Tilllinghast Jr.	TWA	$122,000
5. D. W. Nyrop	Northwest	$115,000
7. W. A. Patterson	United	$100,000
13. C. R. Smith	American	$85,000
15. F. D. Hall	Eastern	$81,142

> Flying, it appears, continues to be a glamorous business for the Aces.[28]

Under the Civil Aeronautics Board, airlines had to report executive salaries and benefits as part of their annual reports to maintain routes, rates, and mail subsidies. While the board did not directly regulate executive salaries, its authority to regulate the industry's "sound economic conditions" and "adequate, economical, and efficient service" meant that excessive paychecks could raise eyebrows at the board. In light of high executive wages and record profits, the Civil Aeronautics Board did not lower air fares. High executive salaries, high profits, and constant fares exacerbated striking workers' frustration.[29] Unlike the union, the airlines faced little pressure from the public or the press to change their position. Four of the five struck airlines were members of the Mutual Aid Pact and therefore had some protection against strike losses. The airlines were willing to settle based on the Presidential Emergency Board recommendations, thus complying with the process of the Railway Labor Act and arguably the wishes of the president himself.[30]

The only further action the president could take was through new legislation. In his State of the Union address in January 1966, Johnson had stated that he would introduce antistrike legislation for situations where strikes "threatened irreparable damage to the national interest." However, congressional pressure for government action to end the strike was growing. Democratic Senator Wayne Morse of Oregon (a member of the Presidential Emergency Board) decried the strike and accused IAM leadership of being unpatriotic: "Any strike called by the officers of this union in this hour of crisis is not reconcilable with the patriotic responsibility of the union to its government, and to the people of our country including our troops in Vietnam." Morse was joined by a fellow Democrat, Ohio Senator Frank Lausche, and Republicans Senator Robert P. Griffin (Michigan), Senator Jacob K. Javits (New York), and Rep. Thomas P. Curtis (Missouri) in calls for antistrike legislation.[31]

On July 22, Morse introduced Joint Resolution 180 to the Senate authorizing court action to end the strike. With the passage of the resolution the president could seek a court order to put the five airlines under court receivership for up to two years or until the strike was settled. Morse argued that the resolution had merit because the strike threatened "essential transportation services to the Nation" and that all procedures under the Railway Labor Act had been exhausted. According to Morse, the strike had created a national emergency, and Congress was obligated to act. Under Morse's resolution a Special Dispute Board would be appointed by the president after the court order was issued. The Special Board would hold hearings and make a recommendation to the president. Thus far the system replicated that of the Presidential Emergency Board and the Railway Labor Act. However, the last section of Morse's resolution put the final responsibility for ending the strike on the president: *if* he determined that the strike created a national emergency, he could stop it for up to two years.[32]

Morse's resolution was met with fury by the IAM and suspicion by Congress. Siemiller announced that the IAM had "never been more militant" and was in full support of its negotiators, and he accused the airlines of sitting back and waiting for congressional action to end the strike rather than working at the bargaining table. Members of Congress and President Johnson were anxious about enacting general strike legislation during an election year.[33] As Senate Joint Resolution 180 went to the Senate Committee on Labor and Public Welfare, the airlines, the union, and politicians wrangled over the impact of the strike and the political fallout over ending it. Had the IAM strike created a national emergency, or had it not? On the first day of hearings Morse submitted a revised resolution. Resolution 181 removed the determination of a national emergency from the president's responsibility. Rather, the signing of the bill would immediately end the strike for 180 days but not place the airlines in receivership. A Special Airline Dispute Board would make recommendations to the president if the two sides had not reached a settlement within 150 days. The president would advise Congress on the terms or procedures for settlement in the public interest and "without further interruption of the continuity of transportation services by these carriers." Labor read this clause to mean compulsory arbitration, while the airlines and Secretary of Labor W. Willard Wirtz believed the clause called for further congressional action.[34]

Hoping to slow down the process so he could weigh the political costs of the antistrike legislation, on July 27 Johnson asked the Senate to wait a few days and let the airlines and the IAM make a final effort toward settlement. In the committee hearing, Wirtz explained that while "the airline strike has confronted the nation with a serious, substantial, adverse impact on the national interest, [it is] an impact which, however, has not yet brought the country to what I suppose most of us would think of an emergency state." Wirtz expressed his strong objection to Morse's bill because of the danger that every labor dispute would go to the White House for settlement.[35]

In response to doubts about a national emergency, Morse offered an amended resolution, under which Congress was no longer obligated to declare a national emergency to pass the resolution. Instead, passage of the bill was possible if the strike threatened "substantially to interrupt interstate commerce to a degree such as to deprive any section of the country of essential transportation services," making it easier for Congress to justify the bill. The language of the act regarding essential transportation services came from the Railway Labor Act (section 10) and was the same language that authorized the creation of a Presidential Emergency Board.[36]

With the amended bill before it, the Committee on Labor and Public Welfare heard testimony from Labor Secretary Wirtz; William J. Curtain, the negotiating chair for the five airlines; Morse, as chair of the Presidential Emergency Board; and IAM president Siemiller, on essential transportation services. Morse and Curtain emphasized the damaging effects of the strike, while Wirtz and Siemiller argued that the strike had caused great inconvenience but not substantial disruption in service to segments of the nation. Siemiller pointed out that less than 0.1 percent of the nation's domestic freight was carried by air and that 97 percent of all intercity passenger travel was not affected by the strike. Curtain warned that "community after community has been choked off from the air transportation it has come to depend upon. The stoppage has imperiled the entire financial structure of the majority of the Nation's air industry, thus endangering not only investor confidence now but also the ability of this industry to expand and renovate as America grows in the future." The strike's impact on the Vietnam War effort was also a central concern. Secretary of Defense Robert McNamara assured the committee that the strike had no adverse effect on the airlift of passengers or cargo for military purposes. The Senate committee voted tentatively to approve the amended version of Morse's bill.[37]

Hoping again to slow down the process so he could weigh the political costs of the antistrike legislation, Johnson asked the Senate to wait a few days and let the airlines and the IAM make a final effort toward settlement. While AFL-CIO president George Meany proclaimed that the request gave "free collective bargaining" the opportunity to work, the *New York Times* decried the request as pure politics and "dictates of organized labor." On July 28, Johnson asked both parties to join him the next day at the White House and engage in a "little introspection" and ask themselves, "What can I do to protect the people I represent but still find an area of agreement?" Johnson spent a half an hour with the two sides urging them to a quick settlement. At 2:30 AM on July 30 the airlines and the IAM reached agreement, and the Senate committee could hold off presenting the antistrike legislation.[38]

What did this settlement look like, and was it inflationary? The three-year agreement included annual 5 percent increases in wages for each year, the elimination of some wage-progression steps, expanded vacation allowances, the Good Friday holiday, increased employer contributions for dependent health and welfare insurance, and a five-cents-an-hour wage differential for mechanics with higher job classifications. Except for the wage increase, these items were all effective in the second or third year of the contract. The contract dismissed all local issues not agreed upon. The increased cost of the settlement was estimated at 4.4 percent, well above the 3.2 percent guidepost. In his statements to the press, Johnson proclaimed, "The fact that production has advanced so rapidly in the airline industry means, according to all the participants in the settlement, that this settlement that has been reached will not be inflationary." IAM leadership worked quickly to promote acceptance of the settlement. Siemiller sent telegrams to all airline locals and a second telegram to all full-time employees on strike strongly recommending ratification, and grand lodge representatives fanned out across the nation to urge members to vote for the contract.[39]

However, IAM rank-and-file airline workers were not so enthusiastic about this settlement. In San Francisco, response to the agreement was "strongly negative"; in Kansas City, the local leadership encouraged members to reject the contract. Andy Shiotta, a local executive board member in New York who supported the contract but recognized that members of his local did not, said, "We don't want to buck the grand lodge and the President of the United States but the membership has got minds of their own."[40] By a margin of two and a half to one, the membership voted down the contract at all five airlines.

The vote was a sharp blow and a direct rejection of the efforts of the Johnson administration and the recommendations of IAM leadership. Siemiller told the press that the strike would continue until there was "something the membership was satisfied with." The Johnson administration had no comment. The largest locals voted down the contract by the greatest margins. Members of Local 1322 in Queens shouted, "Impeach Johnson!" and, "March on Washington!" as votes were cast. Applause erupted when one IAM member called out, "Why can't we get leadership like Mike Quill and John L. Lewis?" Quill, the recently deceased president of the TWU, had led New York Transit workers out on a general transit strike in January 1966, paralyzing the city and winning a 15 percent wage hike over two years, violating the wage guidepost. In response, Frank Cremona, the national IAM representative at the balloting, said, "Mike Quill—may he rest in peace—just defied an injunction of a local court. He did not defy the Federal Government. The highest office of the land and the Congress of the United States is what's involved here. We have already made a mockery of President Johnson's wage-price guidelines. We are stuck with this contract—like it or not." Cremona's statements were met with a resounding "No!" The Queens Local president Charles Kaczinski shouted, "I don't care if you use a pen or ink or if you use blood. Vote No!" Kaczinski explained that the "only benefit to us this year is a 5 percent pay raise. We have to wait until next year for everything else." By a vote of four to one in Queens, IAM members said they did not want to wait.[41]

So why did the IAM rank and file vote down a contract strongly recommended by IAM leadership and well above the 3.2 percent guideline? First, as Kaczinski lamented, the contract offer phased in the gains and lacked a cost-of-living escalator. Workers explained that as things like butter and eggs and taxes went up in price they would be left treading water. Second, the looming back-to-work legislation, the positive spin put on the contract by Siemiller, and Johnson's assessment that the agreement did not actually break the wage guidelines seemed to aggravate an already riled up rank and file. Randy Canale, a baggage handler and strike captain in 1966, remembered, "It wasn't enough, pure and simple. Five percent wasn't enough. We wanted to break the guideline." Kenneth Ahern, a baggage handler in Boston during the 1966 strike, also recalled the strike as one about wages but also the frustration over Johnson's position on the wage guidelines. He explained, "The real thing was that guidepost, the 3.2 percent. We felt a lot of pressure. Johnson was doing a terrible job on us in the press." Vincent Van Dusen, a

IAM members give the thumbs-down sign outside the Massachusetts Air National Guard Auditorium at Logan Airport, Boston. The Boston local voted 425–69 against the White House agreement. July 31, 1966. AP/Wide World Photos.

storekeeper at United Airlines at Kennedy International Airport, complained, "This is a miserable contract. We're going to turn it down. But let the record show that if the President forces us back to work we go under protest." Pat Magarelli of Lodge 1056 in New York City felt that politicians, including Johnson, did not understand the feeling of injustice the wage cap stirred in workers: "The people down there in Washington have got to face reality. The average working man has obligations to meet. You just can't tell him 3.2 percent is all he can get when the companies are making 200 percent. He's got to feed his kids and put them in school and have a little left for some pleasure, too." Others speculated that voting down the first negotiated offer was part of blowing off steam among membership and a longer tradition of autonomy at the local level. Even Siemiller warned, as early returns rolled in, "There's a rebellious attitude. That's what I keep telling everybody."[42]

The next day the Senate returned to the business of antistrike legislation for the airlines. Again senators grappled with the political fallout of ending the strike. President Johnson remained silent on the subject amid speculation as to whether or not he supported such legislation. As senators from both sides of the aisle attempted to compromise over who would be responsible for ending the strike, Congress or the White House, Senator Morse called on Congress to take the lead and pass his bill and stop passing the "hot potato" of antistrike legislation. Public frustration and pressure from the airline industry to pass legislation added to the pressure to pass a bill.[43] On August 5, Senate leaders reluctantly crafted and passed a compromise bill, which gave Congress and the White House shared responsibility for ending the strike. Resolution 186 gave Congress the responsibility for sending the strikers back to work for thirty days and the president responsibility for extending that period up to 150 more days. Senators rejected any compulsory arbitration as part of the bill; however, the bill included language directing the secretary of labor to recommend amendments to the Railway Labor Act to improve procedures for the settlement of strikes.[44]

As Resolution 186 made its way to the House of Representatives, Secretary of Labor Wirtz reported that collective bargaining between the airlines and the union had "fallen on its face" and that there was "little chance" of meaningful negotiations with legislation under discussion.[45] The two sides met again after two weeks away from the table on August 8, and this time bargaining included the presidents of the twelve largest IAM locals in the strike. Wirtz told the press, "I cannot offer one single ounce of encouragement" regarding the state of negotiations. Indeed, the two sides were farther apart than they had been at the end of July: the airlines offered the same settlement they had offered on July 29, and the union returned to its original proposal prior to the Presidential Emergency Board. Democratic Representative Harley O. Staggers of West Virginia, the chair of the congressional committee reviewing Senate Resolution 186, implored both sides to bargain in good faith, warning that reaching a settlement would avoid the passage of a law they would regret "as long as [they] live."[46]

On August 10, the House Interstate and Foreign Commerce Committee tentatively backed the compromise bill to end the airlines strike. President Johnson remained silent on his position on the bill. As the bill made its way through committee, confusion erupted over the possibility of an interim contract and binding arbitration. Congressman Staggers appeared to report that an interim back-to-work agreement was under way and that the airlines and the union had agreed to resolve issues through binding arbitration rather than face legislation. Siemiller countered that any agreement, including issues brought for binding arbitration, would need approval from the IAM membership, and he thought that an unlikely scenario. The airline negotiator William Curtain accused Siemiller of backpeddling and undermining negotiations.

Senate Resolution 186 reached the House floor on August 13. However, as in the Senate, politicians also considered alternate legislation and jostled the blame for ending the strike between the White House and Congress and the inclusion of language defining the strike as a national emergency. Staggers predicted that legislation would pass in the House and then "unexplainably" canceled plans for an evening session to continue the process, blocking support for alternate legislation, which put the onus of stopping the strike on the president. The canceled session slowed down passage of a bill for at least four days.[47]

Negotiations pressed on during the four days as Wirtz oversaw negotiations. The airlines showed some movement toward improving their offer, and the union rolled together a "package" covering its issues. It appeared a settlement was within reach. However, negotiations stopped when Siemiller stormed out, citing an attack on his integrity by the airlines negotiating team. After months of treading lightly, expressing opposition to antistrike legislation, and even expressing theoretical support for the union position, Wirtz admonished Siemiller in the press for the disruption and explained, "Another round of attempts to settle the airline dispute by mediation has come to a disruptive and disturbing conclusion."[48]

In the early hours of the morning on August 15, the IAM and the airlines reached an agreement, and the House Rules Committee canceled a meeting scheduled that day to consider action on the antistrike legislation. In contrast to the July 29 announcements of a strike settlement, few details were released relating to the agreement. IAM leaders gave the rank and file four days to vote on the contract, the president offered no comment, and privately the airlines grumbled that the agreement was more expensive than expected.[49]

Overall, the contract offer equaled a 6 percent increase and cost the airlines approximately eighty-six million dollars over three years. To encourage ratification, AFL-CIO president George Meany sent telegrams to the thirteen largest locals encouraging approval of this "wonderful settlement," and Siemiller sent letters to each striking member explaining that the contract was "by far the best ever secured in the air transport industry" and that it destroyed "all existing wage and price guidelines now in existence." Siemiller upped the ante when he proclaimed that this new offer completely shattered the guidelines for *all* unions. This second agreement met the expectations of most of the largest IAM locals. Local leaders in Minneapolis, Chicago, and Kansas City said they supported the contract and would encourage members to vote for ratification. Local leaders in high-wage areas such as the West Coast were less enthusiastic about the wage gains, and some local leaders in New York City expressed disappointment particularly around health and welfare benefits. Skill, too, played a factor in how airline workers received the new contract offer. Licensed and highly skilled aircraft mechanics were frustrated that the raise was not as substantial as that won by striking Greyhound Bus mechanics on the West Coast. However, the majority of striking IAM members were ready to return to work. The contract offered annual 5 percent increases over three years at earlier points in the contract, a cost-of-living escalator clause, and resolved many issues around working conditions on the individual airlines that were dismissed in the first agreement. On August 19, the IAM rank and file approved the contract by a two-to-one margin.[50]

Back to Work: Costing out the Strike

With the contract ratified, the airlines returned quickly to full operations. As the *New York Times* gleefully reported, the resumption of service meant "a return to the payroll—and to steak instead of salad—for 101,000 airline workers, a scrapping of ingenious travel schemes by anxious businessmen and tourists, standing in ticket lines again for stranded European travelers, and sighs of relief from resort hotel owners who have empty rooms."[51] The *Times* could well have included Labor Secretary Wirtz, President Johnson, and Congress among those exhaling sighs of relief. With the strike over, it was time to count the costs and calculate the implications for the airline industry

IAM members of Local 1781 in San Mateo, California, booed and shouted "no" when L. T. Faircloth, the grand lodge representative from Washington, D.C., recommended a "yes" vote as they gathered to vote on the latest proposed settlement of the airline strike. The meeting of Lodge 1781, which had five thousand members employed by United Airlines, was held in the Hall of Flowers at the San Mateo County Fairgrounds. AP/Wide World Photos.

as well as for other sectors of the economy. According to *Time* magazine, the strike cost the national economy at least three billion dollars; *Time* called it the most serious strike since the 116-day steel strike in 1959.[52]

For striking IAM members, the forty-three-day strike had been stressful and exhilarating. Wage losses for IAM members and other airline employees, furloughed or working reduced hours, totaled $68.8 million. It took the average IAM member sixteen months to recoup the wages lost in the strike.[53] Lost wages aside, the strike was a victory from the perspective of IAM members. Randy Canale recalled being a little nervous about the strike. The sense that "everything you have is on the table," including the right to strike, meant that the stakes were high in terms of personal financial loss during the strike but also the ability to press for future earnings as well. The retired aircraft mechanic Kenneth Thiede remembered the strike as a victory because it broke the wage guidepost that he felt was unfair to labor. Thiede recalled the enthusiasm for the strike among members in Chicago. The union had just completed a new lodge near O'Hare Airport in suburban Des Plaines, and members congregated there for picnics and meetings. Thiede speculated that the strike lasted as long as it did because "people were enjoying the weather too much." Richard Del Boccio, an aircraft radio-and-electronics mechanic for United in Chicago, remembered the strike as a stressful time. During the strike he did his picket duty but also took on a series of other jobs. He delivered phone books and worked construction and landscaping. "I felt like

Dr. Kimball in the *Fugitive.* I think everybody wanted to go [on strike]. After you were out for a while, it was tough." Nonetheless, Del Boccio believed that the victory came in "getting even" because the airlines regularly dragged out negotiations. He explained, "Was it worth it to get 5 percent instead of 3.2 percent? No. Was it worth it that we shut them down? Yes."[54]

For some of these IAM members, the strike also inspired a stronger commitment to the union. In 1963, Randy Canale hired on at United Airlines as a baggage handler in Philadelphia. His first union experience came during a wildcat strike over contracting out during his first few weeks on the ramp. "I was learning my job at the railroad express depot in the airport, and I saw all these ramp folks walking along—I'll never forget. This big fellow, six-foot-three or -four, says, 'Kid, you're outta here! Get your butt out of here!' I figured I'd just lost my job." Instead, he walked out with other IAM members. In 1964, Canale became a union steward after word got around that he was good at talking to supervisors. He served as a steward and strike captain during the strike and was elected local president in 1967 at twenty-two years old. For Canale, the strike "solidified the union" and "unified the workers." The experience was one that IAM members at United would draw on during contract negotiations in 1969 and during a two-month strike in 1979.[55]

Ken Thiede also recalled the strike as marking his increased interest in union activity. Thiede started as an aircraft mechanic at Capital Airlines in 1956 in Chicago and moved to United when the two airlines merged in 1961. He was already a union steward in 1966. Thiede recalled, "I became more and more active through the strike, and I stayed active after the strike. It was interesting work, and I liked helping people, having a common cause. . . . There was togetherness. People really were together. People helped each other. They gave donations, we had picnics. You got to know people."[56] Thiede went on to become recording secretary of Local Lodge 1487 from 1970 to 1976 and president of District Lodge 141 in the 1990s.

The 1966 strike also exposed a growing tension between skilled and unskilled workers on the ground in the U.S. airline industry. Strike observers speculated that the pressure on IAM leaders to break the guideposts and bargain top wages, particularly for highly skilled aircraft mechanics, came from the fledgling independent union, AMFA. Organized in 1962 by three airline mechanics, AMFA petitioned the National Mediation Board for recognition as the bargaining agent for aircraft mechanics at United, Seaboard World, Eastern, and Bonanza Airlines in 1965. AMFA testified that it had collected enough cards from aircraft mechanics to call for an election; however, the National Mediation Board ruled that at United Airlines, the bargaining unit would have to include unskilled workers as well. In response,

AMFA created an Aircraft Technician Division for aircraft mechanics and an Airline Support Division for all employees who were not responsible for the airworthiness of aircraft. In February 1966, aircraft mechanics at Ozark Airlines voted in AMFA over the IAM and the Teamsters. In September 1966, AMFA reported that the IAM strike had brought hundreds of dissatisfied aircraft mechanics to its ranks. According to AMFA's national director, O. V. "Del" Delle-Femine, his eight-thousand-member organization offered a "new look" in labor relations that emphasized the individual skill of aircraft mechanics. During an interview with *Air Transport World* magazine in 1966, Delle-Femine explained,

> We in AMFA are opposed to nineteenth-century labor laws, and to industrial unions headed by cab drivers and unskilled laborers that follow outmoded labor philosophies. . . . [W]e in aviation are a new generation in labor, with new ideas and ideals . . . and we base our philosophy on individual qualification and incentive. . . .
>
> We believe that all airline employe[e]s will benefit from membership in our association. We are "airline-people" and we firmly believe in eight hours' work for eight hours' pay. . . . AMFA members and officials are dedicated to aircraft safety, and both the public and the airline industry stand to benefit from our existence and our future victories.[57]

Delle-Femine's understanding of craft unionism and the mystique of the airline industry harkened back to the early organizing drives of the IAM and the efforts of ALPA to organize across the industry, building on its high-prestige membership.

Richard Del Boccio joined AMFA as an affiliate member in 1963, a year after he started working at United Airlines. For Del Boccio, the IAM "left a bad taste in my mouth, it was too industrial." As he saw it, there were two problems with the size of the bargaining unit at United. First, highly skilled aircraft mechanics carried the unskilled workers "on their coattails." Lesser-skilled workers received raises and differentials similar to those of the mechanics. Del Boccio resented that their top wages began to catch up to those of highly skilled mechanics in later contracts. Second, because the lesser-skilled and unskilled workers in the IAM outnumbered the highly skilled mechanics, Del Boccio felt that skilled mechanics' interests were pushed aside when contracts were ratified.[58]

What did the airlines lose during the Machinists strike of 1966? The fiscal losses were substantial. Estimated reports put revenue losses at $350 million and a profit loss at $28 million for all five airlines during the strike.[59] Some of these losses were offset by participation in the Mutual Aid Pact. In 1966, the pact guaranteed that a struck airline would receive no less than 25 percent of its normal air-transport operating costs during a strike. This revenue would come from windfall payments made by other airlines with traffic gains during the strike and supplemental payments as agreed to in a 1962 revision to the Mutual Aid Pact. In the case of the 1966 strike, the supplemental payment plan could not reach the 25 percent revenue mark because paying pact members needed only to pay up to 0.5 percent of the airline's air-transport operating revenue from the preceding year. Struck members of the Mutual Aid Pact—United, Eastern, Northwest, and TWA—received forty-six million dollars from nonstruck members (Pan Am, American, Continental, and Braniff). National Airlines suffered its losses without revenue from the Mutual Aid Pact.[60]

The airlines had also lost an important political gamble. The airlines had gambled that such an expansive strike would surely be considered a national emergency and bring federal intervention. Instead, President Johnson and Congress had moved slowly toward intervention while pressing both sides to resolution. The enormous profits of 1965 that fueled the strike also returned to haunt the airlines. In comments on the strike settlement, Gardner Ackley, chairman of the President's Council of Economic Advisers, criticized the union for pushing such an "inflationary" settlement but also blamed the airlines for not voluntarily bringing down fares to meet Civil Aeronautics Board profit guidelines, thus creating the tensions that led to the strike. The strike opened up the doors for a full Civil Aeronautics Board review of the industry, its profits, and the impact of the Mutual Aid Pact.[61]

Even with the strike, 1966 proved to be a record year for profits and growth in the airline industry. For the first time, the number of passengers flying on the U.S. scheduled airlines topped one hundred million (up 16 percent from 1965), and cargo shipments were up 26 percent from 1965. Despite increasing wages, new lower-fare specials, and decreasing subsidy from the Civil Aeronautics Board, the airline industry saw a decline in operating expenses through continued investment in new technology (aircraft as well as office). In 1966, the industry grew by thirty thousand employees, and the airlines reported net earnings of over $425 million, a profit rate of 11 percent.[62]

The strike and the settlement did not put an end to whipsawing in the industry. Even during the strike, the TWU used the tentative settlement as a starting point for bargaining at Pan Am and American Airlines. In July 1966 a Presidential Emergency Board convened to examine the labor situation at American Airlines. Perhaps recognizing the futility of making recommendations during the IAM strike, this board recommended only that both sides work vigorously toward a settlement and made no specific suggestions. In

September 1966, under the threat of a strike, American offered the TWU a contract with terms that exceeded those won by the IAM that summer. TWU members threatened to reject the offer, and the two sides continued to bargain. On October 4 TWU members ratified a "clearly inflationary" settlement that cost the airlines 6.5 percent a year over three years. In a press release, the TWU announced, "This is the best contract in the airline industry."[63]

The next day, Johnson created a Presidential Emergency Board to examine the contract dispute between Pan Am and the TWU. A month later, the board recommended a 5 percent annual wage increase, with added fringe benefits at the airline. The board acknowledged that the recommendation was inflationary, but given the settlement at American and the high productivity of the industry, it was the only realistic suggestion they could make. As in the case of the multicarrier bargaining and the IAM, Pan Am agreed to and stood firm on the board's recommendations. As anxious passengers around the world waited for news of a settlement, the two sides came to a tentative agreement. On December 2, the TWU rank and file ratified the agreement that offered up to an 18 percent package increase over eighteen months.[64]

Whipsawing continued as these contracts expired. In February 1969, TWU members at American struck for twenty-one days and won a "pace-setting" contract that included an 8.5 percent annual increase, which was inflationary compared to the 7.5 percent median annual increase in 1968. During 1969, negotiations deadlocked at six of the nine major airlines. At National Airlines, the National Mediation Board stepped in when IAM members called a wildcat strike. The mechanics gained further attention when they interrupted an airline-sponsored golf tournament with a union-hired airplane displaying a "Don't Fly NAL" banner. Adding to the disruption, several strikers surprised golfers at the seventeenth green and fought with police. After a long year, IAM members at United bargained the best contract of the decade. In October, IAM members at United voted overwhelmingly for a three-year contract, which gave a 35 percent increase in wages over the life of the contract. Without a strike and without multicarrier bargaining, the rank and file at United won for "all classifications the highest rates of pay and the greatest earning power to workers in the air transport industry," according to George Robinson, the new president of the IAM.[65]

The Broken Guidepost and the Labor Movement

The 1966 airline strike set the ground floor for later bargaining in the airline industry and ignited further unrest among American workers, a shift that was noted by business and labor alike. A week after the airline settlement, George Meany announced that the 5 percent increase won in the Machinists strike was the new *floor* for bargaining to balance the increasing profits created by increased productivity. President Johnson's economic adviser, Gerald Ackley, acknowledged that the wage guideposts were all but dead.[66]

Congressional leaders and airline executives called for a reevaluation of labor laws and a curb on union power.[67] In January 1967, Secretary of Labor Wirtz expressed deep concern about rank-and-file rejection of bargained contracts, particularly as thirty-two major contracts covering over 1.7 million workers opened that year.[68] The *New York Times* labor writer H. A. Raskin speculated on the rise in militancy and the growing frustration among union members. Raskin asserted that the upsurge in local autonomy stemmed in part from the passage of the Landrum-Griffin Act. The "bill of rights" the legislation included regarding officer elections and contract information had changed the relationship between workers and their unions. The rapid increase in living expenses and the high profits in industry (and the airlines) also contributed to rank-and-file anxiety about keeping up. Further, internal union conflicts, raiding, and dissatisfaction among skilled workers contributed to the push for "more" among rank-and-file union members.[69] In November 1967, *Fortune* magazine warned, "The news about organized labor is a dramatic shift in the balance of power, from the familiar faces to the faceless men of the rank and file. The change signifies an entirely new era in labor relations; in the particular year ahead, it implies a round of very large wage increases—possibly accompanied by strikes—like nothing the U.S. has seen in the last decade."[70] The author was right. Over the next year, the Department of Labor reported more man-days lost to strikes than in any period since 1953. As scholars like Andrew Levison, Jefferson Cowie, and Nelson Lichtenstein have noted, in strikes on the railroads, in auto, at General Electric, among teachers, sanitation workers, farm workers, nurses' aides, and postal workers, the late 1960s and early 1970s rocked with labor activism. These strikes occurred in the context of the civil rights, the Vietnam War, and the antiwar and women's liberation movements. While some of this militancy can be attributed to the contagion of this era of activism, the IAM strike in 1966 offers a formidable example of rank-and-file activism sparked not by liberation politics but rather strident union activism, anxiety over inflation, and consumption and resistance to government intervention.[71]

Epilogue: Deregulation and Beyond

Deregulating and Wages

While profits and wage gains marked 1966 as a record year in the airline industry, such records did not last. By mid-1968 airlines like United, TWA, and Eastern showed earning declines of over 50 percent. In 1970 the industry lost $200 million, marking a steady decline from the $428 million profit mark of 1966. Wage increases, flight delays, discounted "special" fares, and expensive equipment orders ate away at profits, and projected passenger-rate increases failed to materialize. As the airlines took their orders of widebody jets (McDonnell Douglas DC-10s, Boeing 747s, and Lockheed L-1011s), an economic recession cut into the public demand for air travel.

Between 1966 and 1970, wages in the airline industry increased 43 percent, compared to 27 percent for all industries. The ATA, the industry's trade organization, blamed the unions for relentless whipsawing since the 1966 strike, warning that the costs of such huge wage increases would be severe:

> Payroll costs have become a crucial problem for the industry, its employees, the shareholders, and the public. All are affected by it and a satisfactory solution is in their mutual best interest. Without a solution the outlook is bleak indeed. For the airlines, not finding a solution could mean shrinkage instead of the continued growth necessary to meet expanding needs of the traveling public. For airline employees it could mean, inevitably, fewer and fewer jobs, or perhaps no jobs at all for many of them. For the public it could mean higher fares and drastically reduced service. For the shareholders, it could mean little or no return on their investment, a situation many have already endured for years.[1]

In 1971, with Civil Aeronautics Board approval, the industry formed "AIR-Con," the Airline Industrial Relations Conference, to deal with "accelerating labor costs on an industry-wide basis." According to the ATA, productivity had also increased dramatically but was still far outpaced by wage increases. Between 1960 and 1970, productivity increased by 40 percent and wages by 90 percent over the course of the decade. Energy costs dealt another blow to the industry in 1973 when rising oil prices doubled operating costs for the industry. Cancelled flights due to jet-fuel shortages and dramatic pleas by Pan Am and others for fare hikes evidenced an industry in turmoil.[2]

To some extent, declining profits could be met with rising fares during the regulated era. Airlines could expect the Civil Aeronautics Board to set fares to ensure a measure of profitability (up to 10.5 percent). Between 1969 and 1974 the Civil Aeronautics Board approved rate increases for routes less than 1,800 miles and allowed for some changes in discounted promotional fares. The board also authorized reduction in service on highly served routes to decrease capacity to improve load factors. To better compete on these highly served routes, airlines began to "deck out" their new widebody aircraft with lounges and bars and other entertainment.[3]

Several U.S. congressmen challenged these fare and route changes, and the controversy resulted in the Domestic Passenger Fare Investigation (DPFI), a five-year formal investigation of fare rates and structures, aircraft depreciation, and leasing and load factors. The DPFI exposed the root of many of the problems of the regulation system: while the Civil Aeronautics Board held the authority to control entry into the industry, routes, and pricing, it did not regulate schedules or equipment. Airlines could schedule the most convenient and frequent service on nonsubsidized routes and schedule equipment for subsidized (often between smaller markets) routes during off-peak times, creating overcapacity on popular routes and highly inconvenient service on others. Between 1960 and 1975, the airlines successfully lobbied to diminish service to 173 destinations, impacting service between smaller communities. The DPFI took particular interest in these communities and compared regulated fares with unregulated intrastate fares, where fares were much less and the airlines profitable.[4] The DPFI reconfigured the fare structure in an attempt to even out the cost-per-mile fare charges for consumers.

The fare inquiry, the success of the intrastate systems, the collapse of the Pennsylvania Railroad in 1970, and growing interest in consumer advocacy opened the door for further investigation of the regulatory system. Academic professionals, economists in particular, argued for deregulation and found interested listeners in Washington. Movement toward airline deregulation began in earnest in 1974 when Republican President Gerald Ford created the National Commission on Regulatory Reform and Democratic Senator Edward Kennedy and future Supreme Court Justice Stephen Breyer, through the Subcommittee on Administrative Practice, began their investigation of airline regulation. Their investigation led to allegations of illegal political contributions from airline executives. The deregulation process continued under Democratic President Jimmy Carter with the appointment of the Cornell economist Alfred Kahn to the chair of the Civil Aeronautics Board. Kahn began loosening the guidelines for airfare rates and route access in 1977.[5]

Initially the airlines and airline unions stood against deregulation. The legacy airlines, proponents of regulation first in the 1930s, argued that deregulation would create instability in the industry. One of their greatest fears was the entry of new airlines onto profitable routes, while the older airlines remained obligated to fly unprofitable routes. Airline unions feared the entry of non-union airlines into the industry. Before the Senate Commerce Committee Subcommittee on Aviation, airline unions jointly testified, "We are vigorously opposed to legislation which our experience in this industry, our nation's history, human nature, and just plain common sense demonstrates to us will be anti-consumer, anti-industry, anti-labor and therefore, anti-public interest." However, by 1977 the push toward deregulation had broken apart the legacy carriers into two camps. United Airlines, with the nation's largest aircraft fleet, headed a pro-deregulation group that believed it could survive new competition. Pan American supported deregulation to secure domestic routes. The second group, headed by Eastern Airlines, argued that for the smaller legacy carriers, the "sky wars" that would result would lead to collapse.[6]

Profitability returned to the industry with record returns in 1977 with an oil-price freeze and the Civil Aeronautics Board price reforms instituted by its chairman Alfred Kahn. Improved profits and lower fares did not slow the push for deregulation. In 1978 passenger discontent over crowded flights, a pilots' strike at Northwest, and air-traffic-controller slowdowns increased public support for deregulation.[7] That year, with bipartisan support, Congress passed the Airline Deregulation Act, which dismantled the Civil Aeronautics Board in stages and outlawed the Mutual Aid Pact. The process of airline deregulation was complete during the Reagan Revolution in 1985.

After Deregulation

Today it is difficult to imagine, but early critics argued that deregulation would further weaken airlines in the face of union power. Airlines could no longer assume they would last through a strike when competitors could compete on routes, and dramatic fare discounts were now a weekly occurence. In 1979, with deregulation under way, United Airlines faced a fifty-eight-day strike by the IAM that crippled the airline and resulted in a 30 percent wage increase over three years. United faced the strike without the help of the Mutual Aid Pact, which was outlawed in the passage of the Airline Deregulation Act.[8]

Deregulation happened faster than most expected, and the legacy carriers were unprepared for the shock. Intense competition among airlines ensued with daily fare discounting and new non-union airlines entering the market. A second recession in the early 1980s proved deadly to many smaller airlines, and larger airlines responded with new route systems such as the "hub and spoke" and more efficient aircraft. Hostile takeovers and explosive labor relations also marked the 1980s, first with the air-traffic controllers union strike and then airline layoffs, the use of replacement workers, and concession bargaining resulting in two-tier wage scales and outsourcing.

While airline labor maintained high wages rates during the first five years of deregulation, devastating losses followed. The economist David Card estimated a wage drop of 5 percent for aircraft mechanics by 1984. Wages for baggage handlers under shared contracts faced similar shortfalls. The economist Pierre-Yves Cremieux estimated nominal losses for mechanics but more substantial wage losses for pilots and flight attendants. For flight attendants wages dropped 12 percent by 1985 and 39 percent by 1992. For pilots those figures were 12 and 22 percent, respectively.[9] Recent reports suggest that inflation adjusted salaries per employee grew less than 5 percent between 1979 and 2004.[10]

In 1983 airline workers faced the first of a rash of two-tier wages scales. These contracts created a second pay-scale system for workers hired after a specific date. Starting at American Airlines in 1983, this formula was in place at all legacy carriers except Braniff and Continental Airlines by 1986. The average differential between A- and B-scalers was 28 percent. For all workers, the cost of B scales was financial and psychological. In terms of wages, the lower starting rates depressed wages at the top in future bargaining. The climb to equity, if possible, was long for B-scalers as well. Psychologically, a two-tier system relegated some workers as perennial B-scalers. Further, it showed workers at the top of the A-scale that the industry could still attract skilled and unskilled workers at substantially lower wages.[11]

Labor relations in the industry worsened still as financiers like Frank Lorenzo and Carl Icahn purchased and merged various airlines, including TWA, Continental, and Eastern, resulting in extended and bitter battles with labor. Frank Lorenzo's push to build a non-union airline through deep wage cuts and replacement workers and the refusal of President George H. W. Bush to form a Presidential Emergency Board led to a two-year IAM strike at Eastern Airlines. Militant IAM members stayed out "One Day Longer," for nearly two years, than Lorenzo, and the airline collapsed in 1991.[12] Strike activity since then has diminished dramatically, with the National Mediation Board reporting only four strikes on major American airlines between 1992 and 2004.

However, airline employees continued to express their discontent through other means. In 1993, flight attendants at Alaska Airlines instituted "CHAOS," or "Create Havoc Around Our System," an intermittent "spontaneous" strike action on specific routes or at a specific station. The airline fired flight attendants who walked off the job in CHAOS action, but they were reinstated by the National Mediation Board. Subsequently, the Association of Flight Attendants has used or threatened to use CHAOS at U.S. Airways, United, and Northwest Airlines. Pilots at American Airlines called in sick en masse in a "sickout" in February 1999 to protest the integration policy of pilots from the recently acquired Reno Air.[13]

By the early 1990s, with one exception, all the airlines started after deregulation had folded. The "legacy" carriers, such as United, American, TWA, Delta, and Northwest, controlled most of the domestic air market. However, by the late 1990s, low-cost "startup" carriers—sometimes started by the legacy carriers such as Ted by United Airlines and Song by Delta—again with newer equipment and lower labor costs challenged the legacy carriers. With the hijacking of four U.S. airplanes by terrorists on September 11, 2001, the airline industry faced a new crisis. The following severe drop in air travel, high debt levels and labor costs, poor management strategies, and high fuel costs served to push several major carriers to the brink of or into bankruptcy. Between August 2001 and December 2006, the airline industry shrunk by over 150,000 workers.[14]

Since 2001, airline unions and management have struggled over concessions and restructuring plans under the scrutiny of the federal government. These struggles highlight the enormous disparity between workers and airline executives in bearing the burden of massive debt and the pressure this conflict has placed on cross-skill unionism in the industry. TWU members at American Airlines ratified an industry-leading contract just weeks before the 9/11 attacks, only to give back nearly 20 percent of it in 2003 to "share the pain" and help keep the airline out of bankruptcy. In 2006 the airline returned to profitability and offered $170 million of stock options to nine hundred managers as a reward, explaining that stock options offered to rank-and-file workers in 2003 were a comparable expression of cooperation.[15] In December 2002, United Airlines filed for Chapter 11 bankruptcy, the largest bankruptcy in aviation history. IAM members and other workers at the airline faced layoffs and $700 million in wage cuts. Many also lost their pensions, although the IAM bargained to continue a defined-benefits pension plan. The airline exited bankruptcy in 2006.

The concessionary contracts and general anxiety in the industry have also heightened skill-based organizing. Increasingly angry and demoralized aircraft mechanics have turned away from the cross-skill unionism of the IAM and TWU. In 2000, AMFA won representation elections for aircraft mechanics at Northwest Airlines. In 2002 it won elections at ATA Airlines and Southwest Airlines, where mechanics had been Teamsters. In 2003, aircraft mechanics at United voted in AMFA by a substantial margin in an election with less than 50 percent turnout, making it the largest union representative of aircraft mechanics in the United States. In 2007, AMFA is continuing its efforts to build support among aircraft mechanics at American and Delta Airlines.[16] Do AMFA's recent victories mark the end of cross-skill solidarity in the industry? It may be too early to tell; however, the brutal loss in the 2005 AMFA strike at Northwest Airlines signals the costs of the ferocious antagonism between AMFA and the IAM and the collapse of cross-skill unionism at that airline. However, airline unions are reaching out to each other nationally and internationally and arguing for better pay and job security in the name of airline safety. In the 1990s concerns about maintenance and even loading safety after the ValuJet fire and crash in Florida in 1996 and the Alaska Airlines crash in 2000 highlighted the dangers of outsourcing. Concerns over outsourcing grew again in early 2008 as thousands of flights were canceled in response to a Federal Aviation Agency maintenance audit triggered by faulty wiring repairs at Southwest Airlines. After 9/11, fears about inadequate screening, overseas maintenance, and even gang activity among baggage handlers took on new meaning. In response, airline workers and their unions, particularly flight attendants and mechanics, have increasingly emphasized their role as "safety workers" and an important line of defense in air security. The IAM general chairman, Randy Canale, described growing emphasis on building relationships with airline workers' unions overseas. In 2008 the IAM, the TWU, the Association of Flight Attendants–CWA, AFL-CIO, and the Association of Professional Flight Attendants, representing together over ninety thousand flight attendants, met for a three-day summit to coordinate political and bargaining strategy. Despite the volatility in the industry, union density has remained steady in the deregulated era. In 1983, 45.7 percent of airline employees were covered by union contracts. In 2001 that figure was 41.2 percent, and in 2007 it was 45.5 percent. National union density was 23.3 percent, 14.8 percent, and 13.3 percent, respectively.[17]

Conclusions

A study of labor relations on the ground in the American airline industry offers a counter perspective to the myth of labor complacency in the postwar era. Baggage handlers and aircraft mechanics together walked out in sanctioned and wildcat strikes over "small" injustices as well as wages and benefits in the North and the South. Dwarfed by meatpacking, steel, and auto, the industry until recently drew little historical interest among scholars studying twentieth-century labor. Nonetheless, the tremendous energy and resources unions put in to organizing the industry, the constant bargaining, and the confounding application of railway law to the airlines contributes to a new narrative for midcentury labor history—one that examines male workers in service occupations, the deep impact of federal policy on union organizing, and the powerful possibilities of cross-skill industrial unionism in the service economy. Baggage handlers and aircraft mechanics were (and are) often suburbanites. Their social worlds at home, at work, and at their (suburban) union halls are part of the rich history of postwar American working-class life. As scholars like Becky Nicolaides, Thomas Sugrue, and Jeff Cowie ask us to look at suburban workers and militant workers in the 1960s and 1970s, the airlines offers both.[18]

Oral Interviews

Ahern, Kenneth. Telephone interview by author. April 10, 2007.

———. Telephone interview by author. January 24, 2008.

Becker, Otto. Interview by author. Tape recording. Fort Worth, Tex. October 10, 1996.

Canale, Randy. Interview by author. Tape recording. Elk Grove Village, Ill. April 12, 2007.

Coleman, John V. Telephone interview by author. February 27, 2008.

Davies, R. E. G. Telephone interview by author. October 21, 1997.

Del Boccio, Richard. Telephone interview by author. April 19, 2007.

Gales, John. Interview by author. Tape recording. Glendale Heights, Ill. September 26, 2003.

Hall, Eddie. Interview by author. Tape recording. Maywood, Ill. July 29, 1997.

Johnson, Curtis. Telephone interview by author. April 10, 2007.

Kranski, Rob (pseud.). Interview by author. Tape recording. Algonquin, Ill. September 14, 1997.

Okamoto, Roy. Interview by author. Tape recording. Bloomingdale, Ill. August 27, 2003.

Parker, Millard (pseud.). Interview by author. Tape recording. Hillside, Ill. September 16, 2003.

Poulos, George (pseud.). Interview by author. Tape recording. Hanover Park, Ill. July 4, 1997.

Rutledge, George. Interview by author. Tape recording. Los Angeles, Calif. January 19, 1996.

Slouber, Robert. Interview by author. Tape recording. Willow Springs, Ill. July 17, 1997.

———. Telephone interview by author. September 1, 1998.

———. Telephone interview by author. October 13, 1999.

———. Telephone interview by author. March 16, 2000.

Sobczak, Richard (pseud.). Interview by author. Tape recording. Oak Lawn, Ill. September 9, 2003.

Sullivan, James P. "Sully." Interview by author. Tape recording. Brookfield, Ill. August 19, 2003.

Thiede, Kenneth. Interview by author. Tape recording. Des Plaines, Ill. April 26, 2007.

Trizinski, Martin. Interview by author. Tape recording. Schiller Park, Ill. December 5, 1997.

Manuscript Collections and Specialized Libraries

Brotherhood of Railway, Airline, and Steamship Clerks, Freight Handlers, Express, and Station Employees Records. M. Catherwood Library, Kheel Center for Labor-Management Documentation, New York State Industrial Labor Relations Archives, Cornell University, Ithaca.

Cole, Robert F., Papers. M. Catherwood Library, Kheel Center for Labor-Management Documentation, New York State Industrial Labor Relations Archives, Cornell University, Ithaca.

International Association of Machinists and Aerospace Workers Records, 1901–1974. State Historical Society of Wisconsin, Madison.

Kent, Paul, Collection. C. R. Smith Museum, Fort Worth, Tex.

Northwest Airlines Collection. Minnesota Historical Society, St. Paul.

Pan American Airways Collection. Otto G. Richter Library, University of Miami, Coral Gables, Fla.

Republic Airlines Collection. Minnesota Historical Society, St. Paul.

Transport Workers Union Collection. Robert Wagner Archives, Tamiment Institute/ Ben Josephson Library, New York University.

Transportation Library. Northwestern University, Evanston, Ill.

Notes

Introduction

1. This book is titled *On the Ground* because it is about airline workers on the ground as opposed to those who work the skies. The title also alludes to the phrase baggage handlers use when a plane has landed and will soon taxi to the gate. When a plane touches down, a ramp-crew chief will tell his crew they are "on the ground" and need to get ready to park and unload the airplane.

2. In 1967, 75 percent of union members under the age of forty lived in suburbs. *New York Times,* September 1, 1969, 8.

3. I thank the historian Joseph McCartin for pushing me to see baggage handlers this way. His helpful comments on a paper I gave at the American Historical Association in 2004 have contributed to this argument.

4. There is also an expansive body of literature on aircraft by scholars and "buffs." As James R. Hansen has argued, it is time for aviation history to expand beyond the "enthusiast" literature. James R. Hansen, "Aviation History in the Wider View," *Technology and Culture* 30.3 (July 1989): 643–52; Myron J. Smith, *The Airline Bibliography* (West Cornwall, Conn: Locust Hill Press, 1986). Robert J. Serling is one of the most prolific writers of this type of airline history. His works include *Eagle: The Story of American Airlines* (New York: St. Martin's Press, 1985), *Maverick: The Story of Robert Six and Continental Airlines* (New York: Doubleday and Co., 1974), *Howard Hughes' Airline: An Informal History of TWA* (New York: St. Martin's Press, 1983), *The Only Way to Fly: The Story of Western Airlines, America's Senior Air Carrier* (New York: Doubleday and Co., 1976), and *From the Captain to the Colonel: An Informal History of Eastern Airlines* (New York: Dial Press, 1980). Other titles in this category include Ray Scippa, *Point to Point: The Sixty-Year History of Continental Airlines* (Houston: Pioneer Publishers, 1994), Finis Farr, *Rickenbacker's Luck: An American Life* (Boston:

Houghton Mifflin, 1979), Robert Daley, *American Saga: Juan Trippe and His Pan American Empire* (New York: Random House, 1980), Matthew Josephson, *Empire of the Air: Juan Trippe and the Struggle for World Airways* (New York: Harcourt, 1944), David W. Lewis and William F. Trimble, *The Airway to Everywhere: A History of All American Aviation, 1937–1953* (Pittsburgh: University of Pittsburgh Press, 1988), David W. Lewis, *Delta: The History of an Airline* (Athens: University of Georgia Press, 1979), Ernest K. Gann, *Island in the Sky* (New York: Popular Library, 1944), Ernest K. Gann, *Blaze of Noon* (New York: Henry Holt and Co., 1946), Frank K. Smith, *Legacy of Wings: The Story of Harold P. Pitcairn* (New York: Jason Aronson, 1981), Horace Brock, *Flying the Oceans: A Pilot's Story of Pan Am, 1935–1955*, 3d ed. (New York: Jason Aronson, 1983), William S. Gooch, *From Crate to Clipper, with Captain Musick, Pioneer Pilot* (New York: Longmans, Green, and Co., 1939), and William S. Gooch, *Winged Highway* (New York: Longmans, Green, and Co., 1938). Trudy Baker wrote the following series of stewardess "tell-alls": *Coffee, Tea, or Me? Uninhibited Memoirs of Two Airline Stewardesses* (New York: Bantam Books, 1967), *The Coffee, Tea, or Me? Girls' 'Round-the-World Diary* (New York: Grosset and Dunlap, 1970), *The Coffee, Tea, or Me? Girls Lay It on the Line* (New York: Grosset and Dunlap, 1972), *The Coffee, Tea, or Me? Girls Get Away from It All* (New York: Grosset and Dunlap, 1974). See also Paula Kane, *Sex Objects in the Sky: A Personal Account of the Stewardess Rebellion* (Chicago: Follett Publishing Co., 1974), and Captain X and Reynolds Dobson, *Unfriendly Skies: A Pilot Reveals What's Really Going on in Today's Airline Industry* (New York: Berkley Books, 1989).

5. Dominic Pisano, *The Airplane in American Culture* (Ann Arbor: University of Michigan Press, 2003); Janet R. Daly Bednarek, *Reconsidering a Century of Flight* (Chapel Hill: University of North Carolina Press, 2003); Janet Daly Bednarek, *America's Airports: Airfield Development, 1918–1947* (College Station: Texas A&M Press, 2001); Pico Iyer, *The Global Soul: Jet Lag, Shopping Malls, and the Search for Home* (New York: Knopf, 2000); Mark Gottdiener, *Life in the Air: Surviving the New Culture of Air Travel* (Lanham, Md.: Rowman and Littlefield Press, 2001).

6. George Hopkins, *Airline Pilots: A Study in Elite Unionization* (Cambridge, Mass.: Harvard University Press, 1972); Georgia Panter Nielsen, *From Sky Girl to Flight Attendant: Women and the Making of a Union* (Ithaca, N.Y.: ILR Press, 1982); Kathleen Barry, *Femininity in Flight: A History of Flight Attendants* (Durham, N.C.: Duke University Press, 2007); Drew Whitelegg, *Working the Skies: The Fast-Paced Disorienting World of the Flight Attendant* (New York: New York University Press, 2007); Dorothy Sue Cobble, "'A Spontaneous Loss of Enthusiasm': Workplace Feminism and the Transformation of Women's Service Jobs in the 1970s," *International Labor and Working-Class History* 56 (1999): 23–44; Sandra L. Albrecht, "'We Are on Strike!': The Development of Labor Militancy in the Airline Industry," *Labor History* 45.1 (2004): 101–17; Isaac Cohen, "David L. Behncke, the Airline Pilots, and the New Deal: The Struggle for Federal Labor Legislation," *Labor History* 41.1 (February 2000): 47–62; Isaac Cohen, "Political Climate and Two Airline Strikes: Century Air in 1932 and

Continental Airlines in 1983–85," *Industrial and Labor Relations Review* 43.2 (January 1990): 308–23. Unpublished dissertations on airline work include Cathleen Dooley, "Battle in the Sky: A Cultural and Legal History of Sex Discrimination in the United States Airline Industry, 1930–1960" (Ph.D. dissertation, University of Arizona, 2001), and Suzanne Lee Kolm, "Women's Labor Aloft: A Cultural History of Airline Flight Attendants in the United States, 1930–1978" (Ph.D. dissertation, Brown University, 1995).

7. Dana Eischen, "Representation Disputes and Their Resolution in the Railroad and Airline Industries," in *The Railway Labor Act at Fifty: Collective Bargaining in the Railroad and Airline Industries,* ed. Charles M. Rehmus (Washington, D.C.: U.S. Government Printing Office, 1977), 65.

8. I would like to thank the historian Patricia Cooper for her insights on the cultures of work and leisure on the ramp.

9. "More-Mow!" *Time,* September 2, 1966.

Chapter 1: The U.S. Airlines through the 1930s

1. George Rutledge, interview by author, tape recording, January 19, 1996, Los Angeles, Calif. Rutledge retired after almost fifty years with the company. At the time of his retirement, no other employee still working for American Airlines had more seniority than he. Rutledge died in 1998.

2. Joseph J. Corn, *The Winged Gospel: America's Romance with Aviation, 1900–1950* (New York: Oxford University Press, 1983), 3–9.

3. Joseph L. Nicholson, *Air Transportation Management: Its Practices and Policies* (New York: John Wiley and Sons, 1951), 2.

4. Henry Ladd Smith, *Airways: The History of Commercial Aviation in the United States,* 2d ed. (New York: Russell and Russell, 1965), 23–24.

5. Carl Solberg, *Conquest of the Skies: A History of Commercial Aviation in America* (Boston: Little, Brown, 1979), 8.

6. Janet R. Daly Bednarek with Michael Bednarek, *Dreams of Flight: General Aviation in the United States* (College Station: Texas A&M Press, 2003), 5.

7. Smith, *Airways,* 24–35; Corn, *Winged Gospel,* 73.

8. Solberg, *Conquest,* 9; R. E. G. Davies, *Pan Am: An Airline and Its Aircraft* (New York: Orion Books, 1987), 2.

9. Corn, *Winged Gospel,* 11.

10. Smith, *Airways,* 32–39.

11. Ibid., 39.

12. Solberg, *Conquest,* 22.

13. Smith, *Airways,* 39–40.

14. Ibid., 47.

15. Corn, *Winged Gospel,* 51–57; Solberg, *Conquest,* 31.

16. Smith, *Airways,* 86.

17. Solberg, *Conquest,* 30.

18. Myron Smith, *The Airline Bibliography: The Salem College Guide to Sources on Commercial Aviation* (West Cornwall, Conn.: Locust Hill Press, 1986–88), 118.

19. Smith, *Airways,* 87.

20. Solberg, *Conquest,* 32.

21. Ibid., 32.

22. Ibid., 32–34.

23. Smith, *Airways,* 87; Solberg, *Conquest,* 33.

24. R. E. G. Davies, *Airlines of the United States since 1914* (London: Putman, 1972), 8–10.

25. Smith, *Airways,* 54.

26. Patricia Ann Michaelis, "The Development of Passenger Service on Commercial Airlines, 1926–1930" (Ph.D. dissertation, University of Kansas, 1980), 11.

27. Smith, *Airways,* 55. For extensive discussion of the role of airmail in the birth of commercial aviation, see F. Robert van der Linden, *Airlines and Air Mail: The Post Office and the Birth of the Commercial Aviation Industry* (Lexington: University of Kentucky Press, 2002).

28. Michaelis, "Passenger Service," 11.

29. Smith, *Airways,* 56–57.

30. Solberg, *Conquest,* 17–18. F. Robert van der Linden dates this first airmail flight as May 15, 1918 (*Airlines,* 1–2).

31. Smith, *Airways,* 62–63.

32. Solberg, *Conquest,* 20.

33. Ibid., 19; Smith, *Airways,* 74.

34. George Hopkins, *The Airline Pilots: A Study in Elite Unionization,* 2d ed. (Cambridge, Mass.: Harvard University Press, 1998), 19–29.

35. Michaelis, "Passenger Service," 17.

36. Smith, *Airways,* 76.

37. Solberg, *Conquest,* 25.

38. Michaelis, "Passenger Service," 18–19.

39. Ibid., 21.

40. Ibid., 24–25.

41. Smith, *Airways,* 94.

42. Davies, *Airlines,* 39.

43. Smith, *Airways,* 107–11; Davies, *Airlines,* 42–54; Smith, *Airline Bibliography,* 115–218; Michaelis, "Passenger Service," 27–37.

44. Michaelis, "Passenger Service," 29.

45. Davies, *Airlines,* 39.

46. Smith, *Airways,* 117.

47. The amendment to the Air Mail Act made it possible for Western Air Express, a well-run company, to turn a profit. Smith, *Airways,* 119.

48. Davies, *Airlines,* 30.

49. Michaelis, "Passenger Service," 38–39.

50. Smith, *Airways,* 98–99.

51. Michaelis, "Passenger Service," 43.

52. Ibid., 40–69.

53. Smith, *Airways,* 122–23. Patricia Michaelis also describes the American public's overwhelming response to Lindbergh's flight. Michaelis, "Passenger Service," 122–29.

54. Smith, *Airways,* 124–28.

55. Davies, *Airlines,* 54–55.

56. Ibid., 69; Smith, *Airways,* 114–15.

57. Davies, *Airlines,* 43–45.

58. Michaelis, "Passenger Service," 159. Michaelis devotes an entire chapter to the Guggenheim Fund.

59. Davies, *Airlines,* 65.

60. Michaelis, "Passenger Service," 159.

61. Ibid., 160; Smith, *Airways,* 113.

62. Davies, *Airlines,* 57.

63. Ibid., 210–39.

64. Bednarek, *America's Airports,* 30–31.

65. Michaelis, "Passenger Service," 71.

66. Bednarek, *America's Airports,* 73.

67. Michaelis, "Passenger Service," 71. It is not clear how these sites reflect B. Russell Shaw's criteria.

68. Bednarek, *America's Airports,* 35; Archibald Black, "Passenger Facilities at Airway Terminals: These Are Matters of Great Importance Which Require Critical Attention to Details," *Airway Age* 9.9 (1928): 37–38.

69. Michaelis, "Passenger Service," 69–97.

70. Bednarek, *America's Airports,* 98–101.

71. Davies, *Airlines,* 98.

72. Solberg, *Conquest,* 110–11, 127; Davies, *Airlines,* 80–85.

73. W. David Lewis, ed., *Airline Executives and Federal Regulation: Case Studies in American Enterprise from the Airmail Era to the Dawn of the Jet Age* (Columbus: Ohio State University Press, 2000), 3; Van der Linden, *Airlines,* ix.

74. Davies, *Airlines,* 114–15; Smith, *Airways,* 158–60.

75. Smith, *Airways,* 131–32.

76. Van der Linden, *Airlines,* 152–73.

77. Davies, *Airlines,* 116–22; Smith, *Airlines,* 167–86.

78. Smith, *Airline Bibliography,* 127–28.

79. George W. Cearley Jr., *American Airlines: An Illustrated History* (Dallas: George Walker Cearley Jr., 1981), 29.

80. Smith, *Airlines,* 224–47.

81. Davies, *Airlines,* 162

82. Ibid., 156–64, 194; Mark L. Kahn, "Labor-Management Relations in the Airline Industry," in *The Railway Labor Act at Fifty: Collective Bargaining in the Railroad and Airline Industries,* ed. Charles M. Rehmus (Washington, D.C.: U.S. Government Printing Office, 1977), 98–101; Van der Linden, *Airlines,* 260–91; William Leary, ed., *Encyclopedia of American Business History and Biography: The Airline Industry* (New York: Facts on File, 1992), 22–26; Elmer A. Lewis, *Laws Relating to Postal Air Service* (Washington, D.C.: U.S. Government Printing Office, 1951), 15.

83. Lewis, *Airline Executives,* 11.

84. Ibid., 12; Kahn, "Labor-Management," 104.

85. Davies, *Airlines,* 200–201; Solberg, *Conquest,* 199, 210.

86. "History of Pan American World Airways, 1927–1945," Pan American Airways Collection, Otto G. Richter Library, University of Miami, Coral Gables, Florida (hereafter PAA Collection), box 66; Davies, *Airlines,* 240–63.

87. George Rutledge, interview.

88. Cearley, *American,* 11; George Rutledge, interview.

89. Cearley, *American,* 9; George Rutledge, interview.

90. George Rutledge, interview.

91. Ibid.

92. C. B. Allen, "The Airline Attendant's Job," *Aviation* (April 1931): 244–45.

93. Ibid.

94. Solberg, *Conquest,* 211–12.

95. Ibid., 212–14. According to the 1934 American Airlines operations manual, a stewardess had to be between twenty and twenty-eight years old, not taller than five feet, four inches, and weigh no more than 118 pounds. She had to be a registered nurse, have a pleasant personality and appearance, and a good moral character. *American Airlines Operations Manual* 1934 (hereafter *American Manual*), section I, paragraphs 71–74, Paul Kent Collection, C. R. Smith Museum, Fort Worth, Tex. (hereafter Paul Kent Collection). For further discussion of airline-stewardess work in the 1930s, see Barry, *Femininity in Flight,* 11–35.

96. George Rutledge, interview.

97. Claude Puffer, *Air Transportation* (Philadelphia: Blakiston Co., 1941), 642–46.

98. Department of Labor, Bureau of Labor Statistics, "Wages and Hours of Labor in Air Transportation, 1931," *Monthly Labor Review* 35 (August 1932): 339.

99. The wages shown here for pilots are for 110 hours of service. Pilots in this survey flew on average of eighty hours a month. Using that figure, their wages in the East North Central region fall to $550.22 in one month; in the Western region they fall to $614.86 in one month.

100. Department of Labor, Bureau of Labor Statistics, "Wages and Hours of Labor in Air Transportation, 1931" 340–41.

101. Department of Labor, Bureau of Labor Statistics, "Wages and Hours of Labor in the Motor-Vehicle Industry, 1930," *Monthly Labor Review* 33 (September 1931): 149.

102. Department of Labor, "Wages and Hours of Labor in Air Transportation, 1931," 342–44.

103. Department of Labor, Bureau of Labor Statistics, "Wages and Hours of Labor in Air Transportation, 1933," *Monthly Labor Review* 38 (January 1934): 647–65.

104. *American Manual,* section II, paragraph 131.

105. Ibid., section VII, paragraphs 1152 and 1153.

106. Ibid., section VII, paragraphs 1203 and 1204.

107. This conflicts with the recollections of George Rutledge.

108. *American Manual,* section IX, paragraphs 1471–94.

109. Ibid., section IV, paragraph 674.

110. Cearley, *American,* 35–39.

111. Ibid., 39; Davies, *Airlines,* 189–94.

112. *American Manual,* section V, paragraph 802.

113. Solberg, *Conquest,* 25.

114. *American Manual,* section V, paragraphs 802–3.

115. Ibid., section II, paragraphs 134 and 137.

116. Ibid., section II, paragraphs 121–27.

117. Ibid., section II, paragraphs 171–203.

118. As seen in exhibits at the C.R. Smith Museum, Fort Worth, Tex.; Cearley, *American,* 12, 19.

119. Cohen, "David L. Behncke," 47–62; Cohen, "Political Climate," 308–22.

120. Office of Federal Coordinator of Transportation, Section of Research, Section of Labor Relations, *Hours, Wages, and Working Conditions in Scheduled Air Transportation* (Washington, D.C.: U.S. Government Printing Office, 1936) xxi; IAM Aircraft Local 734 to H. J. Carr, telegram, March 16, 1934, International Association of Machinists and Aerospace Workers Records, 1901–1974, State Historical Society of Wisconsin, Madison (hereafter IAM Collection), microfilm, reel 296, vol. 1.

121. Lizabeth Cohen, *Making a New Deal: Industrial Workers in Chicago, 1919–1939* (Cambridge, Mass.: Harvard University Press, 1991); David Brody, *The American Labor Movement* (Lanham, Md.: University Press of America, 1985); Nelson Lichtenstein and Howell John Harris, *Industrial Democracy in America: The Ambiguous Promise* (Washington, D.C.: Woodrow Wilson Center Press, 1996); Melvyn Dubofsky, *The State and Labor in Modern America* (Chapel Hill: University of North Carolina Press, 1994), 92–101.

122. Nelson Lichtenstein, *State of the Union: A Century of American Labor* (Princeton, N.J.: Princeton University Press, 2002), 35–48.

123. Cohen, "David L. Behncke," 53–56.

124. Dubofsky, *State and Labor,* 92–101.

125. William V. Henzey, "Labor Problems in the Airline Industry," *Law and Contemporary Problems* 25.1 (Winter 1960): 44.

126. National Mediation Board, *Fifteen Years under the Railway Labor Act, Amended and the National Mediation Board, 1934–1949* (Washington, D.C.: U.S. Government Printing Office, 1950), 1–7; Robert E. Allen and Timothy J. Keaveny, *Contemporary Labor Relations* (Reading, Mass.: Addison-Wesley Publishing Co., 1988), 63–64; Robert G. Rodden, *The Fighting Machinists: A Century of Struggle* (Washington, D.C.: Kelly Press, 1985), 119; National Mediation Board and Charles M. Rehmus, *The National Mediation Board at Fifty: Its Impact on Railroad and Airline Labor Disputes* (Washington, D.C.: U.S. Government Printing Office, 1984), 9–10.

127. Hopkins, *Airline Pilots*, 46–51; Leary, *Encyclopedia*, 17–19.

128. Leary, *Encyclopedia*, 124; Cohen, "Political Climate," 313.

129. Leary, *Encyclopedia*, 18.

130. Davies, *Airlines*, 122–23; Roger Bilstein, "C. R. Smith: An American Original," in *Airline Executives and Federal Regulation: Case Studies in American Enterprise from the Airmail Era to the Dawn of the Jet Age*, ed. W. David Lewis (Columbus: Ohio State University Press, 2000), 85; Hopkins, *Airline Pilots*, 107–8; Leary, *Encyclopedia*, 125.

131. Rodden, *Fighting Machinists*, 119.

132. Paul Ottman to H. J. Carr, June 27, 1933, IAM Collection, reel 296, vol. 1.

133. Earl Melton to Mr. A. O. Wharton, December 15, 1935, IAM Collection, reel 296, vol. 1.

134. *American Manual*, section II, paragraphs 213–14.

135. Airline Division, International Association of Machinists, "Collective Labor Agreements in Effect between Various Labor Organizations and Principal Scheduled Air Carriers Filed with the National Mediation Board, as of June 30, 1938, 1939, 1940, 1941, 1942, 1943, 1944, 1945, and 1946, Source—Annual Reports of the National Mediation Board," IAM Collection, reel 316, vol. 6.

136. A. D. Durst to Mr. William Green, August 31, 1933, IAM Collection, reel 315, vol. 1; Robert L. Sexton and Louis Needham to A. O. Wharton, November 5, 1933, IAM Collection, reel 315, vol. 1.

137. T. E. Carroll to Mr. Harry J. Carr, October 29, 1934, IAM Collection, reel 315, vol. 1.

138. Thomas E. Carroll to Mr. F. D. Laudermann, August 29, 1936, IAM Collection, reel 315, vol. 1.

139. L. Needham to Mr. H. W. Brown, July 18, 1938, IAM Collection, reel 315, vol. 1.

140. Rufino Lopez to Mr. H. W. Brown, August 11, 1936, IAM Collection, reel 315, vol. 1.

141. A. O. Wharton to Mr. Thomas E. Carroll, October 2, 1936; Thomas E. Carroll to Mr. Fred D. Laudemann, December 4, 1936; L. Needham to Mr. E. C. Yaeger, September 19, 1939, IAM Collection, reel 315, vol. 1.

142. Carl Fricks and Victorino V. Lopez, "Complaint of Violation of the Code of Fair Competition for the Air Transport Industry," April 6, 1934, IAM Collection, reel 315, vol. 1.

143. Rufino Lopez to Mr. E. C. Yaeger, August 28, 1942, IAM Collection, reel 315, vol. 2; Rufino Lopez to Mr. H. W. Brown, August 11, 1936, IAM Collection, reel 315, vol. 1.

144. Unsigned to Mr. R. D. Sundell, May 23, 1938, IAM Collection, reel 315, vol. 1.

145. L. Needham to H. W. Brown, telegram, July 8, 1938; Louis Needham, Steven M. Bernard, and Paul A. Whitiford to Mr. Erwin Balluder, August 2, 1938, IAM Collection, reel 315, vol. 1.

146. Unsigned to Mr. Walter Nash, February 27, 1940, IAM Collection, reel 315, vol. 1.

147. Rodden, *Fighting Machinists,* 120–21.

Chapter 2: Airline Work during World War II

1. Reginald M. Cleveland, *Air Transport at War* (New York: Harper and Bros., 1946), 18–20.

2. Robert Serling, *Eagle: The Story of American Airlines* (New York: St. Martin's/Marek, 1985), 153.

3. R. E. G. Davies, *Airlines of the United States since 1914* (London: Putnam, 1972), 264–65; R. E. G. Davies, telephone interview by author, October 21, 1997; Cleveland, *Air Transport,* 19–20.

4. Cleveland, *Air Transport,* 1, 17–19; Davies, *Airlines,* 276; Serling, *Eagle,* 161.

5. Davies, *Airlines,* 277.

6. Office of War Information, "This Report on U.S. Civil Airlines in the War Is Advance Release: For Wednesday Morning Papers, December 22, 1943," 1–2, Northwest Airlines Collection, Minnesota Historical Society, St. Paul (hereafter NWA Collection), "General Historical Data, 1926–1958" file, box 23.

7. Davies, *Airlines,* 266–68.

8. Alfredo de los Rios, "Flying Freight along the Amazon," *Skyways,* February 1943, 59–62, PAA Collection, box 58; "History of Pan American World Airways, 1927–1945," PAA Collection, box 66.

9. Davies, *Airlines,* 268; Cleveland, *Air Transport,* 23–56; Solberg, *Conquest,* 260–69.

10. Davies, *Airlines,* 276.

11. Cleveland, *Air Transport,* 4, 149–62.

12. Solberg, *Conquest,* 262–63. C-47s had the body of a DC-3, but the new Pratt and Whitney engines were more powerful than those previously put in commercial DC-3s. DC-3s with the older Wright Cyclone engines were designated C-39s when used by the military.

13. Davies, *Airlines,* 276.

14. Office of War Information, "This Report," 10.

15. Ibid., 11.

16. "About the Mod Center," *Field and Hangar,* June 1945, 11, NWA Collection.

Field and Hangar was a newsletter published by Northwest Airlines exclusively for employees of the St. Paul Modification Center.

17. "Center Closes with Brilliant Record," *Field and Hangar,* September 1945, 1, NWA Collection.

18. Solberg, *Conquest,* 262; Cleveland, *Air Transport,* 21.

19. For discussion of the rapid upgrading of airport facilities during the war, see Douglas G. Karsner, "'Leaving on a Jet Plane': Commercial Aviation, Airports, and Post-Industrial American Society, 1933–1970" (Ph.D. dissertation, Temple University, 1993), chap. 2.

20. Serling, *Eagle,* 166.

21. "An Open Letter to the Public!" from Herbert C. Dobbs, Traffic Manager, Miami, Fla., Pan American World Airways, June 20, 1945, PAA Collection, "System Policy" file, box 354.

22. Solberg, *Conquest,* 274–75; Serling, *Eagle,* 166–67.

23. Department of Labor, Bureau of Labor Statistics, *Employment Opportunities in Aviation Occupations, Part 1—Postwar Employment Outlook* (Washington, D.C.: U.S. Government Printing Office, 1945), 7.

24. John Frederick, *Commercial Air Transportation,* 4th ed. (Homewood, Ill.: Richard D. Irwin, Inc., 1955), 87.

25. Solberg, *Conquest,* 274–75.

26. U.S. Bureau of the Census, *Race of Employed Persons (Except on Public Emergency Work) and of Experienced Workers Seeking Work, by Industry and Sex, for Regions: 1940* (Washington, D.C.: U.S. Government Printing Office, 1943).

27. Herbert Northrup, Armand J. Theiboldt, and William N. Chernish, *The Negro in the Air Transport Industry* (Philadelphia: Wharton School of Finance and Commerce, University of Pennsylvania Press, 1971), 56–57.

28. U.S. Bureau of the Census, *Detailed Industry of Employed (Except Emergency Work), and of Experienced Workers Seeking Work, by Color and Sex, for the State, and Cities of 100,000 or More: 1940* (Washington, D.C.: U.S. Government Printing Office, 1943).

29. Ibid.

30. Ibid.

31. Ibid.

32. U.S. Bureau of the Census, *Age of Employed Persons (Exce. Emerg.), and of Experienced Workers Seeking Work, by Industry and Sex, for United States by Regions (with Nonwhite for the South): 1940* (Washington, D.C.: U.S. Government Printing Office, 1943).

33. Pauline Fortune, "Search for the Woman," *Air Transport,* November 1943, 23, Transportation Library, Northwestern University, Evanston, Ill. (hereafter Trans. Library).

34. Ibid., 24.

35. Ibid.

36. Wm. H. Cox to Earl Melton, August 13, 1945, IAM Collection, reel 296, vol. 1.

37. George Rutledge, interview.

38. Memo from Benjamin Bially and Nicholas M. Kiriacon, TWU Local 501, October 6, 1951, "CASE NO. 139–50–10 FLEET SERVICE CLERKS LOCAL 501—A. A.—NEW YORK, NEW YORK, RECLASSIFICATION AND AWARD OF BACK PAY," Transport Workers Union Collection, Robert Wagner Archives, Tamiment Institute/Ben Josephson Library, New York University (hereafter TWU Collection), "Local 501, 1950–1952" file, box 25; Otto Becker, interview by author, tape recording, Fort Worth, Tex., October 10, 1996.

39. *New Horizons,* June 1943, 26–27, PAA Collection, "1941–1960, Women—Ground Jobs" file, box 257.

40. Such designations were common in other industries during the war. See Ruth Milkman, *Gender at Work: The Dynamics of Job Segregation* (Urbana: University of Illinois Press, 1987).

41. *New Horizons,* February 1942, 12, PAA Collection, "1941–1960, Women—Ground Jobs" file, box 257.

42. Fortune, "Search for the Woman," 22.

43. *Northwest Airlines News,* December 22, 1950, 12, NWA Collection, microfilm.

44. U.S. Bureau of the Census, *Detailed Industry of Employed (Except Emergency Work), and of Experienced Workers Seeking Work, by Color and Sex, for the State and Cities of 100,000 or More: 1940* (Washington, D.C: U.S. Government Printing Office, 1943); B. W. King to Mr. Eric Peterson, September, 29, 1943, IAM Collection, reel 315, vol. 2; B. W. King to Mr. Eric Peterson, December 15, 1943, IAM Collection, reel 315, vol. 2.

45. Alex Lichtenstein, "'Scientific Unionism' and the 'Negro Question': Communists and the Transport Workers Union in Miami, 1944–1949," in *Southern Labor in Transition, 1940–1995,* ed. Robert H. Zieger (Knoxville: University of Tennessee Press, 1997), 66.

46. *The Clipper,* February 1949, 2, PAA Collection.

47. *Pan American Alaska Sector Clipper,* September 1944, 3, PAA Collection.

48. Northrup, Thieboldt, and Chernish, *Negro,* 29–30.

49. Lichtenstein, "'Scientific Unionism,'" 66.

50. George Rutledge, interview; Otto Becker, interview; *Agreement between American Airlines, Inc., and Transport Workers Union of America–CIO Covering Airline Mechanic, Plant Maintenance, Fleet Service, and Ground Service Employees of American Airlines, Inc., Effective Date—September 15, 1946,* Paul Kent Collection, C. R. Smith Museum, Fort Worth, Tex. (hereafter Paul Kent Collection).

51. George Herrick, "Postwar Cargo Handling," *Air Transport,* October 1943, 22–27, Trans. Library.

52. *Aviation,* March 1943, 195, Trans. Library.

53. *Air Transport,* December 1944, 92; October 1943, 23; and August 1944, 75, Trans. Library.

54. *Air Transport,* November 1944, 85, Trans. Library.

55. George Rutledge, "Speed by Efficiency Should Rule Postwar Cargo Handling," *Air Transport,* April 1944, 42, Trans. Library.

56. Cleveland, *Air Transport,* 125–35.

57. Office of War Information, "This Report," 11–12.

58. Claude Houser to Mr. E. E. Walker, November 29, 1945, IAM Collection, reel 292, vol. 1.

59. Robert Slouber, telephone interview by author, March 16, 2000.

60. Paul L. Graf, Chief Agent, Ramp—LV, to Public Relations Department—NY, August 31, 1947, Paul Kent Collection.

61. Robert Slouber, interview by author, tape recording, Willow Springs, Ill., July 17, 1997.

62. E. B. McNatt, *Labor Relations in the Air Transport Industry under the Railway Labor Act* (Urbana: University of Illinois Press, 1948), 15–16.

63. Robert H. Zieger, *The CIO: 1935–1955* (Chapel Hill: University of North Carolina Press, 1995), 165.

64. Department of Labor, Bureau of Statistics, *Wage Rates of Union Street Railway Employees, June 1, 1942,* Bulletin No. 731 (Washington, D.C.: U.S. Government Printing Office, 1943), 4; and *Earnings in Ship Construction Yards, Fall 1942,* Bulletin No. 752 (Washington, D.C.: U.S. Government Printing Office, 1943), 7.

65. Department of Labor, Bureau of Statistics, *Wages and Hours of Union Motortruck Drivers and Helpers, June 1, 1942,* Bulletin No. 732 (Washington, D.C.: U.S. Government Printing Office, 1943), 11.

66. H. C. Summers to Mr. H. W. Brown, October 3, 1945, IAM Collection, reel 296, vol. 1. Robert Slouber and Otto Becker recalled very high turnover rates during the war years.

67. E. H. Chambers to Mr. F. D. Laudemann, September 4, 1943, IAM Collection, reel 315, vol. 2.

68. Robert Slouber, telephone interview by author, October 13, 1999.

69. Ibid.

70. Ibid.

Chapter 3: Organizing the Industry, 1945–49

1. Claude Houser to Mr. E. E. Walker, November 29, 1945, IAM Collection, reel 292, vol. 1.

2. Nicholson, *Air Transportation,* 262.

3. This chapter does not address the union organization of airline pilots. ALPA-AFL swiftly organized virtually the entire U.S domestic airline industry between 1939 and 1950.

4. Christopher L. Tomlins, "AFL Unions in the 1930s: Their Performance in Historical Perspective," *Journal of American History* 65.4 (March 1979): 1021–42.

5. Frank Heisler to Mr. H. W. Brown, December 27, 1945, IAM Collection, reel 297, vol. 2; Harold F. Reardon to Frank Heisler, May 14, 1945, IAM Collection, reel 297, vol. 2; Barry, *Femininity in Flight*, 68–72.

6. Nixson Denton, *History of the Brotherhood of Railway and Steamship Clerks, Freight Handlers, Express and Station Employees* (Cincinnati: Brotherhood of Railway and Steamship Clerks, Freight Handlers, Express, and Station Employees, 1965), 7–28, 155, 179, 182–200; Gary Fink, ed., *Labor Unions* (Westport, Conn.: Greenwood Press, 1977), 201–3, 321–22, 400–402.

7. Rodden, *Fighting Machinists*, 28–98; Mark Perlman, *The Machinists: A New Study in American Trade Unionism* (Cambridge, Mass.: Harvard University Press, 1961), 100–105.

8. Rodden, *Fighting Machinists* 99–102; Perlman, *Machinists*, 109–11.

9. "Airline and Related Companies in U.S. Whose Employees Are Represented by IAM (by unit)," Brotherhood of Railway, Airline, and Steamship Clerks, Freight Handlers, Express and Station Employees Records, M. Catherwood Library, Kheel Center for Labor-Management Documentation, New York State Industrial Labor Relations Archives, Cornell University, Ithaca, N.Y. (hereafter BRC Collection), box 450, "Exhibits C-2247/1954 Exhibits Representation Dispute Stock and Storeroom Employees" file.

10. Rodden, *Fighting Machinists*, 122, 161–62.

11. Joshua Freeman, *In Transit: The Transport Workers Union in New York City, 1933–1966* (New York: Oxford University Press, 1989), 39–103, 249–63.

12. Ibid., 262.

13. McNatt, *Labor Relations*, 15–16. Company unions were not permitted under the 1934 amendment to the Railway Labor Act. Douglas Leslie, ed., *The Railway Labor Act* (Washington, D.C.: Bureau of National Affairs, 1991).

14. Nicholson, *Air Transportation*, 251, 261–62.

15. Brad Williams, *The Anatomy of an Airline* (Garden City, N.Y.: Doubleday and Co., 1970), 64.

16. E. H. Chambers to Mr. F. D. Laudemann, September 4, 1943, IAM Collection, reel 315, vol. 2.

17. Charles Kief to George M. Harrison, June 5, 1944, BRC Collection, "1943–1945, Organization—Northwest Airlines, Inc." file.

18. Otto Becker, interview; George Rutledge, interview. Both men noted a change in the type of employee hired during the war. These employees were less likely to share the passion for the airline that these men and their early colleagues held. Furthermore, stemming from their perspective as managers in the airlines, they felt that these workers were not as dedicated to the company, in part because the company could not be as selective in their hiring of employees due to the wartime shortage of workers.

19. "Keep Closer to Employees," editorial, *Air Transport,* March 1945, 21, Trans. Library.

20. George Rutledge, interview.

21. E. H. Chambers to Mr. F. D. Laudemann, September 4, 1943, IAM Collection, reel 315, vol. 2.

22. U.S. Bureau of the Census. *Color, Nativity, and Citizenship of Employed Persons (Except on Public Emergency Work), by Industry and Sex, for the United States: March 1940* (Washington, D.C.: U.S. Government Printing Office, 1943).

23. Freeman, *In Transit,* 261–63; Helen Wood, *Employment Opportunities in Aviation Occupations* (Washington, D.C: U.S. Government Printing Office, 1945), 17–18.

24. The ALMA represented fleet-service clerks from 1943 to 1946, the years he was serving in the military. Robert Slouber, interview.

25. *Agreement between American Airlines, Inc., and Air Line Mechanics Association, International, Representing the Employees of the Company Comprising the Crafts or Classes of Air Line Mechanics, Stores, Fleet Service and Plant Maintenance Personnel,* April 1943, 12, Paul Kent Collection.

26. Robert Slouber, interview.

27. D. J. Omer to Mr. Earl Melton, April 26, 1945, IAM Collection, reel 296, vol. 1.

28. H. C. Summers to Mr. H. W. Brown, October 3, 1945, IAM Collection, reel 296, vol. 1.

29. E. H. Chambers to Mr. F. D. Laudemann, September 4, 1943, IAM Collection, reel 315, vol. 2.

30. Charles Kief to George M. Harrison, June 5, 1944, BRC Collection, "1943–1945, Organization—Northwest Airlines, Inc." file.

31. Philip S. Foner, *Women and the American Labor Movement: From the First Trade Unions to the Present,* 3d ed. (New York: Free Press, 1982); Ruth Milkman, *Gender at Work: The Dynamics of Job Segregation* (Urbana: University of Illinois Press, 1987); Dorothy Sue Cobble, *The Other Women's Movement: Workplace Justice and Social Rights in Modern America* (Princeton, N.J: Princeton University Press, 2004); Alice Kessler-Harris, *Out to Work: A History of Wage-Earning Women in the United States* (Oxford: Oxford University Press, 1983); Karen Anderson, *Wartime Women: Sex Roles, Family Relations, and the Status of Women during World War II* (Westport, Conn: Greenwood Press, 1981); Amy Vita Kesselman, *Fleeting Opportunities: Women Shipyard Workers in Portland and Vancouver during World War II and Reconversion* (Albany: State University of New York Press, 1990); Elizabeth Faue, *Community of Suffering and Struggle: Women, Men, and the Labor Movement in Minneapolis, 1915–1945* (Chapel Hill: University of North Carolina Press, 1991); Nancy Felice Gabin, *Feminism in the Labor Movement: Women and the United Auto Workers, 1935–1975* (Ithaca, N.Y.: Cornell University Press, 1990); Barry, *Femininity in Flight.*

32. Mrs. Lewis to H. A. Schrader, September 13, 1944, IAM Collection, reel 292, vol. 1.

33. "Labor and Airline Transport November 1946," 20, BRC Collection, "July 1946–December 1946, Organization—Air Transport Industry" file.

34. Robert Slouber, telephone interview by author, September 1, 1998. Slouber felt that wages were low compared to those in other industries at the end of the war.

35. "Labor and Airline Transport November 1946," 32–33, BRC Collection, "July 1946–December 1946, Organization—Air Transport Industry" file.

36. During the war and immediately after, certain jobs appeared and disappeared. For example, most of the employees working at the Northwest Airlines Modification Center in St. Paul were laid off at the end of the war. Attempting to organize these workers only complicated organizing drives among employees working in commercial operations. At Pan Am, the job of "beaching crew" or "boatmen," work requiring nautical as well as heavy-machinery skill, disappeared as the airline retired seaplanes from their fleet. In the case of employees working on the ground, particularly for fleet-service clerks, the unions and management struggled not only with the duties they performed but also how to classify their work. "Ashore!" *New Horizons,* December 1940, 22–23; "Pacific Division, Organization, Airport—Maintenance, Boatmen, January 21, 1942," PAA Collection, "Operations Circulars" file, box 400; Smith, *Airline Bibliography,* 173.

37. Freeman, *In Transit,* 261.

38. Elizabeth Whitman to Mr. Douglas L. MacMahon, TWU Collection, "Local 500 AID-1944" file, box 24.

39. Lichtenstein, "'Scientific Unionism,'" 58, 62.

40. The IAM also organized mechanics in Texas in the 1930s, as discussed in chapter 2. During this period the IAM also successfully organized mechanics at Eastern Airlines, a company with a large portion of its employees in Atlanta and Miami.

41. Joseph Besch to Mr. S. L. Newman, August 31, 1943, IAM Collection, reel 315, vol. 1.

42. "Membership Record, Pan American Negroe Workers, Miami, Florida," TWU Collection, "Local 500 ATD-1944" file, box 24.

43. "Enclosing 72 Initiations: Brownsville, Sept. 29, 1945," TWU Collection, "Local 503 ATD, 1945–1960" file, box 25.

44. Transport Workers Union of America, "Application for Local Union Charter," October 6, 1945, TWU Collection, Local 503 ATD, 1945–1960" file, box 25.

45. Lichtenstein, "'Scientific Unionism,'" 58.

46. E. H. Chambers to Mr. F. D. Laudemann, September 4, 1943, IAM Collection, reel 315, vol. 2.

47. B. W. King to Mr. Eric Peterson, August 21, 1943, IAM Collection, reel 315, vol. 2.

48. Ibid.

49. Hilary Ray to Mr. H. W. Brown, June 29, 1946, IAM Collection, reel 292, vol. 1.

50. B. W. King to Mr. Eric Peterson, September 29, 1943, IAM Collection, reel 315, vol. 2.

51. J. B. Jackson to Mr. Eric Peterson, August 23, 1943; Jerry J. Lee to Mr. W. Overton Snyder, August 19, 1943, IAM Collection, reel 315, vol. 2.

52. "Membership Record, Pan American Negroe Workers, Miami, Florida," *TWU Bulletin,* June 1945, 4, June 1946, 9, microfilm, State Historical Society of Wisconsin, Madison, microfilm (hereafter TWU-WI Collection).

53. Lichtenstein, "'Scientific Unionism,'" 64.

54. National Mediation Board, "In the Matter of Representation of Employees of the Pan American Airways, Inc., Mechanics and Helpers, Including Radio Mechanics, Beaching Crew Men, Boatmen, and Seamstresses. Case R-1311, Findings upon Investigation, March 1, 1945," TWU Collection, "Local 500-ATD, January–March 1945" file, box 24.

55. *TWU Bulletin,* June 1945, 4, TWU-WI Collection.

56. Roy Whitman to Douglas L. MacMahon, August 28, 1945; Roy Whitman to Douglas L. MacMahon, April 24, 1945, TWU Collection, "Local 500-ATD, April to December 1945" file, box 24; *TWU Bulletin,* June 1945, 4, TWU-WI Collection.

57. National Mediation Board, "In the Matter of Representation of Employees of the Pan American Airways, Inc., Mechanics and Helpers, Including Radio Mechanics, Beaching Crew Men, Boatmen, and Seamstresses. Case R-1311, Findings upon Investigation, March 1, 1945," TWU Collection, "Local 500-ATD, January–March 1945" file, box 24; National Mediation Board, "In the Matter of Representation of Employees of the Pan American Airways, Inc. (1) Airline Mechanics, (2) Stockroom Personnel, (3) Unskilled Workers. Case No. R-1451, Certification, September 24, 1945," BRC Collection, "September 1945–June 1946, Organization—Air Transport Industry" file.

58. *TWU Bulletin,* October 1945, 8, December 1945, 5, TWU-WI Collection.

59. Grand President (BRC) to Mr. J. R. Abbott, April 24, 1944, referring to NMB Case R-1210, BRC Collection, "1943–1945, Organization—Northwest Airlines, Inc." file; National Mediation Board, "In the Matter of Representation of Employees of the Pan American Airways, Inc. (Miami area), Airline Mechanics and Helpers, Including Radio Mechanics, Beaching Crewmen, Boatmen and Seamstresses. Case No. R-1311, Certification, April 2, 1945," BRC Collection, "1944–August 1945, Organization—Air Transport Industry" file.

60. Lichtenstein, "'Scientific Unionism,'" 58–59.

61. Aaron Spiegel to Mr. Richard Downes, July 10, 1944; "Membership Record, Pan American Negroe Workers, Miami, Florida"; "Miami, Fla., May 5, 1944, Applications," TWU Collection, "Local 500-ATD-1944" file, box 24.

62. Elizabeth Whitman to Mr. Douglas L. MacMahon, March 24, 1945, TWU Collection, "Local 500-ATD, January–March 1945" file, box 24.

63. (TWU) *Contact,* November 1943, IAM Collection, reel 315, vol. 2.

64. TWU, "You Be the Judge," October 1943, IAM Collection, reel 315, vol. 2.

65. IAM, "COPY from the *New York Post,* 'AFL Needs Some Lessons in Social Significance,'" by Victor Riesel, August 3, 1945, IAM Collection, reel 292, vol. 2.

66. J. L. McFarland, International President, Air Line Mechanics Association, to All Council Officers and Keymen, September 4, 1945, IAM Collection, reel 307, vol. 2; J. C. McGlon to Mr. H. W. Brown, September 15, 1945, IAM Collection, reel 307, vol. 2; "As Strong as Vulcan and as Dependable as a Liberator" (pamphlet), October 17, 1945, IAM Collection, reel 307, vol. 2.

67. Robert F. Cole to Mr. G. T. Baker, Mr. J. L. McFarland, Mr. H. W. Brown, October 25, 1945, IAM Collection, reel 307, vol. 2.

68. Edward O. Kimpton to Mr. H. W. Brown (Confirmation Telegram), November 21, 1945, IAM Collection, reel 307, vol. 2; Earl Melton to S. W. Doerner, H. S. Davis (Telegram), November 23, 1945, IAM Collection, reel 307, vol. 2.

69. Robert F. Cole to Mr. H. W. Brown (Telegram), November 28, 1945, IAM Collection, reel 307, vol. 2.

70. Edward O. Klimpton to Mr. H. W. Brown, November 30, 1945, IAM Collection, reel 307, vol. 2.

71. Case No. R-1548, Certification, December 13, 1945, "In the Matter of Representation of Employees of the National Airlines, Inc. (1) Airline Mechanics, Helpers and Apprentices, (2) Commissary and Stockroom Employees and (3) Unskilled Employees," IAM Collection, reel 307, vol. 2.

72. J. C. McGlon to Mr. Edward H. Kimpton, January 28, 1946; D. H. Amos, Manager Personnel, National Airlines, to Mr. J. C. McGlon, March 6, 1946; International Association of Machinists (PROPOSAL) Article VI, Ground Service Employees, March 4, 1946; J. C. McGlon to Mr. H. W. Brown, March 12, 1946, IAM Collection, reel 307, vol. 2.

73. Frank Heisler to Mr. H. W. Brown, January 28, 1945, IAM Collection, reel 296, vol. 1.

74. Mr. William H. Cox to Mr. G. B. Summers, October 19, 1945, IAM Collection, reel 292, vol.1; Frank Heisler to Mr. H. W. Brown, September 18, 1944, IAM Collection, reel 296, vol. 1.

75. G. B. Summers to Mr. William H. Cox, October 23, 1945, IAM Collection, reel 292, vol. 1.

76. Frank Heisler to Mr. H. W. Brown, January 22, 1946, IAM Collection, reel 297, vol. 2.

77. *American Airlines, Inc.; Agreement between American Airlines, Inc., and Air Line Mechanics Association, International, Representing the Employees of the Company Comprising the Crafts or Classes of Air Line Mechanics, Stores, Fleet Service and Plant Maintenance Personnel,* Effective April 7, 1943, 5, Paul Kent Collection.

78. Ibid., 5–17.

79. Frank Heisler to Mr. H. W. Brown, January 28, 1945, IAM Collection, reel 296, vol. 1.

80. Press release from the UAW-CIO, September 2, 1945, IAM Collection, reel 296, vol. 1; "To: All Council Officers and Keymen," from J. L. McFarland, International President, Air Line Mechanics Association, September 4, 1945, IAM Collection, reel 307, vol. 2; Communications Department, Transport Workers Union of America, *TWU at American Airlines—A Record of Success* (1990): 3 (a pamphlet given to new TWU members employed by American Airlines, from the author's personal collection); William H. Cox to Earl Melton, August 13, 1945, IAM Collection, reel 296, vol. 1.

81. Frank Heisler to Mr. H. W. Brown, July 16, 1946, IAM Collection, reel 297, vol. 2; Frank Heisler to Mr. H. W. Brown, September 18, 1944, IAM Collection, reel 296, vol. 1; Frank Heisler to Mr. H. W. Brown, January 28, 1945, IAM Collection, reel 292, vol. 1; Air Line Pilots Association, David L. Behncke, President, to All American Airlines Chairmen (Air Line Labor Is at the Crossroads), October 13, 1945, 3, IAM Collection, reel 296, vol. 1.

82. For discussion of the TWU in New York, see Freeman, *In Transit.*

83. Air Transport Division, Transport Workers Union, American Airlines Organizing Committee, LaGuardia Airport, "For a Real Union Contract in 1945!" December 28, 1944, IAM Collection, reel 292, vol. 1; To "All Maintenance, Stores, Fleet Service and Plant Maintenance Employees" from Manager—Wage and Salary Administration, Labor Relations, January 10, 1945, IAM Collection, reel 292, vol. 1; F. Heisler, O. Klimpton, F. Kenyon, Grand Lodge Representatives, Air Transport Division, International Association of Machinists, AFL, "Mediator Assigned to American Airlines—Oct. 22, 1945," IAM Collection, reel 296, vol. 1; National Mediation Board, "Findings upon Investigation, Case No. R-1447, in the Matter of Representation of Employees of the American Airlines, Inc., Airline Mechanics, Fleet Service Personnel, Stores Department Personnel, and Plant Maintenance Personnel, October 1, 1945," BRC Collection, "September 1945–June 1946, Organization—Air Transport Industry" file.

84. Paul Ottman to H. J. Carr, June 27, 1933, IAM Collection, reel 296, vol. 1.

85. H. W. Brown to David L. Behncke, August 5, 1944, IAM Collection, reel 292, vol. 1; to Mr. David L. Behnke from E. H. Chambers, March 17, 1945, IAM Collection, reel 292, vol. 1.

86. H. W. Brown to David L. Behncke, September 16, 1944, IAM Collection, reel 292, vol. 1; David L. Behncke, "What the American Airlines Mechanics and Kindred Groups of Air Carrier Employees Should Know about the National Mediation Board Conducted Representation Election Soon to Take Place on American Airlines, and Related Problems of Becoming Properly Organized," November 11, 1945, 1–2, IAM Collection, reel 296, vol. 1.

87. Frank Heisler to Mr. H. W. Brown, December 27, 1945, IAM Collection, reel 296, vol. 1.

88. Air Line Pilots Association, David L. Behncke, President, to All American Airlines Chairmen (Air Line Labor is at the Crossroads), October 13, 1945, 3, IAM

Collection, reel 296, vol. 1; David L. Behncke, "For Airline Labor—What?" 1945, IAM Collection, reel 296, vol. 1.

89. Harold F. Reardon to Mr. Frank Heisler, May 14, 1945, IAM Collection, reel 296, vol. 1.

90. *AA Contact,* April 23, 1946, 2, IAM Collection, reel 297, vol. 2.

91. H. C. Summers to Mr. Earl Melton, January 26, 1946, IAM Collection, reel 297, vol. 2.

92. William H. Cox to Mr. G. B. Summers, October 19, 1945, IAM Collection, reel 297, vol. 2.

93. G. B. Summers to Mr. William H. Cox, October 23, 1945, IAM Collection, reel 297, vol. 2.

94. National Mediation Board, "Findings upon Investigation, Case No. R-1447," 3–4.

95. Edward Shils, "Industrial Unrest in the Nation's Airline Industry," *Labor Law Journal* 15.3 (March 1964): 156.

96. National Mediation Board, "Findings upon Investigation, Case No. R-1447," 3.

97. Ibid., 3–4. These are case numbers R-1368, R-1462, R-1464, R-1471, and R-1484.

98. Ibid., 5.

99. Ibid.

100. Ibid., 6.

101. Ibid., 6–8.

102. Ibid., 8.

103. Ibid., 8–9.

104. Ibid., 9.

105. Ibid., 10.

106. Ibid., 9–10.

107. Ibid., 10–12.

108. National Mediation Board, "Case No. R-1447, Certification, November 28, 1945, in the matter of Representation of Employees of the American Airlines, Inc., (1) Airline Mechanics (2) Stores Personnel," 2–3; News Bureau, Air Line Pilots Association, "For Immediate Release in All AM and PM Papers," October 4, 1946, BRC Collection, "August 1946–February 1947, Organization—Northwest Airlines, Inc." file; Air Carrier Mechanics Association pamphlet addressed to mechanics at American Airlines received by the IAM, November 15, 1945, IAM Collection, reel 296, vol. 1.

109. Frank Heisler to Mr. H. W. Brown, December 27, 1945, IAM Collection, reel 296, vol. 1.

110. National Mediation Board, "Case No. R-1640, Certification, July 22, 1946, in the matter of Representation of Employees of the American Airlines, Inc., Airline Mechanics," BRC Collection, "July 1946–December 1946, Organization—Air Transport Industry" file.

111. *TWU Bulletin,* August–September 1946, 10, TWU-WI Collection.

112. H. W. Brown to Mr. H. F. Nickerson, May 10, 1946, IAM Collection, reel 292, vol. 1.

113. Charles Kief to George M. Harrison, June 11, 1943, BRC collection, "1943–1945, Organization—Northwest Airlines, Inc." file.

114. Charles Kief to George M. Harrison, June 14, 1943, BRC Collection, "1943–1945, Organization—Northwest Airlines, Inc." file.

115. George M. Harrison to Charles Kief, June 17, 1943, BRC Collection, "1943–1945 Organization—Northwest Airlines Inc." file.

116. Charles Kief to George M. Harrison, June 24, 1943, BRC Collection, "1943–1945 Organization—Northwest Airlines, Inc." file.

117. Carl L. Dawson to Mr. G. B. Summers, March 23, 1946, IAM Collection, reel 311, vol. 1.

118. Charles Kief to "All Clerical, Office, Station, and Storehouse Employees of the Northwest Airlines, Inc.," July 24, 1943, BRC Collection, "1943–1945 Organization—Northwest Airlines, Inc." file.

119. George M. Harrison to Clerical, Office, Station, and Storehouse Employees, Northwest Airlines, Inc., August 31, 1943, BRC Collection, "1943–1945, Organization—Northwest Airlines, Inc." file.

120. Charles Kief to Clerical, Office, Station, and Storehouse Employees of Northwest Airlines, Inc., February 8, 1944, BRC Collection, "1943–1945, Organization—Northwest Airlines, Inc." file.

121. Air Line Mechanics Association, International, Council No. 17, Organizing Committee, *The Facts Are: A Message of Importance to Each and Every Employee of the Northwest Airlines System,* 1945, 4–7, BRC Collection, "1943–1945 Organization—Northwest Airlines, Inc." file.

122. Status report on IAM organizing, October 1945, IAM Collection, reel 292, vol. 1.

123. Lee Chapman to A. J. Hayer, April 21, 1945, IAM Collection, reel 292, vol. 1.

124. National Mediation Board, "Case No. R-1544, Certification, February 21, 1946, in the matter of Representation of Employees of the Northwest Airlines, Inc., Airline Mechanics," BRC Collection, "September 1945–June 1946, Organization—Air Transport Industry" file.

125. National Mediation Board, "Case No. R-1643, Certification, July 22, 1946, in the matter of Representation of Employees of the Northwest Airlines, Inc., (1) Stores and Stockroom employees, (2) Unskilled employees," BRC Collection, "July 1946–December 1946, Organization—Air Transport Industry" file.

126. National Mediation Board, "Case No. R-1664, Certification, July 22, 1946, in the matter of Representation of Employees of the Northwest Airlines, Inc., Transportation Agents," BRC Collection, "March 1946–July 1946, Organization—Air Transport Industry" file.

127. *Agreement between Northwest Airlines, Incorporated, and All Reservation*

Agents, Transportation Agents, Senior Transportation Agents, Senior Transportation Agents in Charge, and Reservation Supervisors (Senior Control Agents), Represented by Brotherhood of Railway and Steamship Clerks, Freight Handlers, Express and Station Employees, 1946, 2, NWA Collection, box 10.

128. Robert Cherny, William Issel, and Kieran Walsh Taylor, eds., *American Labor and the Cold War: Grassroots Politics and Postwar Popular Culture* (New Brunswick, N.J.: Rutgers University Press, 2004); Elizabeth Fones-Wolf, *Selling Free Enterprise: The Business Assault on Labor and Liberalism, 1945–1960* (Urbana: University of Illinois Press, 1994); Lichtenstein, *State of the Union;* Patrick Renshaw, *American Labor and Consensus Capitalism, 1935–1990* (Jackson, Miss.: University of Mississippi Press, 1991).

129. Zieger, *CIO,* 246–48.

130. *TWU Bulletin,* June 19, 1948, 6, TWU-WI Collection; Freeman, *In Transit,* 294. For extensive discussion of Communism in TWU Local 500, see Lichtenstein, "'Scientific Unionism,'"; and Alex Lichtenstein, "Putting Labor's House in Order: The Transport Workers Union and Labor Anti-Communism in Miami during the 1940s," *Labor History* 39.1 (1998): 7–23; Maria Jurkovic, "Picketing in Paradise: The Garment, Laundry, and Hotel Workers' Unions in 1950s Miami, Florida" (M.A. thesis, Florida Atlantic University, 1995), 11–14.

131. Freeman, *In Transit,* 294; Lichtenstein, "'Scientific Unionism,'" 59–60.

132. *TWU Bulletin,* June 19, 1948, 6, TWU-WI Collection.

133. Ibid., 6.

134. Lichtenstein, "'Scientific Unionism,'" 67–77; Freeman, *In Transit,* 294–95.

135. *TWU Bulletin,* June 19, 1948, 6–7.

136. Lichtenstein, "'Scientific Unionism,'" 76; Freeman, *In Transit,* 296–97.

137. Michael J. Quill to Members of Local 501 and 504, TWU, September 21, 1949, TWU Collection, "Local 504-ATD, 1949" file, box 26; Freeman, *In Transit,* 321–22; *TWU Express,* June 1949, 5, July 1949, 2, 4, 12, TWU-WI Collection.

138. *TWU Express,* July 1949, 1–2, August 1949, 1–2, TWU-WI Collection; Lichtenstein, "'Scientific Unionism,'" 76; Freeman, *In Transit,* 322.

139. Freeman, *In Transit,* 322; *TWU Express,* December 1949, 8, TWU-WI Collection; FAWA, Local 1, "Let's Cut Out Being Mad at Each Other, Brother! We're Workers for PAA Too—And What Hurts You Hurts All of Us!" September 30, 1949, "FAWA Files for Maintenance," October 14, 1949, "Local 504 TWU NEWS," November 1, 1949, TWU Collection, "Local 504-ATD, 1949" file, box 26; *New York Times,* February 25, 1950, 8.

140. Nelson Lichtenstein, "From Corporatism to Collective Bargaining: Organized Labor and the Eclipse of Social Democracy in the Postwar Era," in *The Rise and Fall of the New Deal Order, 1930–1980,* ed. Steven Fraser and Gary Gerstle (Princeton, N.J.: Princeton University Press, 1989),128–35; Dubofsky, *State and Labor,* 192–93; Andrew Kersten, *Labor's Home Front: The American Federation of Labor During World War II* (New York: New York University Press, 2006), 196–222.

141. Zieger, *CIO,* 213–15; George Lipsitz, *Rainbow at Midnight: Labor and Culture in the 1940s* (Urbana: University of Illinois Press, 1994), 99–116; "Jack Metzgar," in *Encyclopedia of Strikes in American History,* ed. M. E. Sharpe (forthcoming); *Air Transport* included editorials by James H. McGraw Jr. of McGraw-Hill publishing regarding the labor turmoil of the late 1940s. See, for example, *Air Transport,* June and September 1946, Trans. Library.

142. The first TWU–Pan Am contract is described in chapter 2.

143. *New York Times,* October 24, 1945, 14; *Chicago Daily News,* October 25, 1945, 1; Lichtenstein, "'Scientific Unionism,'" 66; *Miami Herald,* October 24, 1945, 1A, October 25, 1945, 1A, October 26, 1945, 1A.

144. Lichtenstein, "'Scientific Unionism,'" 71–72.

145. J. W. Ramsey to Mr. H. W. Brown, May 1, 1946, IAM Collection, reel 312, vol. 2.

146. Frank Heisler to Mr. J. W. Ramsey, May 14, 1946, IAM Collection, reel 312, vol. 2.

147. *St. Paul Pioneer Press,* July 15, 1946, IAM Collection, reel 312, vol. 2.

148. J. W. Ramsey to Mr. H. W. Brown, May 18, 1946, IAM Collection, reel 312, vol. 2.

149. J. W. Ramsey to Mr. H. W. Brown, June 18, 1946; C. L. Bentley to H. W. Brown, telegram, July 3, 1946; Tom Temple to J. W. Ramsey, telegram, July 3, 1946, IAM Collection, reel 312, vol. 2.

150. H. W. Brown to Michael Timko, telegram, July 3, 1946, IAM Collection, reel 312, vol. 2.

151. Tom H. Temple to Mr. H. W. Brown, July 4, 1946, IAM Collection, reel 312, vol. 2.

152. J. W. Ramsey to Grand Lodge Representatives, July 4, 1946; *St. Paul Dispatch,* undated, 1; *Minneapolis Star Journal,* July 3, 1946, 1; *St. Paul Pioneer Press,* July 19, 1946, 1, July 20, 1946, 1, July 21, 1946, July 25, 1946; *Minneapolis Tribune,* July 26, 1946, 1; *Washington Post,* August 8, 1946; J. W. Ramsey to H. W. Brown, September 9, 1946, Frank Heisler to J. W. Ramsey, September 4, 1946, IAM Collection, reel 312, vol. 2.

153. In 1947 there were no strikes among ground-service workers employed by the domestic airlines. "Strike Report 1947–2005, U.S. Airlines under the Railway Labor Act," www.nmb.gov/publicinfo/airline-strikes.html (accessed January 10, 2007).

154. TWU Local 501, "If You Fly 'American' You Should Know . . . ," n.d., TWU Collection, "Local 501, 1945–49" file, box 25.

155. TWU Local 501, "Here We Go Again!" August 10, 1948, TWU Collection, "Local 501, 1945–49" file, box 25.

156. C. R. Smith to All American Airlines Employees, August 14, 1948, TWU Collection, "TWU Local 501, 1945–49" file, box 25.

157. TWU Local 501, "Bulletin," August 18, 1948, TWU Collection, "Local 501, 1945–49" file, box 25.

158. Mark L. Kahn, "The National Air Lines Strike: A Case Study," *Journal of Air and Law Commerce* 19.1 (1952): 11–12; George Hopkins, "Fortunate in His Enemies: George T. Baker, National Airlines, and Federal Regulators," in *Airline Executives and Federal Regulation: Case Studies in American Enterprise from the Airmail Era to the Dawn of the Jet Age,* ed. W. David Lewis (Columbus: Ohio State University Press, 2000), 223.

159. Norris P. Thomas to Pres. H. W. Brown, May 17, 1946, IAM Collection, reel 307, vol. 2.

160. H. C. Summers to Mr. Earl Melton, May 14, 1946, IAM Collection, reel 307, vol. 2.

161. J. C. McGlon to Mr. H. W. Brown, March 10, 1947, G. B. Summers, memo to President Brown and Vice President A. J. Hayes, November 12, 1947, IAM Collection, reel 307, vol. 2.

162. Charles M. Mason, "Collective Bargaining Structure: The Airlines Experience," in *The Structure of Collective Bargaining: Problems and Perspectives,* ed. Arnold B. Weber (Chicago: University of Chicago, Graduate School of Business, 1961), 241; Michael H. Cimini, *Airline Experience under the Railway Labor Act* (Washington, D.C.: U.S. Government Printing Office, 1971), 9; Robert M. McGraith (National Airlines) to Mr. George W. Turner, October 22, 1947, IAM Collection, reel 307, vol. 2. Mason and Cimini both state that the Airlines Negotiating Conference was disbanded February 28, 1947. However, correspondence in the IAM Collection clearly states that the conference was at the bargaining table in October 1947.

163. Lee Chapman to Mr. H. W. Brown, October 23, 1947, IAM Collection, reel 307, vol. 2.

164. "The following are names and addresses, including titles . . . ," November 3, 1947, Marty Braun to Brothers and Sisters, November 26, 1947, IAM Collection, reel 307, vol. 2.

165. Kahn, "National Air Lines Strike," 12–13.

166. James Watt, Jos. L. Robison, and Robert W. Cooper to Mr. George W. Turner, November 11, 1947, IAM Collection, reel 307, vol. 2; Kahn, "National Air Lines Strike," 13; Lee Chapman to Mr. H. W. Brown, November 1, 1947, IAM Collection, reel 307, vol. 2.

167. Lee Chapman to Mr. H. W. Brown, November 1, 1947, IAM Collection, reel 307, vol. 2.

168. Kahn, "National Air Lines Strike," 12–13.

169. Ibid., 14.

170. Ibid., 14–15.

171. Hopkins, "Fortunate in His Enemies," 224; Kahn, "National Air Lines Strike," 15–17; Williams, *Anatomy,* 67–70.

172. Kahn, "National Air Lines Strike," 17.

173. *National Airlines, Incorporated, v. International Association of Machinists, Sup-*

plemental Bill for Injunction, In the Circuit Court, Dade County, Florida, in Chancery No. 114,452, IAM Collection, reel 310, vol. 2; *Miami Daily News,* February 24, 1948; *Miami Daily News,* February 25, 1948.

174. Lee Chapman to Mssrs. J. C. McGlon, Frank Heisler, Lloyd Simmons, Hilary Ray, Claude Houser, Carl Dawson, George W. Turner, and H. N. Stephens, March 25, 1948, IAM Collection, reel 310, vol. 2.

175. Williams, *Anatomy,* 67–68.

176. J. C. McGlon to Mr. A. J. Hayes, March 22, 1948, IAM Collection, reel 311, vol. 3; P. N. Stephens to Lee Chapman, J. C. McGlon, April 13, 1948, IAM Collection, reel 310, vol. 2; Hilary Ray to Mr. Lee Chapman, April 7, 1948, IAM Collection, reel 311, vol. 3; Lee Chapman to Mr. H. W. Brown, May 12, 1948, IAM Collection, reel 311, vol. 3; Kahn, "National Air Lines Strike," 15.

177. E. H. Chambers to Mr. A. J. Hayes, February 18, 1948, IAM Collection, reel 310, vol. 2.

178. Lee Chapman to Frank Heisler, J. C. McGlon, Lloyd Simmons, and George Turner, February 3, 1948, IAM Collection, reel 311, vol. 3; E. H. Chambers to the Officers and Membership of All Local Lodges, District 100, February 18, 1948, IAM Collection, reel 311, vol. 3.

179. Lee Chapman to Transport Workers CIO, February 4, 1948, IAM Collection, reel 311, vol. 3; G. B. Summers to President H. W. Brown, March 30, 1948, IAM Collection, reel 311, vol. 3; Claude R. Houser to Mr. Harvey W. Brown, March 17, 1948, IAM Collection, reel 311, vol. 2; George R. Graves, Capital Airlines Shop Chairman, to Mr. Lee Chapman, February 26, 1948, IAM Collection, reel 311, vol. 3.

180. Capital Airlines Employees to Mr. Lee Chapman, February 10, 1948, IAM Collection, reel 311, vol. 3.

181. George W. Turner to Mr. Lee Chapman, April 1, 1948, IAM Collection, reel 311, vol. 3.

182. Martin J. Braun, Local 1901 president, to Honorable Claude Pepper, February 13, 1948, IAM Collection, reel 308, vol. 2; Lee Chapman to the Barry Gray Show, WKAT, March 25, 1948, IAM Collection, reel 311, vol. 3; Hilary Ray to Lee Chapman, March 18, 1948, IAM Collection, reel 311, vol. 3; Lee Chapman to Mr. H. W. Brown, April 28, 1948, IAM Collection, reel 311, vol. 3; Hilary Ray to Mr. Lee Chapman, June 1, 1948, IAM Collection, reel 311, vol. 3; "Striking National Airlines Clerks Use New Method," March 26, 1948, IAM Collection, reel 311, vol. 3.

183. Hilary Ray to Mr. Lee Chapman, April 1, 1948, IAM Collection, reel 311, vol. 3.

184. Lee Chapman to Mssrs. J. C. McGlon, Frank Heisler, Lloyd Simmons, Hilary Ray, Carl Dawson, Claude Houser, George W. Turner, and H. N. Stephens, March 24, 1948, IAM Collection, reel 311, vol. 3. The emphasis on ALPA during the strike extends beyond the contemporary media. Mark Kahn, Brad Williams, and George E. Hopkins all examine the strike in their scholarship and pay scant attention to the IAM strike.

185. Lee Chapman to Mr. H. W. Brown, February 24, 1948, IAM Collection, reel 311, vol. 3.

186. Lee Chapman to Frank Heisler, March 2, 1948, IAM Collection, reel 311, vol. 3; H. W. Brown to Mr. Earl Melton, March 13, 1948, IAM Collection, reel 311, vol. 3; David L. Behncke to Mr. H. W. Brown, March 11, 1948, IAM Collection, reel 307, vol. 3.

187. Kahn, "National Air Lines Strike," 19.

188. Ibid., 18.

189. Ibid., 19; David L. Behncke to Mr. H. W. Brown, April 5, 1948, IAM Collection, reel 310, vol. 2; Report to the President by the Emergency Board, Appointed May 15, 1948, Pursuant to Section 10 of the Railway Labor Act as Amended, to Investigate unadjusted Disputes between National Airlines, Inc., and Certain of Its Employees Represented by the Air Line Pilots Association, International, and the International Association of the Machinists, Washington, D.C., July 9, 1948, No. 62, IAM Collection, reel 310, vol. 2.

190. Kahn, "National Air Lines Strike," 19–20.

191. Ibid., 20.

192. Ibid., 21.

193. Minutes of Negotiating Conference Between IAM and NAL Friday Afternoon, July 16–19, 1948; Agreement by and between National Airlines, Inc., and International Association of Machinists, July 27, 1948, IAM Collection, reel 308, vol. 4.

194. J. C. McGlon to Mr. Edwin J. Hickey, August 21, 1948; Minutes of Negotiating Conference Between IAM and NAL Friday Afternoon, July 16–19, 1948, 12–13, IAM Collection; Lee Chapman to J. C. McGlon, August 10, 1948; Engine Overhaul—Jacksonville, Shop Rules, from D. A. Shropshire, Supt. of Overhaul; David Behncke to Mr. H. W. Brown, August 19, 1948, IAM Collection, reel 308, vol. 4.

195. J. C. McGlon to Mssrs. Lee Chapman, Frank Heisler, Lloyd Simmons, Claude Houser, H. N. Stephens, and George Turner, August 25, 1948, IAM Collection, reel 308, vol. 4.

196. Kahn, "National Air Lines Strike," 21–22.

197. Before the Civil Aeronautics Board, Washington, D.C., In the Matter of Compliance with Section 401 (1) of the Civil Aeronautics Act by National Airlines, Inc., Docket No. 3283, IAM Collection, reel 311, vol. 3; Kahn, "National Air Lines Strike," 22.

198. Ibid., 22.

199. Hopkins, "Fortunate in His Enemies," 225. Such programs were not allowed by the Civil Aeronautics Board until the beginning of deregulation in the early 1970s.

200. Hopkins, "Fortunate in His Enemies," 226–27. While no mention is made of this religious conversion in Brad Williams's study of National Airlines, correspondence between a member of the mechanics local in Miami and the IAM president A. J. Hayes in 1954 refers to Baker's dramatic change of heart in the preceding years. Bob Wright to Mr. A. J. Hayes, February 17, 1954, IAM Collection, reel 309, vol. 6.

201. Hopkins, "Fortunate in His Enemies," 227; Kahn, "National Air Lines Strike," 23.

202. J. C. McGlon to Mr. H. W. Brown, November 29, 1948, IAM Collection, reel 308, vol. 3.

203. J. C. McGlon to Mr. H. W. Brown, November 12, 1948, IAM Collection, reel 308, vol. 3.

204. E. C. Thompson to Mr. Jerome Rosenthal and Mr. H. W. Brown, December 2, 1948, IAM Collection, reel 308, vol. 3; J. C. McGlon to Mr. Robert F. Cole, February 8, 1949, IAM Collection, reel 308, vol. 3; Frank Heisler to All Grand Lodge and Special Representatives Assigned to Airline Industry and Airlines General Chairmen, May 19, 1949, IAM Collection, reel 308, vol. 4; Williams, *Anatomy,* 83; G. B. Summers to Mr. Frank Heisler, August 11, 1949, IAM Collection, reel 308, vol. 4; J. M. Rosenthal to International Association of Machinists, August 19, 1949, IAM Collection, reel 308, vol. 4.

205. H. W. Brown to Representatives and General Chairmen Assigned Air Transport Industry, January 5, 1949, IAM Collection, reel 308, vol. 4; J. M. Rosenthal to Mr. J. C. McGlon, February 9, 1949, IAM Collection, reel 308, vol. 4; J. M. Rosenthal and J. C. McGlon to Mr. Robert F. Cole, February 3, 1949, IAM Collection, reel 308, vol. 4.

206. H. W. Brown to Mr. C. E. Michael, May 26, 1949, IAM Collection, reel 308, vol. 4; G. B. Summers to Mr. Frank Heisler, July 7, 1949, IAM Collection, reel 308, vol. 4; Memorandum of Agreement between National Airlines, Inc., and the International Association of Machinists, July 1, 1949, IAM Collection, reel 308, vol. 4.

207. Formerly the Airlines Negotiating Conference representative.

208. Charles E. Michael to Hilary A. Ray, August 29, 1949, IAM Collection, reel 308, vol. 4; J. M. Rosenthal to Mr. Charles E. Michael, October 3, 1949, IAM Collection, reel 308, vol. 4; (unsigned) Amendment to Memorandum of Agreement between National Airlines, Inc., International Association of Machinists, Original Agreement Dated July 1, 1949, *Company's Proposal,* September 30, 1949, IAM Collection, reel 308, vol. 4; (unsigned) Amendment to Memorandum of Agreement between National Airlines, Inc., and International Association of Machinists, Original Agreement dated July 1, 1949, *Union's Proposal,* IAM Collection, reel 308, vol. 4; Chas. E. Michael to Mr. A. J. Hayes, October 5, 1949, IAM Collection, reel 308, vol. 4; A. J. Hayes to Mr. Charles E. Michael, October 7, 1949, IAM Collection, reel 308, vol. 4.

209. Edward Degnan to Mr. G. B. Summers, September 22, 1949, copy of document attached, IAM Collection, reel 308, vol. 4; Charles E. Michael to Mr. Edward J. Degnan, September 28, 1949, IAM Collection, reel 308, vol. 4.

210. Charles E. Michael to Mr. Edward J. Degnan, September 28, 1949, IAM Collection, reel 308, vol. 4.

211. J. M. Rosenthal to Mr. Frank Heisler, August 19, 1949, IAM Collection, reel 308, vol. 4.

212. W. F. Bevins to All Station Managers, August 5, 1949, IAM Collection, reel 308, vol. 4.

213. Nicholson, *Air Transportation,* 262.

214. The IAM maintained that stock clerks did not want to be represented by the BRC and had signed petitions to that effect. National Mediation Board, "Excerpts from Transcript of the Proceedings of the National Mediation Board, Case No. R-2104, 1953," 32–34, 47–48, BRC Collection, box 450.

215. National Mediation Board, "In the Matter of Representation of Employees of the Northwest Airlines, Inc., Clerical, Office, Stores, Fleet, and Passenger Service Employees, Corrected Copy, Case No. R-2357, Certification, January 18, 1952," BRC Collection, box 104; National Mediation Board, "In the Matter of Representation of Employees of Northwest Airlines, Inc., (1) Stock and Storeroom Employees, (2) Equipment Service Employees, (3) Janitors, Case No. R-2783 (C-2104), Findings upon Investigation, February 16, 1954," BRC Collection, box 448.

216. The TWU argued a case similar to that of the IAM in its own jurisdiction conflict at KLM Royal Dutch Airlines in 1953, in a case filed by the National Mediation Board as case C-2908.

217. National Mediation Board, "Excerpts from Transcript of the Proceedings of the National Mediation Board, Volume No. 4, Case No. R-2104, 1953," 44, 48, 50–51, BRC Collection, box 450.

218. National Mediation Board, "In the Matter of Representation of Employees of Northwest Airlines, Inc., (1) Stock and Storeroom Employees, (2) Equipment Service Employees, (3) Janitors, Case No. R-2783 (C-2104), Findings upon Investigation, February 16, 1954," 13–14, BRC Collection, box 448.

219. Ibid., 14–15.

220. Edward Roers to Mr. George M. Harrison, April 14, 1954, BRC Collection, box 448.

221. Edward Roers to Mr. G. B. Goble, April 30, 1954, BRC Collection, box 448.

222. Edward Roers to Mr. Lawrence Farmer, May 20, 1955, BRC Collection, box 448.

223. Eischen, "Representation," 59–68. Douglas L. Leslie, American Bar Association, and Railway and Airline Labor Law Committee, *The Railway Labor Act* (Washington, D.C.: Bureau of National Affairs, 1995), 104.

224. *New York Times,* February 3, 1954, 1.

225. *American Aviation,* September 18, 1950; Victor J. Herbert, Acting President, ALAA, to All Airline Agent and Clerical Personnel, undated, IAM Collection, reel 309, vol. 5; Cimini, *Airline Experience,* 7.

226. "In the Matter of Representation of Employees of National Airlines, Inc., Clerical, Office, Fleet, and Passenger Service Employees, Case No. R-2858, Certification, July 27, 1954," National Mediation Board, IAM Collection, reel 309, vol. 5.

227. McNatt, *Labor Relations,* 20–22; John M. Baitsell, *Airline Industrial Relations:*

Pilots and Flight Engineers (Cambridge, Mass.: Harvard University Press, 1966), 186–281; Nick Komons, "Flight Engineers International Association," in *Encyclopedia of American Business History and Biography: The Airline Industry,* ed. William Leary (New York: Facts on File, 1992) 179–180.

Chapter 4: Bargaining in Prosperity, 1949–59

1. Lichtenstein, "From Corporatism," 142–44; Dubofsky, *The State and Labor,* 212; James Atleson, "Wartime Labor Regulation, the Industrial Pluralists, and the Law of Collective Bargaining," in *Industrial Democracy in America: The Ambiguous Promise,* ed. Nelson Lichtenstein and Howell John Harris (New York: Cambridge University Press, 1993), 171; Robert H. Zieger, *American Workers, American Unions* (Baltimore: John Hopkins University Press, 1994), 137–68; Mike Davis, *Prisoners of the American Dream: Politics and Economy in the History of the U.S. Working Class* (New York: Verso, 1999), 117, 320; Fones-Wolf, *Selling Free Enterprise,* 3–5; Joel Rogers, "In the Shadow of the Law: Institutional Aspects of Postwar U.S. Union Decline," in *Labor Law in America: Historical and Critical Essays,* ed. Christopher L. Tomlins and Andrew J. King (Baltimore: Johns Hopkins University Press, 1992), 290–93; Howell John Harris, *The Right to Manage: Industrial Relations Policies of American Business in the 1940s* (Madison: University of Wisconsin Press, 1982), 129–33; Lichtenstein, *State of the Union,* 138–40.

2. Mason, "Collective Bargaining," 237.

3. Particularly between ALPA and the FEIA.

4. Davies, *Airlines,* 337–38; Solberg, *Conquest,* 346–47.

5. Davies, *Airlines,* 328–35, 383–84, 658–59.

6. Passenger calculations were somewhat complicated. According to Civil Aeronautics Board statistics, passengers could be overcounted or undercounted depending on how their trip was planned. A person on a round-trip flight was counted as two passengers. A person who made a stopover becomes a second passenger after he or she boards after the stopover. A person who made one trip over several routes by one airline would be one passenger. A person who made one trip by several airlines is a separate passenger on each airline. Frederick, *Commercial Air,* 389.

7. Civil Aeronautics Board, *Handbook of Airline Statistics* (Washington, D.C.: U.S. Government Printing Office, 1961, 1973).

8. Ibid.

9. Gotch and Crawford, *Air Carrier Analyses: A Detailed Analytical Comparison of U.S. Domestic Civil Air Carriers Including Tables of Rank and Relationship,* 6 vols. (Washington, D.C.: Gotch and Crawford, 1947, 1949, 1951, 1953, 1955), Trans. Library.

10. Fones-Wolf, *Selling Free Enterprise,* 67–108.

11. Baitsell, *Airline Industrial Relations,* 239.

12. *Chicago Tribune* Research Division, *Air Travel and Airline Personalities* (Chi-

cago: Chicago Tribune, 1957), 4–6. The airlines included American, Eastern, Northwest, Capital, United, TWA, and Delta.

13. *Clipper,* May 1956, 5, November 1957, 5, May 1956, 1, November 1954, 1, PAA Collection; *Welcome to Pan American!* (1948), PAA Collection, "Personnel Services, 1940–1960" file, box 218; *Northwest Airlines News,* June 1950, 1, NWA Collection, microfilm.

14. *Northwest Airlines News,* June 16, 1950, 1, NWA Collection.

15. *Northwest Airlines News,* May 1953, 4, NWA Collection.

16. *Northwest Airlines News,* January 30, 1953, 1–2, NWA Collection.

17. *Northwest Airlines News,* April 1953, 4–5, NWA Collection.

18. Ibid.

19. Ibid.

20. *Northwest Airlines News,* July 15, 1949, 8, February 24, 1950, 1, 7, 8, NWA Collection.

21. Barry, *Femininity in Flight,* 36–53; R. Dixon Speas, *Technical Aspects of Air Transport Management* (New York: McGraw-Hill, 1955), 224–27; *Northwest News,* July 15, 1949, 8, NWA Collection. A well-trained crew could also cut down on the cost of "ramp rash," the industry term for vehicle-airplane contact, which often results in expensive repairs and lost flying time. In 1997, accidents and incidents on the ramp cost the U.S. airlines an estimated two billion dollars, much of it uninsured losses. D. Harris and T. J. Thomas, "Ramp Rash: Paying More May Cost You Less," *Human Factors and Aerospace Safety* 1.3 (2001): 295–98.

22. Pan American Airways, *Baggage Service, Fleet Service,* 1958, 1, PAA Collection, box 438. This section for fleet services was part of a larger packet for all employees who dealt directly with baggage.

23. Ibid., 1-1, 5-1.

24. Pan American Airways, Latin American Division, *Customer Service Manual* [1954], 25, PAA Collection.

25. Ibid., 26.

26. *Clipper* 16.10 (November 1957): 5, PAA Collection; Robert Slouber, interview; Robert Slouber, telephone interview, September 1, 1998.

27. Martin Trizinski, interview by author, tape recording, Schiller Park, Ill., December 5, 1997.

28. Richard Sobczak (pseud.), interview by author, tape recording, Oak Lawn, Ill., September 9, 2003; James Sullivan, interview by author, tape recording, Brookfield, Ill., August 19, 2003; Roy Okamoto, interview by author, tape recording, Bloomingdale, Ill.; August 27, 2003; Curtis Johnson, telephone interview with author, April 10, 2007; Kenneth Ahern, telephone interview with author, April 10, 2007.

29. George Poulos (pseud.), interview by author, tape recording, Hanover Park, Ill., July 4, 1997.

30. George Poulos, interview; James Sullivan, interview; Robert Slouber, interview;

Martin Trizinski, interview; *TWU Bulletin,* May 1946, 5, February 1954, 7, June 1954, 6, TWU-WI Collection.

31. Mason, "Collective Bargaining," 227.

32. Thomas Wolfe, *Air Transportation: Traffic and Management* (New York: McGraw-Hill, 1950), 29, 484; Davies, *Airlines,* 326–27; Frederick, *Commercial Air,* 85; Cearley, *American,* 51–53. *Air Transport* magazine was filled with advertisements for new loading equipment. See *Air Transport,* August 1944, 75, December 1944, 92, February 1946, 89, April 1946, 62, August 1946, 103, Trans. Library.

33. Wolfe, *Air Transportation,* 410.

34. Ibid., 600–603; *Air Transport,* April 1944, 40–47, Trans. Library.

35. Mason, "Collective Bargaining," 239.

36. Ibid.

37. McNatt, *Labor Relations,* 14–15.

38. Mason, "Collective Bargaining," 243.

39. Ibid., 239; Shils, "Industrial Unrest," 145–46; Cimini, *Airline Experience,* 10.

40. McNatt, *Labor Relations,* 32.

41. *TWU Express,* March 1950, 3, TWU-WI Collection.

42. *New York Times,* December 11, 1950, 47; Agreement between American Airlines, Inc., and Transport Workers Union of America, International-CIO covering Airline Mechanic, Plant Maintenance, Fleet Service, and Ground Service Employees of American Airlines, Inc., Effective Date, December 2, 1950, Paul Kent Collection.

43. *TWU Express,* December 1950, 3, TWU-WI Collection; *New York Times,* March 17, 1950, 47, December 11, 1950, 47.

44. *New York Times,* March 25, 1950, 29, April 4, 1950, 59, April 27, 1950, 59; *TWU Express,* May 1950, 3.

45. *New York Times,* December 27, 1950, 47, December 28, 1950, 45, December 29, 1950, 10, January 16, 1951, 59, March 25, 1951, 50.

46. *New York Times,* June 16, 1951, 31, June 17, 1951, 66, June 18, 1951, 30.

47. *New York Times,* December 16, 1951, 1, December 17, 1951, 1, December 18, 1951, 1; *TWU Express,* December 1951, 2.

48. *New York Times,* December 20, 1951, 30, February 19, 1952, 55.

49. *New York Times,* January 22, 1952, 32. In 1953 there were seven strikes on the airlines, although none at Pan Am, American, Northwest, or National. "Strike Report 1947–2005, U.S. Airlines under the Railway Labor Act," http://www.nmb.gov/publicinfo/airline-strikes.html. (accessed January 10, 2007).

50. TWU Local 501, "Union Meets Mediator . . . Company Plays Hard to Get . . . Cracks Whip," June 12, 1952, TWU Collection, "Local 501: 1950–1952" file, box 25.

51. Michael J. Quill, to National Mediation Board, telegram, June 7, 1952, TWU Collection, "TWU Local 501: 1950–1952" file, box 25; *New York Times,* June 3, 1952, 59, June 6, 1952, 14, June 8, 1952, 1, 69, June 9, 1952, 24.

52. *New York Times,* June 6, 1952, 14.

53. Michael J. Quill to the Executive Secretary, National Mediation Board, tele-

gram, June 7, 1952, reproduced for distribution to the TWU membership by Local 501; G. K. Griffin to James F. Horst, telegram, June 8, 1952, TWU Collection, "Local 501: 1950–1952" file, box 25; *New York Times,* June 9, 1952, 24.

54. James F. Horst to A. DiPasquale, E. C. Thompson, telegram, June 10, 1952, TWU Collection, "TWU Local 501: 1950–1952" file, box 25.

55. *New York Times,* September 20, 1958, 38, September 21, 1958, 41.

56. *TWU Express,* March 1959, 7, TWU-WI Collection; WTLS, February, 17, 1959, PAA Collection, "Pan Am, Labor Relations—Strikes" file, box 64.

57. *TWU Express,* June 1952, 6, TWU-WI Collection; Communication Department, TWU, *TWU at American Airlines—A Record of Success* (1991), author's personal collection.

58. McNatt, *Labor Relations,* 23–24.

59. *TWU Bulletin,* December 1947, 6; *TWU Express,* June 1954, 5, September 1956, 6, October 1958, 6, TWU-WI Collection.

60. Robert Slouber, interview; Martin Trizinski, interview; Richard Sobczak, interview; John Gales, interview by author, tape recording, Glendale Heights, Ill., September 25, 2003.

61. Mason, "Collective Bargaining," 240–41.

62. Ibid., 241; John N. Sheridan to All Maintenance Contract Employees, March 10, 1953, IAM Collection, reel 309, vol. 6.

63. Frederick Locke Johnson, "The 1966 Machinist Airline Strike: A Study in Labor Relations in the Air Transport Industry" (M.A. thesis, University of Illinois at Urbana-Champaign, 1967), 41–42.

64. Cimini, *Experience,* 9–10; Mason, "Collective Bargaining," 241–42; Harold Foster, "Employers Strike Insurance," *Labor History* 12.4 (1971): 513.

65. *Industrial Relations: A Journal of Economy and Society* 1. (October 1961); Dubofsky, *State and Labor;* Lichtenstein, *State of the Union;* Nelson Lichtenstein, ed., *American Capitalism: Social Thought and Political Economy in the Twentieth Century* (Philadelphia: University of Pensylvania Press, 2006); Jack Metzgar, *Striking Steel: Solidarity Remembered* (Philadelphia: Temple University Press, 2000); Davis, *Prisoners of the American Dream;* Cherny, Issel, and Taylor, *American Labor and the Cold War.*

66. Cimini, *Experience,* 36; John William Coffey, "The Airline Industry Mutual Aid Pact" (M.A. thesis, University of Illinois at Urbana-Champaign, 1969), 124–25.

67. Shils, "Industrial Unrest," 165.

68. National Mediation Board, *Annual Report* (Washington, D.C.: U.S. Government Printing Office, 1958); Barry, *Femininity in Flight,* 60.

69. Cimini, *Experience,* 27; Mason, "Collective Bargaining," 242, 245; Vernon Briggs Jr., "The Mutual Aid Pact of the Airline Industry," *Industrial and Labor Relations Review* 19.1 (October 1965): 3–20; Coffey, "Airline Industry," 43–44.

70. Mason, "Collective Bargaining," 245 (Mason calls the Mutual Aid Pact the "Airlines Co-ordinating Committee"); Cimini, *Experience,* 7–11; Frank Pierson, "Recent

Employer Alliances in Perspective," *Industrial Relations: A Journal of Economy and Society* 1.1 (October 1961): 49; Briggs, "Mutual Aid Pact," 3–20; S. Herbert Unterberger and Edward C. Koziara, "Airline Strike Insurance: A Study in Escalation," *Industrial and Labor Relations Review* 29.1 (October 1975): 26–46; Foster, "Employers Strike Insurance," 512–21.

71. *TWU Express,* June 1959, 7, July 1960, 7, TWU-WI Collection; Cimini, *Experience,* 9–11; Coffey, "Airline Industry," 60.

Chapter 5: On the Ramp in the 1950s and 1960s

1. Janet R. Daly Bednarek "The Flying Machine in the Garden: Parks and Airports, 1918–1938," *Technology and Culture* 46.2 (April 2005): 355.

2. Iyer, *Global Soul;* Mark Gottdiener, *Life in the Air: Surviving the New Culture of Air Travel* (New York: Rowman and Littlefield Publishers, 2001).

3. For an analysis of the post-9/11 work culture among flight attendants, see Drew Whitelegg, *Working the Skies: The Fast-Paced Disorienting World of the Flight Attendant* (New York: New York University Press, 2007).

4. I would like to thank the historian Patricia Cooper for her insights on the cultures of work and leisure on the ramp.

5. In the same era, waterfront workers faced the containerization issue as well. See William Finley, *Work on the Waterfront: Worker Power and Technological Change in a West Coast Port* (Philadelphia: Temple University Press, 1988); and William M. Pilcher, *The Portland Longshoremen: A Dispersed Urban Community* (New York: Reinhart and Winston, 1972).

6. Davies, *Airlines,* 511, 661.

7. Ibid., 514.

8. Ibid., 661; *TWU Express,* May 1959, 19, TWU-WI Collection.

9. Solberg, *Conquest,* 405–7; Davies, *Airlines,* 517–18.

10. U.S. Bureau of Transportation Statistics, *Historical Air Traffic Statistics, Annual 1954–1980,* www.bts.programs/airline_information/air_carrier_traffic_statistics/airtraffic/annual/1954_1980.htm. These figures are based on Revenue Passenger Originations.

11. Solberg, *Conquest,* 406–7.

12. George Poulos (pseud.), telephone interview by author, January 28, 2000.

13. Ibid.

14. *TWU Express,* May 1959, 19, July 1960, 20, TWU-WI Collection. The TWU also feared that stewardesses, some of whom were union members, would become "glorified waitresses" thanks to heavier loads and shorter flight times. The union also warned that the new automated baggage-handling systems could threaten fleet-service-clerk jobs.

15. C. L. Dennis to Mr. George M. Harrison, February 27, 1962; "Time Study Survey, Equipment Service Chiefs and Equipment Servicemen, Northwest Airlines, Inc.,

Showing Hours of Work Devoted to Category 'a' and 'b,' MSP, March 7, 1962," BRC Collection, box 448.

16. *Northwest Airlines News,* July 1957, 5, microfilm, NWA Collection.

17. *New York Times,* November 6, 1970; Adele C. Schwartz, "Telecars to Speed Pan Am Baggage," *Airline Management,* May 1971, 90, PAA Collection.

18. "Years of Research Made AirPak a Reality," *Horizons,* September 1961, 1, PAA Collection.

19. "And Now—It's ALL CARGO JETS," *Clipper Cargo Horizons,* May 1962, 1, PAA Collection; Geoffrey Arend, *Original: A Pictoral History of American Airlines Cargo, 1944–1994* (Dallas: American Airlines, 1994), 43, Paul Kent Collection.

20. *TWU Express,* March 1960, 8, TWU-WI Collection.

21. *TWU Express,* July 1960, 20, TWU-WI Collection.

22. Robert Slouber, telephone interview, September 1, 1998.

23. *TWU Express,* February 1960, 8, TWU-WI Collection. Baggage handlers at American Airlines still have their hearing tested annually on company time.

24. *TWU Express,* April 1960, 9, TWU-WI Collection.

25. *TWU Express,* October 1963, 13, TWU-WI Collection.

26. Northrup, Theiboldt, and Chernish, *Negro in the Air Transport Industry,* 61–62, 66–68; Hopkins, *Airline Pilots,* 214–16.

27. Letter to Michael J. Quill from Members of the TWU, Berry Field, Nashville, Tenn. (thirty-three names undersigned), received June 14, 1961; see also letter to Michael J. Quill from TWU Members at Nashville (thirty-eight names undersigned), received July 10, 1961, TWU Collection, "Local 514—1952–53, 1960–65" file, box 29.

28. F. N. Herold, Pres. Local 513 ATD, to Mr. Michael Quill, Int'l. Pres., July 22, 1961, TWU Collection, "Local 513 1949–1969" file, box 28. "Law and order" issues may have also been a factor in the Dallas case. In 1967, Dallas members of Local 513 donated money and food to the cause of striking farm workers in the area. Members of the local also "adopted" a farm-worker family and sent them fifty dollars a month for six months. J. W. Sifford, V.P., TWU Local 513, to Matthew Guinan, received January 25, 1967, TWU Collection, "Local 513 1949–1969" file, box 28.

29. In 1943, the TWU adopted a resolution calling for racial and religious unity in the fight against Hitler. This resolution included an equality clause stating that the union would only support aspirants for public office who believed in "the vital principle of equality for all Americans regardless of race, creed, color or national origin." *TWU Bulletin,* November 1943, 21. Other examples of TWU participation in civil rights agitation include *TWU Express,* October 1946, 6, May 1957, 18, April 1960, 11, Transport Workers Union, *1934–1963, TWU, and the Fight for Civil Rights,* TWU-WI Collection.

30. "The Cancer of Segregation is Urgent TWU Business, an Open Letter from President Quill," *TWU Express,* August 1961, 20, TWU-WI Collection.

31. Vernon Bassom, member Local 514, to "Sirs," November 18, 1963, TWU Collection, "Local 514, 1950–52, 1960–65" file, box 29.

32. Northrup, Thiebolt, and Chernish, *Negro in the Air Transport Industry,* 64–69.

33. Ibid., 60. This geographic factor remained true for some cities into the 1980s or later. In the case of Chicago, O'Hare International Airport was not connected to the city by elevated train until the 1980s; Midway Airport, not until the 1990s, although bus service was available prior to this. In Pittsburgh, city bus service was not available to the airport until the mid-1990s.

34. Eddie Hall, interview with author, tape recording, Maywood, Ill., July 29, 1997.

35. Northrup, Thieboldt, and Chernish, *Negro in the Air Transport Industry,* 92.

36. Ibid., 37.

37. *TWU Express,* May 1963, 12, TWU-WI Collection.

38. Northrup, Thieboldt, and Chernish, *Negro in the Air Transport Industry,* 37; Equal Employment Opportunity Commission, Plans for Progress Program, *Plans for Progress Program: The National Voluntary Equal Employment Opportunity Program of American Business* (Washington, D.C.: U.S. Government Printing Office, 1967), 1–2, 19–28.

39. EEOC data differs from U.S. Census data in an important way. EEOC data is filed by companies that employ more than one hundred people. This information is based on their payroll records. Census data is gathered by enumerators and given by individuals.

40. Equal Employment Opportunity Commission, *Equal Employment Opportunity Report No. 1: Job Patterns for Minorities and Women in Private Industry, 1966,* part 1 (Washington, D.C.: U.S. Government Printing Office, 1966), A2.

41. In some cases airlines counted stewardesses as service workers or blue-collar workers, causing some variation in the numbers. Stewardess was one job in the airline industry that included African American women. Northrup, Thieboldt, and Chernish, *Negro in the Air Transport Industry,* 38–40.

42. Equal Employment Opportunity Commission, *Equal Employment Opportunity Report: Job Patterns for Minorities and Women in Private Industry, 1969,* vol. 1 (Washington, D.C.: U.S. Government Printing Office, 1969), 358; Northrup, Thieboldt, and Chernish, *Negro in the Air Transport Industry,* 57.

43. Department of Labor, "Pan Am to Train 250 Jobless in Three Cities under President's JOBS Program," Press Release, June 27, 1968, PAA Collection, "Arey-Industrial Relations, PAA Co. Employees, 1967–1981" file, box 95; National Alliance of Businessmen, *Training the Hardcore* (New York: Urban Research Corporation, 1969), 7; Northrup, Thieboldt, and Chernish, *Negro in the Air Transport Industry,* 91–102; *Chicago Tribune,* August 27, 1969, 2.

44. Northrup, Thieboldt, and Chernish, *Negro in the Air Transport Industry,* 91–102.

45. Ibid., 111; Eddie Hall, interview; Rob Kranski (pseud.), interview with author, tape recording, Algonquin, Ill., September 14, 1997.

46. Northwest Orient Airlines, Public Relations Department, "You and the Jet Age," April 1959, NWA Collection, "Public Relations records, 1926 to 1980" file, box 23.

47. Eddie Hall, interview; Rob Kranski, interview; "Hiring Hard-Core Unemployed—What Pan Am Is Doing," press release, PAA Collection, "Arey Industrial Relations—Summer and Hardcore Employment, 1968–69" file, box 95; *Chicago Tribune,* August 27, 1969, 2.

48. Pan Am, "Hiring Hard-Core Unemployed—What Pan Am Is Doing," PAA Collection.

49. Rob Kranski, interview.

50. Ibid. Another baggage handler also mentioned "Pops" Courtney as a popular African American old-timer. Roy Okamoto, interview.

51. Martin Trizinski, interview.

52. Millard Parker (pseud.), interview with author, tape recording, Hillside, Ill. September 16, 2003.

53. Curtis Johnson, interview.

54. Roy Okamoto, interview.

55. Ibid.

56. Eddie Hall, interview. It is possible that Hall was employed through the hardcore program despite his army experience because of his low education level. Eddie Hall went to school steadily through the fifth grade. He attended school sporadically after that and had not taken the General Education Degree at the time of the interview.

57. Ibid.

58. Ibid.

59. Wallace W. Price, Corp Director, Personnel Urban Affairs and Equal Opportunity, to George W. Miller, Vice President and Controller, memorandum, May 1, 1973, PAA Collection, "Arey—Industrial Relations—PAA Company Employees, 1967–1981" file, box 95.

60. *New York Times,* October 19, 1969; Frank P. Doyle to the President, Executive Vice President, et al., memorandum, March 29, 1971; Everett M. Goulard, to the President, Executive Vice President, et al., memorandum, December 22, 1969, PAA Collection, "Arey—Industrial Relations, PAA Co. Employees, 1967–1981" file, box 95.

61. Equal Employment Opportunity Commission, *Equal Employment Opportunity Report: Job Patterns for Minorities and Women in Private Industry* (Washington, D.C.: U.S. Government Printing Office, 1969, 1971, 1975).

62. Rob Kranski, interview; Martin Trizinski, interview; Millard Parker (pseud.), interview by author, tape recording, September 9, 2003, Broadview, Illinois.

63. George Poulos, interview; Martin Trizinski, interview; Curtis Johnson, interview.

64. Eddie Hall, interview; Martin Trizinski, interview.

65. Rob Kranski, interview; James Sullivan, interview.

66. Robert Slouber, interview.

67. George Poulos, interview.

68. Eddie Hall, interview.

69. Rob Kranski, interview; Millard Parker, interview.

70. Robert Slouber, interview. I heard similar stories when I worked on the ramp in 1991 and 1992. I was the victim of a similar prank. A more experienced fleet-service clerk told me that I could not drive my tractor and LD-3s, containers used for baggage on wide-body aircraft, through the roadways under the terminal.

71. George Poulos, interview; Roy Okamoto, interview.

72. Richard Sobczak, interview.

73. Ibid.

74. Both Millard Parker and James Sullivan told the story of the baggage handler in the casket. Millard Parker, interview; James Sullivan, interview.

75. Kenneth Ahern, telephone interview; Kenneth Thiede, interview with author, tape recording, Des Plaines, Ill., April 26, 2007.

76. Susan Littler-Bishop, Doreen Seidler-Feller, and R. E. Opaluch, "Sexual Harassment in the Workplace as a Function of Initiator's Status: The Case of Airline Personnel," *Journal of Social Issues* 38.4 (1982): 145.

77. In the 1970s, fleet-service clerks also interacted with pilots while the airplanes were pushed away from the terminal gates. However, this job belonged to mechanics during the period covered in this study.

78. Eddie Hall, interview.

79. Martin Trizinski, interview. He stated that the mechanics became "prima donnas" after the 1970s and demanded a contract separate from the one covering the fleet-service clerks. In 1999, American Airlines' aircraft mechanics split from TWU Local 512 and created their own local.

80. Status relationships among airline employees played a role in the perception of sexual harassment in the workplace. See Littler-Bishop, Seidler-Feller, and Opaluch, "Sexual Harassment"; Randy Canale, interview with author, tape recording, Elk Grove Village, Ill., April 12, 2007; Kenneth Thiede, interview.

81. Rob Kranski, interview. According to Kranski, in the 1980s, after a layoff of pilots, some low-seniority pilots went temporarily to work on the ramp. One pilot worked with Kranski and told him he would never think of fleet-service clerks in the same way again. He said, "I see you're quite human."

82. Roy Okamoto, interview.

83. Richard Sobczak, interview; Eddie Hall, interview; James Sullivan, interview; Curtis Johnson, interview.

84. Kenneth Ahern, telephone interview; Kenneth Thiede, interview; George Poulos, interview; Millard Parker, interview.

85. "Luggage Mishandling Due for Attention," *Air Travel,* January 1962, 18, Trans. Library.

86. "Airlines Cooperate with Manufacturers in Developing Bash-Proof Luggage," *Air Travel,* March 1964, 22, Trans. Library.

87. "Luggage Mishandling Due for Attention," *Air Travel,* January 1962, 18, Trans. Library.

88. "Their Bag: Passenger Luggage," *The Clipper,* July 6, 1970, PAA Collection.

89. "The Masher" appeared as part of "Project '62," a larger employee-improvement campaign at North Central Airlines, Republic Airlines Collection, Minnesota Historical Society, St. Paul, Minn., "North Central misc." file, box 14.

90. Roy Okamoto, interview.

91. Robert Slouber, interview; George Poulos, interview; Eddie Hall, interview; Rob Kranski, interview; Martin Trizinski, interview.

92. George Poulos, interview; Roy Okamoto, interview.

93. Martin Trizinski, interview.

94. Patrick R. Craig and Roger M. Green, "An Analysis of Air Cargo Theft/Pilferage" (M.A. thesis, Air Force Institute of Technology, 1972), 3, Trans. Library.

95. Frederick, *Commercial Air,* 447.

96. Craig and Green, "Analysis," 5.

97. Harvey T. Harris Jr., "International Air Cargo Thefts and Losses: An Identification of Variables" (M.A. thesis, Michigan State University, 1966), 220, Trans. Library.

98. *International Freighting Weekly,* May 8, 1974, Trans. Library.

99. *New York Times,* July 22, 1969, 1, 34.

100. For detailed discussion of freight-theft high-profile robberies and the role of organized crime in airport cargo operations, see James Kaplan, *The Airport: Terminal Nights and Runway Days at John F. Kennedy Airport* (New York: William Morrow and Co., 1994), 209–34.

101. *New York Times,* July 22, 1969, 1, 34.

102. Airport Security Council, Press Release, February 8, 1971, PAA Collection, box 281.

103. Ibid.

104. Robert Slouber, interview.

105. Ibid.

106. Ibid.

107. Eddie Hall, interview; George Poulos, interview; Roy Okamoto, interview.

108. Martin Trizinski, interview.

109. Rob Kranski, interview; George Poulos, interview; James Sullivan, interview.

110. Rob Kranski, interview.

111. James Sullivan, interview.

112. James Sullivan, interview; Martin Trizinski, interview; Richard Sobczak, interview; John Gales, interview.

113. Kenneth Ahern, telephone interview; Millard Parker, interview; Eddie Hall, interview; John Gales, interview.

114. Randy Canale, interview; Millard Parker, interview; Martin Trizinski, interview; Richard Sobczak, interview; Roy Okamoto, interview; James Sullivan, interview.

Chapter 6: Militance and the Mutual Aid Pact, 1960–70

1. "More-Mow!" *Time,* September 2, 1966.

2. Coffey, "Airline Industry," 65–68.

3. Braniff, Continental, Eastern, National, Northwest, Trans World, and United.

4. Johnson, "1966 Machinist Airline Strike," 45–47, 120.

5. *The Machinist,* April 8, 1965, 3, May 6, 1965, 5, IAM Collection.

6. Johnson, "1966 Machinist Airline Strike," 48; *The Machinist,* August 19, 1965, 1; Kahn, "Labor-Management Relations," 110–11.

7. Johnson, "1966 Machinist Airline Strike," 49–50.

8. *New York Times,* July 9, 1966, 31; Rodden, *Fighting Machinists,* 245–49; *The Machinist,* May 19, 1966, 1.

9. Air Transport Association of America, *Air Transport Facts and Figures 1966* (Washington, D.C.: Air Transport Association of America, 1967).

10. National Airlines left the pact in 1961 and rejoined in 1969. Johnson, "1966 Machinist Airline Strike," 56, 48; *The Machinist,* August 19, 1965, 1; Unterberger and Koziara, "Airline Strike Insurance," 29.

11. Johnson, "1966 Machinist Airline Strike," 110–11.

12. Ibid., 61–64.

13. "Excellent, Buoyant, and Ebullient," *Time,* April 23, 1965; "Embattled Guidelines," *Time,* September 10, 1965; "Toward the Fuller Life," *Time,* February 5, 1965; "Bending the Guidelines," *Time,* September 18, 1964.

14. Johnson, "1966 Machinist Airline Strike" 65–72. Average hourly earnings at the five carriers increased 55.7 percent versus 39.1 percent in manufacturing production since 1955.

15. Qtd. in Johnson, "1966 Machinist Airline Strike," 81.

16. Ibid., 81–82.

17. Ibid., 82–87; Lyndon B. Johnson, "Remarks in Response to the Emergency Board Report on the Airlines Labor Dispute, June 7, 1966," in John Woolley and Gerhard Peters, *The American Presidency Project,* http://presidency.ucsb.edu/?pid=27633 (accessed June 20, 2007).

18. *The Machinist,* June 16, 1966, 1.

19. Johnson, "1966 Machinist Airline Strike," 88.

20. Number of passengers carried daily by the five struck airlines. *New York Times,* July 9, 1966, 1.

21. *New York Times,* July 9, 1966, 1, 10–11.

22. *New York Times,* July 9, 1966, 1, 10–11; *Aviation Week and Space Technology,* July 18, 1966, 34–36.

23. *New York Times,* July 10, 1966, 1, 44, July 13, 1966, 23, July 14, 1966, 1, 21, 37.

24. *New York Times,* July 10, 1966, 45, July 14, 1966, 34.

25. Randy Canale, interview; *The Machinist,* July 21, 1966, 1; *New York Times,* July 12, 1966, 31; *Aviation Week and Space Technology,* July 25, 1966, 42.

26. *New York Times,* July 14, 1966, 1, 20.

27. *New York Times,* July 20, 1966, 20.

28. *New York Times,* May 22, 1966, 64. This quote includes selected salaries only; *The Machinist,* May 19, 1966, 2, 12; *The Machinist,* July 28, 1966, 8.

29. Puffer, *Air Transportation,* 311; Robert Burkhardt, *CAB: The Civil Aeronautics Board* (Dulles International Airport, Chantilly, Va.: Green Hills Publishing Co., 1974), 15; John V. Coleman, telephone interview with author, February 27, 2008 (Coleman worked for the Civil Aeronautics Board in the Essential Air Service department from 1963 to 1984); W. W. Rostow, *The Diffusion of Power: An Essay in Recent History* (New York: Macmillan Co., 1974), 321–22.

30. *New York Times,* July 17, 1966, E11, July 22, 1966, 13; Rodden, *Fighting Machinists,* 240.

31. *The Machinist,* July 21, 1966, 1.

32. *New York Times,* July 22, 1966, 13; Johnson, "1966 Machinist Airline Strike," 89–92; President Lyndon B. Johnson's Annual Message to the Congress on the State of the Union, January 12, 1966, http://www.lbjlib.utexas.edu/Johnson/archives.hom/speeches.hom/660112.asp (accessed June 20, 2007).

33. *New York Times,* July 24, 1966, 63.

34. Johnson, "1966 Machinist Airline Strike," 90–93.

35. *New York Times,* July 28, 1966, 1.

36. *New York Times,* July 29, 1966, 1.

37. Johnson, "1966 Machinist Airline Strike," 93–94.

38. *New York Times,* July 29, 1966, 1, July 30, 1966, 8; Johnson, "1966 Machinist Airline Strike," 98.

39. Johnson, "1966 Machinist Airline Strike," 99–101; *New York Times,* July 30, 1966, 8.

40. *New York Times,* July 31, 1966, 62; Johnson, "1966 Machinist Airline Strike," 100.

41. *New York Times,* August 1, 1966, 16; Freeman, *In Transit,* 334–38; "Back to Normal," *Time,* January 21, 1966.

42. Randy Canale, interview; Kenneth Ahern, interview; *New York Times,* August 1, 1966, 16, August 3, 1966, 16; *The Machinist,* August 11, 1966, 3.

43. *New York Times,* August 3, 1966, 1.

44. *New York Times,* August 4, 1966, 17, August 5, 1966, 1, 28.

45. *New York Times,* August 7, 1966, 24.

46. *New York Times,* August 9, 1966, 1, 23.

47. *New York Times,* August 12, 1966, 1, 16.

48. *New York Times,* August 12, 1966, 16, August 13, 1966, 1, August 14, 1966, 1.

49. *New York Times,* August 16, 1966, 1, 32.

50. *New York Times,,* August 17, 1966, 1, 21, August 18, 1966, August 19, 1966, 1, 17; Johnson, "1966 Machinist Airline Strike," 104–8.

51. *New York Times,* August 21, 1966, 1.

52. "Back to Work through an Open Gate," *Time,* August 26, 1966.

53. Johnson, "1966 Machinist Airline Strike," 104; *Aviation Week and Space Technology,* August 8, 1966, 40; "Back to Work"; *New York Times,* August 16, 1966, 32.

54. Kenneth Thiede, interview; Richard Del Boccio, telephone interview with author, April 19, 2007.

55. Randy Canale, interview; *New York Times,* August 22, 1963, 56.

56. Kenneth Thiede, interview.

57. Hank Borner, "AMFA: Budding New Union for Mechanics?" *Air Transport World,* September 1966, 22–23.

58. Richard Del Boccio, interview. While Del Boccio supported AMFA all these years, in 2007 he was contacted through the IAM retirees club in Des Plaines, Illinois. Del Boccio retired before AMFA won recognition at United Airlines in 2003.

59. "Back to Work."

60. Unterberger and Koziara, "Airline Strike Insurance," 28.

61. Johnson, "1966 Machinist Airline Strike," 114–15; "Airline Strike Repercussions," *Aviation Week and Space Technology,* August 29, 1966, 19; "Strike Clouds Airlines' Economic Future," *Aviation Week and Space Technology,* August 29, 1966, 25–26; *New York Times,* November 24, 1967, 85.

62. Air Transport Association, *1967 Air Transport Facts and Figures* (Washington, D.C.: Air Transport Association, 1967), 152–55, 186; *New York Times,* January 23, 1967, 86.

63. *New York Times,* September 26, 1966, 20, September 27, 1966, 93, October 5, 1966, 58.

64. *New York Times,* December 1, 1966, 93, December 2, 1966, 30, December 3, 1966, 1, December 24, 1966, 40; "Public Relations Department Strike Kit for Pan Am-TWU Contract Negotiations 1966 *FOR INTERNAL USE* ONLY," PAA Collection, "Arey, Industrial Relations, Transport Workers Union of America" file, box 96.

65. *New York Times,* March 20, 1969, 94, October 29, 1969, 84; "Up, Up and Away with Wages," *Time,* April 11, 1969.

66. *New York Times,* August 25, 1966, 1, 20; "Gone Guideposts," *Time,* August 12, 1966.

67. *New York Times,* December 6, 1966, 93, January 12, 1967, 20, April, 30, 1967, 37, April 16, 1967, 41, June 2, 1967, 80.

68. "A Need for Jawboning," *Time,* December 30, 1966; *New York Times,* January 3, 1967, 16.

69. *New York Times,* January 8, 1967, sec. IV, 6.

70. *Fortune* 74.6 (November 1966): 151.

71. Lichtenstein, *State of the Union,* 136–38; Andrew Levison, *The Working-Class*

Majority (New York: Penguin Books, 1975) 225–29; Jefferson Cowie, "Vigorously Left, Right, and Center," in *America in the Seventies,* ed. Beth Bailey and David Farber (Lawrence: University Press of Kansas, 2004), 75–106.

Epilogue

1. Air Transport Association of America, *Rising Employment Costs in Air Transport: A Concern for All* (Washington, D.C.: Air Transport Association of America, 1972), 2–3.

2. "More of Everything but Earnings," *Time,* September 20, 1968; Donald R. Whitnah, "Airline Deregulation Act of 1978," in *Encyclopedia of American Business History and Biography: The Airline Industry,* ed. William Leary (New York: Facts on File, 1992), 15–16; Air Transport Association of America, *Rising Employment Costs.* AIRCon continues to exist. See its website: http://www.aircon.org/what_is_aircon/index.htm (accessed June 20, 2007); *New York Times,* April 4, 1974, 61.

3. Richard H. K. Vietor, "Contrived Competition: Airline Regulation and Deregulation, 1925–1988," *Business History Review* 64.1 (1990): 61–108.

4. Elizabeth E. Bailey, David R. Graham, and Daniel P. Kaplan, *Deregulating the Airlines* (Cambridge: Massachusetts Institute of Technology Press, 1986), 1–25; George W. Douglas and James C. Miller III, "The CAB's Domestic Passenger Fare Investigation," *Bell Journal of Economics and Management Science* 5.1 (Spring 1974): 205–22.

5. "Again, Political Slush Funds," *Time,* March 25, 1975; Barbara Sturken Peterson and James Glab, *Rapid Descent: Deregulation and the Shakeout in the Airlines* (New York: Simon and Schuster, 1994), 35–48.

6. "No Cheers for Decontrol," *Time,* October 20, 1975; Peterson and Glab, *Rapid Descent,* 49–63; "Sky Wars over North America," *Time,* September 12, 1977; Vietor, "Contrived Competition," 364.

7. "Flying the Snarled-Up Skies," *Time,* July 3, 1978.

8. *New York Times,* May 21, 1979, 16; Herbert Northrup, "The New Employee-Relations Climate in the Airlines," *Industrial and Labor Relations Review* 36.2 (January 1983): 169; Peter Cappelli, "Airline Union Concessions in the Wake of Deregulation—37th Annual Meeting of the Industrial Relations Research Association, Dallas, December 1984—transcript," *Monthly Labor Review* 108.6 (June 1985): 32–41.

9. David Card, "The Impact of Deregulation on the Employment and Wages of Airline Mechanics," *Industrial and Labor Relations Review* 39.4 (July 1986): 527; Pierre-Yves Cremieux, "The Effect of Deregulation on Employee Earnings: Pilots, Flight Attendants, and Mechanics, 1959–1992," *Industrial and Labor Relations Review* 49.2 (January 1996): 223.

10. U.S. Government Accountability Office, "Airline Deregulation: Regulating the Airline Industry Would Likely Reverse Consumer Benefits and Not Save Airline Pensions," June 2006 (GAO-06-630), 13.

11. David J. Walsh, "Accounting for the Proliferation of Two-Tier Wage Settlements in the U.S. Airline Industry, 1983–1986," *Industrial and Labor Relations Review* 42.1

(October 1988): 50–53. In 2003, A-scale baggage handlers would still refer to workers hired in 1983 as B-scalers. Almost all the retired baggage handlers interviewed for this book referenced 1983 as an important turning point. Several felt that the B-scale marked a loss of union power and was an example of when the "bean counters" really took over from "airline people" in the industry.

12. Martha Dunagin Saunders, *Eastern's Armageddon: Labor Conflict and the Destruction of Eastern Airlines* (Westport, Conn.: Greenwood Press, 1992); Ernie Mailhot, Judy Stranahan, and Jack Barnes, *The Eastern Airlines Strike: Accomplishments of the Rank-and-File Machinists and Gains for the Labor Movement* (New York: Pathfinder Press, 1991); Cohen, "Political Climate," 308–23.

13. Lisa Catherine Tulk, "The 1926 Railway Labor Act and the Modern American Airline Industry: Changes and 'CHAOS' Outline the Need for Revised Legislation," *Journal of Air Law and Commerce* 69.3 (Summer 2004): 615–45.

14. Air Transport Association of America, "U.S. Passenger Airline Employment," www.airlines.org/economics/labor/ (accessed May 16, 2007).

15. *USA Today,* April 1, 2003; *International Herald Tribune,* Business Section, April 18, 2007.

16. "UAL Mechanics Change Unions: Victory Makes AMFA No. 1 Representative of Mechanics," *Chicago Tribune,* July 15, 2003.

17. Whitelegg, *Working the Skies,* 99–125; *Wall Street Journal,* April 8, 2003, D1; *New York Times,* December 17, 2000, 45; Susannah Frame, KING 5 News, "Investigators: Gang Graffiti Exposed in Alaska Air Jet Cargo Holds," February 16, 2006, http://www.king5.com/topstories/stories/NW_021606INKalaskagraffitiJK.340e4092.html (accessed March 17, 2008); Association of Flight Attendants, "Joint Statement of the Coalition of Flight Attendant Unions Following the First-Ever Flight Attendant Strategic Bargaining Summit, January 10, 2008," http://www.afanet.org/aefiles/011008JOINT_STATEMENT.pdf (accessed March 17, 2008); "Airline Safety: A Whistleblower's Tale," *Business Week,* February 11, 2008, 48–52; *Washington Post,* March 13, 2008; *New York Times,* April 9, 2008; *Rocky Mountain News,* April 3, 2008; Barry Hirsch and David Macpherson, Union Membership and Coverage Database from the Current Population Survey, www.unionists.com (accessed October 10, 2008).

18. Jefferson R. Cowie, "Nixon's Class Struggle: Romancing the New Right Worker, 1969–1973," *Labor History* 43.3 (2002): 257–83; Cowie, "Vigorously Left, Right, and Center," 75–106; Kevin Michael Kruse and Thomas J. Sugrue, *The New Suburban History,* Historical Studies of Urban America (Chicago: University of Chicago Press, 2006); Becky Nicolaides, *My Blue Heaven: Life and Politics in the Working-Class Suburbs of Los Angeles, 1920–1965* (Chicago: University of Chicago Press, 2002); Richard Harris, "The Suburban Worker and the History of Labor," *International Labor and Working-Class History* 64 (Fall 2003): 8–24; Minna P. Ziskind, "Labor Conflict in the Suburbs: Organizing Retail in Metropolitan New York, 1954–1958," *International Labor and Working-Class History* 64 (Fall 2003): 55–73.

Index

Note: Page numbers in *italics* refer to illustrations and page numbers followed by *t* indicate tables.

LIESL MILLER ORENIC is associate professor of history and director of the American Studies Program at Dominican University. Her publications include articles and reviews in the *Journal of Urban History* and the *Journal of Social History*. She has served on the board of directors of the Labor and Working-Class History Association and is co-chair of the 2009 LAWCHA-sponsored labor conference in Chicago. She is co-chair of the Chicago Center for Working-Class Studies and is on the Board of Trustees of the Illinois Labor History Society.

THE WORKING CLASS IN AMERICAN HISTORY

Worker City, Company Town: Iron and Cotton-Worker Protest in Troy and Cohoes, New York, 1855–84 *Daniel J. Walkowitz*

Life, Work, and Rebellion in the Coal Fields: The Southern West Virginia Miners, 1880–1922 *David Alan Corbin*

Women and American Socialism, 1870–1920 *Mari Jo Buhle*

Lives of Their Own: Blacks, Italians, and Poles in Pittsburgh, 1900–1960 *John Bodnar, Roger Simon, and Michael P. Weber*

Working-Class America: Essays on Labor, Community, and American Society *Edited by Michael H. Frisch and Daniel J. Walkowitz*

Eugene V. Debs: Citizen and Socialist *Nick Salvatore*

American Labor and Immigration History, 1877–1920s: Recent European Research *Edited by Dirk Hoerder*

Workingmen's Democracy: The Knights of Labor and American Politics *Leon Fink*

The Electrical Workers: A History of Labor at General Electric and Westinghouse, 1923–60 *Ronald W. Schatz*

The Mechanics of Baltimore: Workers and Politics in the Age of Revolution, 1763–1812 *Charles G. Steffen*

The Practice of Solidarity: American Hat Finishers in the Nineteenth Century *David Bensman*

The Labor History Reader *Edited by Daniel J. Leab*

Solidarity and Fragmentation: Working People and Class Consciousness in Detroit, 1875–1900 *Richard Oestreicher*

Counter Cultures: Saleswomen, Managers, and Customers in American Department Stores, 1890–1940 *Susan Porter Benson*

The New England Working Class and the New Labor History *Edited by Herbert G. Gutman and Donald H. Bell*

Labor Leaders in America *Edited by Melvyn Dubofsky and Warren Van Tine*

Barons of Labor: The San Francisco Building Trades and Union Power in the Progressive Era *Michael Kazin*

Gender at Work: The Dynamics of Job Segregation by Sex during World War II *Ruth Milkman*

Once a Cigar Maker: Men, Women, and Work Culture in American Cigar Factories, 1900–1919 *Patricia A. Cooper*

A Generation of Boomers: The Pattern of Railroad Labor Conflict in Nineteenth-Century America *Shelton Stromquist*

Work and Community in the Jungle: Chicago's Packinghouse Workers, 1894–1922 *James R. Barrett*

Workers, Managers, and Welfare Capitalism: The Shoeworkers and Tanners of Endicott Johnson, 1890–1950 *Gerald Zahavi*

Men, Women, and Work: Class, Gender, and Protest in the New England Shoe Industry, 1780–1910 *Mary Blewett*

Workers on the Waterfront: Seamen, Longshoremen, and Unionism in the 1930s *Bruce Nelson*

German Workers in Chicago: A Documentary History of Working-Class Culture from 1850 to World War I *Edited by Hartmut Keil and John B. Jentz*

On the Line: Essays in the History of Auto Work *Edited by Nelson Lichtenstein and Stephen Meyer III*

Labor's Flaming Youth: Telephone Operators and Worker Militancy, 1878–1923 *Stephen H. Norwood*

Another Civil War: Labor, Capital, and the State in the Anthracite Regions of Pennsylvania, 1840–68 *Grace Palladino*

Coal, Class, and Color: Blacks in Southern West Virginia, 1915–32 *Joe William Trotter, Jr.*

For Democracy, Workers, and God: Labor Song-Poems and Labor Protest, 1865–95 *Clark D. Halker*

Dishing It Out: Waitresses and Their Unions in the Twentieth Century *Dorothy Sue Cobble*

The Spirit of 1848: German Immigrants, Labor Conflict, and the Coming of the Civil War *Bruce Levine*

Working Women of Collar City: Gender, Class, and Community in Troy, New York, 1864–86 *Carole Turbin*

Southern Labor and Black Civil Rights: Organizing Memphis Workers *Michael K. Honey*

Radicals of the Worst Sort: Laboring Women in Lawrence, Massachusetts, 1860–1912 *Ardis Cameron*

Producers, Proletarians, and Politicians: Workers and Party Politics in Evansville and New Albany, Indiana, 1850–87 *Lawrence M. Lipin*

The New Left and Labor in the 1960s *Peter B. Levy*

The Making of Western Labor Radicalism: Denver's Organized Workers, 1878–1905 *David Brundage*

In Search of the Working Class: Essays in American Labor History and Political Culture *Leon Fink*

Lawyers against Labor: From Individual Rights to Corporate Liberalism *Daniel R. Ernst*

"We Are All Leaders": The Alternative Unionism of the Early 1930s *Edited by Staughton Lynd*

The Female Economy: The Millinery and Dressmaking Trades, 1860–1930 *Wendy Gamber*

"Negro and White, Unite and Fight!": A Social History of Industrial Unionism in Meatpacking, 1930–90 *Roger Horowitz*

Power at Odds: The 1922 National Railroad Shopmen's Strike *Colin J. Davis*

The Common Ground of Womanhood: Class, Gender, and Working Girls' Clubs, 1884–1928 *Priscilla Murolo*

Marching Together: Women of the Brotherhood of Sleeping Car Porters *Melinda Chateauvert*

Down on the Killing Floor: Black and White Workers in Chicago's Packinghouses, 1904–54 *Rick Halpern*
Labor and Urban Politics: Class Conflict and the Origins of Modern Liberalism in Chicago, 1864–97 *Richard Schneirov*
All That Glitters: Class, Conflict, and Community in Cripple Creek *Elizabeth Jameson*
Waterfront Workers: New Perspectives on Race and Class *Edited by Calvin Winslow*
Labor Histories: Class, Politics, and the Working-Class Experience *Edited by Eric Arnesen, Julie Greene, and Bruce Laurie*
The Pullman Strike and the Crisis of the 1890s: Essays on Labor and Politics *Edited by Richard Schneirov, Shelton Stromquist, and Nick Salvatore*
AlabamaNorth: African-American Migrants, Community, and Working-Class Activism in Cleveland, 1914–45 *Kimberley L. Phillips*
Imagining Internationalism in American and British Labor, 1939–49 *Victor Silverman*
William Z. Foster and the Tragedy of American Radicalism *James R. Barrett*
Colliers across the Sea: A Comparative Study of Class Formation in Scotland and the American Midwest, 1830–1924 *John H. M. Laslett*
"Rights, Not Roses": Unions and the Rise of Working-Class Feminism, 1945–80 *Dennis A. Deslippe*
Testing the New Deal: The General Textile Strike of 1934 in the American South *Janet Irons*
Hard Work: The Making of Labor History *Melvyn Dubofsky*
Southern Workers and the Search for Community: Spartanburg County, South Carolina *G. C. Waldrep III*
We Shall Be All: A History of the Industrial Workers of the World (abridged edition) *Melvyn Dubofsky, ed. Joseph A. McCartin*
Race, Class, and Power in the Alabama Coalfields, 1908–21 *Brian Kelly*
Duquesne and the Rise of Steel Unionism *James D. Rose*
Anaconda: Labor, Community, and Culture in Montana's Smelter City *Laurie Mercier*
Bridgeport's Socialist New Deal, 1915–36 *Cecelia Bucki*
Indispensable Outcasts: Hobo Workers and Community in the American Midwest, 1880–1930 *Frank Tobias Higbie*
After the Strike: A Century of Labor Struggle at Pullman *Susan Eleanor Hirsch*
Corruption and Reform in the Teamsters Union *David Witwer*
Waterfront Revolts: New York and London Dockworkers, 1946–61 *Colin J. Davis*
Black Workers' Struggle for Equality in Birmingham *Horace Huntley and David Montgomery*
The Tribe of Black Ulysses: African American Men in the Industrial South *William P. Jones*
City of Clerks: Office and Sales Workers in Philadelphia, 1870–1920 *Jerome P. Bjelopera*
Reinventing "The People": The Progressive Movement, the Class Problem, and the Origins of Modern Liberalism *Shelton Stromquist*
Radical Unionism in the Midwest, 1900–1950 *Rosemary Feurer*

Gendering Labor History *Alice Kessler-Harris*
James P. Cannon and the Origins of the American Revolutionary Left, 1890–1928 *Bryan D. Palmer*
Glass Towns: Industry, Labor, and Political Economy in Appalachia, 1890–1930s *Ken Fones-Wolf*
Workers and the Wild: Conservation, Consumerism, and Labor in Oregon, 1910–30 *Lawrence M. Lipin*
Wobblies on the Waterfront: Interracial Unionism in Progressive-Era Philadelphia *Peter Cole*
Red Chicago: American Communism at Its Grassroots, 1928–35 *Randi Storch*
Labor's Cold War: Local Politics in a Global Context *Edited by Shelton Stromquist*
Bessie Abromowitz Hillman and the Making of the Amalgamated Clothing Workers of America *Karen Pastorello*
The Great Strikes of 1877 *Edited by David O. Stowell*
Union-Free America: Workers and Antiunion Culture *Lawrence Richards*
Race against Liberalism: Black Workers and the UAW in Detroit *David M. Lewis-Colman*
Teachers and Reform: Chicago Public Education, 1929–70 *John F. Lyons*
Upheaval in the Quiet Zone: 1199/SEIU and the Politics of Healthcare Unionism *Leon Fink and Brian Greenberg*
Shadow of the Racketeer: Scandal in Organized Labor *David Witwer*
Sweet Tyranny: Migrant Labor, Industrial Agriculture, and Imperial Politics *Kathleen Mapes*
Staley: The Fight for a New American Labor Movement *Steven K. Ashby and C. J. Hawking*
On the Ground: Labor Struggle in the American Airline Industry *Liesl Miller Orenic*

The University of Illinois Press
is a founding member of the
Association of American University Presses.

Composed in 10.5/13 Adobe Minion Pro
with FF Meta display
at the University of Illinois Press
Manufactured by Thomson-Shore, Inc.

University of Illinois Press
1325 South Oak Street
Champaign, IL 61820-6903
www.press.uillinois.edu